CLINICIAN'S THESAURUS, 5TH EDITION

THE CLINICIAN'S TOOLBOX™
A Guilford Series
Edward L. Zuckerman, Series Editor

BREAKING FREE OF MANAGED CARE
A Step-by-Step Guide to Regaining Control of Your Practice
Dana C. Ackley

THE PAPER OFFICE, 2nd Edition
Forms, Guidelines, and Resources
Edward L. Zuckerman

THE ESSENTIAL GUIDE TO GROUP PRACTICE IN MENTAL HEALTH
Clinical, Legal, and Financial Fundamentals
Simon H. Budman and Brett N. Steenbarger

OUTCOMES AND INCOMES
How to Evaluate, Improve, and Market Your Psychotherapy Practice
by Measuring Outcomes
Paul W. Clement

THE INSIDER'S GUIDE TO MENTAL HEALTH RESOURCES ONLINE
2000/2001 Edition
John M. Grohol

TREATMENT PLANS AND INTERVENTIONS FOR DEPRESSION
AND ANXIETY DISORDERS
Robert L. Leahy and Stephen J. Holland

AUTHORITATIVE GUIDE TO SELF-HELP RESOURCES IN MENTAL HEALTH
*John C. Norcross, John W. Santrock, Linda F. Campbell, Thomas P. Smith, Robert Sommer,
and Edward L. Zuckerman*

CLINICIAN'S THESAURUS, 5th Edition
The Guidebook for Writing Psychological Reports
Edward L. Zuckerman

CLINICIAN'S ELECTRONIC THESAURUS, Version 5.0
Software to Streamline Psychological Report Writing
Edward L. Zuckerman

CLINICIAN'S THESAURUS

5th Edition

The Guidebook for Writing Psychological Reports

EDWARD L. ZUCKERMAN, PhD

THE GUILFORD PRESS
New York   London

© 2000 Edward L. Zuckerman

Published by The Guilford Press
A Division of Guilford Publications, Inc.
72 Spring Street, New York, NY 10012
www.guilford.com

Printed in Canada

This book is printed on acid-free paper.

Last digit is print number: 9 8 7 6 5 4 3 2 1

Library of Congress Cataloging-in-Publication Data is available from the Publisher.

ISBN 1-57230-569-X

About the Author

Edward L. Zuckerman received his PhD in clinical psychology from the University of Pittsburgh and remained there as an adjunct teacher of personality psychology and human sexuality for 14 years. He taught abnormal psychology at Carnegie Mellon University for 9 years and now consults to the Social Security Disability Determination Division. He was in the independent general practice of clinical psychology for more than 15 years and has worked in state hospitals and community mental health centers. He lives on a small farm in Pennsylvania with his wife, two daughters, and their horses, chickens, dogs, cats, geese, and ducks.

Contents

Acknowledgments
and an Invitation

I must first express my continuing appreciation to my editors at The Guilford Press, without whom this work would be much less clear, organized, and precise. I am very grateful for their expertise, experience, and enormous efforts. Thank you, Anna Brackett, Marie Sprayberry, and Barbara Watkins.

With appreciation for their expertise and generosity, I am happy to give credit here to the following professionals for their contributions to this revised edition:

Dolores Arnold, MEd, NCC, of Lawton, OK
Judy Bomze of Wynnewood, PA
Renee F. Bova-Collis of Richmond, VA
Richard L. Bruner, PsyD, of Hightstown, NJ
Jeffry Burkard of Colvis, CA
Kathryn Elkins of Victoria, Australia
Patricia Hurzeler, MS, APRN, CS, of Bloomfield, CT
Mustaq Khan, PhD, of London, Ontario, Canada
Dorothy H. Knight of Jacksonville, IL
Bryan Lindberg of Portsmouth, RI
Susan G. Mikesell, PhD, of Washington, DC
Ilene D. Miner, CSW, ACSW, of New York, NY
Robert W. Moffie, PhD, of Los Angeles, CA
Fay Murakawa, PhD, of Los Angeles, CA
Michael Newberry, MD, of Palm Bay, FL
James L. Pointer, PhD, of Montgomery, AL
Joseph Regan, PhD, of Toronto, Ontario, Canada
Daniel L. Segal, PhD, of Colorado Springs, CO
Judith Shea, MA, of Lawrence, MA
Janet L. Smigel, RN, CD
Henry T. Stein, PhD, of San Francisco, CA
Frank O. Volle, PhD, of Darien, CT
Marcia L. Whisman, MSW, ACSM, of St. Louis, MO
Leslie J. Wrixon, PsyD, of Cambridge, MA
Nora F. Young of Sedro Wolley, WA

I must also clearly acknowledge my debt to many other colleagues, from whose clearest thinking and best writing I have borrowed liberally to fill these pages. More than 200 of you have furnished the more than 40,000 reports from which I have culled the 25,000 or so unduplicated wordings incorporated here. Although you are too numerous to credit individually, please accept my gratitude and appreciation. While I have borrowed many of the words and phrases, I alone must assume responsibility for the content and organization of the *Clinician's Thesaurus*, whatever its merits or limitations.

Now, you are invited to contribute. What is missing from this book? What would you have put in or taken out? What have I gotten wrong? Please let me know by mail or e-mail, and—if your suggestions are adopted into the next edition—three good things will happen:

1. You will get **a free copy of the next edition**.
2. Your contribution will be fully acknowledged here.
3. You will receive my (and our fellow clinicians') sincere appreciation for adding to our knowledge, and for making our work easier.

Send mail to P.O. Box 222, Armbrust, PA 15616 and e-mail to edzuckerman@ information4u. com, or edzuckerma@aol.com.

*   *   *

The following copyright holders have generously given permission to quote or adapt material from these copyrighted works:

"Alzheimer's Disease Updated" by B. Reisberg, 1985, *Psychiatric Annals, 15*, 319–322. Copyright 1985 by Slack, Inc.

"Assessment of Coma and Impaired Consciousness" by G. Teasdale and B. Jenvet, 1974, *Lancet, 2*(7872), 81–83. Copyright 1974 by The Lancet Ltd.

"Benign Senescent Forgetfulness" by V. A. Kral, 1978, in R. Katzman, R. D. Terry, and K. L. Bick (Eds.), *Alzheimer's Disease: Senile Dementia and Related Disorders* (New York: Raven Press). Copyright 1978 by Raven Press.

"Cyclothymic Temperamental Disorders" by H. S. Akiskal, M. K. Khani, and A. Scott-Strauss, 1979, *Psychiatric Clinics of North America, 2*, 527–554. Copyright 1979 by W. B. Saunders Co.

"Detecting Physical Illness in Patients with Mental Disorders" by R. S. Hoffman and L. M. Koran, 1984, *Psychosomatics, 25*, 654–660. Copyright 1984 by the American Psychiatric Press.

Diagnostic and Statistical Manual of Mental Disorders (4th ed.) by the American Psychiatric Association, 1994 (Washington, DC: Author). Copyright 1994 by the American Psychiatric Association.

"Distinguishing Psychological Disorders from Neurological Disorders: Taking Axis III Seriously" by M. Bondi, 1992, *Professional Psychology: Research and Practice, 23*(4), 306–309. Copyright 1992 by the American Psychological Association.

"Enhancing Motivation for Treatment of Addictive Behavior: Guidelines for the Psychotherapist" by A. T. Horvath, 1995, *Psychotherapy, 30*, 475–480. Copyright 1995 by the Division of Psychotherapy (29) of the American Psychological Association.

"The False Patient: Chronic Factitious Disease, Munchausen Syndrome, and Malingering" by T. Nadelson, 1986, in J. L. Haupt and H. K. H. Brodie (Eds.), *Consultation–Liaison Psychiatry and Behavioral Medicine* (Philadelphia: Lippincott). Copyright 1986 by J. B. Lippincott.

Handbook of Psychiatric Emergencies (4th ed.) by A. E. Slaby, J. Liev, and L. R. Tancredi, 1994 (Norwalk, CT: Appleton & Lange). Copyright 1994 by Appleton & Lange.

Handbook of Psychodiagnostic Testing: An Analysis of Personality in the Psychological Report (3rd ed.) by H. Kellerman and A. Burry, 1997 (Boston: Allyn & Bacon). Copyright 1997 by Allyn & Bacon.

"Homosexual Identity Formation: A Theoretical Model" by V. C. Cass, 1979, *Journal of Homosexuality, 4*(3), 219–235. Copyright 1979 by The Haworth Press.

"Levels of Cognitive Functioning" by C. Hagen, D. Malkmus, and P. Durham, 1979, in *Rehabilitation of Head Injured Adults: Comprehensive Physical Management* (Downey, CA: Los Amigos Research and Education Institute, Inc., Rancho Los Amigos National Rehabilitation Center). Copyright 1974 by Los Amigos Research and Education Institute, Inc.

"The Masking and Unmasking of Depression" by J. J. Lopez-Ibor, Jr., 1990, in J. P. Feighner and W. F. Boyer (Eds.), *The Diagnosis of Depression* (New York: Wiley). Copyright 1990 by John Wiley & Sons, Ltd.

CLINICIAN'S THESAURUS, 5TH EDITION

Getting Oriented
to the *Clinician's Thesaurus*

WHAT IS THE *CLINICIAN'S THESAURUS* AND WHAT DOES IT DO?

This book is more than a giant collection of synonyms; it is a treasury of the terms, standard phrasings, common concepts, and practical information clinicians use in their daily work. *In breadth and in depth, this book covers the language of American mental health.* It is organized to help you, first, collect the client information you need; second, find the most precise terms to express your findings; and, third, structure those findings into a high-quality report.

If you create psychological or psychiatric evaluations, progress notes, testing-based reports, intakes, psychosocial narratives, managed care reports, summaries of treatment, or the like, the *Clinician's Thesaurus* will ease your workload as it sharpens your writing because it does the following:

- Presents dozens of related terms to enhance the clarity, precision, and vividness of your reports.
- Offers behavioral descriptions for a range of psychopathology to help you illustrate your formulations and conclusions.
- Suggests phrasings and observations that can individualize and personalize a report or description.
- Stimulates your recall of a client's characteristics (we all can recall more when we prompt our memories by reading related terms).
- Suggests "summary statements" where only a brief indication is needed, such as when cognitive functioning is within normal limits.

- Contains extensive cross-references and a helpful index for ease in locating materials and ideas.
- Replaces the drudgery of narrative reporting with playfulness, spontaneity, and serendipity. (I know this is a big promise, but when you skim the book you will find both the familiar and the novel.)

In addition, because of its format and structure, the *Clinician's Thesaurus* can help you do these things:

- Structure an interview or assessment to ensure that you have not missed any important aspect.
- Organize your thoughts when writing or dictating a report to ensure that you have addressed all the issues of relevance for that client.
- Access the knowledge base you have built from your training and experience for use in treatment planning or other clinical decisions you have to make.
- Help you rewrite, elaborate on, or tighten up a report you have drafted. The wide diversity of terms offered allows you to refresh and vary your writing, even about a familiar topic or point.
- Learn, do, or teach report writing (see below).

The *Clinician's Thesaurus* can be thought of as an enormous 25,000+-item checklist. It is designed to approximate your internal checklist—the one on which you draw to conduct interviews, understand and respond to questions, and construct your reports. However, because it is far easier to work from an external checklist, it converts the demanding free-recall task into a much simpler recognition task. You just have to read and select the best wording for the task at hand.

HOW THIS BOOK IS ORGANIZED—ITS STRUCTURE

This book is organized into three main parts. Part I helps you to collect the client information you need. Parts II and III help you structure and phrase your reports.

The three chapters in Part I offer a guide for interviewing, plus hundreds of questions and aids for eliciting specific kinds of client information.

- Chapter 1 provides pointers for conducting a valid and ethical interview and guidance for beginning and ending the interview.
- Chapter 2 covers all the traditional aspects addressed in a **Mental Status Evaluation (MSE).** It offers common questions (and many variations on them when needed) for examining cognitive functioning.
- Chapter 3 offers hundreds of questions designed to elicit information about all kinds of **signs, symptoms, and behavior patterns**, including ones that are particularly difficult to address in the interview context (such as paranoias, dissociative experiences, and sexual history).

Part II of this book is designed to guide your writing of a report. It is organized in the sequence of the traditional evaluation report. (For more on this format and on constructing reports, see below.) The chapters in Part II offer a range of descriptors and phrases by topic area. Almost any report can be shaped from the terms and areas covered. Useful clinical tips and common wording pitfalls also appear throughout the text.

- Chapters 4–6 cover **introducing the report**: preliminary information; the reasons for the referral; and background information.
- Chapters 7–13 address **the person in the evaluation**: behavioral observations; responses

to aspects of the examination; presentation of self; emotions/affects; cognition and mental status; abnormal symptoms; and personality patterns.
- Chapters 14–19 cover **the person in the environment**: Activities of Daily Living (ADLs); social/community functioning; couple and family relationships; vocational and academic performance; recreational functioning; and other dimensions clinicians are often asked to evaluate.
- Chapters 20–25 cover **completing the report**: summaries, diagnostic statements, recommendations, prognosis, and professional closings.

Part III of this book offers useful clinical resources. These include the following:

- Formats for treatment plans
- Formats for writing a wide range of reports and summaries
- A list of common medications, by generic and brand names
- Cues for recognizing the psychiatric presentation ("masquerade") of medical conditions

In addition, there are Appendices containing useful abbreviations; a table for converting test scores into other formats for interpretation; and an annotated list of readings in assessment, interviewing, and report writing.

UNDERSTANDING THE STYLE AND FORMAT OF THE CHAPTERS

As just described, each chapter in this book covers broad aspects of evaluation questions (in Part I), areas of a report (in Part II), or clinical resources (in Part III). Each chapter is then subdivided into more specific, useful topics, and each begins with a list summarizing these main section topics. For example, Chapter 10, "Emotional/Affective Symptoms and Disorders," begins with a list of its 11 main sections (each addressing a specific affective symptom or disorder, ranging from anger to depression to panic). Each of these main topics has its own section number (e.g., the third section in Chapter 10, "Anxiety/Fear," is numbered 10.3). Cross-references throughout the book are to section numbers.

To find terms and descriptors for an anxious client, you could turn to the title page of Chapter 10, see that Section 10.3 is "Anxiety/Fear," and then turn to that section for a full range of terms relating to anxiety and fear grouped by manifestation. You could also look up "anxiety" in the index for a quicker search.

Please note that not all section topics within a chapter will need to be covered in every report. The section topics represent a range of possible options across different types of clients and different types of reports. Select from these topics and terms those relevant to the particular client and type of report you are writing.

Types of Information in the Sections

Most of this book consists of lists and groupings of the standard terms used in American mental health. The format for these is explained below. It is from these descriptors that you may select the ones most appropriate for incorporation into your reports. Other kinds of useful information also appear throughout the chapters. They following different types of information are provided:

- Introductory and explanatory comments
- Cross-references to related sections of the book
- Practice tips, reminders, and cautions
- References to the standard works in the field or area
- Descriptors, terms, and phrases for wording reports

- Sample "summary statements" that are the most common ways of summarizing findings or other information
- Sample evaluation questions and tasks (primarily in Chapters 1, 2, and 3)

Figure 1 (see below) offers a quick visual guide to identifying these various types of information within the chapter format.

The descriptors and phrasings offered in this book are standard American English usage and are the conventional language of the mental health field. Because the terms offered are only rarely defined here, you may find useful a specialized psychiatric dictionary (e.g., Campbell, 1996; *Stedman's Medical Dictionary*, 1999; *Stedman's Psychiatry/Neurology/Neurosurgery Words*, 1999).

As you will see in Figure 1 and throughout the book, the descriptors and terms in this book may appear in different formats, such as in a paragraph, in a list, or as columns of words across the page. Specific formats indicate that the terms have been ordered according to degree of meaning. Understanding the arrangements gives you further information about those terms. These formats are explained next.

Formats for Descriptors and Terms

The terms and descriptors offered in the *Clinician's Thesaurus* are always shown in a sans serif font to set them off from other kinds of text. They are arranged in one of four ways. These range from an unordered grouping of related words to increasingly ordered arrangements, as follows:

1. **Unordered groups of similar but not synonymous words and phrases** in a line or paragraph. Example:

   Presentable, acceptable, suitable, appearance and dress appropriate for age and occupation, businesslike, professional appearance, nothing was attention-drawing, modestly attired.

   These words are often used as alternatives for each other. They are presented in a line or paragraph with no ordering principle. In the example above, the terms and phrases are all possible descriptors for "appropriateness" of clothing/attire.

2. An **ordered spectrum of words and phrases,** indicated by a double-arrow graphic (↔), in a line or paragraph. Example:

   (↔ *by degree*) Awkward, clumsy, "klutzy," often injures self, "accident-prone," inaccurate/ ineffective movements, jerky, uncoordinated, <normal>, purposeful, smooth, dextrous, graceful, agile, nimble.

   When words are sequenced by degree of the trait or behavior, this is indicated by a double arrow (↔). In the example above, a client's movement or activity is characterized along a spectrum of ability from uncoordinated ("awkward") to coordinated ("nimble"). Occasionally, the word <normal> enclosed in arrowheads appears in such a grouping of terms to indicate the midpoint of the spectrum.

3. **Columns of words ordered by degree (↔) across the page.** Example:

   ### Qualities of Clothing (↔ *by degree*)

filthy	seedy	needing repair	plain	*neat*	*stylish*
grimy	disheveled	threadbare	out of date	careful dresser	fashionable
dirty	neglected	rumpled	old-fashioned	clothes-conscious	elegant

   When introduced by a double arrow (↔), word columns are sequenced along a spectrum of degree of the trait—in this example, from "*filthy*" to "*stylish*." Each individual column contains one or more unordered clusters of alternative terms with slightly different shades of meaning. However, when a word is the standard term used by clinicians for a cluster, it is presented at the top of the cluster and *italicized*. In the example above, the three words in the first column all indicate the same relative degree of "Qualities of Clothing," but have different nuances. "*Filthy*" is the standard term for this degree in quality.

4. **Lines or paragraphs sequenced by degree (↔) and staggered downward across the page.** Example:

> Unable to recognize the purposes of the interview/the report to be made . . .
>
> Indifferent, bland, detached, distant, uninvolved, uncaring . . .
>
> Dependent, sought/required much support/reassurance/guidance . . .
>
> Anxiety appropriate/proportionate to the interview situation . . .
>
> Understood the social graces/norms/expectations/conventions . . .

When lines or paragraphs are staggered down the page as in the example above, each level represents a degree of the quality along an ordered spectrum. In the example above, the quality of a client's response to the evaluation ranges from "Unable to recognize the purposes . . . " to "Understood . . . "

Typographic Conventions

- **Double-arrow (↔):** Indicates that the terms or phrases are ordered along a spectrum of degree for the trait, quality, or behavior.

- **Slash mark (/):** Indicates that an alternative word or words immediately follow. Example:

  > Understood the social graces/norms/expectations/conventions . . .

  Here the terms "social graces," "norms," "expectations," and "conventions" are alternative descriptions, each of which can be used with the term "Understood" to indicate a quality of client response to the evaluation.

- **Quotation marks (" "):** Indicate that a word is slang or inappropriate in a professional report. Example:

  > Awkward, clumsy, "klutzy," often injures self, "accident-prone," . . .

  Slang and similar inappropriate words are frequently offered by persons being evaluated. They are placed in the *Clinician's Thesaurus* under appropriate headings to assist the clinician unfamiliar with such phrasings in understanding their meanings. For example, the descriptors for uncoordinated movement in the example above include "klutzy" and "accident-prone." Their placement indicates their meaning, but the quotation marks should alert you NOT to use the terms in your report.

- **Check mark with or without square brackets ([✓] or ✓:** Indicates comments, advice, cautions, and clinical tips. These range from brief comments to tables of information; they are useful in understanding the client or phenomena, but are not to be borrowed for the report. Example:

  > Client has persistent physical symptoms that do not respond to medical treatments. [✓ Note especially headaches, digestive disorders, and chronic and migratory pains.]

- **Braces ({ })**: Indicate words or phrases that are obsolete, obscure, or only of historical interest. Example:

  (↔ *by degree*) Gregarious, likeable, dramatic, entertaining, pleasant, vivacious, seductive, cracks jokes, prankish, naive, infantile, silly, {witzelsucht}.

  The descriptors above constitute a spectrum of terms relating to mania. The word "*witzelsucht*" is now considered an obsolete description, and so it appears in braces. (Italics in this case indicate the word's foreign origin.)

- **Underlining and capitalization of the initial letters of a phrase**: Indicate a commonly used acronym. For example, Activities of Daily Living are often referred to as "ADLs."

- **Special headings**: Most wordings apply to both adults and children. However, words used only in the evaluation of children are listed at the end of each area where they apply, and are indicated by the heading "For a Child." Similarly, other uses are indicated, such as "For a Disability Report." Finally, in some instances sample sentences are provided to indicate how you might sum up a situation; these are indicated by the heading "Summary Statements."

- **Blank space**: Provided in much of the text so that you may customize the entries with your favorite phrases and statements.

Figure 1 illustrates many of the formats and typographic conventions described above. The figure represents a composite of several pages, so as to include a wider range of types of format. Some content has been omitted in this composite.

Notes on Grammar

For compactness and simplicity, adjectives, adverbs, verbs, and nouns are sometimes mixed in a listing. Just modify the word to suit the sentence you have in mind.

The **pronoun forms** used here are intended to lessen the sexist associations and implications whose harmful effects are well documented in this field. This book uses combinations such as "her/him" and "he/she" in varying order, or alternates in turn between "he" and "she," to avoid furthering gender associations. When pronouns of a single gender are employed, that phrasing should not be taken to imply any association of gender with behavior.

Attributions

References to professionals may be phrased as follows:

The clinician, therapist, psychologist, social worker, psychiatrist, nurse, counselor, behavior specialist, consultant, evaluator, interviewer, writer, undersigned, author, reporter, correspondent.

The professional can be said to do the following:

Report, offer, observe, note, document, record, state, summarize, etc.

References to the client may be phrased as follows:

The client, patient, claimant, {examinee}, resident, {subject}, individual, person, citizen, consumer, man, woman, child, student, etc.

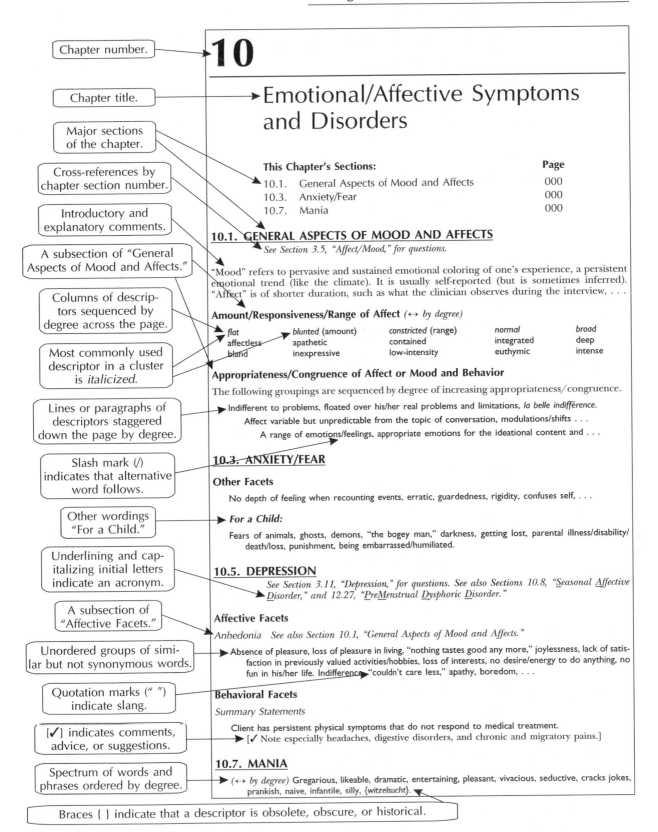

Chapter number.

Chapter title.

Major sections of the chapter.

Cross-references by chapter section number.

Introductory and explanatory comments.

A subsection of "General Aspects of Mood and Affects."

Columns of descriptors sequenced by degree across the page.

Most commonly used descriptor in a cluster is *italicized*.

Lines or paragraphs of descriptors staggered down the page by degree.

Slash mark (/) indicates that alternative word follows.

Other wordings "For a Child."

Underlining and capitalizing initial letters indicate an acronym.

A subsection of "Affective Facets."

Unordered groups of similar but not synonymous words.

Quotation marks (" ") indicate slang.

[✔] indicates comments, advice, or suggestions.

Spectrum of words and phrases ordered by degree.

Braces { } indicate that a descriptor is obsolete, obscure, or historical.

10

►Emotional/Affective Symptoms and Disorders

This Chapter's Sections:	Page
10.1. General Aspects of Mood and Affects	000
10.3. Anxiety/Fear	000
10.7. Mania	000

10.1. GENERAL ASPECTS OF MOOD AND AFFECTS
See Section 3.5, "Affect/Mood," for questions.

"Mood" refers to pervasive and sustained emotional coloring of one's experience, a persistent emotional trend (like the climate). It is usually self-reported (but is sometimes inferred). "Affect" is of shorter duration, such as what the clinician observes during the interview, . . .

Amount/Responsiveness/Range of Affect *(↔ by degree)*

flat	*blunted* (amount)	*constricted* (range)	*normal*	*broad*
affectless	apathetic	contained	integrated	deep
bland	inexpressive	low-intensity	euthymic	intense

Appropriateness/Congruence of Affect or Mood and Behavior

The following groupings are sequenced by degree of increasing appropriateness/congruence.

Indifferent to problems, floated over his/her real problems and limitations, *la belle indifférence.*

Affect variable but unpredictable from the topic of conversation, modulations/shifts . . .

A range of emotions/feelings, appropriate emotions for the ideational content and . . .

10.3. ANXIETY/FEAR

Other Facets

No depth of feeling when recounting events, erratic, guardedness, rigidity, confuses self, . . .

► **For a Child:**

Fears of animals, ghosts, demons, "the bogey man," darkness, getting lost, parental illness/disability/death/loss, punishment, being embarrassed/humiliated.

10.5. DEPRESSION
See Section 3.11, "Depression," for questions. See also Sections 10.8, "Seasonal Affective Disorder," and 12.27, "PreMenstrual Dysphoric Disorder."

Affective Facets

Anhedonia See also Section 10.1, "General Aspects of Mood and Affects."

Absence of pleasure, loss of pleasure in living, "nothing tastes good any more," joylessness, lack of satisfaction in previously valued activities/hobbies, loss of interests, no desire/energy to do anything, no fun in his/her life. Indifference, "couldn't care less," apathy, boredom, . . .

Behavioral Facets

Summary Statements

Client has persistent physical symptoms that do not respond to medical treatment.
► [✔ Note especially headaches, digestive disorders, and chronic and migratory pains.]

10.7. MANIA

► *(↔ by degree)* Gregarious, likeable, dramatic, entertaining, pleasant, vivacious, seductive, cracks jokes, prankish, naive, infantile, silly, {*witzelsucht*}. ▼

FIGURE 1. Reduced composite page from Chapter 10, illustrating various formats and typographic conventions.

The client can be said to do the following during an interview:

> Say, state, report, note, speak of, describe, indicate, mention, tell me, concede, present, disclose, elaborate, maintain, offer, deny, disavow, disclaim, exhibit, evidence, register, reveal, etc.

Or, for more legalistic language, you can use these terms:

> Allege, submit, claim, contend, aver, opine, certify, etc.

The use of first names, given names, or nicknames is unprofessional except for children. For adults, Mr. or Ms. (yes, even for married women) is the professional standard. For confidentiality reasons, it may be preferable to use the client's full name on the first page and from then on to use "Mr. A" or "Ms. B." This usage offers the advantage that if you ever need to send a copy of the report to a reader who may not share your understanding of or constraints on confidentiality, you will need to remove the name only once.

Use "Dr." and other titles only where necessary to prevent misunderstanding or where they are relevant to the purpose of the report.

A FUNCTIONAL GUIDE TO REPORT CONSTRUCTION

The Nature of Reports, the Steps of Their Construction, and the Corresponding Portions of the *Clinician's Thesaurus*

The purpose of a report is to communicate the results of your assessments (and, for therapy summaries, interventions) to someone who has a need for this information. To accomplish this purpose, you, the writer, must simultaneously attend to two aspects:

1. Creating a coherent, integrated narrative. What you have to say should be relevant, should be important, and should fit within a familiar professional structure. In addition, the specific contents and writing style should vary with each reader's needs, and so this takes us to the second aspect.
2. Focusing on the needs of the reader. That reader may be a referrer, a supervisor, the client's next therapist, a court or lawyer, a teacher or school system, a physician, or another professional, and each will understand your words from her/his background and experience.

Keeping these two aspects in mind is essential to producing reports that communicate well and are useful.

The next few pages move from looking at the most general to the most specific aspects of a report's narrative. You will see how the flow of information is organized to produce a report whose ideas are of value to the report's reader(s), and whose expression is precise, tailored to the individual, and meaningful. The narrative flow here is matched by the organization of Part II of the *Clinician's Thesaurus*, and this organizational scheme is used to assist your learning of this process.

Report construction begins when you begin to organize your data. In general, the sequence of data presentation in a report begins with old information, such as the client's history and the referral reasons. It proceeds to the new information you have gathered in the interview or assessment. It then presents the new understanding you have formed of the client, based on both the old and the new information. This integrated picture finally leads to new planning, which involves the generation of appropriate and effective interventions. This stepwise process corresponds to the main components of a traditional evaluation report, as seen below:

The process of constructing a report	The main components of an evaluation report	Subdivisions of Part II of the Clinician's Thesaurus
Old information	Introducing the report	A
New information–personal	The person in the evaluation	B
New information–social	The person the environment	C
New understandings and plans	Completing the report	D

The model above is an extremely general version of the logic of constructing reports. Let us now examine a generalized format for a report. Table 1 shows how the components listed above, and their subcomponents, are organized into a report. Each of the four main components of a report includes a range of specific issues or concerns that you can address. Of course, no single report will include all of these. Rather, you must use the report's purpose combined with your clinical judgment to select those issues of most use to the reader of the report.

Table 1 illustrates the flow of the main components of a report (here called A through D, as they are in Part II of this book). The major subcomponents within those components address the familiar concerns of any examining clinician. Now let us look even more closely at these concerns (and their parallel chapters and sections of the *Clinician's Thesaurus*), so as to understand the nature of the clinical work involved in each.

The Clinician's Analysis and Synthesis

Using the framework of the report laid out above, let us look at the clinician's thought processes regarding each concern. What is a clinician doing when he/she considers each area of personal and social functioning? What are the questions implicitly or explicitly asked by the reader that will help her/him to do what is best for the client? The chapters and sections of Part II of the *Clinician's Thesaurus* are designed to offer ways of framing the answers. The following discussion is intended to guide you in framing the questions.

A. Introducing the Report

The beginning of a report covers old information: facts, issues, and background before this evaluation took place. Don't include every piece of historical information you may have. Rather, include only the information relevant to the goals of the report. Use the information to clarify why you are doing an evaluation or writing a summary.

Reports usually begin with identifying information (the client's identity, age, marital status, etc.). In addition, important aspects of your meeting with the client, such as the client's competence and consent to participate in the interview, are customarily included here although they are not historical. This is done here to remove them from the flow of clinical information; they could as well be integrated into B, "The Person in the Evaluation."

For each of the following areas, there are examples of the kinds of questions clinicians ask themselves during the process of report construction. You will also find some additional comments to guide the process.

BEGINNING THE REPORT: PRELIMINARY INFORMATION (CHAPTER 4)

Who are you? When and where did you gather data? From where did you get this information? Who is the client? How well does the client understand the interview process and outcomes? (See Chapter 1, Sections 1.3 and 1.4, for assistance with explaining the purposes, conse-

TABLE 1. Generalized Format for an Evaluation Report

Components of a report	Chapters/sections of the *Clinician's Thesaurus*
A. Introducing the report (old information)	
Preliminary information	Chapter 4
Could include these:	
Headings and dates	Section 4.1
Sources of your information about the client	Section 4.2
Identifying information about the client	Section 4.3
Self-sufficiency in appearing for the examination	Section 4.4
Statements of consent to be evaluated	Section 4.5
Reliability of the client	Section 4.6
Confidentiality notices about the report	Section 4.7
Referral reasons	Chapter 5
Could include these:	
Nature of the problem(s) faced by the client or the referrer	Section 5.1
Who referred the client, for what services, and for what purpose(s)	Sections 5.2 to 5.4
Background information and history	Chapter 6
Could include these:	
History of the presenting problem or chief concern	Section 6.1
Medical, family, social, adjustment histories	Sections 6.2 to 6.5
Using a genogram	Section 6.6
B. The person in the evaluation (new information—personal)	
Could include these:	
Behavioral observations	Chapter 7
Responses to aspects of the examination	Chapter 8
Presentation of self	Chapter 9
Emotional/affective symptoms and disorders	Chapter 10
Cognition and mental status	Chapter 11
Abnormal signs, symptoms, and syndromes	Chapter 12
Personality patterns	Chapter 13
C. The person in the environment (new information—social)	
Could include these:	
Activities of Daily Living	Chapter 14
Social/community functioning	Chapter 15
Couple and family relationships	Chapter 16
Vocational/academic skills	Chapter 17
Recreational functioning	Chapter 18
Other specialized evaluations	Chapter 19
D. Completing the report	
New understandings	
Could include these:	
Summary of findings and conclusions	Chapter 20
Possible psychiatric masquerade of medical conditions	Chapter 28
Diagnostic statement/impression	Chapter 21
New plans	
Could include these:	
Recommendations	Chapter 22
Prognostic statements	Chapter 23
Detailed treatment plan	Chapter 25
Closing statements	Chapter 24

quences, and confidentiality of the interview to the client.) Were there any limitations on the interview? How reliable was the client?

REFERRAL REASONS (CHAPTER 5)

What is the nature of the problem(s) faced by the client or the referrer? Who referred the client, when, for what services, and for what purpose(s)? The greater the precision of this goal, the easier the report is to write, because you will always be returning to it. Spend as much time as necessary to refine your understanding of the referrer's needs.

BACKGROUND INFORMATION AND HISTORY (CHAPTER 6)

What led up to this evaluation? What do you know about this person's previous functioning and the context in which he/she has lived?

B. The Person in the Evaluation

The goal of the next main component of the report is to state how this person is doing in her/his life at present or in the recent past. The component, like the one that follows it, consists of *new information*. Here, that information is about the client's functioning in her/his contacts with you (during the assessment or therapeutic interviews).

What did you observe of this person's appearance, behavior, ways of relating to you, cognitive functioning, emotional reactions, symptoms, and personality? Your findings might be either test data for a psychological evaluation, or things you learned about the client's dynamics, personality, or functioning during therapy sessions you are now reviewing.

The central question for each of the first three areas covered below is this: What do these observable behaviors indicate or illustrate about important aspects of the client's mental state and interpersonal functioning? Information irrelevant to these aspects should be excluded.

BEHAVIORAL OBSERVATIONS (CHAPTER 7)

In what ways might the client's appearance, clothing, movement, speech, etc., indicate clinical phenomena?

RESPONSES TO ASPECTS OF THE EXAMINATION (CHAPTER 8)

How did the client relate to you and the your questions or materials? How much effort and persistence did he/she demonstrate? How did the client respond to difficulties, failure, frustration, success, or feedback?

PRESENTATION OF SELF (CHAPTER 9)

How friendly or forthcoming was the client? How self-confident was the client? How dependent or independent? How knowledgeable about socially appropriate behaviors? How warm or cold? How socially skilled?

The last four areas covered here are those usually seen as the most psychological: emotions; thinking; other signs, symptoms, and syndromes; and personality patterns.

EMOTIONAL/AFFECTIVE SYMPTOMS AND DISORDERS (CHAPTER 10)

What were the client's mood and affects? How did these change during the interview, in response to topics discussed or for other reasons? Did the client display or recount anger, anxiety/fear, depression, mania, guilt/shame, or other feelings?

COGNITION AND MENTAL STATUS (CHAPTER 11)

How well was the client able to think, to process information, to come to conclusions, to make decisions, and to take actions? Could she/he recall and integrate relevant information and exclude the irrelevant? Did she/he understand the world, her-/himself, and what was happening in common ways? Did he or she organize thoughts and words normally and communicate effectively? What evidence did you see of judgment, insight, and higher-level functioning? (For questions to evaluate all aspects of cognitive functioning, see Chapter 2.)

ABNORMAL SIGNS, SYMPTOMS, AND SYNDROMES (CHAPTER 12)

What other symptomatic behaviors (i.e., not purely emotional/affective or purely cognitive) have you been alerted to, observed, and investigated, and want to tell the referrer about? How severe are these? How limiting? (For questions to evaluate abnormal and symptomatic behaviors, see Chapter 3.)

PERSONALITY PATTERNS (CHAPTER 13)

What enduring and cross-situational patterns of attending, thinking, feeling, and acting did you observe? What evidence did you see of traits or patterns of the better-known personality disorders and character patterns (e.g., aggressive, authoritarian, codependent, sadistic, self-defeating, etc.)?

C. The Person in the Environment

Continuing with new information, the purpose of the third main component of the report is to describe how this person functions in the larger world of everyday activities, close and formal relationships, and similar areas. The central question to be answered is this: How successful or impaired is this person in each area?

ACTIVITIES OF DAILY LIVING (CHAPTER 14)

Can this person take care of him-/herself? How well accomplished are the daily tasks of self-care, cooking, cleaning, child care, shopping, and getting around?

SOCIAL/COMMUNITY FUNCTIONING (CHAPTER 15)

What has the client or others told you about social and community relationships? How skilled and involved is the client? How much conflict and failure does she/he experience?

COUPLE AND FAMILY RELATIONSHIPS (CHAPTER 16)

What did the client or others tell you about more intimate and persistent relationships with the members of his/her family of origin, spouse/partner, and/or children? How effective or limited is this person in these areas? If you evaluated family members, how competent were they? What were their structural and systemic patterns?

VOCATIONAL/ACADEMIC SKILLS (CHAPTER 17)

What do you know of the client's academic and vocational adjustments and accomplishments? What are her/his current reading, mathematical, and vocational skill levels? What kinds of problems or conflicts have occurred?

RECREATIONAL FUNCTIONING (CHAPTER 18)

How does this person spend his/her free time? What activities are engaged in, and at what level of performance or intensity? How satisfying are they?

OTHER SPECIALIZED EVALUATIONS (CHAPTER 19)

You may be asked to evaluate the client's competence to manage his or her finances, make a will, cope with stress, or adapt to being a refugee, among other things. Or you may be asked to describe her/his spiritual or religious concerns, problems, and issues.

D. Completing the Report

The last main component of the report covers new understandings and the resulting new plans. Groth-Marnat (1997, p. 631) says that a good report should "integrate old information as well as provide a new and unique perspective on a person." This is a daunting task. It requires an organization of the data around topics of interest, but there are a very large number of topics or ideas on which you can focus. If a report is to have value, it will be in the integration of the information and the formulation of accurate diagnoses, well-considered recommendations, and achievable plans for treatment.

Do not be afraid to do outlines and drafts (Ownby, 1997). You might start with summaries of the old and newly acquired information. You can then create a longitudinal picture: In your initial review of the client's life's trajectory, how do his/her background and history fit with the current findings (of a single slice of time) and lead to your prognosis and treatment recommendations? A later review should edit the materials into a tight narrative that clearly links the pieces of evidence to the conclusions drawn from it. Finally, use your understanding of the referral reasons or the readers' needs to pare down the report to the answers to their needs.

New Understandings

SUMMARY OF FINDINGS AND CONCLUSIONS (CHAPTER 20)

Offer an integration of history, findings, and/or observations, and your understanding of the client's functioning in the areas most relevant to the referrer's or reader's needs. Condense this information into a paragraph: the relevant demographic information, referral reason, history, and your major findings most relevant to the referral question, treatment history, or any other purpose of the report.

Additional issues may need to be addressed at this point in some reports. For example, what additional information do you need and from whom? Also, might the psychological symptoms presented be due to a medical condition? (See Chapter 28, "Psychiatric Masquerade of Medical Conditions.")

For testing reports, findings should be organized by topic (integrating the results of different tests, such as cognitive functioning, emotional controls, interpersonal relations, etc., depending on the referral questions). A statement about the probable reliability of the findings is also needed (see Chapter 4, Section 4.6, "Reliability Statements").

DIAGNOSTIC STATEMENT/IMPRESSION (CHAPTER 21)

A diagnosis is professional shorthand that integrates many kinds of data. Generally you should include all five axes of a DSM (or ICD) diagnosis and any "rule-outs." Placing it here orients the reader to the recommendations and treatment planning that follow.

New Plans

The last few elements of the report involve using your fuller and newer understanding of the client (generated above) to do new planning for services that are in the client's best long-term interest: recommendations and treatment planning (for more detail on the latter, see chapter 25, "Treatment Planning and Treatment Plan Formats").

RECOMMENDATIONS (CHAPTER 22)

Are any further evaluations needed to clarify diagnoses or other points? What levels and areas of current functioning indicate the need for treatment? What supports might the client need? What kinds of treatment would best restore functioning? How motivated is the client for treatment? In general terms, what intensity of treatment, approaches, and methods would be best? (For creating a detailed treatment plan, again, see Chapter 25. For a listing of common psychiatric medications, see Chapter 27, "Listing of Common Psychiatric and Psychoactive Drugs.")

PROGNOSTIC STATEMENTS (CHAPTER 23)

What course do you expect for this client if she/he does not receive the recommended treatments and services? More specific predictions belong in the treatment plan. What course do you expect for this client if she/he does receive the recommended treatments and services?

CLOSING STATEMENTS (CHAPTER 24)

Thank the referrer, indicate your continued availability, and sign the report.

Further Guidelines and Advice on Report Writing

Unlike reports of the past, which emphasized precise diagnosis and understanding of etiology, current models focus more on descriptions of the person and his/her specific behaviors. Current report models have shifted away from a focus on symptoms, maladjustments, and areas needing change; they now emphasize assessing strengths and coping mechanisms and maintaining a balanced perspective.

As to writing style, Ownby (1997) calls for a "professional style," by which he means avoiding jargon, using shorter words with precise meanings, writing short paragraphs focused on a single concept, and employing a variety of sentence lengths and structure to maintain readers' interest.

Take into account how the intended readers of your report will interpret it. Consider their level of psychological sophistication, their theoretical or professional orientation, their decisions and options, and their relationship with you.

Only those details that are relevant and have meaning for "point/purpose" of the report should be given.

Do not report as facts what you have only been told. Instead specify where the information came from. (For various phrasings, see "Attributions," above.)

It is sometimes useful to convey a client's personal style by reference to characters in the mass media, but this is easy to overdo.

Remember to report negative (absent) as well as positive (present) findings.

Avoid the unclarified use of acronyms, abbreviations, and names for local service providers and programs if the report is addressed to or might be useful to those unfamiliar with such references. Instead, use the local language and then describe the program in general terms—for example, "TSI, a transitional community residential services provider" or "7 West, the alcohol detoxification ward."

Where you are concerned about confidentiality and yet know you will be releasing the report to readers with whom you wish to maintain the subject's anonymity, you might use this method: Write the subject's name at the top of page 1 only, and use the subject's first (for a child) or last (for an adult) initial in all subsequent references to the subject. This way, you will have only one occurrence of the name to remove. (See also Section 4.7, "Confidentiality Notices.")

For the prevention of tampering with and loss of the pages of a report, they can be numbered as "Page 1 of 6," "Page 2 of 6," etc.

Because of concerns with test security and copyrights, do not repeat the questions from standardized tests or the mental status questions in your reports, but only the responses you received.

Make sure your statements are consistent. Don't make different judgments in the narrative and on a check-off form. Don't state different conclusions based on different data.

Be neat and legible, or get a word processor for everything. Use correct spelling and grammar, and use a dictionary or spelling checker.

Get feedback on your reports no matter how intimidating this may seem. Ask peers and report recipients for their input.

It is customary to write intakes and similar contemporaneous evaluations (e.g., progress notes) in the present tense, and to use the past tense for events reported from the past (as in closing summaries and histories). However, it is preferable to use careful phrasings in the present tense for material that is controversial or potentially untrue, and for which you have no confirming evidence beyond the client's report. For example, phrasings like "The client describes her parents as severe alcoholics" or "He reports having been sexually abused by his priest" are preferable to "Her parents were alcoholics" or "He was sexually abused by his priest."

Sattler's (1988) advice on writing reports is worthwhile:

- Prefer the specific to the general, the definite to the vague, the concrete to the abstract.
- Do not take shortcuts at the cost of clarity.
- Avoid fancy words.
- Omit needless words. Make every word tell.
- Express coordinate ideas in similar form. The content, not the style, should protect the report from monotony.
- Use a clear order of presentation so that your ideas can be followed.
- Avoid the use of qualifiers. "Rather," "somewhat," "possible," "may"—these are the leeches that infest the pond of prose, sucking the blood of words.
- Put statements in positive form. Make definite assertions; avoid tame, colorless, hesitating, noncommittal language.
- Do not overstate. Avoid overgeneralization, overinterpretations, and "Barnum statements" (see Meehl, 1954/1996).

Esser (1974) points out these common problems with reports:

- Failure to answer referral questions or provide desired information.
- Making the report too long or too short. The report should be the shortest way to convey the essential information. Balance brevity and thoroughness.
- Telling the referrer what he/she already knows, or, conversely, failing to use referrer-provided information.
- Providing just pure data: findings without interpretations, judgments, or impressions.
- The presence of contradictions in the report.
- Reluctance to provide realistic or negative findings.
- Making unrealistic plans for the client.
- Failure to back up recommendations and plans with facts and reasons.
- Failure to consider alternative recommendations, courses of action, and objectives.
- Giving a summary that isn't one: It fails to bring together the information and to create a composite picture from it.

Zimmerman and Woo-Sam (1973) offer other points:

- State the information simply and concisely.
- In your writing style, reflect the human elements over the scientific objectivity.
- Tailor the report to the reader's needs.
- Minimize the use of jargon.
- If you cite an authority, make certain she/he is qualified and neutral.
- Do not go beyond your data.
- Do not hedge so much that your statements are meaningless.
- Identify the substantiated bases of your cause–effect conclusions, and beware of fads in these interpretations.

SOME WAYS TO USE THE *CLINICIAN'S THESAURUS*

To use the Clinician's Thesaurus most efficiently, please understand that it is organized in the sequence of actions you would take to approach a client, assess the client's functioning, and then construct the report. Part I covers conducting a mental health evaluation. Part II offers ways to begin, develop, and end the report; it includes all of the standard topics addressed in mental health reports, presented in the sequence they are addressed in a typical report, as described above. Part III offers treatment plan formats, alternative report formats, and other useful resources.

When You Interview

You can use Part I of this book to guide your interview. You might simply read some of the mental status or symptom questions to the client; you might copy out a few to ask; or you might use them to refresh your memory of the questions appropriate to the referral's concerns. In contrast to structured interviews, these chapters offer many questions for each area; if a particular question does not result in a satisfactory response, you will have many similar ones to use.

When You Write or Dictate a Report

As described above, Part II of this book is organized in the same sequence as the "classic" mental health report. You can use it to organize the data you have collected during an interview or testing. The individual chapter titles correspond to the major headings of standard reports such as Behavioral Observations, Mental Status, or Diagnostic Summary. Within each chapter, the numbered sections cover the aspects that are typically evaluated in that area. Paging through the major numbered sections within each chapter will remind you to address each relevant area in your report. If you need to do a very comprehensive evaluation, you can use all the numbered headings within each chapter as a checklist to make certain you haven't overlooked any important point.

The chapters in Part II contain numerous ranges of specific words and phrases. From these, you can select the best descriptors for your patient in these areas. You can turn to a specific chapter and its numbered sections to focus on a particular topic for writing a more fine-grained description.

As you use the *Clinician's Thesaurus,* you may find it worthwhile to highlight in color, underline, or box the words or phrases that best suit your writing style and are most relevant to your practice and setting. You may find it practical to use the black thumb tabs on the edge of each page to access sections of the book more quickly. On several pages, some space is purposely left blank so that you can easily add your notes, comments, and especially suggestions (see "Acknowledgments and an Invitation," above).

When You Teach

As a teacher, you simply cannot offer your students more than a fraction of the behaviors a clinician must understand. When you focus on a few diagnoses or processes, students may miss the breadth they will need. If you discuss theory, your students may miss the concrete; if you offer cases, they may learn only a few examples and not the larger picture of the disorder. As a teacher, I have struggled with these choices myself. This book provides another option: All the aspects of each syndrome and pattern are in the *Clinician's Thesaurus*. The whole language of the mental health field is in here.

When students need to interview, the questions here will enable them to follow up (almost) any referral question. When they sit down to write up their findings, all the language options are here. They and you can concentrate on the higher-level functions—weighing, winnowing, and adapting—not on reinventing the standard language.

Students love this book because it reduces their anxiety, as well as making them more competent. When they see that (almost) everything they will need is in this one book, they breathe a sigh of relief. The book does not replace their clinical education, but it does assist the process. It is equivalent to giving a calculator to a math student: The student can concentrate on the nature of the problem, not the details of the calculation.

When You Supervise

Less skilled professionals or students may sometimes fail to think deeply or may write glib reports. The usual supervisor's response to this situation is to interview the students, trying to pull from them observations of the patients that they probably never made because they lacked the terms for labeling the phenomena of interest. Even Socrates couldn't always ask the right questions, and so this approach is usually frustrating and unproductive (except that it produces bad feelings between supervisors and students).

When you supervise, try this instead: Refer such students to the appropriate sections of the *Clinician's Thesaurus* and ask them to find, say, three or more words to describe the cognitive aspects of a patient's depression. Not only does this make the supervision problem into a game instead of a contest over who is smarter, but also it puts the burden of discrimination on the students, where it belongs. Moreover, this process of weighing the alternatives trains a kind of clinical judgment that I find almost impossible to teach in other ways.

The *Clinician's Thesaurus* is not a "cheat sheet" or a crutch. Reports written by clinicians using it are not "canned." Few individuals have 25,000 words and statements in mind to choose from, and there is no limitation on entering new ones into the book. It does not write reports for anyone; students still have to learn the words' meanings and evaluate their appropriateness for each client.

A CAUTIONARY NOTE AND DISCLAIMER

The entries of this book are presented simply as sample questions and lists of terms that have been used in the field. Their presence here does not imply any endorsement by the author or publisher. These wordings are offered without any warranty, implied or explicit, that they constitute the only or the best way to practice as a professional or clinician.

When individuals use any of the words, phrases, descriptors, sentences, or procedures described in this book, they must assume the full responsibility for all the consequences—clinical, legal, ethical, and financial. The author and publisher cannot, do not, and will not assume any responsibility for the use or implementation of the book's contents in practice or with any person, patient, client, or student. The author and publisher shall not be liable in the event of incidental or consequential damages in connection with or arising out of any use by purchasers or users of the materials in this book. By employing this book, users signify their acceptance of the limits of the work and their acceptance of complete personal responsibility for all such uses.

The author and publisher presume (1) that the users of this book are qualified by education and/or training to employ it ethically and legally, and (2) that users will not exceed the limits of documentable competence in their disciplines as indicated by their codes of ethical practice.

If more than the material presented here is needed to manage a case in any regard, readers are directed to engage the services of a competent professional consultant.

I would be grateful for and attentive to your suggestions and improvements, and will send you a free copy of the next revision of the *Clinician's Thesaurus* if these are implemented. Please see "Acknowledgments and an Invitation," above, for further information, or use the feedback form on page 367.

Part I

Conducting
a Mental Health Evaluation

1

Beginning and Ending
the Interview

1.1. STRUCTURING THE INTERVIEW

There are dozens of specialized interview methods (see Hersen & Turner, 1994) and numerous structured interviews, which should be used to increase reliability and validity over more open-ended approaches. An excellent guide for a clinician seeking this direction is Rogers (1995).

The format below addresses some points crucial to beginning all interviews, whether structured or unstructured. Because a client may not understand a question's goal, or the answer may not be as informative as you hoped, Chapters 2 ("Mental Status Evaluation Questions/Tasks") and 3 ("Questions about Signs, Symptoms, and Behavior Patterns") offer multiple questions under each topic so that you can ask a second or third question.

1.2. INTRODUCING YOURSELF AND NOTING POSSIBLE COMMUNICATION DIFFICULTIES

See Section 7.5, "Qualities of Communication."

Make eye contact and introduce yourself to each client as follows: "Hello, I'm (Title) (Name). And you are . . . ?"

With each client, be alert to the client's possible **limitations of hearing and vision,** and inquire if you have any reason to suspect a disability. Ask about any need for glasses/contact lenses or hearing aids if not worn, and comment in your report on the effects on the client's performance. Ask the client for suggestions to improve conditions, such as minimizing the background noise or changing the lighting. Don't cover your mouth; be sure to speak clearly. When you are interviewing hearing-impaired clients or users of American Sign Language (who call themselves deaf), it is far preferable to obtain the services of a certified interpreter than to force clients to read or write in a language structure other than ASL or to lip-read. There are far too many examples of hearing-impaired people being misdiagnosed as mentally retarded or psychotic for any examiner to be complacent about this.[1]

1.3. ASSESSING THE CLIENT'S UNDERSTANDING OF THE INTERVIEW SITUATION

Ask early, especially if the subject seems unforthcoming:

> "What have you been told about this interview/our meeting?"
> "What do you expect to happen here?"
> "What did you think and feel before you came in here/met me?"

> "Because I have spoken with _____ /read reports from _____ /know you from _____, I already know some things about you/why you have come here/why we are talking. However, I'd like to hear from you why you have come to see me/come here."

> "I'd like to talk with you for a few minutes in order to _____."

Assess and report, with your conclusions, the presence of any of the following:

> Visual impairment: Near-/farsightedness, astigmatism, cataracts, hemianopsia, blindness, etc.; totally/partially/not compensated for with glasses.
> Hearing impairment: Total/partial deafness in left/right/both ears, necessitating hearing aids/lip reading/signing/total communication/American Sign Language; understands amplified/simplified/repeated conversational speech.
> Impaired speech. *(See Section 7.4, "Speech Behavior.")*
> Unfamiliarity with the English language, English as a second language, non-native speaker.

1.4. OBTAINING INFORMED CONSENT

See Section 4.5, "Consent Statements."

Obtain fully informed and voluntary consent to the interview or evaluation.

Explain the purposes of the interview. Attend to the client's and examiner's perceived expecta-

---

[1] I am grateful to Ilene D. Miner, CSW, ACSW, of New York, NY, for this information.

tions of the referring agent; what information is to be gathered, by what means; what is then to be done; and, if a report is written or made, who will see it.

As you explain each relevant aspect, ask the client: "Would that be all right with you?"

Once some private fact is revealed, it cannot be ignored, so you must fully explain the likely consequences of your evaluation and subsequent report and then offer the client the opportunity not to participate and let him/her know he/she can stop participating at any point. I usually use statements such as "Consider what will be in your long-term best interests" or "If you have any reservations let us discuss them before we proceed any further." Do encourage questions if you detect or suspect any reluctance.

Of course, issues may arise as you proceed, in which case you might say something like, "You can stop me at any time during our interview if you don't understand me or what I am asking you to do."

For situations in which you are a consultant, you should explain that your interview will not be for treatment, you will not prescribe anything or refer the client to other therapists, nothing is off the record, and the client may choose not to answer any of your questions.

1.5. OTHER ASPECTS TO BE CONSIDERED AT THE BEGINNING OF THE INTERVIEW

Current medication prescribed/taken: name(s), dosage(s), frequency.

Current use of alcohol and other drugs.

Handedness/preference/dominance: Comment here or later (*see the "Praxis" heading under Section 7.3, "Movement/Activity"*).

Understanding and use of English or whatever language the interview was conducted in (ASL, etc.)

Use of or need for an interpreter, and possible consequences of this: ambiguity, distortions, psychological naivete or sophistication of interpreter, the influence of the interpreter's opinions of client's language and thoughts, etc.

✓ It may be hard for clinicians to understand that up to half their clients, depending on the setting, lack basic literacy. However, because illiteracy is socially negative, few clients will acknowledge it when asked. Appropriate evaluation should be routine. Administering an instrument called the Rapid Estimate of Adult Literacy in Medicine (Davis et al., 1993) is more relevant than having a client read aloud and summarize the content of a few paragraphs from a magazine. Low literacy and its resulting misunderstanding and low compliance should not be mistaken for resistance.

1.6. UNIQUE ASPECTS OF YOUR SETTING

Space is provided below for you to note any things you should do because of the nature of your professional setting.

Because of my setting, **I should always remember the following:**

Do:

Say:

Warn about:

Explain:

Remind the client of:

1.7. ELICITING THE CHIEF CONCERN/COMPLAINT/ISSUE
See Section 6.1 for descriptors of the Chief Concern.

"Would you please tell me why you are here/we are meeting/you are being evaluated?"
"What brings you to the hospital/the clinic/my office?"
"What concerns you most?"
"What has been going on?"
"Why have you come to see me?"
"What has happened to you?"
"What do you hope to have happen because we have met?"

1.8. ELICITING THE CLIENT'S UNDERSTANDING OF THE PROBLEM
See also Section 19.5, "Cultural Sensitive Formulations."

Some initial questions to elicit the client's understanding of the presenting problem (based on similar questions by Reimer et al., 1984) are as follows:

"What do you think caused your problem?"
"Do you have an explanation for why it started when it did?"
"What does your problem do to you?" "How does it work?"
"How severe is your problem/disorder/complaint/sickness?"
"How long do you expect it to last?"
"What problems has your problem/disorder/complaint/sickness caused you?"

"What do you fear about your problem/disorder/complaint/sickness?"
"What kind of treatment do you think you should receive?"
"What are the most important results you hope to receive from this assessment/treatment?"

1.9. DIMENSIONALIZING THE CONCERN/PROBLEM

"For how long has this been happening?"   (Duration)
"How often does this happen?"   (Frequency)
"Think back to the last time this happened
  and tell me:

  "What led up to its happening?"   (Antecedents, cues, controlling stimuli,
  latency, sequences, progression, chains)

  "What were you thinking and feeling?"   (Expectations, beliefs, meanings, affects)
  "Who else was around, and what did they   (Social support, who defined problem)
  think and feel?"
  "What happened next/afterward?"   (Sequences, reinforcers, consequences)
  "How typical was this occasion?"   (Development of the problem, intensity)
  "Was the first time it happened different?"   (Client's understanding of development)
  "What could have made a difference in   (Expectations of outcome, changeability,
  this incident?"   treatment, treaters, understandings of
  causation)

1.10. ENDING THE INTERVIEW

It is best to develop a standard set of closing statements for your interview. These will ensure that potentially important information is not lost, that consistency across clients and occasions is maintained for reliability and validity, and that important legal or patient care issues are discussed.

"Is there anything else that you want to add/tell me/want me to know/understand?"
"Is there anything important/relevant that we have not covered?"

"Do you have any questions about what we have done today/this evaluation/the report I will be writing?"

"Do you have any questions about what the next step will be/what happens next?"
"The next step is that _____ will contact you about _____ by mail/phone."
"_____ will see you later to discuss _____."
"You will need to make an appointment with _____ to _____."

"I want to thank you for your time and efforts."
"I appreciate your taking the time to come to this interview and the efforts you made to provide the information I needed."
"Thank you for your time and efforts in coming here and talking to me."
"I expect that you will receive some benefit from all of this." Or "Although you will not benefit directly from what we have done today, you will be assisting in the training of professionals who/the collection of research data that will help others in your situation."

2

Mental Status Evaluation Questions/Tasks

These questions are about **cognitive functions**. Questions about **symptoms** and **abnormal behaviors** are in the **next** chapter.

2.1. INTRODUCTION TO THE MENTAL STATUS QUESTIONS

Over the years, clinicians have discovered questions for assessing mental status (especially cognitive function) that seemed face-valid, heuristic, or revelatory, and have passed them down to their students. With empirical examination, most of these have been found to lack reliability, validity, or both, and the whole area of interpreting the patient's responses is unstandardized. Therefore, for higher reliability, a number of standardized brief mental status tests and short batteries are available, such as those by Folstein et al. (1975), Erkinjunti et al. (1987), Ables et al. (1983), Davis et al. (1990), Favier (1986), Hays (1984), Jacobs et al. (1977), Lefkovitz et al. (1982), Miller et al. (1988), Mueller (1995), Pfeiffer (1975), Reisberg (1983, 1985), Reisberg et al. (1982), Sovner and Hurley (1983), Robertson et al. (1982), and Whelilan et al. (1984). You could, of course, use the questions from the age-appropriate sections of the Stanford–Binet, or the Wechsler subtests of Information, Arithmetic, Comprehension, Similarities, or Digit Span, for the advantage of precise scoring and interpretation of the responses. Even with these tests, however, norming and validity may still be less than desired for the important consequences that flow from MSE's.

The questions offered below may be suitable alternatives for clients who have recently been formally tested on the instruments cited above, or they may be used for other reasons. These questions are appropriately used only as screening devices; unusual responses must be investigated further with standardized tests, and patterns of unusual responses must be investigated with neuropsychological, neurological, or other appropriate scientific methods.

No assertion or implication of any kind of validity is made or should be inferred about the use of the questions presented here. As far as I know, no research has been conducted on them, and no published norms are available to guide clinicians in interpreting the responses obtained to the questions asked. The internal "norms" of experienced and well-trained professionals are the only basis for evaluating such responses. Although you will find guidance in almost any psychiatry text, the best books for learning to do MSEs are Trzepacz and Baker (1993) and Morrison (1995a). The latter has a simple but excellent eight-page outline that integrates the process of data gathering and the formal structure of the interview. Rogers (1995) offers reviews of MSEs and structured interviews.

The following areas of mental functioning with numbered sections are presented in rough order of increasing complexity and demand on the client's cognitive abilities. For each subsection that asks about a specific cognitive function, such as memory, similarities, or social judgment, a cross-reference is included to the appropriate section of Chapter 11, "Cognitive and Mental Status." There you will find the terms for describing the cognitive function.

2.2. BACKGROUND INFORMATION RELATED TO MENTAL STATUS

See also Chapter 6, "Background Information and History."

✓ **Note**: If the client is incapable of providing this information, a family member or other informant should be sought.

"How far did you go in school/How many grades did you finish in school/Did you finish high school?"

"In school, were you ever left behind a year/not promoted to the next grade/did you have to take a grade over again?"

"Were you ever in any kind of special classes/special education/classes for the learning-disabled/ slow learners/mentally retarded/socially and emotionally disturbed or disabled?"

2.3. RANCHO LOS AMIGOS COGNITIVE SCALE

This scale can be used to assess the level of function in carrying out purposeful behavior. Adapted from Hagen, Malkmus, and Durham (1979). Used by permission.

Level I	No response to pain, touch, sound, or sight.
Level II	Generalized reflex response to pain.
Level III	Localized response. Blinks to strong light, turns toward/away from sound. Responds to physical discomfort. Inconsistent response to commands.
Level IV	Confused–agitated. Alert, very active, aggressive, or bizarre behaviors. Performs motor activities, but behavior is nonpurposeful. Extremely short attention span.
Level V	Confused–nonagitated. Gross attention to environment. Highly distractible; requires continual redirection. Difficulty learning new tasks. Agitated by too much stimulation. May engage in social conversation, but with inappropriate verbalizations.
Level VI	Confused–appropriate. Inconsistent orientation to time and place. Retention span/recent memory impaired. Begins to recall past. Consistently follows simple directions. Goal-directed behavior with assistance.
Level VII	Automatic–appropriate. Performs daily routine in highly familiar environment in a nonconfused but mechanical, robot-like manner. Skills noticeably deteriorate in unfamiliar environment. Lacks realistic planning for own future.
Level VIII	Purposeful–appropriate.

2.4. GLASGOW COMA SCALE

This scale can be used for more precise numerical rating of core mental functioning, particularly after brain trauma. It is for an older child (age 4 and up) or adult and is adapted from Teasdale and Jenvet (1974). It is used by permission.

Eyes:	Open:	Spontaneously	4
		To verbal command	3
		To pain	2
		No response	1
Best motor response:	To verbal command:	Obeys	6
	To painful stimulus:	Localizes pain	5
		Flexion–withdrawal	4
		Flexion–abnormal	3
		Extension	2
		No response	1
Best verbal response:		Oriented and converses	5
		Disoriented and converses	4
		Inappropriate words	3
		Incomprehensible sounds	2
		No response	1

Total (3–15): ___

✓ Generally, ratings of 12 or above indicate mild injuries, and ratings of 8 or less indicate severe injuries.

2.5. ORIENTATION

See Section 11.3, "Orientation," for descriptors.

To assess the period of disorientation and confusion after <u>T</u>raumatic <u>B</u>rain <u>I</u>njury, you can use the <u>G</u>alveston <u>O</u>rientation and <u>A</u>mnesia <u>T</u>est (Levin et al., 1979). Or use the following questions:

To Person

"Who are you?"
"What is your name?"   [✔ Pay attention to nicknames, childhood versions of name, hesitations, aliases.]
"Are you married?"
"What kind of work do/did you do?"

For a Child:

"What school do you go to?"
"What grade are you in now?"

To Place

"Where are we/you?" (Setting, address/building, city, state/province.)
"Where do you live?" (Setting, address/building, city, state/province.)
"How far is this place from where you live?"

To Time

Observe whether the client wears a watch and, if so, whether the time indicated is correct and the client can read the time correctly. If the client wears no watch and indicates not knowing the time, ask for a guess or an approximation.

"What time is it? Is that A.M. or P.M.? Is it day or night?"
"How old are you?" "When is your birthday?"
"What day is today? Which day of the week is today? What month is it now? What is today's date?"
"What season is it? What year is it?"
"When did you first come here? How long have you been here? Have you ever been here before?"
    (If yes:) "How long were you here then?"

To Situation

"Who am I?"
"What am I doing here?"
"What is the purpose of our talking?"
"Why are you here?"

To Familiar Objects

[Hold up your hand and ask, "Is this my right or left hand?" "Please name the fingers of my hand."
Hold up/point to a pencil, a watch, and eyeglasses, and ask the client to name each object, its uses, and its parts.

To Other People

"What is your mother's/father's/spouse's name?"
"What is your child's name/are your children's names?"
"What is my name?"
"What is my title/job?"
"When was the last time we met?"
"What are the names of some staff members?"   [✔ Ask about their titles, functions, etc., as well.]
"What are the names of some other persons here/patients?"

2.6. ATTENTION

See Section 11.4, "Attention," for descriptors.

The questions and tasks below, arranged in order of increasing difficulty (↔ *by degree*), cover active information processing about a single or particular stimulus with filtering out of irrelevant stimuli.

For attention span questions, see Sections 2.7, "Concentration," and 2.10, "Memory."

"Please say the alphabet as fast as possible."   (Note the time taken; normal speed is 3–10 seconds.)
"Spell 'world'/'house.'" "And now please spell it backward."
"Repeat your Social Security number backward, please."   [✔ You may need to clarify this by adding "One number at a time, from the end."]
"Tap a pencil on the table each and every time I say the letter C." (Present a series of random letters at the rate of about one each second, with the letter C randomly distributed but occurring about every three to eight letters.)   [✔ Normal performance is making one or two errors (not noticing a C) in 45 seconds/45 letters.]
Digit span, forward and reverse: In other words, ask client to listen to, repeat, then repeat in reverse an arbitrary series of digits you say first. *(See Section 2.10, "Memory.")*
Name three objects and have the client repeat them, or repeat all three to the client until all are learned. Record the trials until the client is able to repeat all of them accurately.   [✔ This can also be used for delayed recall.] *(See Section 2.10.)*
"Count and then tell me the number of taps I have made." (Tap the underside of the table, or in some other manner make several trials of 3–15 sounds out of the client's sight.)

2.7. CONCENTRATION (↔ *by degree*)

See Section 11.5, "Concentration," for descriptors.

The questions and tasks here cover the maintenance of/holding of attention, or the performance of linked mental acts that require the excluding of irrelevant stimuli.

"Please spell your last name." "Now please spell it backward."
"Name the days of the week backward, starting with Sunday."
"Please name the months of the year. Now please say them backward."
"Say the alphabet backward as fast as you can."
Ask the client to write a fairly long and complex sentence from your dictation.
Ask the client to tell you when a minute has passed while you talk/don't talk to him/her, and record the time taken.

Ask the client to point to/underline each A in a written list presented on a full page of letters: for
example, B, F, H, K, <u>A</u>, X, E, P, <u>A</u>, etc.

Have the client do mental arithmetic problems. *(See Section 2.16, "Calculation Abilities," for example–including the famous "serial sevens.")*

2.8. COMPREHENSION OF LANGUAGE

Receptive

Receptive language abilities can be assessed by the response to a series of commands such as
these:

"Close your eyes. Open them. Raise an arm. Raise your left arm."

"Show me how you brush your teeth/comb your hair."

"Put your right hand on your left knee three times, and then touch your left ear with your right
hand."

"If today is Tuesday, raise one arm; otherwise, raise both."

(A three-stage command:) "Pick up that paper, fold it in half, and put it on the floor."

"Please read and obey this sentence." (Presented on a card: "Close your eyes.")

Fluency

"Please tell me as many words as you can think of that begin with the letter F. Don't give me
names/proper nouns or repeat yourself, and keep going until I stop you." (Stop the client after
30 seconds, and perhaps repeat with the letters A, P, or S. Score is the total number of words
meeting the criteria on each trial.)

Expressive

Have the client repeat the following, one at a time: "One, top, pipe, basket, cabinet, affection, sten-
torian, pleurisy, Methodist Episcopal; No ifs, ands, or buts; liquid linoleum; Third Royal Riding
Artillery Brigade."

Ask the client to read and explain some sentences from a magazine or newspaper.

Show her/him a photograph (e.g., in a magazine) and ask for the name(s) of the item(s) depicted.

Ask her/him to describe a picture portraying several actions.

2.9. EYE–HAND COORDINATION/PERCEPTUAL–MOTOR INTEGRATION/DYSPRAXIA/CONSTRUCTIONAL ABILITY

Ask the client to:
Pick up a coin with each hand.
Spin a paper clip on the tabletop, using each hand.
Touch each thumb to each finger as you name them (not in order).

Ask the client to:
Copy a design of two overlapping pentagons from an illustration on a card.
Draw a house/a tree/a person/a person of the opposite sex/yourself.   [✓ These are known as
the <u>H</u>ouse–<u>T</u>ree–<u>P</u>erson and <u>H</u>uman <u>F</u>igure <u>D</u>rawing tests.]

MENTAL STATUS
QUESTIONS

Ask the client to draw, from your dictation:

a diamond   the outlines of a cross
a smoking pipe   the edges of a transparent cube

Ask the client to draw a clock face and then indicate the present time as he/she estimates it to be, or "twenty after six."   [✔ This is known as the Clocks Test. See O'Rourke et al., 1997.]

2.10. MEMORY

See Section 11.7, "Memory," for descriptors.

If possible, it is probably best to use the Wechsler Memory Scale—III (Wechsler, 1998) or a similar validated test for accurate and precise evaluation.

Introductory Questions

"Has your memory been good?"
"Have you had any difficulty concentrating or remembering what you read/watch on television/recipes/telephone numbers/appointment times?"
"Have you recently gotten lost/forgotten an important event/forgotten something you were cooking/left some appliance on too long?"
"Have you had any difficulty recalling people's names or where you know them from?"
"Have other people said to you that your memory is not as good as it was?"

Immediate Memory

Immediate memory covers a period of about 10–30 seconds in the experimental laboratory, or what was just said, done, or learned during the evaluation in the clinic.

Digit span, both forward and reverse, is a common but complex task requiring perhaps more concentration than immediate memory.[1] Begin by telling the client:

"I would like to check your memory. I am going to say some numbers one at a time. When I finish, please repeat them back to me. Ready?"

Start with two digits ("1, 7," not "17, 36," etc.). When the client repeats these correctly on a first or second attempt (with different digits), increase the length of the list by one digit until the client fails both trials/number sequences offered. Write the numbers down as you say them.

✔ Speak at a consistent rate of one digit per second; do not emphasize ending numbers with changes in your voice; and avoid consecutive numbers and easily recognizable dates or familiar sequences, or use your own Social Security number or telephone number.

Then say:

"Now I am going to say some more numbers, but this time I want you to repeat them backward. For example, if I said '6, 2,' what would you say?"

✔ The score is the maximum number of correctly recalled digits in correct order on either trial. "Five forward with one mistake" is four forward.

✔ Normal digit span is about five to eight digits forward and four to six backward. A difference of three or more in maximum forward minus maximum backward suggests concen-

---

[1]I am grateful to James L. Pointer, PhD, of Montgomery, AL, for this clarification.

tration deficits. Five or more forward is considered unimpaired in younger or middle-aged adults.

Short-Term Retention

Short-term retention covers a period from a few minutes up to 1–2 hours.

- Name (for auditory retention) or point to (for visual retention) three items (e.g., Broadway–New York City–taxi; book–pen–tablet; scissors–stapler–pad, apple–peach–pear). Tell the client that you will ask him/her about them later, and then ask for recall after 5 minutes of interspersed activities.
- Offer four items from four categories (e.g., house, table, pencil, dictionary) and record the number of trials taken to learn the list. Ask for recall in 5 and 10 minutes. If the items are not recalled, prompt with category descriptions (e.g., a building, a piece of furniture, a writing tool, a kind of book). If they are still not recalled, ask the client to select the words from a list of four similar items (e.g., for pencil offer pen, crayon, pencil, paintbrush).
- Give the client three colors or shapes to remember, and ask her/him to recall them in 5 minutes.
- Tell the client your name and ask him/her to remember it because you will ask for it later. Ask in 5–10 minutes. If it is not correctly recalled, reinform and teach; then ask again every 5 or 10 minutes more, and note the number of trials to mastery or your abandoning the test.
- Ask the client to read a narrative paragraph from a magazine or newspaper, and to produce the gist of the story upon completion without being able to refer to the source.
- Ask about events at the beginning of the interview. (For example, were any other people present? What was asked first and next? Which history items were sought?)

Recent Memory

Recent memory covers a period from a few hours up to 1–4 days, and so also today's events.

- Ask about yesterday's meals/television programs/activities/companions (but only if these can be verified).
- Ask about the route taken/distance to this office, your name (if not overused in the interview), events in the recent news.

Recent Past Memory

Recent past memory refers to the last few weeks and months. Ask the following questions only if the answers can be verified:

- "What did you do last weekend?"
- "Where and when did you take your last vacation?"
- "What presents did you get on your last birthday/Christmas?"
- "What were you doing on the most recent national holiday (July 4th, Labor Day, Christmas)?"
- "Name any other doctors you have seen/any hospitalizations/tests received, when the present illness began/you first felt troubled/ill, etc."

Remote Memory

Remote memory extends from approximately 6 months ago up to all of the client's lifetime, including the premorbid period (before symptom onset). Ask about the following:

- Childhood events (in their correct sequence), places lived, schools attended, names of friends.
  - "Where were you born?"
  - "What is your birth date? Your first memory?"
  - "What was the name of your high school?"

Life history: parents' full names, siblings' names and birth order, family deaths, first job, date(s) of marriage, names/birth dates/ages of children.

More difficult alternatives: siblings' birthdays, dates of hospitalizations, names of doctors, school teachers' names, "how you dressed up for Halloween."

Activities on holidays about a year ago or on other dates that stand out.

Local historical events.

Historical events: Sputnik (1957); first men on the moon (July 20, 1969); name of the U.S. president who resigned (Nixon, Aug. 9, 1974); the fall of Saigon (Apr. 29, 1975); U.S. presidents during wars (WW II—F. D. Roosevelt; Korean War—Truman, Eisenhower; Vietnam—Johnson, Nixon); *Challenger* disaster (Jan. 28, 1986); collapse of Berlin Wall (Nov. 9, 1989); Tiananmen Square massacre (June 4, 1989); Operation Desert Storm (Jan.–Feb. 1991); Nelson Mandela becomes president of South Africa (1994); Oklahoma City bombing (Apr. 19, 1995), etc.

2.11. FUND OF INFORMATION

See Section 11.8, "Information," for descriptors.

Basic Orientation Information

"What is your birth date? Social Security number?"
"What is your phone number? Area code?"
"What is your address? Zip code?"
"What is your height? Weight? Shoe size? Dress/suit size?"

"Tell me the time." "What time will it be in an hour and a quarter?"
"How long will it be until Christmas?"
"How many days are there in a month/year?"
"Name the days of the week/months of the year."

"Where are we?"   [✓ Ask for state, county, city, hospital/building, floor, office.]
"Name the local sports teams."
"What is the capital of this state?"
"Which states border this one?"
"Name the five largest U.S. cities."
"How far is it from here to ____ (one of the large cities named above)?"
"How far is it from New York City to San Francisco?"
"In which country is Rome/Paris/London/Moscow?"
"Name three countries in the Middle East/Europe/South America."
"What is the current population of this city/state/the United States (about 268 million in 1999), the world (about 6.2 billion in 1999)?"

Information about People

"Who is the current president? And before him? And before him? Name the presidents backward, starting with the current one." (U.S. Presidents since 1901 in reverse order: Clinton, Bush, Reagan, Carter, Ford, Nixon, Johnson, Kennedy, Eisenhower, Truman, F. D. Roosevelt, Hoover, Coolidge, Harding, Wilson, Taft, T. Roosevelt.)   [✓ Note: The failure to recall most of these is not pathognomonic.]
"Where does the president live?" (In the White House; Washington, D.C.)
"Who was the first president of the United States?"
"Who is the governor of this state/mayor of this city?"
"Who is Bruce Springsteen/Gloria Estefan/Michael Jackson/Michael Jordan/Mark McGwire/Martina Hingis?"

"What was Booker T. Washington/Thomas Edison/Jonas Salk/Albert Einstein famous for?"
"Who invented the airplane?" (The Wright brothers, Wilbur and Orville.)
"What does a pharmacist do?"
"Who is/was John F. Kennedy/Mikhail Gorbachev/Martin Luther King, Jr./Indira Gandhi/Fidel Castro?"

For a Child:

"Who is Mickey Mouse/Mr. Rogers/Big Bird/Ronald McDonald/Barney?"
"What are your teachers' names?"

The names in several of these questions can of course be varied depending on a client's age, gender, and ethnicity, as well as on the current popularity or importance of various figures.

Information about Things

"Name five foods."
"Name five animals."
Ask about local geography: rivers, mountains, streets, downtown, parks, highways, stores, malls, schools.
"How many sides does a pentagon have?" (Five.)
"Name three animals beginning with C."
"Name three cities beginning with D."
"How many ounces in a pound?" (16.)
"What are houses made of?"
"Which is the longest river in the United States?" (The Mississippi.)
"In what direction does the sun rise?" (The east.)
"Please identify these." (Show some coins and bills of common U.S. currency.)
"Who/whose face is on a penny/nickel/dime/dollar bill/five-dollar bill?" (Lincoln/Jefferson/F. D. Roosevelt/Washington/Lincoln.)
"At what temperature does water freeze?" (32 degrees Fahrenheit or 0 degrees Celsius.)
"From what do we get gasoline?" (Oil, crude oil.)

Information about Events

"What do we celebrate on the 4th of July/Christmas/Thanksgiving Day/Labor Day/Memorial Day/ Easter/Passover/Ramadan/Kwanzaa?"
"Who won the last Super Bowl/World Series?"
"Please name some events/big stories that are currently in the news/that you have read about in the papers or seen on the TV news."
"What has happened recently in (specify a place)?"
"What did (person's name) do recently? What happened to (person's name) recently?"
"In about what years did the United States fight in World War II/Korea/Vietnam/the Persian Gulf?" (1941–1945, 1950–1953, 1965–1975, and 1990–1991, respectively.) "What were the issues involved in each war?"
(For those over 60 Years of Age:) "What was the date of the attack on Pearl Harbor?" (Dec. 7, 1941.)
(For those over 40 Years of Age:) "What was the date President John F. Kennedy was assassinated?" (Nov. 22, 1963.)

2.12. OPPOSITES

"Please tell me the opposite of each of these words."
Hard   fast   large   out   high   child

2.13. DIFFERENCES

Use the format "What is the difference between a _____ and a _____?" or "In what ways are a _____ and a _____ different or not the same?"

lie–mistake	midget–child	kite–airplane
duck–chickadee	orange–baseball	water–land

Ask: "Which of these is the different one and why?"

Desk, *apple*, chair, lamp. (Apple is not furniture, not artificial, is edible.)
Pottery, *statue*, painting, *poem*. (Poem is not tangible; statue does not begin with P.)

2.14. SIMILARITIES

Use the format "In what ways are a _____ and a _____ the same or similar?" Pairs of words, grouped by difficulty, are listed below.

✓ Question any vague responses until you obtain a clear estimate of the level of comprehension and abstraction involved. For example, "bus–bicycle" can be interpreted on a spectrum of increasing abstraction: "Both have wheels/People ride on both/Both are means of transportation/Both are technological artifacts."

✓ In ambiguous cases, ask the client: "Please tell me more about that." If necessary, add: "What type/class of things do they belong to?"

Easy

truck/car–bus	duck–chicken	dollar–dime	shoes–pants
scissors–saw	book–newspaper	bucket–mug	violin–piano
apple–orange	bottle–can	work–play	happy–sad
car–airplane	ship–airplane	elbow–knee	candle–lamp
stone–egg	wheel–ball	mountain–lake	joy–anger

Moderately Difficult

door–window	moose–whale	telephone–radio	sun–moon
fox–dog	ladder–steps	lamp–fan	barn–house
cat–lion	bread–milk	tree–forest	prison–zoo

Difficult

paper–coal	tree–branch	theater–church	wings–legs

2.15. ABSURDITIES

You can, of course, use Absurdities from the Stanford–Binet, Intelligence Scale, 4th edition (Thorndike, Hagen, & Sattler, 1986), or you might select from your experience examples tailored for the particular person being examined.

Ask the client: "What is wrong with/is foolish/doesn't make sense about this?"

"The doctor rushed into the emergency room, got out the bandages, and after eating a sandwich, bandaged the bleeding man."

"Bill's ears were so big he had to pull his sweaters on over his feet."
"An airplane pilot ran out of gas halfway across the ocean, so to be safe, he turned around and flew back to land from where he took off."
"A man was in two auto accidents. The first accident killed, him but the second time he got well very quickly."

Only if you believe it useful, ask about absurdities/contradictions/paradoxes in everyday life:

"The government pays farmers to grow tobacco and also pays for programs to reduce tobacco consumption."
"Please give me an example of 'Catch-22.'"
"Prevention is more effective than treatment, yet is underfunded."

2.16. CALCULATION ABILITIES
See Section 11.11, "Arithmetic," for descriptors.

The questions below require attention, concentration, memory, and education. On all math problems, make note of the actual answers given; the effort required/given; time needed; accuracy; changed performance when given a prompt of the next correct answer in a sequence, or when given paper and pencil to perform the calculations; etc. Also note self-corrections, use of fingers to count upon, requests for paper and pencil, complaints, excuses, etc.

Basic Examples of Arithmetic Questions *(↔ by degree)*

"How much is 2 + 2? And 4 + 4? and 8 + 8?"   [✓ Continue in this sequence and note the limits of skill. More difficult versions are 3 + 3's and 7 + 7's.]
One-step: "3 + 4 = ?" "6 + 4 = ?"
Two-step: "7 + 5 − 3 = ?" "8 + 4 + 9 = ?" "4 + 6 + 3 = ?"
"Which is larger: ⅓ or ½?"

Verbally Presented Arithmetic Problems *(↔ by degree)*

"How many quarters are there in $1.75?" (7)
"If oranges are priced at 2 for 18 cents, how much would half a dozen cost?" ($0.54)
"How much is left when you subtract $5.50 from $14.00?" ($8.50)
"How many nickels are there in a dollar?" (20)
"How many nickels are there in $1.95?" (39)

Serial Subtractions/"Serial Sevens"

"Starting with 100, subtract 7, and then subtract 7 from that, and continue subtracting 7."

✓ Normal performance is 1 minute or less in subtracting to 2 with two or fewer errors, not including spontaneous self-corrections. In reporting responses to this, it is clearer to the reader if you underline the errors, as in this set of responses: 93, 84, 77, 70, 62.

Simpler Alternatives to "Serial Sevens"

Ask the client to count to 20 by twos or to count from 1 to 40 by threes.
Ask the client to subtract serial threes from 31, serial fives from 100, serial fours from 100.

2.17. ABSTRACT REASONING/PROVERBS

See Section 11.10, "Reasoning/Abstract Thinking/Concept Formation," for descriptors.

The selection of which proverbs to offer depends on your initial assessment of the client's deficits and diagnosis. Some are more difficult to interpret satisfactorily, while others reveal coping strategies, the intensity of the cognitive dysfunction, or personalization.

Ask, "What do people mean when they say _____?", followed by a proverb such as the following:

"All that glitters is not gold"/"You can't judge a book by its cover." (Appearances can be deceiving.)

Make hay while the sun shines"/"Strike while the iron is hot." (Using an opportunity, taking initiative.)

"Don't cry over spilled milk." (Mature resignation and priorities.)

"The grass is always greener on the other side." (Optimism, pessimism, envy, regret, dissatisfaction.)

"Every cloud has a silver lining." (Optimism, hopefulness, trust, patience.)

"Rome wasn't built in a day"/"Great oaks from little acorns grow." (Patience, frustration tolerance, deferral/delay of gratification.)

"People who live in glass houses shouldn't throw stones." (Arrogance vs. tolerance, humility, guilt, impulse control.) (Or more casually: What goes around comes around.)

"Birds of a feather flock together"/"Like father, like son"/"The apple doesn't fall far from the tree." (The effects of history, genetics, or learning.)

"Don't count your chickens before they are hatched"/"A bird in the hand is worth two in the bush." (Caution, realistic hopes/plans.)

"The squeaking wheel gets the grease." (Excessive modesty vs. attention-seeking behavior, self-assertion.)

"When the cat's away, the mice will play." (Control and rebellion.)

"A rolling stone gathers no moss." (Either positive or negative interpretations of stones/moss/rolling.)

✓ It is often advisable to ask whether the client has heard these proverbs before.

2.18. PAIRED PROVERBS

These proverbs can be used to further evaluate the client's abstraction abilities. Present one on the left and then the paired one on the right. Ask the client, "What do people mean when they say . . . " before each proverb.

✓ Note when and how the client recognizes the conflicts presented by the pairs. Does she/he fail to notice the conflicts; seem to notice but then ignore the conflict; make some joke; comment on human nature, proverbs in general, the examiner, or the examiner's questions; try to resolve the conflict at a higher level of abstraction; offer other conflicting proverbs spontaneously?

"Don't change horses in midstream."	and	"If at first you don't succeed, try, try again."
"A bird in the hand is worth two in the bush."	and	"Nothing ventured, nothing gained."
"Look before you leap."	and	"He who hesitates is lost."
"Out of sight, out of mind."	and	"Absence makes the heart grow fonder."
"A stitch in time saves nine."	and	"Don't cross a bridge until you come to it."

"Haste makes waste."	and	"Strike while the iron is hot"/ "Make hay while the sun shines."
"Do unto others as you would have them do unto you."	and	"To each his own"/"Different strokes for different folks."

2.19. PRACTICAL REASONING

General Questions

"Why do we refrigerate many foods?"
"Why do we have newspapers?"
"Why do people buy life/fire insurance?"
"Why should people make a will?"

Hazard Recognition (↔ *by degree*)

"What should you do before crossing the street?"

"Why shouldn't people play with matches/smoke in bed?"
"What should you do when paper in a wastebasket catches fire?"
"What should you do if food catches on fire when you are cooking at the stove?"

"What should you do when you cut your finger?"
"What should you do if you smell gas in your house?"

2.20. SOCIAL JUDGMENT

See also Section 2.19, above; see Sections 11.13, 11.14, and 11.15 for descriptors.

The questions below require increasing social understanding.

"What should you do if you lose/find a library book?"
"What should you do if you see a purse or a wallet on the sidewalk/in the street?"
"Why should people go to school?"
"What should you do if you are stopped by the police?"

"Why do we have to put stamps on letters we mail?"
"Why do people have to have license plates on their cars?"

"Please tell me of a situation/incident in which you made a bad/foolish/mistaken choice."
"Have you ever been taken advantage of/been a victim?"
"Have you ever made any bad loans?"

"What should you do if someone is very critical of a job you have done?"
"What would you do if someone threatened/tried to hurt you?"
"Please tell me the name of a close friend of yours/someone you would confide in/talk with if you had a personal problem/talk over a serious problem with."

"How would you spend $10,000 if it were given to you/you won the lottery?"

"Who is or was the most important person in the world/history? Why?"
"What is the role of a free press in a democracy?"
"Why do people feel so strongly about the subject of abortion?"
"What do you think are the major differences between the Republican and Democratic parties?"

For a Child:

"If you could have anything you wished for, what three things would you wish for?"
"If you could be any animal, which would you choose and why?"
"If you could live anywhere in the world, where would you want to live?"
"If you could change anything about yourself, what would you change?"
(For aggression:) "What would you do if another student pushed/hit/teased you?"

"What would you do if someone you didn't know offered you a ride home from school/a video
    game/to show you a puppy or kitten?"[2]

"Do you think you have enough friends?"

2.21. DECISION MAKING

See Section 11.19, "Decision Making," for descriptors.

"Are you satisfied with the decisions you make?"
"Do you have a hard time coming to some decisions? Which are hardest? Why?"
"Do you decide too quickly or take too long to make a decision?"
"Do you think you usually make good or bad decisions?"
"Have other people ever said you were indecisive/wishy-washy? Do you agree?"

2.22. SELF-IMAGE

For descriptors, see Section 9.2, "Self-Image/Self-Esteem."

"Which three words best describe you?"
"What are your strengths as a person?"
"How would you describe yourself?"
"Please describe your personality."

"What was the most important thing that ever happened in your life?"
"What would be written on your tombstone/in your obituary if you were to die today?"
"Has life been fair to you?"
"Please identify the turning points in your life."

2.23. INSIGHT INTO DISORDER

For descriptors of responses, see Section 11.16, "Insight."

"Why are you here? What causes you to be here?"
"How well is your mind working?"
"What kind of place is this? What goes on here?"
"Why are you talking to me?"

"Do you think there is something wrong with you?" (If so:) "What? Do you think you are ill?"
"What do you think has caused your troubles/pain/confusion/being disabled/being hospitalized?"

---

[2]Some of these questions are from Judy Bomze of Wynnewood, PA.

"What is your diagnosis?" "What does that mean?"
"Did you ever have a nervous breakdown/bad nerves/something wrong with your mind?"

"Do you think you need treatment?"
"Did you come here voluntarily?"
"Why did/do you need to take medicines?"

"What role or part do you think/believe you have played in this problem/your problems?"[3]
"What are your suggestions for your treatment?"
"What changes would help you most?"

"How would you describe your childhood/family/earlier life?"

2.24. MENTAL STATUS EVALUATION CHECKLIST

The checklist presented on the next two pages (Form 1) is reprinted from my 1997 book *The Paper Office*, 2nd ed. (Zuckerman, 1997). I have found it a concise and helpful form for recording the results of an MSE. You may photocopy and adapt it for your work with clients without obtaining written permission, but you may not use it for teaching, writing, or any commercial venture without such permission.

---

[3]This way to assess the client's degree of taking responsibility or blaming comes from Michael Newberry, MD, of Palm Bay, FL.

Mental Status Evaluation Checklist

Directions: Rate current observed performance, not reported, historical, or projected. Circle the most appropriate descriptive terms in part C, and feel free to write in others. If an aspect of mental status was not assessed, cross out the heading. Write additional observations, clarifications, and quotations in part D.

Client: _____ Date: _____ Evaluator: _____

A. Informed consent was obtained about:

❑ The recipient(s) of this report ❑ Confidentiality ❑ Competency ❑ Other: _____

B. Evaluation methods

1. The information and assessments below are based on my observation of this client during:

   ❑ Intake interview ❑ Psychotherapy ❑ Formal mental status testing ❑ Group therapy
   ❑ Other: _____

2. We interacted for a total of _____ minutes.

3. Setting of the contact: ❑ Professional office ❑ Hospital room ❑ Clinic ❑ School ❑ Home ❑ Work
   ❑ Jail/prison ❑ Other: _____

C. Mental status descriptors (Circle all appropriate items)

1. Appearance and self-care

Stature	Average	Small	Tall	(For age, if a child)		
Weight	Average weight	Overweight	Obese	Underweight	Thin	Cachectic
Clothing	Neat/clean	Careless/inappropriate	Meticulous	Disheveled	Dirty	
	Appropriate for age, occasion, weather		Seductive	Inappropriate	Bizarre	
Grooming	Normal	Well-groomed	Neglected	Bizarre		
Cosmetic use	Age appropriate	Inappropriate for age	Excessive	None		
Posture/gait	Normal	Tense	Rigid	Stooped	Slumped	Bizarre Other: _____
Motor activity	Not remarkable	Slowed	Repetitive	Restless	Agitated	Tremor

Other notable aspects: _____

2. Sensorium

Attention	Normal	Unaware	Inattentive	Distractible	Confused	Persistent	Vigilant
Concentration	Normal	Scattered	Variable	Preoccupied	Anxiety interferes		
	Focuses on irrelevancies						
Orientation	×5	Time	Person	Place	Situation	Object	
Recall/memory	Normal	Defective in: Immediate/short-term Recent Remote					

(cont.)

3. **Relating**

Eye contact	Normal Fleeting Avoided None Staring
Facial expression	Responsive Constricted Tense Anxious Sad Depressed Angry
Attitude toward examiner	Cooperative Dependent Dramatic Passive Uninterested Silly Resistant Critical Hostile Sarcastic Irritable Threatening Suspicious Guarded Defensive Manipulative Argumentative

4. **Affect and mood**

Affect	Appropriate Labile Restricted Blunted Flat Other: _____
Mood	Euthymic Pessimistic Depressed Hypomanic Euphoric Other: _____

5. **Thought and language**

Speech flow	Normal Mute Loud Blocked Paucity Pressured Flight of ideas
Thought content	Appropriate to mood and circumstances Personalizations Persecutions Suspicions Delusions Ideas of reference Ideas of influence Illusions
Preoccupations	Phobias Somatic Suicide Homicidal Guilt Religion Other: _____
Hallucinations	Auditory Visual Other: _____
Organization	Logical Goal-directed Circumstantial Loose Perseverations

6. **Executive functions**

Fund of knowledge	Average Impoverished by: _____
Intelligence	Average Below average Above average Needs investigation
Abstraction	Normal Concrete Functional Popular Abstract Overly abstract
Judgment	Normal Common-sensical Fair Poor Dangerous
Reality testing	Realistic Adequate Distorted Variable Unaware
Insight	Uses connections Gaps Flashes of Unaware Nil Denial
Decision making	Normal Only simple Impulsive Vacillates Confused Paralyzed

7. **Stress**

Stressors	Money Housing Family conflict Work Grief/losses Illness Transitions
Coping ability	Normal Resilient Exhausted Overwhelmed Deficient supports Deficient skills Growing
Skill deficits	None Intellect/educ. Communication Interpersonal Decision making Self-control Responsibility Self-care Activities of daily living
Supports	Usual Family Friends Church Service system Needed: _____

8. **Social functioning**

Social maturity	Responsible Irresponsible Self-centered Impulsive Isolates
Social judgment	Normal "Street-smart" Naive Heedless Victimized Impropriety

D. Other aspects of mental status

_____
_____
_____

This is a strictly confidential patient medical record. Redisclosure or transfer is expressly prohibited by law.

This report reflects the patient's condition at the time of consultation or evaluation. It does not necessarily reflect the patient's diagnosis or condition at any subsequent time.

3

Questions about Signs, Symptoms, and Other Behavior Patterns

Questions here do not address **cognitive functioning** or **mental status**; those are covered in Chapter 2, "Mental Status Evaluation Questions/Tasks." For interviewing and evaluating **couples or families,** see Chapter 16, "Couple and Family Relationships."

Topics here are arranged in alphabetical order.

3.1. INTRODUCTION TO THE QUESTIONS ABOUT SIGNS, SYMPTOMS, AND BEHAVIOR PATTERNS

The questions in this chapter address two kinds of phenomena: (1) signs and symptoms (such as anxiety, hallucinations, and mania) and the disorders with which they are associated; and (2) behaviors that are considered the province of the clinician but are not psychopathological (such as gay and lesbian identity formation, chronic pain syndromes, and sleep disorders).

These questions are generally open-ended and address the issues from several directions. This allows you to ask a second or third question about the same phenomenon, to get a fuller sense of it or allow the client to offer more information.

Some of the phenomena covered in this chapter are of great clinical importance, but formulating nonleading or nontransparent questions about them is most difficult. Examples of these include dissociative experiences, delusions, and sexual identity; this chapter provides questions that will make it far easier for you to address such topics. The chapter also includes full sets of questions for taking a sexual history and for assessing substance use of all kinds. Finally, most of the symptom sections here are cross-referenced to sections in Chapter 10, "Emotional/ Affective Symptoms and Disorders," or Chapter 12, "Abnormal Signs, Symptoms, and Syndromes." There you will find the terms for describing your findings.

If you are engaged in screening persons for the presence of psychopathology, one general strategy is first to use a symptom checklist and then use an interview to follow up on what the screening checklist has found. There are hundreds of well-validated checklists for any kind of symptomatic behavior, and they are time- and effort-efficient. Expensive interview time should be reserved for in-depth evaluations of the severity, impact, development, dynamics, and duration of the psychopathology. As an interviewer, you might also use the referral question or historical records to select which topics to address with a client. The layout of the book even allows you to refer to the book during the interview if something the client says or does suggests the need for a more thorough evaluation.

The questions about sexual abuse, substance abuse, suicide, and impulse control/violence are considered essential to the assessment of risk; ask them of *every* client you interview.

SYMPTOM QUESTIONS

3.2. ABUSE (NONSEXUAL)/NEGLECT OF SPOUSE/ELDER

See also Section 3.15, "Impulse Control/Violence." See Section 12.1, "Abuse, Physical," for descriptors. For nonsexual abuse/neglect of a child, see Section 3.3, just below.

Opening Questions

Inquire of all patients about physical and sexual abuse, threats, fights, arguments.

"How are things at home?"
"Are you alone at home a lot?"
"Are you afraid of anyone at home?"

✓ **Note**: Neglect/abuse may show as weight loss, dehydration, withdrawal, etc.

Battering by Partner

These questions are based on similar questions by NiCarthy and Davidson (1989).

"Has your partner ever[1] hit, punched, slapped, kicked, pushed, or bitten you/your children/anyone else at home?"
"Have you had bruises from being hit, held, or squeezed?"
"Have you ever had to stay in bed or been too weak to work after being hurt?"
"Have you ever seen a doctor as a result of injuries from your partner?"

Emotional/Psychological/Financial Abuse

"Has your partner
'tracked' all of your time?"
controlled all the money in the household and forced you to account for everything you spent?"
repeatedly accused you of being unfaithful when you weren't?"
bragged to you about his/her affairs with others?"

interfered with your relationships with family and friends?"
prevented you from working or attending school?"
humiliated you, called you names, or made painful fun of you in front of others?"

gotten very angry or frightened you when drinking or using drugs?"
threatened to hurt you or the children?"
threatened to use a weapon against you or the children?"
repeatedly threatened to leave you?"
punished the children or pets when he/she was angry at you?"
destroyed personal property or sentimental items?"
forced you to have sex against your will?"

3.3. ABUSE (NONSEXUAL)/NEGLECT OF CHILD

See also Section 3.2, above, and Section 3.4, "Abuse (Sexual) of Child or Adult," below. For DSM-IV diagnoses, see V codes in Section 21.21.

Opening Questions[2] for a Child

"Are you a happy kid?"
"How do you get along with your father/mother/caregiver?"

---

[1]You can use "ever" for emphasis or to reduce denial.
[2]This stepwise approach and wording are suggested by Nora F. Young of Sedro Wolley, WA.

"Are your parents strict?"
"What happens when you get into trouble?"
"Are you afraid of anyone at home?"
"Do you have problems with a teacher, babysitter, or minister?"

Physical Abuse

✓ **Note**: Obtain experienced medical consultation if you have suspicions about injuries.

Look for evidence of injuries, and inquire how they occurred and what was done about them. Attend to:

Explanations of the cause of the injury—especially any reluctance to explain, or different explanations by different caregivers.
Whether treatment was sought in a timely and effective fashion.
Previous similar or suspicious injuries.
Cooperation with previous treatments prescribed.
If the injury was the result of disciplining the child: When caregivers discipline and how; what so annoyed a caregiver as to result in the injury; rationale for the punishment; caregivers' present view of the previous situation/undesired behaviors/punishment.
Psychological patterns in the child, such as depression, anxiety, avoidance, preference for isolation, acting out, etc.
Risk factors: unwanted birth; prematurity; poverty; developmental delay; "difficult baby"; colicky baby; inappropriate expectations; ignorance of developmental sequence and schedule; misfit or poor match between parent and baby; many small children at home; few supports; shortage of diapers/clean clothes; previous involvement with the authorities; drug or alcohol abuse; etc.

3.4. ABUSE (SEXUAL) OF CHILD OR ADULT
See also Sections 3.2 and 3.3, above.

The relevant DSM-IV codes are V61.21, Sexual Abuse of Child, and V61.1, Sexual Abuse of Adult.

✓ **Note**: This is a specialty area; if you are not experienced and trained, get consultations or refer clients before going very far into the topic, in order to avoid contaminating the memories or interpretations.

Initial Inquiry

✓ Sometimes, in the right context, a gentle inquiry like "What has happened to you?" will open the door to these issues. This is preferable to "What is your problem?", as sexual abuse may not be seen as a "problem."[3]

"What do you call your private parts? What do you call the other sex's private parts?"

For a Child:

"Who has touched your private parts?"   [✓ **Note:** Do not add "when you didn't want them to," as that may not have been true or may as yet be unrecognized.]

[3]This sensitive approach is recommended by Nora F. Young of Sedro Wolley, WA.

SYMPTOM
QUESTIONS

"How did that make you feel?"
"Whom did you tell? What did they do about it?"
Ask other "who, when, where, why" questions.

For an Adult:

"Have you ever been forced into sexual acts as a child or adult?"
"Has your partner ever insisted on sex when you didn't want to?"
"Was your first experience with sex by choice, or were you forced?"

Sexual Victimization

"Did anyone ever touch you sexually when you didn't want them to?"
"Who, if anyone, have you had a sexual experience with who was also a relative of yours?"
"Have you ever been forced to have any kind of sex with anyone?" (If so:)
    "What happened? With whom?"
    "Where? When?"
    "How many times did it happen?
    "Whom did you tell?" (If no one:) "Why not?"
    "What did you do about this?"
    "How did this affect you, etc.?"

Consider the interventions needed and required.

Sexual Offenses

"Have you ever forced anyone to have any kind of sex with you?"
"What happened? With whom? Where? When?" (Continue with the questions under "Sexual Victimization," above.)
"Have you had any kind of sex with anyone who was under 18 years of age?"

3.5. AFFECT/MOOD

See Sections 10.3, "Anxiety/Fear," and 10.5, "Depression," for descriptors.

"How would you describe your mood today?"
"Are you happy, sad, or what right now?"
"Using a scale where plus 10 is as happy as you have ever been, 1 is not depressed at all, and minus 10 is as depressed as you have ever been, please rate your mood today."   [✔ Less educated persons may need a scale from 0 to 10.]

"What is your usual mood like?" (If negative, ask:) "When was it last good?"
"When are/were you happiest?"

"In the last month, how many times have you cried/yelled/been afraid?"
"How long does it take you to get over a bad mood/upset?"

"What was your mood like during your childhood/adolescence/earlier life?"
"Were there ever times when you couldn't control your feelings?"

ALCOHOL USE/ABUSE   *See Section 3.26, "Substance Abuse: Drugs and Alcohol."*

<u>**ANOREXIA**</u>   *See Section 3.12, "Eating Disorders."*

3.6. ANXIETY

See Section 10.3, "Anxiety/Fear," for descriptors; see Section 28.2, "Anxiety," for possible medical causes.

"Is there something you are very concerned about/afraid of happening?"
"What do you worry about?"
"How does the future look to you?"

"When you get frightened, what happens to you?"
"Do you ever have times of great fear or anxiety/panic attacks?"   [✔ If so, inquire about cues/ triggers, frequency, duration, whether observed by others, specific physiological symptoms, the sequence of the symptoms, etc.]

"Are there any distressing memories that keep coming back to you?"
"Is there any situation you avoid because it really upsets/scares you?"

<u>**BULIMIA**</u>   *See Section 3.12, "Eating Disorders."*

<u>**CHILD BEHAVIOR DISORDERS**</u>
See Chapter 6, "Background Information: History," and Sections 5.2–5.4 (covering typical problems of children).

3.7. COMPLIANCE–NONCOMPLIANCE WITH TREATMENT

The relevant DSM-IV code is V15.81, Noncompliance With Treatment.

"What medications are you taking? What medications should you be taking?"
"What problems have you had in getting treatment/finding an understanding doctor/taking the medicine as it was prescribed/keeping scheduled medical appointments?"
"Have you ever stopped taking medications prescribed for you before they ran out/because of some reason?" (If so:) "What was the reason?"
"Is there anything that makes you reluctant to take medications/treatments prescribed for you?"

3.8. COMPULSIONS

See also Section 3.18, "Obsessions"; see Section 12.7, "Compulsions," for descriptors.

The questions below are based in part on similar questions by Goodman et al. (1989).

Initial Inquiries

"Do you ever have to do the same thing over and over, or in a certain way?"
"Is there anything in your house/at work that you have to check on frequently?"
"Are you a person who is especially careful about safety?"

Behaviors

"Do you have any habits/frequent actions/behaviors that you must/feel compelled to do in a particular way or very often?"
"Are there some things you must do in order to fall asleep/to get ready to go out?"
"Are there any actions you have to do before or while you eat/go to the bathroom?"
"Do you ever have to arrange your clothes in certain ways?"
"Are you very careful about/afraid of poisons/dirt/germs/diseases?"

Repetition

"Are there any words or phrases you feel that you have to say in a certain way or at certain times?"
"Do you have to check the doors/windows/locks/kitchen/house/your family's safety?"
"Do you have to wash or clean often?"

Client Awareness of Excess/Irrationality

"Do you feel uncomfortable until these actions are done, even though you may know them to be unimportant/foolish/ineffective?"
"Do these actions seem reasonable to you/more than you should be doing? Do they involve more than the usual number of times a day/take up a long time each day?"
"Do you spend more time on these than you would like to?"
"How does doing these things affect your life/routines/job/relationships/family members?"
"How much control do you feel you have over these actions? Do you resist them or yield to them?"

CONDUCT DISORDERS IN CHILDREN

See Sections 5.2–5.4 (covering typical problems of children).

3.9. DELUSIONS

See also Section 3.21, "Paranoia"; see Section 12.9, "Delusions," for descriptors.

Mind Control

"Did anyone try to read your mind/use unusual means to force thoughts into your mind/try to take some of your thoughts away/stop or block your thoughts?"

Grandeur/Special Abilities

✓ Note person's reports of a large number of cars or other possessions, exaggerated abilities, titles/degrees/education/high positions, dramatic or unlikely consumption of alcohol or drugs, or history of unlikely or criminal activities.

"Are you an especially gifted person?"
"Do you have great wealth/unusual strengths/special powers/impressive sexual qualities?"
"Are you able to influence others/read people's minds/put thoughts into their minds?"
"Have you ever received personal messages from heaven/God/someone unusual?"
"Have you been in communication with aliens/dead people/God/Christ/the Devil/the Blessed Virgin/any Biblical persons?"
"Do you think you are immortal/cannot be harmed/hurt/killed?"

Imposter

"Are you a fake?" [✓ Separate a delusion from beliefs of inadequacy based on low self-esteem—the "imposter" phenomenon.]
"Do you think people recognize who you really are?"
"Are you concerned about being discovered/identified/exposed?"
"What is your real rank?"

Monomania

Is this person preoccupied with certain ideas, themes, events, or persons? Does all his/her conversation return to a single topic/false idea?

Nihilism

"Do you think everything is lost/hopeless?"
"Do you think that tomorrow will never come? Do you think that the world has stopped?"
"Do you think that things outside no longer exist?"
"Do you suspect that nothing is real?"
"Do you still have all the parts of your body?"

Persecution   *See Section 3.21, "Paranoia."*

Reference

"Do people do things/do things happen that only you really understand/have special meanings for you/are designed to convey or tell you something no one else is to know?"
"Are things on the TV/the radio/in the papers especially meaningful to you/contain special messages just for you?"
"Have you ever been forewarned/known that something would happen before it did?"

Somatic/Hypochondriacal

"How is your health? How often are you ill? How often do you see a physician? Do you have many illnesses/medical or health problems?"
"Do you have a lot of pain or unusual pains?"
"Which medicines do you take regularly? Which medicines do you take regularly that don't need a prescription?"

"Is there some illness you are worried about getting, or some illness you already have, that concerns you?"
"How often do you think about it?"
"How does it make you feel when you think about it?"
"What do you do about it?"

"Do you think you might or do have a serious disease like cancer or AIDS or multiple sclerosis or a brain tumor?"
"Do you think you might or do have some serious disease that hasn't been diagnosed correctly?"
"Do you think you have a serious disease, but haven't been able to find a doctor to treat it?"

Self-Deprecation   *See also Section 10.5, "Depression."*

"Do you think you are worthless/ugly/emitting bad or noxious odors?"
"Are you afraid you will be punished because you have sinned unforgivably?"

3.10. DISSOCIATIVE EXPERIENCES

See Section 12.11, "Depersonalization and Derealization," for descriptors.

For standardized evaluation, you can use Ross et al.'s (Ross, 1989; Ross et al., 1990) Dissociative Disorders Interview Schedule, or Bernstein and Putnam's (1986) Dissociative Experiences Scale.

Dissociative Experiences

"Have you ever walked in your sleep?"

"Did you have imaginary playmates as a child?"

"Have you ever remembered a past event so vividly that it seemed you were actually re-experiencing it?"

"Have you ever suddenly realized that . . .
>   you don't remember earlier parts of the trip you are on?"
>   you are in a place and have no recall of how you got there?"
>   you are wearing clothes you would not have chosen?"
>   some of your personal possessions were missing?"
>   there are items in your possession you don't recall acquiring?"

"Have you ever been greeted by people who call you by another name and really seem to know you?"

"Have you ever been unable to recall major events in your life?"

"Have you ever been unable to decide whether you actually did something or just imagined doing it?"

Depersonalization

"Are you aware of any significant change in yourself?"

"Do you feel normal/all right/natural/real?"

"Did you ever feel detached from yourself/unattached/divorced from yourself?"

"Did you ever act in so strange a way you considered the possibility that you might be two different people?"

"Did you ever feel that you have lost your identity/like you were someone else?"

"Are you always certain who you are?"

"Do you ever wonder who you really are?"

"Did you ever feel that you were no longer real/you were becoming someone or something different?"

"Have you ever suddenly realized that you don't recognize your face/body in a mirror?"

"Did you ever feel that your self/body was different/changed/unreal/strange?"

"Have you ever felt that your body doesn't belong to your self?"

"Ever feel like you were/your mind was outside/watching/apart from your body?"

"Have there been times you felt your mind and body were not together/linked?"

"Do you ever feel like someone else is moving your legs as you walk/ever feel like a robot?"

Derealization

"Did you ever get so involved in a daydream that you couldn't tell if it were real or not?"

"Do people, trees, houses, etc., look as they usually do/always did to you?"

"Did you ever feel like you weren't really present?"

"Did you ever feel you were detached/alienated/estranged from yourself or your surroundings/everything around you?"

"Have you ever been in a familiar place but found it strange/peculiar/weird/unfamiliar/somehow changed?"

"Did you ever feel that things around you/the world were/was very strange/remote/unreal/changing?"

"Do things seem natural and real to you, or does it seem like things are make-believe?"
"Did things or objects ever seem to be alive?"

DEPERSONALIZATION AND DEREALIZATION   *See Section 3.10, just above.*

3.11. DEPRESSION

See Section 10.5, "Depression," for descriptors; see Section 28.4, "Depression," for possible medical causes.

Somatic/Vegetative Symptoms

"How is your general health? Has it changed recently?"   [✔ Follow up reports of symptoms.]

"Has your interest in food increased or decreased?" *(See Section 3.12, "Eating Disorders," for questions.)*
"Have you gained or lost weight?"

"How is your sleep? Do you have trouble falling asleep? On how many nights in a week?" *(See Section 3.25, "Sleep," for questions.)*
"Do you wake in the middle of the night, other than to go to the bathroom, and then can't get back to sleep?"
"Do you wake up early and then can't fall asleep again?"
"Do you regularly nap during the day?"   [✔ Count this into the total number of sleep hours, which generally decreases with age.]

"Have your bowel or bladder habits changed?"
"Has your interest in sex changed?"   [✔ Libido is desire, not performance.]

Affective Symptoms

"How are your spirits generally?"
"When was the last time you felt really down?"
"Do you ever get pretty discouraged/depressed/blue? Are you blue/feeling low now?"
"When you get sad or down, how long does it last?"
"Have you had a time when you felt very tired or very irritable?"
"Have you suffered some personal losses recently?"
"How did you feel about (specific event)?"
"Do you think you are more depressed in the winter than the summer, or only in one season?"
    (See Section 10.8, "Seasonal Affective Disorder.")

Social Functioning

See also Chapter 15, "Social/Community Functioning," and Chapter 18, "Recreational Functioning."

"Do you find yourself avoiding being with people?"
"Do you go out less than you used to?"
"Have you given up any friendships?"

Self-Deprecation

"Are you hard on yourself?" Are there times when you call yourself names?" (If so:) "Which?"
"Have you been harder on yourself lately?"
"Do you think you are a wicked person?/have sinned?" (If so:) "Why?"

Suicidal Ideation

> *See also Section 3.28, "Suicide and Self-Destructive Behavior"; see Section 12.37, "Suicide," for descriptors.*

"What do you see for yourself in the future?"
"Do you think you will get well/over this problem?" (If so:) "How long will it take?"

"When people are depressed, they sometimes think about dying. Have you had thoughts like that?"
"Have you ever thought of hurting yourself?"

Optimism–Pessimism

"What is the worst thing that ever happened to you?"
"What is the best thing that ever happened to you?"
"If you could have three wishes come true, what would you wish for?"

Anhedonia

"What do you do to enjoy yourself/have a good time/for fun?"
"Has your interest in this/these things changed?"

DRUG ABUSE   *See Section 3.26, "Substance Abuse: Drugs and Alcohol."*

Always ask every client about past and present use of medications/street drugs/alcohol/other chemicals.

3.12. EATING DISORDERS

> *See Section 12.12, "Eating Disorders," for descriptors.*

✓ Evaluate weight, fat percentage, and proportion. Also evaluate self-efficacy, preoccupation, or hypervigilance around eating; terror over weight gain; typical cognitive distortions (e.g., body image); odd eating behaviors; etc. See also Garner and Garfinkel (1979) for evaluating anorexia nervosa.

Opening Questions

"What is your present weight? The most you ever weighed? Your lowest weight as an adult?"
"Have you gained or lost weight in the last year or two?" (If so:) How much?"

Thoughts and Feelings about Weight

"How often do you think about your weight/eating/dieting?"
"How do you feel about your current weight?"   [✓ Note any disparity between client's statements and your judgments of appearance.]
"Do you feel you are too fat?" (If yes:) "How long have you felt that way?"
"Are you afraid of being/becoming overweight?"
"How much control over your eating do you feel you have?"
"Do you avoid certain foods (foods with sugar, fat, salt, cholesterol, etc.)?"
"How would your life be different if you lost/gained the weight you want to?"

History of Food Restriction

"What kinds of diets have you tried?"   [✓ Take a diet history: dates, losses, regaining, kinds of restrictions used, weight at initiation and at termination, etc.]

"Have you ever gotten so upset or desperate about your weight that you have done something drastic?"

"Have you ever: gone on eating binges, vomited after you've eaten, fasted for long periods, used diet pills/cathartics/laxatives/diuretics to lose weight, lost a great deal of weight, or felt guilty after eating?"

Alternative Questions[4]

"Do you think your eating habits are unusual?"

"Do you eat when you're not hungry? Do you eat to escape from worries or troubles?"

"Is your life dominated by thoughts of food?"

"Is your eating out of your control? Is your weight or eating pattern affecting the way you live your life?"

"Do you look forward with pleasure to the times when you can eat alone?" (If so:) "Do you plan these occasions?"

"Do you have a fear of becoming fat or losing control of your eating?"

"Do you feel fat when your weight is at or below that of your friends?"

"Do you feel guilt or remorse after overeating?"

"Do you eat sensibly when others are present and then binge when alone?"

"Is your life a series of diets?"

"Do you vomit, take laxatives or diuretics, or exercise to control your weight?"

"Do you have times when you alternate between eating binges and fasting to control your weight?"

"Does your weight often change as much as 10 pounds because you radically change your eating habits?"

"Do you resent being told to 'use your willpower' to stop overeating?"

"Have you said you can 'diet on your own' despite the evidence?"

"Do you have 'food binges' where you eat a large amount of food in a short time period?"

"If you have binged, was it on high-calorie foods such as sweets, desserts, or salty or fatty foods?"

"Have you stopped a binge by vomiting, purging, or sleeping, or because of pain?"

FEARS   *See Sections 3.6, "Anxiety," and 3.22, "Phobias."*

A listing of 100 common fears with suitable research basis can be found in Braun and Reynolds (1969).

3.13. GAY AND LESBIAN IDENTITY

See also Section 19.9, "Stages in the Formation of Homosexual Identity," and the "Sexual Adjustment" heading under Section 6.4, "Adjustment History."

The questions in this section cover normative homosexual identity development.[5]

[4]The following questions are modified from the Alcoholics Anonymous/Overeaters Anonymous literature.

[5]I am grateful to Leslie J. Wrixon, PsyD, of Cambridge, MA, for these questions and for guidance regarding the stages of identity development.

General Questions

"Did you ever have a sense of not belonging or of feeling sexually different from most people?"

"Do you know any gay men? Any lesbians?" (If so:) "What are they like?"
"What images of gay men and lesbians do you have?"

"Have you ever thought you might be gay?" (If so:) "When did you first think this?"
"What was it like to consider this idea/recognize such feelings?"

Attraction

"Do you find yourself attracted to gay/lesbian relationships or to specific gays/lesbians?"
"Have you ever acted on your feelings? (If so:) "What did you do?"
"Have you tried to ignore or change these thoughts and feelings and/or convince yourself that you may not be gay?"

Understanding

"Why do you think gay people are that way?" (Example: "They can't help it/are born that way.")
"Do you see yourself as gay and accept it without liking it?"

Identity Activism

"Tell me about the pressures from society you feel/are aware of."

"Are you out (i.e., "out of the closet"—not concealing one's homosexuality) to friends/family/coworkers/the public?"
"Are you considering coming out to them?"
"Are you involved in any gay activities—social, political, or otherwise?"

3.14. HALLUCINATIONS

See Section 12.16, "Hallucinations," for descriptors; see Section 28.7 "Psychosis," for possible medical causes.

✓ **Note**: Look for behaviors that suggest hallucinating: return of gaze to a spot, sudden head turning, staring at one place in room, eyes following something in motion, mumbling or conversing with no one else present, etc. If there is an indication of the presence of hallucinations, ask questions to discriminate those that are apparently due to entering or leaving sleep, delirium, alcohol or drug withdrawal or abuse, medications, etc.

General Questions

"Do you have a vivid imagination?"
"Do you dream so vividly that you aren't sure it was a dream?"
"Did you ever think/act in really strange/odd/peculiar ways?"
"Have you had any uncanny/eerie/bizarre/unexplainable experiences?"
"Has your mind ever played tricks on you?"
"Did you ever see or hear things others did not?"
"Have you had visions?"
For any of these: "Where did you first experience this?"

Auditory

"Were you ever surprised that you could hear some sounds other people couldn't hear? (e.g., whispering voices, echoes, melodies, parts of conversations, etc.)"

"Have you ever heard noises in your head that disturb you?"
"Have you ever heard voices coming from inside your head?" (If yes:)
  "Was this like voices speaking your own thoughts or someone else speaking?"
  "Where do the voices come from?"
  "Whose voices? Men's or women's? How old were they?"
  "What did they say?"
  "When does this happen? How often do you hear them?"
  "When did this start?"
  "What brings these on?"

Visual

"Have you ever seen anything so unusual that other people didn't believe it?"
"Did you ever have visions/see apparitions/ghosts?"
"Did you ever see anything like in a dream when you were awake?"
"Have you ever seen things that no one else saw?" (If so:)
  "What? What did you feel then?"
  "What do you call these experiences?"
  "What causes these things to happen?"
  "When was the first time this happened?"

Kinesthetic

"Have you ever felt strange sensations (e.g., electricity)/odd feelings in your body/anything crawling on you (e.g., bugs)?"

Gustatory

"Have you ever felt strange tastes in your mouth (metal, electricity, poisons, etc.)?"

Olfactory

"Have you ever smelled strange odors that you could not account for (poisons, death, something burning, sewage, odd smells from your own body, dead spirits, etc.)?"

Other

"What was the strangest experience you ever had?"
"Did you ever visit another planet? Ever die and return to life?" (If so:) "How/why do you think these things come about?"

HOMOSEXUAL IDENTITY DEVELOPMENT

See Section 3.13, "Gay and Lesbian Identity," and Section 19.9, "Stages of the Formulation of Homosexual Identity."

3.15. ILLUSIONS

See also the "Derealization" heading under Section 3.10, "Dissociative Experiences"; see Section 12.19, "Illusions," for descriptors.

"Does the world look very different to you?" (If yes:) "In what way(s)?"
"Do any things feel different, in some way, at certain times?"
"Do things ever seem to change size/look smaller or larger?"

"Do parts of your body ever seem to change in size or shape or texture?"
"Do things sometimes seem nearer or farther away than they should?"
"Does time ever seem to move very slowly or very fast?"

3.16. IMPULSE CONTROL/VIOLENCE

See Sections 12.18, "Homicide Risk Factors," and 12.20, "Impulse Control Disorders," for descriptors.

"Do you find yourself suddenly doing things before you have thought about or decided to do them?"
"Does money 'burn a hole in your pocket'?"
"Do you feel compelled/driven to do things you don't want to do?"
"Do you feel unable to stop yourself from doing some things?"

"Have you ever been involved in sexual behaviors you regretted?"
"Do you ever steal/shoplift?"
"Please tell me about all the times you have had contact with the police."
"Have you ever been fired/evicted/arrested?" (If yes:) "Why did that happen?"

"What do you usually do when you get very upset and angry?"
"Do you have a bad temper/fly off the handle/flare up?"
"Have you ever lost control of yourself? Ever thrown/broken things? Ever hit/attacked anyone?"
"Do you get involved in more fights than others in your neighborhood?"

INSIGHT   *See Section 2.23, "Insight into Disorder"; see Section 11.16, "Insight," for descriptors.*

3.17. MANIA

See Section 10.7, "Mania," for descriptors; see Section 28.5, "Mania," for possible medical causes.

"Was there ever a time when you . . .
    stayed very excited?"
    were too happy without any reason?"
    were too full of energy?"
    talked too much and couldn't stop?"
    started things you couldn't finish?"
    did without sleep for a day or two?"
    seemed to be oversexed?"
    were overworked/held several jobs at the same time?"
    spent money recklessly/spent money you didn't have/made extravagant gifts?"
"Have you ever found yourself pacing and couldn't stop/stop for long?"
"Was there ever a time when you were too impatient/irritable/couldn't concentrate/couldn't stop your mind's racing?"

(If yes to any of the above:) "When did this start? How long did this last? What happened because of this?"
"Were you ever treated for these conditions?"

<u>NONCOMPLIANCE</u>   *See Section 3.7, "Compliance–Noncompliance with Treatment."*

3.18. OBSESSIONS

See also Section 3.8, "Compulsions"; see Section 12.22, "Obsessions," for descriptors.

✓ Differential diagnosis must distinguish obsessions from depressive ruminations and from delusions. For standardized recording, you can use the <u>Y</u>ale–<u>B</u>rown <u>O</u>bsessive–<u>C</u>ompulsive <u>S</u>cale (Goodman et al., 1989), which covers contents, distress, time spent, insight, indecisiveness, avoidance, and resisting thoughts. A children's version is also available.

Initial Inquiries

"Are there any thoughts you just seem unable to forget/get rid of/keep out of your mind/stop thinking about?"
"What do these thoughts revolve around or continually come back to?"
"Are there any phrases/names/dates/slogans/rhymes/titles/music that continually run through your mind/you can't seem to control?"
"Are there any prayers/numbers/names/phrases you feel you have to repeat?" (If so:) "Which? When?"

Thoughts

"Is there any possibility you keep thinking about/considering/mulling over/speculating about?"
"Are there any everyday decisions you seem unable to make or take too much time to make?"
"How often do you think about your health/how your body is working/whether you are sick?"

Client Awareness of Excess/Irrationality

"Do these thoughts seem reasonable to you, or do you think about them more than you should/ more than a sensible number of times a day? Do they take up a long time each day?"
"How does thinking these things affect your life/routines/job/relationships/family members?"
"Do you feel uncomfortable until you think these thoughts, even though you may know them to be nonsensical/unimportant/foolish/ineffective?"

"How much control do you feel you have over these thoughts? Do you resist them?"
"How do you try to get these thoughts out of your head/make them stop?"
"Where do you think these thoughts come from?"

Contents of the Obsessions

Body parts or illness.
Cleansing.
Checking.
Contamination: Bodily waste, dirt, germs, animals, etc.
Hoarding or saving.
Religious scrupulosity.
Repetition, counting, arranging, hoarding/collecting, etc.
Sexual: "Perverse" or forbidden acts, incest, homosexuality, etc.
Symmetry, precision.
Violence: Self or other harm, horrific images, blurting out obscenities/insults, etc.

3.19. ORGANICITY/COGNITIVE DISORDERS

See Chapter 11, "Cognition and Mental Status," for descriptors; see Chapter 2, "Mental Status Evaluation Questions/Tasks," for guidance in conducting an MSE.

Ask for a history of:

Sunstroke.	Head injuries.	Syphilis.
Near-drowning.	Head surgery.	AIDS/AIDS-Related Complex.
Electrocution.	Apnea.	High fevers/delirium.
Poisonings.	Vertigo/dizziness.	Seizures/convulsions/fits.

Exposure to toxic chemicals in the workplace/home/garden.
Substance use/abuse/IV drugs/overdoses. *(See Section 3.26, "Substance Abuse: Drugs and Alcohol.")*
Periods of unconsciousness/being "knocked out"/having fainted.
Episodes of alteration of levels of consciousness, "out cold," "weirded out," "falling out."

Do a complete MSE, and consider neuropsychological testing and/or neurological evaluations.

3.20. PAIN, CHRONIC

See Section 12.24, "Pain Disorders/Chronic Pain Syndrome," for descriptors.

The usual medical interview asks these questions, using the mnemonic OPQRST:

Onset: "What brings it on?"
Palliative and Provocative: "What makes it better or worse?" (Time of day, cold, movement?)
Quality or character: e.g., "Is it throbbing or steady?"
Region and Radiation: e.g., "Is it located on one or both sides?" "Does it spread?"
Severity: Use comparisons (toothache, wound from a . . .) from the person's history.
Timing and duration. "How often do you get it?" "How long does it last?"

For a more standardized and thorough measurement of pain, Hase (1992) offers a revision and improvement of the classic McGill–Melzack Pain Questionnaire. You may also find the following questions useful.

"Do you frequently have pain somewhere in your body?" (If so:) "Where?"
"Has the pain affected your sleep?" (If so:) "How?"
"Has the pain affected your eating? Has your weight changed?"
"Has the pain changed your thinking or concentration abilities?" (If so:) "Please explain."
"Do you have to lie down and rest because of the pain, or does it force you to keep moving?"
"Do you find that you are thinking about the pain a lot?"

"Tell me about your activities in a 24-hour day, such as cooking, laundry, shopping, cleaning, reading, exercise, hobbies, etc. When do you wake up?" (And so on.)
"Does the pain affect your ability to take care of yourself/your day-to-day needs?" (If so:) "Please explain."
"What activities have you had to restrict or stop because of pain?"
"Do you need to use any assistance device? Anything to walk with?" (If so:) "When did you start using it? Which physician gave it to you?"

"How has the pain changed in the last year?"

"What medications do you take for the pain?"   [✔ Ask for names, dosages, over-the-counter or physician source, location and phone number of source.]

"How does the medicine affect the pain?"
"Do you get any side effects from these medications?"

"What other treatments have you had? How well did they work?"
"Have you been treated in any pain management program or pain clinic?" (If so:) "When? Where? To what effect/with what result?"
"Have you ever been referred to a psychologist or psychiatrist to help you to learn to cope with the pain?"   [✓ Ask for name, dates, location, phone number, dates of treatment.]
"Do doctors seem to have helped or failed you?"
"Has some doctor said your pain was 'imaginary' or 'all in your head'?"
"Do you secretly think your case is hopeless?"

3.21. PARANOIA

See Section 12.25, "Paranoia," for descriptors.

Being Monitored

"When you get on a bus/eat in a restaurant/enter any public place, do people notice you/turn around to look at you?"
"Have you ever been singled out for special attention/watched/spied on?"
"Do people sometimes follow you for a while?"

Suspicion

"Would you say that you are more suspicious than other people, perhaps with good cause?"
"Have you been attacked/been shot at?"
"Would you feel safer if you carried a gun/knife/Mace or hired a bodyguard?"

"Do you think there is someone or something out to get you?"
"Do you think anyone is against you? Do you have enemies?"
"Does any organization or group of people have it in for you? Is anyone plotting against you?"

"Is there anything about you that has made other people jealous of/prejudiced against you/out to get or harm you/want to damage your property?"
"Do people talk about you more than they talk about others?"
"Do people say things about you behind your back? What do they say?"
"Are people making insulting/derogatory/critical/negative remarks about you?"
"Do people laugh at you?"

"Do you believe you have to be extra careful/extra alert/vigilant around people?"
"Have you had to take any special precautions?"
"Have you changed your way of doing things to feel safer?"

Being Controlled (↔ *by degree*)

"Do people try to trick you/play tricks on you?"
"Are people doing things that affect you and that you do not understand?"
"Have drugs been put in your food or drinks?"

"Do other people seem to know your thoughts? Can other people read your mind?"
"Have you ever had thoughts in your mind that were not your own?"
"Are people controlling your thoughts or your mind?" (If so:) "What are they doing? How are they doing/attempting this? Why is this happening?"
"Is your mind controlled by others/thought waves/electricity/radio or television waves?"

3.22. PHOBIAS

See Section 12.26, "Phobias," for descriptors.

"Are you afraid of any things that do not frighten most people as much?" (If so:) "What are they?"

"Is there any activity or any place that makes you very uncomfortable or anxious, and so you avoid it?" (If so:) "Tell me more about it or them."

"Do these fears/avoidance behaviors seem reasonable and appropriate to you?" (If not:) "How have you tried to overcome these fears?"

3.23. SEXUAL HISTORY

If a client presents with a sexual problem, see the "Sexual Adjustment" heading under Section 6.4, "Adjustment History," or Section 10.10, "Sexuality." If sexual abuse is suspected, see Section 3.4, "Abuse (Sexual) of Child or Adult."

This section is for a non-problem-focused history and is arranged in developmental order. See Pomeroy et al. (1982), Masters and Johnson (1970, Ch. 2), or H. S. Kaplan (1983) for how to take a very complete sexual history.

Always ask every client about a history of sexual abuse.

Childhood

"When were you first aware of the sexes' differences?"

"What toys did you play with as a child?"

"Were you ever called a 'tomboy' (for females)/'sissy' (for males)?"

"Did you ever wear the clothes of the other sex as a child?"

"What were your first sexual experiences/feelings? How old were you? What was the situation? What thoughts did you have then?"

"What sex games did you play with girls and with boys?"

"When did you first masturbate? How did you learn about masturbation? What did it feel like and what did you think when you started?"

"What sexual behaviors did you see between adults? What were your feelings and thoughts about these?"

Adolescence

"From whom or what did you first learn/learn the most about sex?"

"Did you have sex education classes in school?" (If so:) "What did you learn about?"

"Did you feel free to ask sexual questions in your home?" (If not:) "To whom/where did you go with your questions/for information?"

(For females:) Ask about age of menarche, regularity of menstrual cycle, changes in menstrual cycle, pregnancies/miscarriages/abortions/deliveries.

(For males:) Ask about age of puberty (voice cracking, nocturnal emissions, body hair, ejaculation/orgasm by masturbation, etc.).

"How and when did you learn about menstruation, intercourse, and pregnancy?"

"How prepared were you for menstruation/wet dreams/the changes in your body?"

"Have you ever engaged in voyeurism/watching someone get undressed, exhibitionism/showing off your genitals, sex with animals?"

"What erotic materials (or 'pornography'[6]), such as books, magazines, or videotapes, have you

---

[6]A useful distinction (made by Steinem, 1980) is as follows: Of all artifacts made by humans, some are designed to arouse viewers sexually—these are erotica. Some erotica shows a large difference in power between the *(cont.)*

seen? What was shown in this material?" (Heterosexual or homosexual intercourse, oral sex, child sex, etc.?)

"At what age did you start to date?"
"How many people have you dated and for how long?"
"What was your first experience with petting ('necking,' 'making out') like?"

"How old were you when you first had sex with another person?"
  "Was this heterosexual or homosexual?"
  "What were your feelings and thoughts?"   [✓ Attend to issues of force.]

"What methods of birth control have you used?"
"Do you want to become pregnant/father a child?"
"How often do you have unprotected intercourse?"
"What sexually transmitted diseases have you had?"

Adulthood

"How many times in your life do you guess you have had intercourse without using a condom?"
"Have you had any kind of sexual intercourse with men, women, or both in the last 15 years?"
"Have you had a male sexual partner who has had sex with other men in the last 15 years?"[7]

"What are your sexual fantasies about?"
"Do any of your sexual fantasies distress or frighten you?"

"Do you have any sexual problems now? Did you in the past?" (If so:) "Which?"
  (For men:) "When have you had difficulty with erection/'getting and staying hard,' or orgasm/ejaculation/'coming' too soon?"
  (For women:) "When have you had difficulty with arousal/'getting excited/hot,' or orgasm/'coming'/'climaxing,' or painful intercourse?"
"As you see it, do these problems affect you alone, mainly you, both you and your partner, or mainly your partner?"
"What have you done to try to overcome this/these problem(s)?"

"As you look back over your past history, what have been the sexual high and low points?"
"What things about your sexual development do you wish could have been different?"

For Women Only:

"How does your menstrual cycle affect your mood/attitudes/behavior/sexual desire?"
"Please describe all your pregnancies."

✓ **Note**: Because medications and illnesses affect libido and performance, ask about medications (prescription and over-the-counter), street drugs, and alcohol (by referring to Section 3.26), and illnesses (especially diabetes and circulatory diseases).

---

partners—this is pornography. Thus closeup pictures of intercourse can be erotica and beautiful (and likely harmless), while fully clothed depictions of rape can be pornographic and ugly (and likely harmful).

[7]Based on the responses to these questions, consider asking for information to assess HIV risk:
  "Have you ever shared or borrowed a needle to inject yourself with a drug, or do you think that someone you had sex with did this?"
  "Have you ever had a sexual partner who you knew, or later learned, was HIV-infected or had AIDS?"
  "Did you receive a blood transfusion or treatment for a blood-clotting problem between 1977 and 1985?"
  "Did a sexual or needle partner receive a blood transfusion or treatment for a blood-clotting problem between 1977 and 1985?"
  "Are you at all concerned that you may have picked up HIV?"
  "Have you ever had a test for HIV or AIDS?"

Relationships

"In each of your previous relationships, how was the sexual relationship?"
"What was the reason each relationship ended?"
"In your present relationship, how has the sexual adjustment been?"
"How attracted to your partner do you feel?"
"How attractive do you feel to your partner?"
"Are you satisfied with the frequency of sexual relations? Is your partner?"
"What images or fantasies do you think of when you are with your partner?"
"What conflicts do you have with your partner in any aspect of your sexual relationship?" (Oral sex—either kind; positions; frequency; amount of stimulation; the circumstances of sex; communication of preferences; initiation; etc.?)
"What incompatibilities or conflicts exist in other aspects of the relationship?"

3.24. SEXUAL IDENTITY/TRANSSEXUALITY

See also the "Sexual Adjustment" heading under Section 6.4, "Adjustment History."

✓ Distinguish transsexuality from transvestism, cross-dressing, dissatisfaction with one's body, and delusions.

"At what age did you first know you were a boy/girl?"
"Did you ever dress in the other sex's clothes/play with the other sex's toys?"

"Do you want to look like someone of the other sex?"
"Do you dislike your sex's clothes or bodies?"
"Do you think you really should have been/are of the other sex?"
"Do you want to marry a person of your sex?"
"Are your sex organs normal? Do you dislike them? Do you feel disgust at your genitals?"
"Have you ever sought to change your sex?"
"Have you ever tried to injure your genitals?"

For Females Only:

"Were you a tomboy? Are you still?"
"Do you feel more comfortable/better when you wear masculine clothing?"
"Do you stand up to urinate?"
"Do you feel like a man trapped in a woman's body?"

For Males Only:

"Do you dress in women's clothes or underclothes/use makeup?"
"When do you do this? How does it make you feel? What do you get from this?"
"Do you feel like a woman trapped in a man's body?"

3.25. SLEEP

See Section 12.35, "Sleep Disturbances," for descriptors.

Data can also be collected from a sleep–wake diary and from questionnaires like Edinger's (1985).

General Questions

"Do you have any trouble with your sleep?" (If so:) "What kind?" (Interruptions, restlessness, parasomnias, nightmares, confusional episodes, seizures, sleep paralyses, awake frightened, vivid images, hypnagogic or hypnopompic illusions, cataplexy, sleep attacks, bruxism, etc.?)
"How does this affect your life?"

"Do you wake up refreshed, or irritable and tired?"
"What time do you usually go to bed? Fall asleep? Wake up? Get up?"   [✓ Compute the client's total sleep time and compare it with that of age peers and the client's own lifelong patterns. This is more likely to be accurate than asking, "How much sleep do you usually get each night?"]
"Has there been any change in the ways you sleep?"
"Are you sleepy during the day? Do you usually/have to take a nap during the day?" (If so:) "For how long?"
"What do you dream about? Do you have bad or unusual dreams?"
"Do you usually have the same dream every night for a while?"
"Are there dreams you dream over and over?"

Difficulty Falling Asleep (Initial Insomnia)

"What do you just before you go to bed?"
"Typically, what time do you go to bed?"
"What do you do in bed?" (Watch TV, read, study, eat, use telephone, have sex, etc.?)
"Typically, what time do you fall asleep?"
"How long does it take you to fall asleep after you go to bed?"   [✓ 15–20 minutes is usual.]
"What keeps you awake?" (Activities, partner, rehearsing the day, conditions of bedroom, etc.?)
"What do you think about before you fall asleep?"
"Do you see or hear or feel unusual things before falling asleep?"
"Do you do anything to help yourself fall asleep?/What do you do to fall asleep?"

Sleep Continuity Disturbance (Middle Insomnia)

"How well do you sleep? Are you a very light/light/sound/very sound sleeper?"
"Do you awaken in the middle of the night?" (If so:) "How many times, on the average?"
"Is there anything that wakes you so you can't sleep through the night?" (Need to urinate, bed partner's behavior, a needy child, street noises, etc.?)
"How long is it before you fall back to sleep?"
"What do you think about as you lie in bed?"
"What have you tried to help you return to sleep?"

Early Morning Awakening (Terminal Insomnia)

"What time do you usually wake up/awaken?"
"Do you awaken too early in the morning and are unable to go back to sleep again?" (If so:) "What do you do then?"
"What do you think about as you lie in bed?"

Other

"How much coffee/cola/tea do you drink each day?"
"Do you use any caffeine-containing medications/over-the-counter medicines/drugs, such as Midol (for premenopausal females), Bufferin, Anacin, etc.?"
"How many cigarettes do you smoke in a day?"

"What medications are you taking? Do you use any sleeping aid or sleeping pill?"
"What do you eat and drink before going to sleep?"
"Do you work shiftwork/changing/rotating shifts?"
"Are you under a lot of stress?"
"Did anyone in your family have problems with sleeping/similar problems?"
"Do you snore loudly?"
"Do you awaken gasping for air/with leg jerks/cramps/pain?"

For a Child:

Ask about regular bedtimes, fears (of the dark, of the "bogeyman," relatives, dangerous animals, violence, harm to caregivers), bedtime rituals, reluctance to fall asleep, need for lights/company, entry into parents' bed, bad dreams/nightmares/night terrors, sleepwalking, incontinence.

3.26. SUBSTANCE ABUSE: DRUGS AND ALCOHOL

See Section 12.36, "Alcoholics, Types of," and 17.37, "Substance Abuse and Use," for descriptors. See Section 3.27 for tobacco and caffeine use.

There are no sharp demarcations or agreed-upon criteria among use, misuse, and abuse, or between being a "problem drinker/drug user" and an "alcoholic/drug addict," because people now enter treatment at all stages/levels. In this section, abuse and misuse issues concern any of these substances:[8]

Alcohol in beer, wine, liquor, over-the-counter medications, nonpotable forms, etc.
Prescription/legal drugs, such as amphetamines, barbiturates, antidepressants, opioids, sedatives, hypnotics, and anxiolytics.
"Street"/illegal/unidentified/synthetic ("designer") drugs, including cannabis/marijuana/"weed"/"grass"/"pot," etc., cocaine, crack, hallucinogens, narcotics.
Over-the-counter medications such as stimulants.
Substances inhaled ("huffed"), such as glues, chemical thinners, gasoline.

Although the questions in the next few pages are useful, more precise tools for screening, diagnosing, treatment planning, and outcome assessment are available. Carey and Teitelbaum (1996) provide a good overview.

The CAGE criteria are a simple set of questions that can and should be asked of every new patient:

"Have you ever felt the need to   Cut down your drinking?"
"Have you ever felt   Annoyed by criticism of your drinking?"
"Have you ever had   Guilty feelings about your drinking?"
"Have you ever taken a morning   Eye-opener?"

Screening Questions about Effects

"What happens to you when you drink/use drugs? Do you change a lot/act very differently/do strange things/have other parts of your personality come out?"
"Has drinking/drug use affected your school/work/job/career, caused you legal problems or in your friendships/family/marriage, health, or changed any other area of your life?"

---

[8]Bernard (1991) provides a very complete checklist of substances-by-when-consumed, which can be used for screening.

"What problems has the use of alcohol/drugs caused in your life at any time? During the last month?"

"Which of these have you had: shakes, blackouts, visions or voices, aches and fevers, injuries from falls/fights/car accidents?"

"Are you or other people concerned/worried about your drinking/drug use? Have other people tried to get you to stop drinking/using?" (If so:) "How do you feel about them?"

History/Consumption Patterns

Because an individual's patterns of use/overuse/misuse/abuse change with availability, resources, setting, choice, treatment, and aging, and may involve cross-addictions, temporary substitutions or preferences, and many other factors, a detailed and individualized history is desirable. However, such tailoring is not possible in the format here. Therefore, follow your clinical intuition and the client's lead (or avoidances) in history taking to get all the relevant facts and experiences.

✓ It may be useful to construct a table like this as you obtain the history, especially if the history is complex.

Drug name/type	Age started	Amount	Frequency	Route	Last dose	Control efforts and outcome

Begin with this question: "What is/are your drugs of choice/preference?" Depending on the answer, go to "Alcohol" or to "Drugs," below.

Alcohol

"When and where did you first drink any kind of alcohol?"
"When and where did you first drink to drunkenness/intoxication?"
"When did you first start drinking regularly?"
"How did you progress to the quantity you now drink?"

"What is your preferred drink? What else will you drink?"
"Do you ever drink substances such as shaving lotion, cough medicine, or hair tonic?"
"Where do you get your alcohol?" (From peers, stores, bartenders, steal it, sneak it from others?)
"Where do you drink?" (At work, home, parties, bars?)
"With whom do you drink?" (Alone, with buddies, friends, spouse?)
"Do you drink without eating anything?"
"Do you drink every day or every other day or only on weekends?"
"Do you stay drunk during the day? Most days? When?"

"When you drink, how much do you consume? Do you drink more than a case of beer/fifth of whiskey[9] in a day?"
"At what time of day do you start drinking?" (Upon awakening, all day long, no particular time, at lunch, after work, with dinner, late at night?)
"Do you ever feel you need a drink to get going/can't get through the day without a drink?"
"What are the usual situations or moods just before you start drinking?"

---

[9]Starting with a large amount may reduce defensiveness and inaccuracy.

"Do you ever drink heavily after a fight or disappointment?" (Other possible precipitating emotions: angry, frustrated, lonely, bored, agitated.)

"Do you drink more when you feel under a great deal of pressure?"

"When you are drinking at a party or social occasion, do you sneak a few extra drinks?"[10]

"Have you huffed/ever gulped your drinks to get drunk quickly?"

"Have you ever concealed/lied about the amount of your drinking?"

Drugs

"What street drugs have you used?" (Marijuana, cocaine, crack, heroin, "ice," hallucinogens, LSD, "Ecstasy," "uppers," "speed," "downers," pain killers, "ludes," "Reds," "Black Beauties," tranquilizers, etc?)

"Have you huffed/used inhalants, such as glue, gasoline, butane, naphtha, etc.?"

"What drugs or medications have you used in the last month/6 months? How did you get them?"

"Have you ever used drugs prescribed for you (pain killers, sleeping pills, tranquilizers, barbiturates, etc.) in a way that the doctor didn't prescribe?"

"Have you ever taken medications prescribed for someone else?"

"When did you first use street drugs/misuse medications/sniff chemicals?"

"What effects did they have on you?"

"What did you use at first?"

"When did you first start using it/them regularly?"

"How did you progress to the quantity you now use?"

"What are the usual situations or moods just before you start using?"

"How often do you use? When do you start using? Do you ever feel you need to do some drug just to get going/get through the day or night?"

"Where do you use?" (At work, home, parties, friends' houses?)

"With whom do you use?" (Alone, with buddies, friends, spouse?)

"How do you take each drug/chemical? What is the usual/maximum amount you take?"

Positive and Negative Effects

See the "Points in a Cost–Benefit Analysis Approach" heading under Section 12.36, "Substance Abuse and Use."

"What kind of person are you when you are drunk/high?"

"What are the effects of your drinking/drug use you like most?"

"What are the effects you like least?"

Control

"When was the first time you became concerned about your use of drugs or alcohol?"

"Do you think you need to drink to function normally/get through the day?"

"Once you start drinking, what stops you?" (Internal forces such as self-control/decisions, self-created rules as to location or time; external forces such as intoxication, unconsciousness, lack of money, other people, etc.)

"Have you ever tried to cut down or stop and couldn't? What thoughts/feelings/urges did you have when you tried to stop or refrain?"

"What means have you tried to control your drinking/drug use?" (Relocating, prayer/religion,

---

[10]Janet L. Smigel, RN, CD, suggests adding: "Do you drink one or several drinks before the party because you fear that there won't be alcohol or enough alcohol at the social gathering, or that someone might think you drink too much if you have your usual amount?"

switching to another form of alcohol/another drug, willpower, scheduling, detoxification, reha-
bilitation programs, <u>A</u>lcoholics <u>A</u>nonymous, new friends, isolation, etc.)
"Do you think you have lost control of your drinking/drug use? When?"
"What was the longest period of sobriety/staying clean you have had?"
"Have you ever attended an <u>A</u>lcoholics <u>A</u>nonymous meeting?"

Emotional or Psychological Aspects

"Have you ever regretted what you have done or said when you were drunk/high?"
"Do you feel guilty/embarrassed/remorseful/apologetic about the way you drink/use drugs?"
"Do you ever lie about/conceal/justify/avoid discussion of your actual drinking/drug use?"

Health Consequences

"Did a doctor ever tell you to stop drinking/using drugs for your health?"
"Is your drinking/drug use worsening a health problem you have?"
"Has using drugs/alcohol ever changed your eating/weight? Your sleeping?" (Irregular patterns,
    day–night reversal, interruptions, staying up 24 hours or more when using?)
"Have you ever had any of these when you drank/used drugs or stopped doing so: cramps, sweats/
    fevers, runny nose/watery eyes, diarrhea, dry heaves, seizures/convulsions, tremors/shakes,
    <u>D</u>elirium <u>T</u>remens, weight loss (without dieting), hearing voices, seeing things that others
    didn't, feeling things crawling on your skin?"
"Have you ever been diagnosed with cirrhosis, pancreatitis, jaundice, or other drug-related dis-
    eases?"
"Have you ever had blackouts/times where you couldn't remember what you did or how you got
    to where you were?" (If so:) "When did these first happen and when most recently? How
    often?"
"Have you ever become very drunk when you had only one or two drinks?"

Family/Social Consequences/Impacts

"Have you ever gotten into a serious fight with/hit/beaten/been beaten by your spouse/children/
    relatives/friends when drunk/high?"
"Is your partner also a problem drinker/alcoholic/drug abuser?"
"Do any family members, like your brothers/sisters/parents/children, have a problem with alcohol
    or drugs?"
"Does or did drinking/drug use cause strained relations with your children or family/neglect/ver-
    bal/sexual/physical abuse?"
"Does drinking ever spoil family gatherings/create an atmosphere of tension/make your children
    afraid of you/cause others to talk about you?"
"Do you avoid your family when you are drinking/high?"
"Has drinking/drug use caused you any sexual problems?" (Erectile/arousal problems, high-risk
    behavior, etc.?)
"How would you describe the overall effect of drinking/drugs on your marriage/children/family/
    friends?"
"How do you spend your leisure/free time and with whom?"

Vocational/Financial Consequences

"Did your drinking/drug use ever cause problems when you were in school?"
"How much work have you missed because you were drunk/high/hung over?"

"Did you ever get into arguments or problems at work because you were drunk/high/hung over?"

"Have you ever been disciplined/been fired/damaged anything/hurt anyone because of your drinking/drug use?"

"If you were in the military, did you drink there? Did your drinking cause problems there?"

"Did your work suffer because of your drinking/drug use, such as being less productive, losing out on a promotion or a raise, or other problems?"

"How did/do you get the money to buy drugs?"

Legal Consequences

"Have you been arrested for disorderly conduct, Driving While Intoxicated/Driving Under the Influence, assault, or destructive behavior when you were drunk/high?"

"Have you ever been arrested for possession, sale, or distribution of drugs?"

"How much dealing in drugs have you done?"

"Have you run up large debts/been evicted because of drinking or drug use?"

Identity

"Would you say you are a 'social drinker' or 'have a drinking problem'? Or how would you describe your use?"

"Do you think you are an alcoholic/drug addict? Why or why not?"

Other Aspects

"Has your drinking/drug use caused you any spiritual problems?" *(See Section 19.7, "Religious and Spiritual Concerns.")*

Treatment[11]   *See also Section 25.6, "Treatment Plan Components for Substance Abusers."*

"Have you ever attended an Alcoholics Anonymous/Narcotics Anonymous meeting?" (If so:) "When was that? What was it like? Why did you stop going?"

"What treatments have you received for drug/alcohol use?"

✓ It may be clarifying to construct a table to record this information.

Date	Kind of treatment[12]	Duration	Location/provider	Duration of sobriety	Relapse trigger	Client's comments[13]

"What brought you into (or back into) treatment?"

---

[11]I am grateful to Bryan Lindberg, of Portsmouth, RI, for ideas for this section.

[12]For example: inpatient, outpatient, detoxification, residential/"halfway house," medications (methadone, disulfiram [Antabuse], etc.), marital or couple therapy, motivational interviewing (Miller & Rollnick, 1985), harm reduction (Marlatt, 1998), etc.

[13]Here I would listen for attitude toward treatment (such as pessimism, distancing, frustrations, disappointments, or other barriers) and for expectations (both reasonable and distorted).

3.27. SUBSTANCE USE: TOBACCO AND CAFFEINE

Tobacco

"Do you smoke cigarettes/cigars/a pipe? Do you chew/dip snuff/use smokeless tobacco?" (If so:) "How many/how much do you smoke/use each day?"

"When do you have your first smoke/tobacco use of the day?"

"Where and when do you always/never smoke/use tobacco?"

"What positive things does smoking/tobacco use do for you?"

"When did you start smoking/using tobacco?"

"Did you ever smoke/use more or less than you do now?"

"Have you changed the brand you smoke/use to cut down?"

"Have you tried to stop smoking/using tobacco?" (If so:) "How? How many times? For how long? What has and hasn't worked for you?"

Caffeine

"How many cups of coffee (except decaffeinated/Sanka) or cola drinks (Coke, Pepsi, Dr. Pepper, Mountain Dew, etc.—diet or regular) do you drink in a day?"

"How often do you take Anacin/Bufferin/(for premenopausal females) Midol?"

"How often do you eat chocolate? Do you have some chocolate when you feel down?"

"How much tea/iced tea do you drink each day?"

"How often do you use caffeine tablets like No-Doz?"

3.28. SUICIDE AND SELF-DESTRUCTIVE BEHAVIOR

See Section 12.37, "Suicide" for descriptors.

Initial Inquiry

Begin by saying to the client:

"You have told me about some very painful experiences. They must have been hard to bear, and perhaps you sometimes thought of quitting the struggle/harming yourself/even ending your life. Is that true?"

If this idea is accepted by the client, ask about the following areas.

Death Wish

"When was the last time you wished you would not wake up/were dead/thought you/others/the world would be better off if you were dead?"

"Have you ever thought this way before?"

Ideation

"Have you recently said to yourself or others words like 'Life is not worth living,' 'I can't take any more of this,' 'Who needs this crap/pain?', 'You won't have to worry about me much longer,' 'Soon it will all be over'?"

"When was the first time you thought of/considered ending it all/harming/killing yourself?"

"When was the last time you thought of/considered ending it all/harming/killing yourself?"

"Have you recently/in the last month made any plans to harm or kill yourself?"

"When you have suicidal thoughts, how long do they last?"

"What brings on these thoughts?"

"How do you feel about these thoughts?"

"Do you feel you have control over these thoughts?"
"What stops/ends these thoughts?"

Affects and Behaviors

"How often have you felt lonely/fearful/sad/depressed/hopeless[14]?"
"Are there more themes of despair in your writing/what you are reading/art work/music you listen to than there were before?"
"Are you now very happy after coming out of a depression?"[15]

"Have you lost someone close to you?" (Through moving away, breakup, divorce, death?)
"Have you lost interest in/given up some of your interests/hobbies/activities?"
"Have your grades dropped/your work performance fallen off?"
"Are you more careless with/have you changed for the worse your grooming, eating, and sleeping?"
"Are you taking more risks than you used to?"

"Because of a bad mood, have you ever . . .
    not eaten? slept poorly? Gotten drunk or high? Run away?"
    gotten into a physical fight or trouble in/been kicked out of school? Damaged property?"
    gotten into trouble with the police or been arrested?"
    been involved in physical or sexual abuse or actions you have regretted later?"
    gotten pregnant/gotten someone pregnant?"
    increased your use of alcohol or drugs?"

Motivation

"Why are/were you thinking of killing yourself?"
"Have you felt 'My life is a failure' or 'My situation is hopeless'?"
"What would happen to you after you were dead?"
"What effects would your suicide have on your family/friends/coworkers/others who care about you?"
"Has any relative or friend of yours ever tried to kill/succeeded in killing himself/herself?"   [✔ If any, determine number, age/time when tried, reasons, most recent attempt.]
"Under what conditions would you kill yourself?"

Deterrents/Demotivators

"What reasons do you have to continue to live?"
"What would prevent you from killing yourself?" (Possibilities: "I'm a coward/no courage," "my children," religious convictions, shame, "I wouldn't give her/him the satisfaction," wish to live/enjoyment, hope for improvement.)

Gestures/Attempts

"When was the first time you tried to harm or kill yourself?"
"Have you tried more than once?"
"When was the last time you tried to harm or kill yourself?"
    "What were you thinking at the time about death or dying?"
    "Did you intend to die then?"
    "How did you try to do it?"

[14]Hopelessness seems to be the crucial factor in suicide, not depression.
[15]This is a high-risk period.

"Were you alone?"

"Were you using drugs or alcohol?"

"What happened before each attempt?" (An argument, conflicts with family, a humiliating experience, disappointments, school difficulties, incidents with police, a pregnancy, an assault, physical/sexual abuse, being told "I wish you would die"?)

"What happened afterward?" (Hospitalization [intensive care unit, psychiatric, general medical]; effects on family and friends, on self; counseling or therapy?)

Preparations

"Have you . . .
   given away any (prized) possessions of yours?"   written a will?"
   checked on your insurance?"   made funeral arrangements?"
   told anyone about your plans?"   written a suicide note?"

Plan/Means/Method

"Have you thought about how/where/when you might kill yourself?"

"Have you thought about how easy or difficult it would be to kill yourself?"

"Have you made any plans to harm or kill yourself?"   [✓ If so, assess the degree of practicality/ effort.]

"How would you do it? Do you have the means?"   [✓ If means are present, assess the availability, opportunity, and lethality.]

"What preparations have you made?" (Collecting pills, keeping a gun loaded, etc.?)

A most interesting approach to the evaluation of suicidal intention is the Firestone Voice Scale for Self-Destructive Behavior (Firestone, 1991), which ranks thoughts on an 11-point scale from self-critical to cynical, vicious, urging substance abuse, withdrawal, self-injury, and suicide.

Part II

Standard Terms and Statements for Wording Psychological Reports

Part II of this book is grouped into four subdivisions—A, B, C, and D—that correspond to the format and sequence of a typical evaluation report. The first main component of every report (A) has to cover what is known to you—old information. Upon this base you present your findings (B and C) and go on to your conclusions and recommendations (D).

The section on "Functional Guide to Report Construction" in "Getting Oriented to the *Cinician's Thesaurus*" provides step-by-step assistance with using Part II of this book to generate a report format. If you have decided not to use the sequence offered by Part II, you can go to Chapter 26 to select a different format.

A. Introducing the Report

Every report should begin with orienting information about you, the client, and the examination or treatment. Chapter 4 offers a suggested structure for this information, standard phrasings, and some ethical issues about which you should comment. Chapter 5 lists possible reasons the client was referred to you, and Chapter 6 suggests ways to present the client's histories (medical, social, educational, family, and adjustment).

4

Beginning the Report: Preliminary Information

This chapter covers the **basic information** with which you would **begin** any report. **Reasons for the referral** are covered in Chapter 5; more detailed **background information about the client** is covered in Chapter 6.

4.1. HEADING AND DATES FOR THE REPORT

Use prepared stationery or include full identification of the evaluator by name, degree, and title; agency address; and, where appropriate, affiliation, supervisor, license number, address, and phone number.

Use a title for the report that fits the report's contents and audience—for example, "Psychological Evaluation" or "Case Closing Summary." Most titles are combinations of the words provided below. Always choose those favored by your practice setting.

Choose a word describing the discipline or activity:

Psychosocial, Social Work, Psychiatric, Psychological, Neuropsychological, Psychoeducational, Nursing, Multidisciplinary.
Forensic, Rehabilitation, Habilitation, Diagnostic, Testing, Case, Mental Status, Intake, Progress, Discharge, Closing.
Educational, Intellectual, Personality, Ecological, Individualized, Behavioral, Treatment, Management, Life Management.

And then choose a word describing the kind of document:

> Summary, Evaluation, Assessment, Report, Examination, History, Plan, Update, Note, Formulation.

Always date the report. In addition, give all dates and locations (e.g., in the hospital room, school's office, private office, home) of examination/evaluation/interview(s)/testing. Indicate time of day, total time of testing, duration of interview, etc., as relevant.

4.2. SOURCES OF INFORMATION FOR THE REPORT

Begin describing information sources with one or more of these statements, as appropriate:

> In preparation for/advance of the interview, I received and reviewed the following records...
> The records I received were without clear provenance/were from a source I could not establish.
> Records were destroyed/unavailable/scant/unhelpful/scattered/adequate/pertinent/voluminous.

Sources of information may include the following:

> Review of documents furnished—charts, treatment summaries and reports, school records, previous evaluations, etc.
> Observations of the client during a clinical interview.
> Collateral interviews with friend/spouse/parents/family/relatives/caregiver/interpreter/etc.
> Testing: List each test or questionnaire separately by its full name, and use abbreviations/ acronyms in the body of the report. *(See Sections 11.21, "Evaluation of Intellect and Cognitive Functions," and 13.27, "Personality Assessment," for tests' names.)* [✓ If appropriate, add this statement: "All tests were administered, scored, and interpreted by this report's author without the use of assistants or supervisees."]
> Consultation with other professionals.
> Observation by other professionals of/interview with the client/child/family.

4.3. IDENTIFYING INFORMATION ABOUT THE CLIENT

The description should be so detailed as to enable the identification of the unique individual. *See Chapter 7, "Behavioral Observations," for specific language.*

Name

Always state the client's given name and surname. As appropriate, also specify family of origin/maiden name, changes, aliases/<u>A</u>lso <u>K</u>nown <u>A</u>s.

> *For a Child:* Indicate preferred name/nickname(s).

Other Identification

Give the client's address, phone number, case number (if any), and name of current therapist/ physician/referrer (as appropriate).

Gender/Sex

Specify the client's gender or sex (the term "gender" is more accurate here).

Age

Give age in years, for adults.

> *For a Child:* Use 9 years and 3 months, 9 3/12, or 9'3", not the ambiguous 9.3 years.

Marital Status

Be consistent in reporting marital status for males and females. Give number and duration of marriages/common-law marriages, separations/divorces.

> Current: Never married [✓ preferable to "single" because it is less ambiguous]/living with a paramour or partner/married/common-law marriage/separated/divorcing/divorced/widow/widower/unknown.
> Childless/parent of _____ children.

Occupation

Specify whether the client is employed/unemployed/underemployed, a student, retired, etc. Also describe other occupations, part-time work, previous occupations, etc.

> *For a Disability Report:* Give date of alleged industrial/other injury, date last worked.

Nationality/Ethnicity

> ✓ In reporting nationality/ethnicity, note also place of birth and what language is used in the home.

Race

> ✓ Be consistent across reports in reporting race; do not report it only for minorities. Race does not equal skin color. If in doubt about a person's race or about currently, locally, or personally acceptable terms, ask.

> African-American, white/European-American/"Anglo," Asian/Asian-American,[1] Hispanic/Latino,[2] Native American, Inuit ("Eskimo"), Oceanic, etc., biracial/multiracial/of mixed races.

Residence/Living Circumstances

Religion

Report on religion only as relevant.

> Parents' religion/born into, religion baptized into/raised in/converted to/recent if changed, current.
> No preference: Unimportant, unaffiliated, nonpracticing, rejected, agnostic, atheist.
> Preference (↔ *by degree*): Practicing, pious, devout, righteous, zealous, proselytizing, evangelizing, preoccupied, delusional.

Legal Mental Health Status

> Involuntary/voluntary admission/treatment/commitment. (Perhaps give the number or name of the applicable section of the local law.)

REFERRAL REASON *See Chapter 5, "Referral Reasons."*

---

[1]My thanks to Fay Murakawa, PhD, of Los Angeles, CA, for clarification and correction.

[2]Be wary of using any global term to indicate the psychological/cultural diversity of this or other large population groups.

4.4. SELF-SUFFICIENCY IN APPEARING FOR EXAMINATION

Came to first (or second, etc.) appointment, late by _____ minutes/excessively early/appropriately early for examination/on schedule/exactly on time for examination.

Came alone/without escort, came with friend/spouse/children/escort/caseworker/etc. [✓ If companion is present, specify role of companion in examination, if any.]

Had _____ degree of difficulty finding the office.

Drove/was driven/used other mode of transportation (specify).

4.5. CONSENT STATEMENTS

Consent to Assessment or Treatment

With regard to the information you should provide to your patients, the guideline is this: "What would a reasonable, prudent adult need to know to decide whether to agree to engage in this assessment or treatment or to refuse it?"

For assessments, the client has to be informed of who will see the report (e.g., the courts, managed care staff, the referrer, an adolescent client's parents, etc.); to be advised of what decisions these persons or organizations will be making based on it; and to be offered the opportunity to refuse to participate or discontinue participation if the client decides that specific revelations would not be in her/his best interests.

As regards a course of treatment, you must discuss the risks and benefits that can reasonably be anticipated. You might couch your statements to the patient in terms like these, based on ones suggested by the Group for the Advancement of Psychiatry (1990):

"Although no completely satisfactory statistics are available, I believe that this combination of treatments offers the best chance of success."

"The success rate of this treatment is about 85%.[3] That is, about 85% of all patients receiving this treatment experience complete or substantial relief of their symptoms."

The discussions and handouts in Zuckerman (1997) can be very helpful in this regard.

Informed Consent

We discussed the evaluation/treatment procedures; what was expected of both the client and the evaluator/therapist; who else would be involved or affected; the treatment's risks and benefits; and alternative methods' sources, costs, and benefits.

This client understands the risks and benefits of giving and withholding information.

The client understands the procedures that he/she is being asked to consent to and their likely consequences/effects, as well as alternative procedures and their consequences.

I have informed the client that the information he/she provides will be incorporated into my report, which I will send to _____, who referred him/her to me for evaluation.

I advised the client that I am not her/his treating psychologist, that we will not have a continuing professional relationship, and that no records will be kept at this/my office.

The client knows that the results of this evaluation will be sent to . . . and used for . . .

In a continuing dialogue, these have been explained in language appropriate to his/her education and intellect.

---

[3]Obviously this figure would differ with each proposed treatment.

Voluntary Consent

This client understands and willingly agrees to participate fully.
The client understands that she/he may withdraw her/his consent at any time and discontinue the evaluation/treatment.

Competency to Consent

I have no reason to suspect that this person is not competent to consent to the evaluations/procedures/treatments being considered.
The client is not a minor or mentally defective; nor does he/she have any limitation of communication, psychopathology, or any other aspect that would compromise his/her understanding and competency to consent.

4.6. RELIABILITY STATEMENTS

Basis of Data

On the basis of ...
    observations of this person for ___ hours on ___ occasions in (specify settings) ...
    internal consistency of the information and history ...
    absence of omissions/deletions of negative information, contradictions ...
    the character and cohesiveness of the client's responses, spontaneous comments, and behaviors ...
    consistency of information from different sources ...
    client's ability to report situations fully ...
the data/history are felt to be completely/quite/reasonably/rather/minimally/questionably reliable.
I consider her/him to be an adequately/inadequately reliable informant.

This report reflects this person's condition at the time of this consultation and may not reflect this person's condition at the time of discharge or final diagnosis, or at any later or earlier time period.

The information above was provided by the informant/(give name)/client/claimant and should not be considered as the opinions of the writer.

Representativeness

Results are believed to be a valid sample of/accurately represent this person's current level of functioning/typical behavioral patterns/behaviors outside the examination setting.
Because this client refused no test items/questions, worked persistently/was most cooperative and helpful, and had no interfering emotions such as anxiety or depression, test findings/results of this evaluation are felt to be representative of her/his minimal/usual/optimal level of functioning.

Consistency

His/her appraisals tended to be supported/corroborated by my observations/others' records. She/he presented personal history in a spontaneous fashion, organized in a chronological sequence and with sufficient detail, consistency, logic, and attention.
He/she was a poor/adequate/good/excellent historian.

($\leftrightarrow$ *by degree*) Complete/quite organized presentation, accurate recall of details/names and sequences, sparse data/stingy with information/only sketchy history, disorganized/scattered/haphazard, nebulous/vague/ambiguous, illogical/contradictory/facetious.

Accuracy

I believe he has been honest/truthful/factual/accurate.
Although somewhat dramatized, the core information appears to be accurate and valid for diagnostic/evaluative purposes.

The client tries hard to be accurate in recalling events, but . . .
She/he is not an astute observer.
He/she tried to provide meaningful responses to my question, but . . .

She/he had difficulty presenting historical material in a coherent and chronological manner.

Client was questioned extensively and creatively, but it was not possible to determine/get a clear picture of/obtain more information on _____.
Impossible to obtain any delineation of symptoms other than his/her informal description of "I lost it."
She/he becomes tangential when pressed for specifics.

The patient gave what she seemed convinced was an accurate account of her personal situation, although she seemed unaware of her many limitations and deficits.
He expresses himself with great confidence, as though totally unaware of any mistakes or confusions.
Although the client seemed to present the information above in an honest manner, its accuracy must be questioned because of possible difficulties with accurate perception of social/consensual/chronological reality/the accepted meaning of behaviors/patterns in relationships/etc., or the very unusual nature of her/his accusations/reported experiences.

She/he gave a history that did not so much appear to describe symptoms as to describe a major characterologically disturbed style of living.

Trustworthiness/Honesty/Malingering

She seemed to be honest in her self-descriptions of her strengths and weaknesses.
He appeared to be a truthful witness and an accurate historian.
She did not appear to be fabricating any of her history.
His response to questions appeared to be free of any deliberate attempts to present a distorted picture.
She gave no evidence of a deliberate distortion of her test-taking efforts.

The history offered should be taken with a grain of salt/was fabricated/grandiose.
Much of what he said sounded like it was what someone told him/sounded rehearsed.
Responded eagerly to leading questions, endorsing the presence of symptoms or problems if suggested.

Ganser's syndrome {hysterical pseudodementia}/{vorbeireden}.

It should be noted that in each of these complaints her description was vague, self-contradictory, and not completely consistent with any recognized clinical pattern.
She is motivated only to obtain benefits/malingering.
Despite allegations of pain and deficiency, he is able to get up and down from a chair without difficulty.
She offered an exaggerated/minimized description of her behaviors.
Client is deliberately deceptive/malingering/faking bad.
This examiner believes the client is very capable of claiming conditions and reporting experiences that will enhance his application for disability but that bear little relation to reality.
Client was a willfully poor historian.

She lies with panache.

He indicated a sense of righteous entitlement to his (e.g., alcoholism, violence, irresponsibility, etc.).

Client's attitude toward her illness/disability suggests indifference/tolerance/acceptance/transcendence.

✔ **Note:** In some medical education, terms and concepts other than "reliability" (or "validity") are used for these headings (Coulehan & Block, 1987). "*Objectivity* is the removal of systematic biases due to the observer's beliefs, prejudices, and preconceptions" (p. 5). "*Precision* is how widely observations are scattered around the 'real' value" (p. 9), due to random error. "The *sensitivity of a test*" expresses its ability to "'pick up' real cases of the disease in question" (p. 11)—that is, the ability to separate true positives from false ones. "*Specificity*, by contrast, refers to a test's ability to 'rule out' disease in normal people" (p. 11)—that is, the ability to separate true negatives from false ones.

4.7. CONFIDENTIALITY NOTICES

Guidelines

In order to ensure confidentiality, it is *not* sufficient to stamp the pages of a report "Confidential" or "For professional use only," because these are too general and vague. Instead, provide a notice on each page (perhaps by placing it in a footer in your word processor) that makes the following points clear:

1. The contents of this report are considered a legally protected medical document.
2. The information in this report is to be used for a stated/specific purpose.
3. The report is to be used only by the authorized recipient.
4. The report is not to be disclosed to any other party, including the patient/client.   [✔ Any exceptions to this must be clearly and specifically stated.]
5. The report is to be destroyed after the specified use has been made/stated need has been met.

Examples

Any of these examples may be reworded as necessary to meet the requirements of your own setting.

This information has been disclosed to you from records protected by federal confidentiality rules (42 C.F.R. Part 2, P.L. 93-282) and state law (e.g., Pennsylvania Law 7100-111-4). These regulations prohibit you from making any further disclosure of this information unless further disclosure is expressly permitted by the written consent of the person to whom it pertains or as otherwise permitted by 42 C.F.R. Part 2. A general authorization for the release of information is *not* sufficient for this purpose. The federal rules restrict any use of the information to criminally investigate or prosecute any alcohol or drug abuse patient.

This is privileged and confidential patient information. Any unauthorized disclosure is a federal offense. Not to be duplicated.

This report may contain client information. Release only to professionals capable of ethically and professionally interpreting and understanding the information it contains.

Persons or entities granted access to this record may discuss this information with the patient only insofar as necessary to represent the patient in legal proceedings or other matters for which this record has been legally released.

I have in my possession a signed and valid authorization to supply these records to you and you alone.

This information is not to be used against the interests of the subject of this report.

This is strictly *confidential* material and is for the information of only the person to whom it is addressed. No responsibility can be accepted if it is made available to any other person, including the subject of this report. Any duplication, transmittal, redisclosure, or retransfer of these records is expressly prohibited. Such redisclosure may subject you to civil or criminal liability.[4]

It is inappropriate to release the information contained herein directly to the client or other parties. If this information is released to interested individuals before they are afforded an opportunity to discuss its meaning with a trained mental health professional, it is likely that the content of the report may be misunderstood, leading to emotional distress on the part of the uninformed reader.

This report is to be utilized only by professional personnel. Any information released to others will require interpretation.

For a Child:

The contents of this report have/have not been shared with the child's parent(s)/guardian. She/he/they may review this report with the evaluator or his/her specific designee. Copies of this report may be released only by the evaluator or his/her departmental administrator, or in accord with the school district's policy.

The information contained in this report is private, privileged, and confidential. It cannot be released outside the school system except by the examining psychologist/evaluator/creator of this report, upon receipt of written consent by the parent or guardian. Not to be duplicated or transmitted.

[4]This is from *The Paper Office* (Zuckerman, 1997).

5

Referral Reasons

This chapter covers **reasons for referral only.** Everything else that should be included in the introduction to a report is covered in Chapters 4 and 5.

After a suggested phrasing for a referral statement, this chapter concentrates on **referral reasons for children**. This has been done because adult referral reasons are thoroughly covered in Chapter 12, "Abnormal Signs, Symptoms, and Syndromes," and many other chapters.

5.1. STATEMENT OF REFERRAL REASON

A statement of the reason for referral should cover the referral source, date, type of evaluation/service, and purpose, as well as the referral reason itself.

> Client was referred by _____ (referral source/person and agency) on _____ (date of referral), for _____ (type of evaluation or other service), to _____ (rationale/purpose) in regard to _____ (referral reason).

The rest of this section gives descriptors that can be used to fill in the blanks for type of evaluation or other service and for rationale/purpose in this basic statement. As noted above, the remainder of the chapter gives descriptors that can be used as referral reasons for children.

Types of Evaluations/Services

Mental Status Evaluation.
Clinical interview.
Diagnostic determination.
Competency evaluation.
Forensic evaluation.

Custody evaluation.
Pretreatment evaluation and recommendations.
Reevaluation.
Educational placement.
Vocational recommendations.

Rationales/Purposes

Determine the nature and extent of psychiatric/psychological disabilities.
Assist with the development of a treatment/rehabilitation/education program.
Evaluate suitability for entry into _____ program.
Assess extent of neuropsychological losses and coping abilities.
Determine benchmarks of current functioning.
Meet organizational needs for evaluation/state and federal regulations/Joint Commission on Accreditation of Healthcare Organizations guidelines.
Assist with legal/forensic decisions.

5.2. COMMON REFERRAL REASONS FOR CHILDREN AT HOME

For problems at school, see Section 5.3, below. See also the adult symptoms listed in Chapter 12, "Abnormal Signs, Symptoms, and Syndromes."

These are presented in alphabetical order, as no theory provides an agreed-upon structure.

Abuse: Suspected, reported being investigated, founded/confirmed/supported, by whom/relationship, duration.
Attention-seeking behaviors: Tattling, baiting, provoking others, taunts, teases, overly demanding of attention from siblings/peers/adults, craves _____'s attention, tantrums, disruptive noises, "clowning around," pranks, "daredevil," interrupts, compulsive talking, manipulates.
Autistic withdrawal: Lack of responsiveness to people, resistance to change in the environment.
Conflicts with parents over: Persistent rule breaking, spending money, doing chores, doing homework, school grades, choices in music/clothes/hair/friends.
Dawdles/lingers/procrastinates/wastes time/starts late in dressing/eating/bedtimes.
Eating: Poor manners, refuses, appetite changes, odd combinations.
Imaginary playmates/fantasy.
Legal difficulties: Truancy, loitering, panhandling, hangs out with peers, underage drinking, vandalism, fighting, drug sales, "joyriding," auto theft, burglary, extortion.
Need for _____ degree of supervision at home over play/chores/schedule.
Oppositional/resists/noncompliant.
Parent's role as disciplinarian: Uses lectures/threats/guilt inductions/force/spankings/groundings/allowance reductions/privilege losses as a consequence irregularly/arbitrarily/regularly, with good/mixed/poor success at control.
Relationships with sibs/peers: Rivalry, competition, fights, teases/provokes, bullies, tyrannizes, assaults.
Running away/wandering off.
Shyness.
Sleep problems: Parasomnias, refusing to go to bed, nightmares, night terrors, sleepwalking, excessive drowsiness, refusal to get out of bed.
Steals, shoplifts.
Verbal abuse: Criticized, berated, belittled, humiliated.
Violence: Abusing, aggressive, threatening, bullying.

5.3. COMMON REFERRAL REASONS FOR CHILDREN AT SCHOOL

Academic Performance

Fails tests, difficulty with _____ (specify subject), subject matter appears too difficult, extracurricular activities interfere with academics.

Failure in subjects, kept back, retention in grade, underachievement, social promotion.

Lacks order and system in work and method of study, disorganized, careless/sloppy, lacks precision/neatness, is irregularly/rarely/never prepared.

Does not seek help when appropriate, copies from peers.

Cheating.

Poor academic progress due to low attendance/dropping out.

Social Factors

With Peers

Loner, relates to few students, isolates self, "different," doesn't belong/fit in, relates to adults only on request.

Clique membership/exclusion.

Is easily influenced/led, suggestible, engages in risky activities.

Sexual inappropriateness.

Verbally criticizes/abuses/insults peers, name-calling, unprovoked attacks, fights with _____, bullies.

Does not respect rights and property of others.

Does not participate in group activities.

Interacts inappropriately with peers.

With Teachers

Noncompliant, resists, disobeys, refuses to complete work assignments, seldom prepared, unmotivated, reluctantly participates, requires 1:1 supervision.

Does not follow classroom rules and procedures, challenges disrupts.

Attention-seeking behaviors: Tattling, baiting, lying, provoking others, overly demanding of attention from teachers/peers/adults, craves _____'s attention, tantrums, disruptive noises, "clowning around," pranks, "daredevil," "class clown."

Overly dependent on teacher.

Conduct/Deportment/Behavior

Oral aggression/interrupts/talks out.

Disruptive: Agitates/disturbs/disrupts other kids.

Low respect for authority/confronts teachers/defiant, insults, defies, lies, troublemaker.

Bullies/intimidates, teases, manipulates.

Overactive, inappropriate, out-of-seat behaviors/in-seat behaviors, restlessness, fidgety. *(See Section 12.3, "Attention-Deficit/Hyperactivity Disorder.")*

School's response to behavior problems: Expulsions/suspensions/disciplinary conferences.

Motivation/Initiative

Does not try, makes little effort, content to "get by."

Has ability to do better work, but lacks interest to do so—"That's too hard."

Does not persevere, needs great encouragement, gives up too easily/at first sign of difficulty, low frustration tolerance.

Doesn't pay attention, daydreams, preoccupied, stares out of window, slow to respond.

Does not complete homework/in-class assignments.
Does not make up missed assignments.
Turns in assignments late.
Shows no interest in subject matter, in learning.
Careless work.
Does not spend enough time on work.
Copies assignments from others, does not do own work.
Comes to class without necessary work materials.
Forgetful.

Attendance: Misses excessive days, absenteeism, tardy, tardiness, cuts classes, truancy.

School "phobia"/avoidance. *(See Section 12.31, "School Refusal/'Phobia.'")*

Student's Perceptions

Perceptions of grades, source of problems, other problems, fairness of system, attitude of peers/
teachers/administrators.
Sense of identity, self-esteem, confidence.

Other Aspects

Behavior deteriorates when confronted by academic demands.
Inappropriate behavior in structured/unstructured situations.
Is too tired during the school day to put forth best effort.
Hearing, sight, coordination problem.
Behaviors inimical to other students' welfare or exercise of rights (specify).

5.4. COMMON REFERRAL REASONS FOR CHILDREN AT BOTH HOME AND SCHOOL

Cognitive

Distractible, hyperactive, inattentive, handles new or exciting situations poorly, lacks foresight, low
frustration tolerance, gets confused in group, does not finish his/her work, daydreams, low
concentration. *(See Section 12.3, "Attention-Deficit/Hyperactivity Disorder.")*

Behavior

Alcohol/drug abuse. *(See Section 12.36, "Substance Abuse and Use.")*
Encopresis, enuresis.
Fire setting, plays with matches/cooking equipment.
Hypochondriasis.
Overactive/restless.
Self-abusive/self-harming behavior: Bites, hits, head banging, nail biting, lacerates self, tattooing, self-
mutilation, scarring, cutting, burning, bondage, piercing, insertion of objects into the body.
Sexual behaviors:
Sexual preoccupation, public masturbation, inappropriate sexual behaviors, obscenity/swear-
ing.
Molests/molestation/molested, threatened, touched, fondled, battery.
Intercourse/entry: Oral/vaginal/anal/femoral.
Repeated/single episode/recurrent.
Assault/rape/force used/damage.
Protective services/police/court/medical/school/family interventions.

(↔ *by degree*) Slow-moving or responding, lethargic, hypoactive, <normal>, impulsive, hyperactive/overactive.

Speech difficulties, stuttering. *(See Section 7.4, "Speech Behavior.")*

Thumb sucking.

Tics: Involuntary rapid movements, noise or word productions.

Violence/aggression. *(See below.)*

Social

Aggression/violence: Verbal aggression, intimidation, bullying, repeated threats, throwing things, destructiveness of own/others/peers/teacher's/school property, physical fights/attacking/violence, hits parents/caregivers. *(See Section 12.20, "Impulse Control Disorders.")*

Antagonistic, "smart-aleck."

Noncompliance: Disobedience, negativism, resistive, oppositional, argues, "sasses/talks back/mouthy," ignores, defiant of authority, lying in regard to chores/house rules, complies only when threatened, independent/autonomous/"stubborn."

Immaturity: Impaired judgment; does not take responsibility for own work/belongings, own words/actions, own behavior and consequences; does not demonstrate positive/resilient self-concept.

Lying.

Mutism (elective/selective).

Prejudiced, bigotry, insults, vandalism, threats, hate crimes.

Lacks respect for authority, insults, dares, provokes, acts out.

Swearing/blasphemy.

Temper tantrums: Falls to floor and bangs heels/head, breath-holding episodes, throws objects, screams, weeps, destructive.   [✓ Note duration, as well as how handled: time out, spanking, ignored, punished, mocked.]

Timid/shy/dependent/anxiety-prone.

Is not accepted/valued as friend, doesn't sustain friendships.

Is an object of scorn/ridicule/mockery/teasing/name calling/insults/threats/physical attacks, is scapegoated/picked on, does not defend self when attacked, ostracized.

Isolation, withdrawal.

Affects

Anxiety, fears, phobias; nervous habits (tics, tapping, restlessness, mannerisms, drumming); avoids certain things/actions/situations, "freezes" in these situations. *(See Section 10.3, "Anxiety/Fear.")*

Angry, irritable, outbursts, rage, tantrums.

Cries easily, pouts, "thin-skinned," whines, feelings are easily hurt.

Depressed, sad, unhappy, cries, hurt, low energy, easy fatigue, apathy, withdrawn, suicidal. *(See Section 10.5, "Depression.")*

Emotional constriction: Has limited range of emotions, expresses only high-intensity feelings.

Physical

Problems with fine motor coordination (cutting, drawing, writing, etc.), alternates right–left/ambidextrous.

Problems with gross motor coordination (walking, running, climbing, etc.).

Many physical/medical complaints, accident-prone.

Dysgraphia, dyslexia, eye preference, hand preference.

6

Background Information
and History

This chapter covers the client's **history and adjustment** in many areas. **Referral reasons** are covered in Chapter 5, **other preliminary information** is covered in Chapter 4.

6.1. HISTORY/COURSE OF THE PRESENT/CHIEF COMPLAINT/CONCERN/PROBLEM/ILLNESS

This section covers the patient's view of the problem in his/her own words, and beliefs about the source(s) of the complaints. It can also cover the following:

For a Child: Parents'/teachers'/authority's perception of problem(s).

For a Disability Report: Claimant's view of the impairment created by the injury/complaint/disorder.

Onset, Circumstances, and Effects

Formal statement of presenting/Chief Complaint.
Circumstances, precipitating stresses/triggers/cues/situations/events, anniversary reactions.
Premorbid personality and functioning levels.
Development of signs/symptoms/behavioral changes, longitudinal/chronological/biographical sequence, periods of/attempts to work/return to functioning since onset, current status.

Duration, progression, and severity of presenting complaint.

Effects of the complaint on the functioning of the patient.
Effects of treatments on complaint.
Reasons and goals for seeking treatment at this time.
Evaluator's clarification/reformulation/elaboration of complaint.

Summary Statements:

Reason for current admission/Current admission is result of . . .
This is the ___ (#) admission to (name of hospital) and the ___ (#) lifetime psychiatric hospitalization.

Course   *See also the "Course Descriptors" heading under Section 23.1, "General Prognostic Statement."*

Single episode, or multiple episodes? If the latter describe as:
    Recurrences, relapses, exacerbations, worsenings, flareups, fluctuating course.
Duration of each episode?
Remissions, if any:

    Therapeutic or spontaneous.
    Duration?
    Return to what level of function/symptomatology? Describe as (↔ *by degree*)
        Decompensation, damage, recompensation, recovery, adjustment, overcompensation, growth.

6.2. PERTINENT MEDICAL HISTORY AND OTHER FINDINGS

Medical History

Current/recent illnesses.
Symptoms. [✓ Consider using a checklist such as the Symptom CheckList 90 (Derogatis, 1977) for completeness.]
Diseases/disorders with known psychological aspects: e.g., thyroid, mitral valve prolapse, AIDS, diabetes, cancer of the pancreas, alcohol abuse, etc. *(See Chapter 28, "Psychiatric Masquerade of Medical Conditions.")*
Surgeries.

(For women:) Live births, stillbirths, spontaneous/induced abortions. Gravida (#), para (#), abortio (#).

Injuries/accidents, especially Traumatic Brain Injury, Closed Head Injury, and all unconsciousness-producing incidents.
Drug treatment, use, and abuse, especially street/illegal/illicit drug use. *(See Section 3.26, "Substance Abuse: Drugs and Alcohol," for questions, and Section 12.36, "Substance Abuse and Use," for descriptors.)*
Exposure history: Risk, toxins, duration, type.

Psychiatric History

Psychological difficulties in the past, and treatment(s)/professional help sought.
Hospitalizations: Date(s), name(s), location(s), condition on admission(s), therapies instituted and response to treatment(s), duration(s) of hospitalization(s), condition on discharge(s), time before next hospitalization(s), course *(see above).*

Current and past medications/therapies/treatments received, effects of/response to/ treatments, side effects, condition on discharge(s) from treatment.
After discharge: follow-up treatments, referral, lost to follow-up?

Previous Testing or Evaluations

Evaluations: <u>H</u>istory <u>and</u> <u>P</u>hysical, neurological, intellectual, educational, vocational, neuro-psychological, personality, projectives, organicity, other/specialized.
Results/findings: Availability, scores, comparisons with current results, omissions and contradictions, "<u>Rule-Out</u>(s)."

Previous Psychotherapy or Counseling

Dates, nature of problems.
Provider(s) and nature of services.
Outcome(s).

6.3. PERSONAL, FAMILY, AND SOCIAL HISTORIES, AND CURRENT SOCIAL SITUATION

✓ Construction of a genogram *(see Section 6.6)* may be useful to guide inquiries and to record findings as you interview.

Parents' Qualities

General physical and mental health during client's childhood; present health; chronic or severe illnesses, disabilities.
Ages, birth dates.
Year and cause of death (if deceased); client's age and reaction to death and its consequences (if applicable).
Personality characteristics, manner of relating to client, disciplinary methods, client's perception of parents' influences.
Marriages/divorces/separations.
Qualities of the marital relationship—describe as:
    Stormy, close, distant, warm, functional, abusive, demonic, etc. *(See also Chapter 16, "Couple and Family Relationships.")*
Other: Extended family, patterns, obligations, familial "debits and credits."
Occupation(s), effects of employment/career on client.
Parental history of substance abuse or misuse, physical or sexual abuse, traumas.
Composition of family during patient's childhood and youth.
Family's response to patient's behavior/problems/illness.

Client's Development and Early Health/Medical History

Pregnancy—describe as:
    Eagerly anticipated/planned, unplanned, unaccepted/accepted.
    Full-term, premature/postmature by ___ weeks.
    Uncomplicated/complicated (specify difficulties/illnesses before/during pregnancy).
Delivery—describe as:
    Natural, prepared, unprepared, difficult, uneventful, easy.
    Normal duration/prolonged (specify ___ hours' duration).
    Uncomplicated/complicated (specify difficulties).

Birth weight, Apgar scores, birth defects.
Exposure to toxins, drugs, alcohol, diseases, other insults pre-, peri-, postnatally.
Development:
  Postnatal difficulties, weight gain, eating, sleeping, daily routines.
  Milestones: Timing of crawling, sitting up unaided, walking, toilet training, speech and language acquisition; delays in development, loss of previously acquired skills (specify); immature behavior patterns.
Childhood illnesses, medication(s), disabling/handicapping conditions.

Siblings/Stepsiblings/Half-Siblings

Ages, genders, locations in birth order/sibline/sibship/confraternity/constellation of ___ children/sibs/siblings.[1]
Relationships among sibs in past and at present.
General physical and mental health during client's childhood; present health; chronic illnesses, disabilities.

Social Context for a Child

Cultural/ethnic background and, as appropriate, country of birth and language spoken in the home.
Living arrangements: Specify applicable relationship/legal issues. Describe situation as:
  Lives with both parents/stepparent and remarried parent/blended family/single parent/grandparents/other relatives (specify), is adopted, lives in foster home/institution, other (specify).
Location—describe as:
  City/metropolitan/urban, suburban, rural, institution, military base, other (specify).
Home supports—describe as:
  Destitute/homeless, poverty, welfare, Social Security (Supplemental Security Income, SS Disability Income), "working poor," one/both parents working part-time/full-time/several jobs, etc.
SocioEconomic Status (specify).
Social relationships—describe as:
  Organizational memberships, cultural interests, many/few/no friends, close/best friends, buddies/clique/peer group membership, isolation/exclusion/rejection/"loner." (See also Chapter 15, "Social/Community Functioning.")

Social History and Situation for an Adult

Marriage(s): Age at/date of each marriage, termination reason (if applicable). (See Chapter 16, "Couple and Family Relationships.")
Number, age, gender of children.[2]
Relationship with ex-spouse (if applicable), spouse/partner, children.
Adultery/extramarital relationships/satellite relationships, exclusivity/monogamy.
Living circumstances—describe as:
  Lives independently, lives with family/relatives/friends/other persons, lives alone but with much family support.

---

[1]Possible language: "The client has a brother aged 18, and two sisters aged 22 and 16; he is the second of the four children."
[2]Possible language: "She has sons aged 3 and 5, and a daughter aged 6."

Vocational/occupational factors:
> History of sheltered/adapted employment, competitive employment.
> Nature, demands, duration of previous jobs (if any).
> Present occupation: Chosen/not chosen, duration, satisfaction, intellectual demands, social–behavioral requirements/demands, advancement, aspirations, frustrations.

Military service:
> None, rejected, alternate service, avoided, enlisted/volunteer, draftee.
> Branch of service, training, work performed, promotions/demotions.
> Combat/combat zone/noncombat location.
> Reenlistments, duration of service, final grade, kind of discharge.
> Military adjustment: Article XVs, time spent in the stockade (Army)/brig (Navy), court(s)-martial.

Legal/criminal history: Warnings from police, charges as a minor, charges/indictments, arrests, prosecutions, convictions, incarceration/probation/parole, civil suits, current litigation/lawsuits, bankruptcy, violence directed against others (specify).

Other: Special skills, career goals, debts/burdens, adequacy of income to meet responsibilities/needs.

Recreational activities. *(See Chapter 18, "Recreational Functioning.")*

Sexual History and Situation   *See Section 3.23, "Sexual History," for questions.*

Educational Situation for a Child or Adult

Nature of enrollment—describe as:
> Day, full-time, part-time, other (specify).

Type of school/study—describe as:
> Public, private, parochial/religious/sectarian, special (indicate needs met), itinerant teacher, home study.

Location of school—describe as:
> Rural, suburban, metropolitan/urban/inner-city.

Name(s) of teacher(s), relationship(s) with teacher(s), teacher report/description of problems.

Class assignment/level (specify), age–grade differential (if any).

Nature of educational placement—describe as:
> Regular classes, special education (life skills, learning support/learning disability, Socially and Emotionally Disturbed), mainstreamed, scholar's program, gifted in _____ (specify subject or subjects).

Overall level of academic achievement/performance/grades, Quality/Grade Point Average, standing in class.

Major area of study and its relationship to present employment (if any).

Type of educational program—describe as:
> Academic, technical/vocational, General Equivalency Diploma, college preparatory, etc.

Extracurricular activities—describe as:
> Athletics, social service, music, scholarly, religious, political, special interests (specify), other (specify).

Other aspects: Favorite subjects, peer and teacher relationships, position in peer group, aspirations.

Level/highest grade completed—describe as:
> Preschool/kindergarten, elementary/middle/junior high/high school, technical school, 2- or 4-year college, graduate school; ___ grades completed; dropped out of school in grade ___ at age ___.

Summary Statements:

The client has received special services/educational support through his/her whole school history/ since the ___ grade/in grades _____.
Her/his attainment of developmental milestones was within the normal range of expectation.
There are no remarkable factors to suggest the presence of unmeasured potential.

REFERRAL REASON   *See Chapter 5, "Referral Reasons."*

SEXUAL HISTORY, NONSYMPTOMATIC
See Sections 6.4, below; see also Section 3.23, "Sexual History."

SUBSTANCE ABUSE HISTORY   *See Section 3.26, "Substance Abuse: Drugs and Alcohol."*

6.4. ADJUSTMENT HISTORY

Sexual Adjustment   *See also Sections 3.4, 3.13, 3.23, and 3.24 for questions and issues.*

Dysfunctions/disturbed sexual performance—describe as:
   Loss of desire, inhibited arousal, primary/secondary/occasional difficulty getting or keeping an erection/"impotence," fast/premature/delayed ejaculation, inhibited orgasm, dyspareunia, vaginismus.
History of physical and/or sexual abuse, molestation, violence/victimization, traumas.
Orientation and object choice—describe as:
   Celibate, "sex addict," heterosexual, homosexual, gay, lesbian, bisexual, asexual, etc.

Paraphilias/sexual minorities/variations/special interests—describe as:
   Pedophilia, hebephilia, exhibitionism, voyeurism, pornography, prostitution, Sadism and Masochism, Slave and Master, zoophilia, frottage, Bondage and Domination/Discipline, Domination and Submission, fetishism, TransVestism, "water sports"/"golden showers"/"toilet service"/urolagnia, Greek (anal)/French (oral)/English (whipping) sex, transsexualism, etc.

Summary Statements:

The client reports no/some traumatic sexual/traumatizing experiences (if any, specify).
The patient was not questioned about sexual preferences/orientation, history, or interests.

Social Adjustment

Acquaintances, clique membership/exclusion, friends/buddies/best friends, relationship with sibs/friends/enemies.
Ability to adjust to marriages, childbirth/parenthood, losses, aging, illness, health care/services/treatments.
Ability to conform to social standards; hold employment; advance in a career; adjust to superiors/bosses, peers/coworkers/fellow workers, schedules, work load, and task changes.

Summary Statements:

The client denied the presence of any environmental or circumstantial, precipitating, or contributing event that could have thrown her/him out of balance/destabilized her/his normal adjustment.

His/her history is remarkable only for ... (specify findings).

The client has no history of military service/drug or alcohol difficulties/special training/police involvement.

_____ is present in the client's bloodline/consanguinity/relations/family tree.

The client has a history of having lived for ___ years in an agonizing/tormenting/abusive/sociopathic/criminal/tumultuous/chaotic/pathogenic family.

The family environment was unstable, unstimulating, and unstructured.

The client's early life situation was victimizing/traumatic/tragic/disastrous.

6.5. SOCIAL HISTORY FOR A DISABILITY EXAMINATION

See also Chapter 17, "Vocational/Academic Skills."

Applicant's description of industrial/workplace stressors, onset of complaints, and (alleged) injuries or illness associated with onset.

Psychological response to (alleged) injury situation:
  History of mental health problems since (alleged) injury.
  History of treatment(s) since (alleged) injury.
  Current treatment and medication, including medication taken on day of examination.

For each of the following areas, distinguish baseline, periinjury, and postinjury events:

Educational level and training: professional, technical, etc.
Sequential description of occupations pursued (including military service):
  Training and skills required.
  Supervisory responsibilities.
  Career advancement: upward, downward, lateral, static.

Difficulties and/or accomplishments in each occupational setting.
Previous occupational injuries, time lost, and outcome.
Previous life changes (external stresses and losses) and responses to these.
Legal history, when applicable:
  Previous worker's compensation and other personal injury claims, with the circumstances and outcome.
  Criminal history if relevant to diagnosis and/or disability.
Substance use and abuse.
Applicant's description of a typical day.

6.6. FAMILY GENOGRAM/FAMILY TREE/PEDIGREE

Constructing a genogram can guide and record the results of history taking. Enter any relevant information in spaces next to symbols; use as many copies of the genogram as necessary. Some typical information might be demographics (name, gender, date of birth, marriages, separations, divorces, deaths/causes of deaths), current health/psychological status, nodal events (moves, separations, financial changes, illnesses), functioning levels, critical events, ethnicity, religion or religious change, education, occupation, legal difficulties, medical risk factors/illnesses/conditions, dates left home, triangulations, and balances. Listing these events in chronological order on another page may help clarify the history.

The figure below shows the conventions for recording a genogram.

Draw a line around members of the current household.

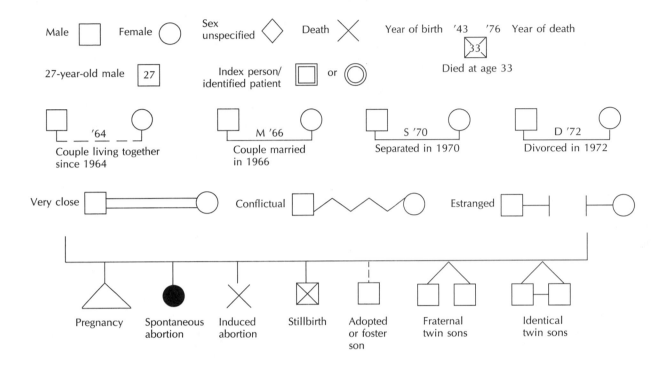

Other family information for evaluations can be found in Chapter 16, "Couple and Family Relationships." The design and use of genograms[3] in family therapy is explored in McGoldrick and Gerson (1985) and Kaslow (1995).

[3]If you do a lot of genograms or want to use them in family therapy, there are programs for IBM and Macintosh computers (including paper forms, checklists, and other quite useful materials) available from Humanware, 2908 Nancy Creek Road, NW, Atlanta, GA 30327.

B. The Person
in the Evaluation

7

Behavioral Observations

This chapter covers the following areas: **appearance**, including clothing; **movement** of all kinds; and **speech behaviors** (but not content).

How the client **responded to the evaluation interview**, and how he/she **presented him-/herself** in the examination, are covered in Chapters 8 and 9, respectively. **Speech behaviors** that reflect abnormal cognition are covered in Section 11.9, "Stream of Thought."

7.1. PHYSICAL APPEARANCE

✓ **Note**: Because physical beauty is so tightly associated in North American culture with goodness and health, and has such an impact on a person's life course, all clinicians should be fully informed about the distortions of judgment caused by socially supported prejudices (e.g., sexism, racism, ageism, beautyism) and cautiously circumspect of wordings supportive of these.

Overall Appearance: Summary Statements

The client seems to be well kept, well nourished, in No Apparent Distress.
Hygiene is managed independently, effectively, and appropriately.
His/her appearance is not unusual.
No unusual physical features; unremarkable, clean, well groomed, well dressed.
No dysmorphic features. No deformities.
The client took good care of her/his appearance in regard to dress, hygiene, and grooming.
Nothing unusual/remarkable/noticeable about his/her posture, bearing, manner, or hygiene.
Her/his hygiene and grooming habits were adequate and normative for a socially conscious individual with an active self-interest and common social concerns.

This client shows some signs of self-neglect, specifically . . .
Client appears about/older/younger than chronological/stated age.
Haggard, weak, pale and wan, frail, sickly, sleepy/tired.   [✓ Note time of day; ask about sleep.]
Disfigured, disabled, "handicapped," "maimed."
Shows the ravages of drug/alcohol/illness/stress/overwork/age/disease, dissipated, ill-looking, wasted-looking, out of shape.

Client shows evidence of current alcohol or drug use/physical dependence.   [✓ Note presence of recent needle marks, needle tracks, thrombosed veins, piloerection/"goose bumps," sweating, lacrimation/tearing, diarrhea, rhinorrhea/"postnasal drip," pupils dilated/constricted.]

For a Child:

Appears to be well cared for/well trained in self-care/assisted/supervised, ignored/neglected.

For a Vocational Evaluation:

The client has a suitable appearance for work involving contact with the public.
He/she would not be identified as unusual in a group situation on the basis of physical appearance alone.

Build (↔ by degree)

emaciated	*thin*	*average*	stocky	formidable
sickly	lean	well developed/built	chubby	hulking
malnourished	wiry	weight proportionate	heavy-set	enormous
undernourished	slender	to height	husky	
underweight	lanky	well nourished	heavy	multiple chins
cachectic	skinny	within usual range	pudgy	jowly
frail	bony	"healthy"	barrel-	"beer belly"
gaunt			chested	pot-bellied
		large-boned	chunky	flabby
	petite	rangy	portly	fat [✓See note
	small-boned	large-framed	fleshy	on obesity
	diminutive	robust	burly	below]
		full-framed	beefy	rotund
		rugged		overweight

Height

✓ It is preferable to state height objectively (i.e., to give measurement) rather than to use relative terms ("short/average/tall"), unless you also include your own height.

Weight

Ask: "What do you now weigh?" and "Is this your usual weight?"

✓ **Note:** "Obesity" and "hardly/mildly/moderately/extremely/massively/morbidly obese" are all misleadingly subjective and subject to changing tastes and styles. It is far preferable to report measured height, weight, and general "build." Remember, obesity is *not* a psychiatric diagnosis.

Common labels for obesity: Mild = 20–40% over, moderate = 41–100% over, and severe = more than 100% over the published height-to-weight tables.
Body types: Android/abdominal/"apples," truncal obesity, or gynoid/femoral/"pears."

BEHAVIORAL OBSERVATIONS

For a Child:

Stature in relation to age is short/normal/tall.
Child is at the ___ percentile of the standard tables for height and weight for children.
Child is at Tanner stage _____ (of sexual development; Tanner, 1962).

Complexion

Ruddy, tanned, sunburned, wan, sallow, jaundiced, sickly, pale, pallid/pallorous, leathery, pimply, warty, scarred, shows negligence, birthmarks/port-wine marks, scars.

Face

General: Pinched, puffy/swollen, washed out, emaciated, old/young-looking for chronological/true age, baby-faced, long-faced, moon-faced.
Movement: Tics, twitches, drooping, mobility during interview/over topics.
Head: Odd-shaped, microcephalic/macrocephalic, dolichocephalic/mesocephalic/brachycephalic, normal, cretinous, damaged.
Teeth: Unremarkable hygiene, dentures, gaps and missing teeth, carious, edentulous, unusual dentistry, bad breath/breath odor/"halitosis."
Chewed gum/toothpick/other items.
Notable features: Ears, nose, cheeks, mouth, lips, teeth, chin, neck. (Examples: Dark circles under eyes, bulbous/red/richly veined nose, large/small features, toothy grin.)

Facial Expressions   *See also Chapter 10, "Emotional/Affective Symptoms and Disorders."*

Attentive, alert, quizzical.
Tense, worried, indrawn, frightened, alarmed.
Sad, frowns, downcast, in pain, grimaces, forlorn, drawn.
Tearful, watered/tears up, tears falling, open crying/sobbing.
Apathetic, preoccupied, inattentive, unspontaneous, withdrawn, vacuous, vacant, absent, detached, mask-like, did not smile/change expression during the long interview, lacks spontaneous/appropriate/expected facial expression, flat, expressionless, lifeless, frozen, rigid.
Calm, composed, relaxed, dreamy, head bobbed as if nodding off.
Smiling, cheerful, happy, delighted, silly/sheepish grin, beaming.
Angry, disgusted, distrust, contempt, defiance, sneering, scowling, grim, dour, tight-lipped, hatch marks between his/her eyes, a chronic sour look.

Eyes   *See also "Eye Contact/Gaze" under Section 7.3, "Movement/Activity."*

Size, shape, etc.: Large, small, close-set, wide-set, almond-shaped,[1] sunken, bloodshot, red, pink, bleary-eyed, bulging, hooded, wide-eyed, cross-eyed, "wall-eyed," disconjugate gaze.
Expression: Staring, unblinking, glassy-eyed, vacant, penetrating, vigilant, nervous/frequent blinking, darting, squinting, tired, "eyes twinkled," limpid, unusual.
Brows: Beetling brows, heavy, massive, raised, pulled together, pulled down, shaven, plucked.
Glasses: Regular corrective lenses, half-lenses, bifocals, reading glasses, contact lenses, sunglasses, needed but not worn, broken/poorly repaired.

Hair

Hairstyle: Fashionable length and style, long, ponytail, "pigtails," plaits, cornrows, braided, crew/brush cut, natural/"Afro," frizzy, curly, finger curls, dreadlocks, wavy, straight, uncombed, tou-

[1]This is preferable to "slanted." My thanks to Fay Murakawa, PhD, of Los Angeles, CA, for this clarification and correction.

sled, "punk," "Mohawk," pageboy, currently popular haircut, stylish, unusual hair cut/style/ treatment, moused, permed, "relaxed," unbarbered, simple/easy-to-care-for cut, unremarkable.

Color: Bleached, colored/dyed, frosted, streaks of color, different-colored roots, flecked with gray, salt-and-pepper, gray, white, faded color, albino, platinum/blonde/fair-haired, red-haired, auburn, chestnut, brunette, brown, black.

Hair-loss: Thinning, receding hairline, high forehead, widow's peak, male-pattern baldness, balding, bald spot, bald, head shaven, alopecia.

Artificial hair: Wig, toupee, hairpiece, "a rug," implants, transplants, an obvious hairpiece.

Other: Clean, dirty, unkempt, greasy/oily, matted.

Beard: Clean-shaven, unshaven/needs a shave, had the beginnings of a beard/wispy/scraggly, stubble, cultivated/deliberate stubble, poorly/well maintained/groomed, stylish, neatly trimmed, full, closely trimmed, mutton chops, goatee, chin beard, unbarbered, Van Dyke/ZZ Tops/Santa Claus style, wore his facial hair in a _____.

Moustache: Wore/sported a moustache/moustached/moustachioed, handlebars, pencil-thin, neat, drooping, scraggly, just starting/light.

Other Aspects of Appearance

Grooming/hygiene/cleanliness: Excellent/good/unremarkable/fair/marginal/poor/awful, scruffy, bedraggled, neglected, indicating indifference, acceptable but not optimal, unremarkable/as expected/neat, tidy, meticulous.

Grooming reflective of: impoverishment/very limited resources/cultural background, physical limitations, cognitive limitations, pride in appearance.

Odor (body or clothing): Musty, noticeable, offensive, excess perfume, smells of alcohol, ineffective deodorant.

Nails: Clean, tobacco-stained, dirty, grimy, bitten down to the quick, overlong, broken, painted/ colored, polished, manicured, artificial/extensions.

Skin: Bruises, cuts, abrasions, scabs, sores, damage, tattoos, acne, acne vulgaris scars, birthmarks/ port-wine stains, mottled.

Breathing: Noisy, wheezed, Shortness Of Breath, used a mechanical assisting device.

Notable aspects: Shoulders, chest, breasts, back, pelvis, legs, feet, hands, fingers.

Other: Jewelry (rings, earrings, bracelets, pins, piercings, etc.), makeup, hearing aid, prosthesis, colostomy bag, catheter, other device.

Bearing   *See also Section 7.3, "Movement/Activity."*

Suggests chronic illness, appeared weak/frail, low stamina/endurance/easily winded, listless, labored, burdened.

7.2. CLOTHING/ATTIRE

✓ The relevant perspectives are not fashion, cost, or newness, but what clothing means about the client's ability to care for herself/himself and her/his judgment of appropriateness.

Appropriateness

Appropriate for situation/occasion/weather, nothing unusual for a visit to a professional appointment/office.

Presentable, acceptable, suitable, appearance and dress appropriate for age and occupation, businesslike, professional appearance, nothing was attention-drawing, modestly attired.

Client's idea of suitable, not suitable for age/suitable for a younger person, not suitable for his/her station in life, too casual to be acceptable, care of person and clothing was only fair.

Other: Institutional, odd, unusual, eccentric, peculiar, unique combinations, carefully disordered, dressed to offend, un/conventional, attention-seeking/drawing, outlandish, garish, bizarre.

Qualities of Clothing (↔ *by degree*)

filthy	seedy	needing	plain	*neat*	*stylish*
grimy	disheveled	repair	out of date	careful	fashionable
dirty	neglected	threadbare	old-fash-	dresser	elegant
smelly	wrong size	rumpled	ioned	clothes-	dandified
dusty	ill-fitting	clean but	old	conscious	natty
musty	unkempt	worn		in good taste	dapper
		worn	regional/		
food-spotted	messy	shabby	foreign	overdressed	meticulous
greasy	slovenly	tattered	designs	seductive	immaculate
oily	sloppy	torn	eccentric	revealing	
	baggy		"grunge"	flashy	
	bedraggled	shows		too tight-	
	raggedy	unilateral		fitting	
		neglect		tasteless	
		unzipped		design	
		unbuttoned			

Other

Dressed in a manner typical of today's youth/of the 1940s/1950s/1960s, attired in the style of her/his contemporaries.
Overly prim, somber.

7.3. MOVEMENT/ACTIVITY

Speed/Activity Level

(↔ *by degree*) Frozen, almost motionless, little animation, psychomotor retardation, slowed, slowed reaction time/latency to questions, <normal>, normokinetic, restless, squirming, fidgety, fretful, constant hand movements, continual flexing of _____, hyperactive, agitated, frenetic.

For a Child:

High activity level, motorically active, fidgets, difficult to redirect/redirectable, difficulty remaining in his/her chair/seat, many out-of-seats, restless and distractible, investigated all the contents of the room/desk/testing materials/intrusive, overactive/hyperactive/aggressive, a darter, tantrums/tantrumming. (*See Section 12.3, "Attention-Deficit/Hyperactivity Disorder."*)

Coordinated–Uncoordinated

(↔ *by degree*) Awkward, clumsy, "klutzy," often injures self, "accident-prone," inaccurate/ineffective movements, jerky, uncoordinated, <normal>, purposeful, smooth, dextrous, graceful, agile, nimble.

✓ Note degree of body awareness, body ego, body confidence.

Noticeably poor manual dexterity, held objects such as pencils awkwardly, difficulty coordinating hands and fingers when asked to copy designs, hands shaky on tasks, problems in drawing lines (specify).

For a Child:

Coordination delayed by ___ months/years, good/poor gross and fine motor coordination.

✓ Note handedness/preference/dominance, presence of astereognosis.

Dominance: Right/left/mixed, as seen in hopping on a foot, preferred use of one eye, using only one hand to flip a coin/catch a thrown object.

Praxis

Grip: Held pencil in the usual grip/atypical/awkward/in a fist-like grip, in a palmar grasp, perpendicular to the table, down by the graphite, with fingers too close to the point/thumb overlapping the forefinger/forefinger overlapping the thumb, with two fingers and the thumb, with three fingers and thumb, between the forefinger/index/pointer and third/middle finger, tensely.

Handwriting (↔ *by degree*): Elegant, precise, stylized, legible, sloppy, primitive, prints, scrawls, illegible, no recognizable letters.

Handshake (↔ *by degree*): Avoided, "fishy," moist/sweaty/nervous, limp, tentative, weak, delayed, normal, firm, exaggerated, painfully hard.

✓ Ask client to walk, write a sentence, and/or tie shoes/tie, and observe skill/difficulties.

Mannerisms/Oddities

This subsection covers peculiarities of motor behavior, automatisms, unusual uses of hands/body. *(See also "Symptomatic Movements," below.)*

Stereotyped movements: Twirling, rocking, self-stimulation, hand flapping, aimless/repetitious/unproductive/counterproductive movements, head bobbing, wriggling, hand or finger movements, bounces leg, posturing, picks/pulls at clothing, rocking.

Perseverations: Pauses and repeats movements at choice points, as when leaving the room/in doorway.

Manneristic mouth movements: Tongue chewing, lip smacking, whistling, made odd/animal/grunting sounds, belching, pulls lips into mouth.

Squints, made faces/grimaced.

Childlike facial expressions/speech (e.g., "Gol-lee").

Sniffles repeatedly/loudly, uses/needs but does not use tissues/handkerchief, freely and frequently picks his/her nose, repetitively "cleans" ears with fingers.

Yawned excessively/regularly/elaborately, rubbed eyes.

Made audible breathing sounds.

Smoked incessantly/carelessly/dangerously/compulsively/selfishly.

Deliberately dropped items so she/he could retrieve them.

There were no mannerisms, tics, or gesticulations (movements) indicative of any psychopathology or physical distress.

For a Child:

Kept thumb in mouth for ___ minutes of the ___ hour session, sucked fingers.
Covered face with hands and peeked out.

Symptomatic Movements

Waxy flexibility (*cerea flexibilitas*), tardive dyskinesia, dysdiadochokinesia, Parkinsonian/Extra-Pyramidal Symptoms/movements, athetoid, athetotic, akathesias, choreiform, akinesia, "pill rolling," "chewing," "restless leg syndrome," opened and closed legs repeatedly, paced, restlessness, hyper/hypotonic, hyper/hypokinetic, echopraxia, cataplexy, denudative behavior. *(See also Section 12.34, "Side Effects of Medications.")*

BEHAVIORAL OBSERVATIONS

Tremor: None/mild/at rest/of intent/familial, quivers, shivers, twitches, tics, shakes. Autonomic hyperactivity. *(See Section 10.3, "Anxiety/Fear.")*

Mobility

(↔ by degree) Confined to bed/bedfast, uses wheelchair/adaptive equipment, requires support/assistance/supervision, uses a gait aid (cane, leg/back brace, walker, crutches/Canadian crutch), walks, slow, careful, avoids obstacles, runs, athletic.

Stood up frequently, roamed the room, walking on tiptoe/heels, stretching/walking around periodically, attempted to leave.

Gait, Carriage, and Station

(↔ by degree) Astasia, abasia, awry, shuffles, desultory, effortful, dilatory, stiff, limps, drags/favors one leg, awkward, walks with slight posturing, lumbering, leans, lurching, ataxic, collides with objects/persons, broad-based, knock-kneed, bow-legged, <normal>, ambled, no visible problem/no abnormality of gait or station, fully mobile (including stairs), springy, graceful, glides, brisk/energetic, limber.

Mincing, exaggerated, strides, dramatic/thespian/for effect, unusual.

For a Child:

Difficulty climbing stairs, brushed ankles against each other, unsteady forward gait, stumbled at intervals. [✓ **Note:** Observe the wear patterns on shoes.]

Balance *(↔ by degree)*

Dizzy, vertigo, staggers, sways, fearful of falling/unsure, unsteady, positive Romberg sign, complains of light-headedness, normal, no danger of falling, steady.

Posture

"Hunkered down," hunched over, slumped, slouched, stooped, round-shouldered, limp, hangs head, cataplexy, relaxed, <normal>, stiff, tense, guarded, rigid, erect, "military," upright, sat on edge of chair, leans, peculiar posturing/atypical/inappropriate (sat sideways in the chair, reversed chair to sit down).

Eye Contact/Gaze *(↔ by degree)*

None, avoided, stared into space, kept eyes downcast, broken off as soon as made/passing/intermittent, wary, alert, looked only to one side, brief, flashes, fleeting, furtive, evasive, appropriate, normal, expected, modulated, lingering, staring, steady, glared, penetrating, piercing, confrontative, challenging, stared without bodily movements or other expressions.

Other *If any movement or posture indicates pain, see Section 12.24, "Pain Disorder/Chronic Pain Syndrome."*

7.4. SPEECH BEHAVIOR

Give quotes/verbatim examples. *(See also Section 11.9, "Stream of Thought.")*

Articulation

Unintelligible, stammer/stutter, stumbles over words, mumbles, whispers to self, mutters under breath, lisp, sibilance, slurred, "juicy," garbled, understandable, clear, precise, clipped, choppy and mechanical, poor diction, poor enunciation, misarticulated, unclear, dysfluencies, dysarthrias (spastic, flaccid, ataxic), aphasias.

Pace/cadence/rate: Too slow/fast, _____ rhythm.

Accent: Noticeable, mild, strong, foreign, regional, odd, intense, confusing, drawl, burr.

For a Child:

Immature, simpler sentences/formation than expected, expected/age-appropriate/inappropriate articulation errors, difficulty in speech articulation (especially sounds such as r, sh, th, z, or ch), slid over some consonant sounds.

Voice's Qualities

Loud/noisy/almost screaming, strident, brassy, harsh, gravelly/hoarse/raspy, throaty, nasal, screechy, squeaky, shrill, staccato, mellifluous, quiet, soft, weak, frail, thin, "small" voice, barely audible, whispered/aphonic, affected, tremulous/quavery, low/high pitched, sing-song, whiny, odd inflection/intonation, monotonous pitch/tone, sad/low tone of voice, muffled, bass/baritone/alto/soprano.

Phraseology: Summary Statements

Client spoke in almost "babytalk"/infantile/childish/immature style.

He mispronounced words, used uneducated vocabulary/uncultured language/vocabulary reflective of limited education/cultural deprivation, used slang words, made grammatical mistakes, used nonstandard/substandard English.

She used dialect, regionalisms, colloquialisms, provincialisms, foreign words/idioms.

Speech was notable for cliches, habitual expressions, repetition of catch phrases, much use of "You know"/"like."

Client's vocabulary was pedantic, pseudointellectual, stilted, excessively formal, jargon.

Inappropriately familiar terms were used (e.g., "dear," "honey").

Client engaged in punning, rhyming, contrived language.

Speech included casual and familiar swear words, epithets, hostile cursing, racial/ethnic/religious slurs.

Anomia, agrammatism, syntactical errors were present.

Misspoke; confused words (e.g., "wall" for "while"), requiring repetition and inquiry for clarification.

For a Child:

Child has underdeveloped vocabulary for his/her age.

Conversation consisted of three- or four-word phrases rather than sentences.

Speech Amount/Productivity/Energy/Flow/Rate/Rhythm (↔ by degree)

halting	slowed	normal	pressured	verbose
hesitant	minimal	initiates	loquacious	overproductive
delays/ed	response	alert	garrulous	long-winded
inhibited	unspontaneous	productive	excessively	bombastic
blocked	reticent	animated	wordy	nonstop
lags	terse	talkative	exaggerated	vociferous
slowed	sluggish	fluent	hurried	overabundant
reaction time	paucity	well spoken	voluble	copious
	sparse	easy	talkative	overresponsive
mute	impoverished	spontaneous	expansive	excessive detail

selective mutism | laconic | smooth | blurts out | voluminous
only nods | economical | crisp | run-together | hyperverbal
unresponsive | taciturn | even | raucous |
word-finding difficulties | single-word answers | | | *flight of ideas*
word searching | | | rapid |
difficulty generating | | | fast |
| | | rushed |

Speech Manner (↔ *by degree*)

distant	*normal*	candid	empathic
hurried	responsive	open	touching
pedantic		frank	insightful
somber	well modulated	guileless	wise
inarticulate	articulate	free	charming
whiny	gets ideas across well	untroubled	witty
	good-natured	easy	jovial
expressionless	engaging	warm	
mechanical	well spoken	sincere	
	eloquent	self-disclosing	
dramatic	realistic	in touch with	
	measured	own feelings	
naive	thoughtful		

Summary Statements for Communication/Speech Behaviors

I noted no impairments in language functioning reflecting disordered mentation.

The client could comprehend and carry out the test/evaluation instructions and tasks, and didn't misinterpret or misunderstand the test materials or questions.

He displayed no language impairment, either receptively or expressively.

Communication was not impeded in any way; satisfactory/adequate/normal expressiveness.

Auditory comprehension was adequate, and oral delivery was effective.

The client's speech was without articulatory deficit.

The client's comprehension of English/spoken words was normal/defective/abnormal.

His ability to understand the spoken word was adequate within the context of this examination, but might not be in other situations, such as . . . (specify).

Client did not have to have the questions/instructions rephrased/simplified/repeated.

She is a reciprocal conversationalist/dialogued spontaneously/is able to carry on a conversation.

He is able to initiate topics appropriately.

She follows the conventions/social rules of communication (including appropriate phrasing and turn taking), and understood the suppositions and expectations of native speakers of American English.

Client participated/did not participate in appropriate social dialogue.

He engaged in little/normal/expected/excessive small talk.

She did not initiate conversation or develop spontaneous themes.

Summary Statements for Conversational Style   *See also Section 8.7, "Other Statements."*

The client's speech was sophisticated, with considerable emphasis on intellectual/personal/medical/historical/family matters.

Client used a paragraph where a word would do.
He was an excessively verbal person who needed more braking than prompting.

Client assumed that I, the listener, knew more than I did about her history/ideas/the subject of the conversation.

Speech was slow, deliberate, and at times evasive.
All of the client's speech was defensive/designed to emphasize his degree of disability.
Her answers were not to be relied upon, but were pertinent and to the point. *(See also Sections 4.6, "Reliability Statements," and 8.2, "Rapport/Relationship to Examiner.")*

Client uses vulgarity/blasphemy/scatology/sexuality to shock.
Speech reflects preoccupations. *(See Section 11.9, "Stream of Thought.")*
Client engaged in rote retelling of an often-told story.
Uses psychiatric language sophisticated enough to suggest a person who is system-wise.
Speech was excessively colloquial for our relationship.
His language choices were, in reality, more odd than I am able to reproduce here.

She was reluctant to expand on/denies her complaints/problems/symptoms.
Client offered little information but responded readily to direct questions. He was very verbal but not articulate.
Where one word would suffice/answer the question asked, she produced a paragraph.
Client attempted to be helpful by trying to tell a great deal, and so created pressured speech.

For a Child:

The child was perseverative/echolalic/mimicked examiner's speech.
Delayed language acquisition is evident.
Child had difficulty in comprehending or expressing oral language.

7.5. QUALITIES OF COMMUNICATION

Good Communication

Asked permission/made "appointment" for best opportunity to communicate.
Showed understanding, offered feedback/reflections/rephrasings, showed patience/didn't fore-close/close off prematurely, tolerated others' emotions, nonaccusatory style.
Used "I" messages, "owned" feelings, took risks, was honest, no facade, was present, could ventilate.

Problematic Communication

As Speaker

Overly critical, overly logical, accusatory, changed topics, sarcastic.
Automatic/play-acting/irrelevant emotionality, overblown emotions, overly dramatic.
Withdrawing, "tuning out," "stonewalling," subterfuge/evasion.
Jumping to conclusions/"mind reading," second-guessing speaker.
Righteousness, condescending, nagging, reminding, overfocus on the past, threatening.
Excessive repetitions, overwhelmed listener with quantity of words, hogging the floor/refusing to relinquish the floor, used time to criticize/lobby the professional.

As Listener

Insincere "agreement," missed the point too often/"thick-headed," silent/didn't know what to say, had to be reminded of the rules too often, failed to recall what was said, assumed the speaker role by arguing/criticizing/reacting/questioning, etc.

7.6. OTHER BEHAVIORAL OBSERVATIONS/DEMEANOR

Brought items to the examination: Possessions, cigarettes, presents, papers, briefcase, coffee/refreshments/candy/food.

Anxious behaviors: Fidgety, nervous and inappropriate laughter/smiling, titters, giggles, nervous habits. *(See also Section 10.3, "Anxiety/Fear.")*

Depressed behaviors: Audible sighs, tearful, tears, crying, sobbing, hand wringing. *(See also Section 10.5, "Depression.")*

For a Child:

Tantrum: Assaultive, destructive to property, aggressive to others, not redirectable.

8

Responses to Aspects
of the Examination

This chapter describes **face-to-face**, one-on-one, **interpersonal behaviors** reflecting the client's **responses to aspects of the examination**, including responses to the procedures of evaluation, rapport with the examiner, response to the methods of evaluation, concentration, motivation, response to failure, and approach to the tasks of the examination. The next chapter covers **self-presentation** of the client to the evaluator. Other chapters of relevance are Chapters 15, "Social/Community Functioning," and 16, "Couple and Family Relationships."

8.1. RESPONSE TO THE EVALUATION'S CONTEXT

See also Sections 8.2 and 8.4, below.

The following five paragraphs are sequenced by increasing degree of responsiveness.

Unable to recognize the purposes of the interview/the report to be made, unaware of the social conventions, did not understand or adapt to the testing situation, did not understand give and take of question-and-answer format, did not grasp nature of questions, gave inappropriate responses, not relevant, nor logical, not goal-directed, was not able to comprehend or respond to questions designed to elicit _____ symptoms of _____, low attending skills, just able to meet the minimum requirements for appropriate social interaction, misconstrued what was said to him/her, unaware, withdrawn, unresponsive, echolalic, preoccupied, estranged, didn't grasp essence or goal, autistic.

Indifferent, bland, detached, distant, uninvolved, uncaring, lackadaisical, no effort, did not try, no interest in doing anything but playing out her/his time, haphazard, insensitive, bored, showed the presence of an interfering emotion, overcautious, related obliquely.

Dependent, sought/required much support/reassurance/guidance/encouragement from the examiner, desperate for assistance, self-doubting, ill at ease.

Tense, anxiety appropriate/proportionate to the interview situation, initially responded only to questions but later became more spontaneous, began interview with an elevated level of anxiety that decreased as the evaluation progressed, needed assistance to get started.

Understood the social graces/norms/expectations/conventions/demand characteristics of the examination situation, comfortable, confident, relaxed, interested, curious, eager, intense, carefully monitored the testing situation, oriented, aware, alert, cooperative, no abnormalities, attended, responded, reciprocated, continued, participated, initiated, communicated effectively, clear and efficient, high quality of interaction, with depth.

For a Child: Summary Statements

✓ Note that "parent" in these statements should be taken to mean biological/custodial parent/grandparent, foster parent, or any other caregiver/major attachment figure.

Parental Interaction with Examiner

Parent's manner of relating to examiner was arrogant/threatening, suspicious, impatient, cooperative/trusting, controlling/manipulative, seductive, dependent, other (specify).
Parent took _____ role and assigned _____ role to examiner during interview (specify).
Parent's attitude did/did not change during interview (if it did, specify).

Behavior When with Parent

Child played easily/unwillingly/not at all in the waiting room, did/did not put away the toys used.
Child exhibited _____ level of play, with playthings appropriate for ___ age.
Parent used control in the following ways . . . (specify degree, kind/methods/means, timing), over issues of . . . (specify).
Parent's relationship to child was supportive/unsupportive, negotiated/unilaterally controlling.
Parents showed agreement/disagreement/conflict over discipline, rewards, language, attention given, etc.

Separation from Parent

Upon separation, child showed excessive/expected/limited/no anxiety, expressed as . . . (specify).[1]
Child used appropriate/a few/no coping mechanisms upon separation (if any, specify).
Child was reluctant/willing to separate from parent and accompany examiner into the interview room/testing room/office.
Child separated easily/poorly/reluctantly from the examiner.
Child's reaction upon rejoining parent was . . . (specify).

Child/parent described symptoms of separation anxiety: worry over possible harm to parent/parent deserting child/disaster keeping child away from parent, school refusal in order to stay with parent, refusal to sleep without parent, "clinging" or "shadowing" behaviors, nightmares

---

[1]John Bowlby (1969) described three stages of separation: (1) Initial protest with crying, screaming, and general activity; (2) despair with dejection, stupor, withdrawal, and decreased activity; and (3) detachment with indifference and hostility.

about separation, physical complaints when separated, tantrums/pleading not to separate, excessive homesickness, not easily redirected/distracted from parent, need for much reassurance, discomfort with other adults, inability to master own anxiety.

Playing Observed

Child played eagerly/willingly/unenthusiastically/not at all with same-age/younger/older peers.
Child showed eager/expected/limited/no approach to and interest in toys/materials.
Toys/materials actually used were . . . (specify).
Mode of play was incorporative/extrusive/intrusive/other (specify).
Manner of play was constructive/disorganized/mutual/parallel/distractible/disruptive/other (specify).
Child was tractable/intractable to discipline, such as . . . (specify).

Child's Attitudes and Feelings

Child did/did not grasp purpose of clinic visit(s).
Child did/did not seem aware of own difficulties.
He showed excessive/expected/limited/no reaction to own symptoms.
She showed positive/negative/no feelings about returning to clinic.

Child showed positive/negative/no feelings/attitudes about/toward . . . (specify aspects of self, as appropriate: behavior, appearance, body, gender/sex, intellect, worries/fears, preoccupations).

Child showed positive/negative/no feelings/attitudes about/toward parents/siblings/school/peers/authorities/others (specify).

Feelings Aroused in Examiner by Child

Child caused examiner to feel sympathetic/protective, concerned, pitying, admiring, curious, etc. (specify).
Child aroused feelings of irritation, anger, dislike, etc. (specify) in examiner.

For an Adolescent:

✓ Note any limited spontaneity that is excessive but not inappropriate/abnormal for the adolescent's age and evaluation/evaluator.

8.2. RAPPORT/RELATIONSHIP TO EXAMINER

Cooperation/Positive Behaviors (↔ *by degree*)

pleasant	*cooperative*	*dependent*	*indifferent*	seductive
affable	helpful	institutionalized	noncommittal	
friendly	easy to	agreeableness	nonchalant	practical joker
familiar	interview	docile	blase	clowned around
			neutral	
chummy	enjoyed	deferential	minimal	exhibitionistic
outgoing	interview	ingratiating	cooperation	
socially graceful	responded with-	trying to please		spooky
amiable	out hesitation	eager to please	submissive	
	responsive	accommodating	passive	curt
	answered readily			monosyllabic

tactful	obliging	effusive	plaintive	legalistic
cordial	agreeable	obsequious	help-seeking	passive–
solicitous	amicable	pleading		aggressive
warm	conciliatory	oversolicitous	careless	"sassy"
		compliant		flippant
genial	civil	obedient		
joked around	polite			
breezy	courteous	oily		
playful	well-mannered	fawning		
easy		flattering		
"upbeat"	appropriate			
	engageable	eulogistic		
inoffensive	available	apple-polishing		
"laid-back"	open	deferential		
low-key		humble		
"mellow"	frank	overpolite		
placid	forthright	overapologetic		
	candid	mealy-mouthed		
	confidential			
		bartered affection		
		wanted to please		

Summary Statements about Cooperation

The client made every effort to be cooperative and maintained a cordial attitude toward the examiner.

She put forth good effort to collaborate in the evaluation.

He was aware of the social norms and was able to conform to them.

Resistance/Negative Behaviors (↔ *by degree*)   *See also Section 10.2, "Anger."*

guarded	surly	defensive	demanding	hostile	argumentative	belligerent
reserved	sulky	subtle	imposing	irritating	territorial	insulting
reticent	petulant	hostility	insistent	instigating	possessive	defiant
recalcitrant	balky	uncoopera-	indignant	obnoxious	antagonistic	obstreper-
resistive	touchy	tive	confronta-	tested limits	contentious	ous
reluctant	pouty	"sick and	tive	rebellious	oppositional	scolding
	peevish	tired"	presump-	had an		
inaccessible	sullen	resentful	tuous	"attitude"	manipula-	name-calling
distant	brooding	noncompli-		bristled	tive	vilifying
remote	crabby	ant	frustrated	when	provocative	slandering
evasive	testy	refused	complaining	questioned	quibbled	menacing
wary	gruff		domineering		questioned	intimidating
withdraws	snappish		rude	*superior*	hypercritical	venomous
withholding			nagging	condescend-	irascible	threatening
avoidant	grouchy			ing	quarrelsome	nasty
not forth-	scowled		*stubborn*	pitying	challenging	malicious
coming	"snippy"		mulish			caustic
tight-lipped			intractable	aloof	*abusive*	loathing
	childish		unbending	disdainful	derisive	
suspicious	immature		unyielding	egocentric	scornful	
cagey			unadaptable	entitled	overbearing	
sneaky			rigid	cocky	arrogant	

overcon-	adamant	contemp-	sarcastic
trolled	obtuse	tuous	carping
businesslike	inflexible	supercilious	berating
stiff	negativistic	toyed with	derogatory
unfriendly	abrasive	examiner	mocking
desultory	opinionated	"knows it	taunting
habit-bound	willful	all"	sneering
only perfunctory/	contrary	smart-	facetious
superficial	pushy	alecky	teasing
cooperation		cantankerous	sarcastic
		"chutzpah"	quips
		"brassy"	
		smug	

For a Child:

"Mouthy," "mouthed off," "sassed," talks back, mimicked examiner's speech, noncompliant, threw things, hit.

Other Summary Statements about Rapport   *See also Chapter 9, "Presentation of Self."*

Rapport was easily/intermittently/never established and maintained.
Response to authority was cooperative/respectful/appropriate/productive/indifferent/hostile/challenging/undermining/unproductive/noncompliant/contemptuous.
The client required/allowed another to answer none/some/all of the questions posed.
She seemed to enjoy the attention received.

I could easily understand his/her meanings.
I found it hard to like/feel for this person.

Client was cooperative within limits; she refused some test items/tests/topics.
He was fully cooperative with the examination only after determining my credentials.

Client would not accept direction from people in authority.
She repeatedly/irrelevantly/provocatively interrupted the interviewer.
He talked over me/interrupted, made efforts to control the interview.

Client showed inappropriate forwardness toward male/female staff.

The testing/questions/history taking/examination was particularly trying for this client.

Eye Contact   *See "Eye Contact/Gaze" under section 7.4, "Movement/Activity."*

8.3. RESPONSE TO THE METHODS OF EVALUATION/TESTS/QUESTIONS

Comprehension of Instructions/Questions

See also Section 8.5, "Motivation/Persistence/Perseverance," ans Section 8.1, "Response to the Evaluation's Context."

The following two groupings are sequenced by increasing degree of comprehension.

Rarely understood instructions, required much repetition/elaboration, needed to have instructions repeated often, became confused, required restructuring of my questions in a manner to make them more concrete and simplistic, required elaboration of the standard instructions before comprehending the nature of the tasks, required excessive time and repetition to understand what was required of him/her.

Attentive, understood, good comprehension, quickly grasped problem/demands/goals/point of situation, anticipated the response expected/desired.

Approach/Attack/Strategy *(↔ by degree)*

random	*indifferent*	*scattered*	*organized*	*rigid*
haphazard		inconsistent	coordinated	compulsive
distracted	flippant	careless	controlled	ritualistic
guessed at	giggled	disorganized	goal-oriented	perseverative
answers		sloppy	active	perfectionistic
	acted without	uncoordinated	diligent	manneristic
distrusted own	instructions		caught on fast	
ability		*baffled*	well ordered	tense
self-doubting	thought aloud	nonplussed	thought through	
second-guessed	absent-minded		before acting	plodding
self	used trial-and-	*perplexed*	notes details	
insecure	error approach	bewildered	orderly	
unsure		confused	methodical	
refused to guess/	*hurried*	uninformed	deliberate	
take chances	fast		persistent	
underestimated	rapid		neat	
own abilities	speedy		contemplative	
	rushed		matter-of-fact	
impulsive			thoughtful	
agitated			efficient	

Summary Statements about Approach/Attack/Strategy

The client waited for full instructions.
He listened attentively to the interviewer's questions.
No problems with test directions or instructions.
Directions/instructions did not have to be repeated or rephrased/simplified.
Only repetition/slowed presentation, not simplification, of test directions was required.
She was able to follow multistep directions.
He responded fully to all tasks' demands.

The client was consistent and organized.
He organized his ideas before responding to test questions.
She stepped back and reviewed behavior when she failed; did not stick with an obviously ineffective approach.

The client worked quickly, with little deliberation.
She took a marginal approach to the evaluation, reflective of . . .
    mildly/moderately/severely reduced intellectual capacity.
    poorly developed cognitive strategies.
    generalized undisciplined mental processing.
    lack of self-evaluation/little concern for the quality of her responses.

He gave impulsive responses with poor organization and planning skills, without forethought, minimal reflection/consideration before answering.

She was not task-oriented.

The client used a random approach on most tasks, showed little comprehension/visualization/analysis of the overall tasks, little learning from attempts, low planning skills.

She was not flexible in problem approaches/lacked problem attack skills/perseverated in manner of problem attack.

Client perseverated, in that he had difficulty adjusting and responding appropriately to the next task's demands/instructions.

There was no change in her approach toward the more difficult items.

He does not have a well-trained or logical mind.

She used avoidance techniques in the examination, such as dropping test materials, starting conversations between tasks/subtests, attending to sounds in the hallway, asking repeated questions regarding the test materials and procedures, wandering off task, etc.

8.4. EFFORT/ATTENTION/CONCENTRATION

See also Sections 8.3, "Response . . . , " 8.5, "Motivation . . . , " 11.4, "Attention," and 11.5, "Concentration/Task Persistence."

apathetic	*sluggish*	*distractible*	*normal energy*	*eager*
dull	worked slowly	low attending	cooperative	animated
uninvolved	in slow motion	skills	interested	fascinated
uninvested	slow reactions	easily distracted	adequate	initiates
passive	slowed	from task	good effort	inquisitive
anergic		lost concentration	spontaneous	enthusiastic
	flat		attentive	
shunned effort	no originality	did not stick	alert	
bored	unchanging	with task		
uninterested	expressionless	had great		
inattentive	uncreative	difficulty		
indifferent	paucity of	following		
	worthwhile	directions		
tired	ideas	nonpersistent		
listless				
exhausted				
resigned				

inconsistent
skimpy responses
sporadic efforts
varied with task

Summary Statements:

The client showed adequate attention span/concentration, with little distractibility, anxiety, or frustration.

The source of distractions were . . . and the client was successfully able to resist distraction by . . . (specify).

8.5. MOTIVATION/PERSISTENCE/PERSEVERANCE

The following groupings are sequenced by increasing degree of involvement in tasks.

Refused test items/subtests/questions, withdrew, showed irritation/anger, complained.

Only brief responses, had to be prompted to elaborate, gave up on easy items, sought to terminate interview, quit quickly, gave up easily, "defeatist," terminated effort following minimal concentration, responded slowly/gave purposefully erroneous responses as a form of resistance, performed halfheartedly, showed minimal compliance.

Variable level of interest/motivation, slowed/varying reaction time to questions, hesitant, sustained effort only for _____ time period, often discouraged, low frustration tolerance, preferred only easy tasks, little tolerance for ambiguity, initially refused to attempt tasks but upon re-presentation later was cooperative, no motivation to succeed with difficult tasks/perform well for the examiner, became frustrated and wanted to give up when the test materials became necessarily too difficult.

Took breaks and recovered willingness to continue, began to lose interest in the evaluation tasks and in conversing with the examiner after _____ time, offered only perfunctory cooperation.

Average perseverance and effort demonstrated, only rarely discouraged or inattentive, completed all tasks fully and competently, work-oriented, applied herself/himself to the tasks presented, was cooperative and put forth best effort on each evaluation task administered, willingly/eagerly attempted each task presented, participated well and fully in the evaluation process, demonstrated serious efforts to respond to tasks' demands, became quite involved in the tasks.

Changed tasks appropriately, eager to continue, challenged by difficult tasks, concentrated on one task for a long time, finished every task, distracted only by extreme circumstances, sustained effort, persisted, diligent, systematic, conscientious, wanted to do well, evaluation seemed to be challenging and interesting to him/her.

8.6. RESPONSE TO SUCCESS/FAILURE/CRITICISM/FEEDBACK

The items in this section describe the client's response to his/her performance and to the evaluator's reaction; they also describe self-awareness/self-monitoring/self-criticism. *See also Section 8.2, "Rapport/Relationship to Examiner."*

The following groupings are sequenced by increasing degree of unresponsiveness.

Oblivious to failure, no response to either success or failure, unaware of/unconcerned about/failed to recognize errors, unaware of the low level at which he/she performed, low self-monitoring/error correction skills, accepted own inferior performance, satisfied with inadequate work, minimal concern and care about doing well on evaluations, indifferent, hypocritical, inappropriately overconfident, examiner's questions/suggestions/hints didn't improve performance.

Flustered, embarrassed, ashamed, chagrined, apologetic, self-reproached, self-derogated, feelings easily hurt, reluctant to expose weaknesses, rationalized failures, extremely critical of own work/hypercritical, disparaged own performance, not satisfied with less than perfection, vulnerable to humiliation, loath to say he/she didn't know so clammed up instead, discouraged/dejected/very angry at failure.

Normal responsiveness and coping with failure, tried his/her best, surprised at failure, accepted mistakes with regret, accepted need to go on despite failure/mistake/incorrect answers, confident, calm, understood easily, adapted, modulated, good balance of self-criticism and self-confidence, self-sufficient, learned from errors/experience, accepted own limitations so failure had little effect.

Self-congratulatory, proud, took pride in accomplishments, delighted with success, persisted, worked harder, self-monitored, sought errors in own work and self-corrected, gave up only on items clearly beyond ability, refused to concede defeat, wasn't discouraged by errors, was easily motivated by "Try again."

Summary Statements:

The client required/did well with/ignored no/usual/copious praise.
Needed frequent/constant reinforcement/encouragement/reassurance/praise/commendation for continued performance.

The client was not so skillful as he thought.
Her perception of her status and abilities was somewhat inflated.
Efforts at compensation through _____ (e.g., a pedantic style) created a negative impression of which he was apparently unaware.

The evaluation setting, which was generally empathic, reinforcing, and accepting of the client's behavior, proved to be . . . (specify).

8.7. OTHER STATEMENTS

This section provides further statements about approach/attack/strategy, task performance, attention, attitude, motivation, persistence, and response to criticism beyond those above. *Perhaps see also Section 4.6, "Reliability Statements."*

Productive

The client related each presented test item to some direct experience in his/her own life.
She asked relevant/insightful/helpful questions.

Counter-/Nonproductive

Client took a great deal of time, showed a longer/shorter than usual reaction time/latency of response to questions.
He worked at an even pace throughout, regardless of the task at hand.

The results showed the long-term effects of defective innate ability, low expectations, an unstimulating environment, and poor/minimal formal training.
Her performance was depressed by poor application of skills she already possesses/by fatigue.
Client completed tasks in a mechanical fashion with little comprehension of what he was doing/the goal.
Client stressed details but missed main point/"couldn't see the forest for the trees"/didn't "catch on"/"missed the boat."

Defective performance was present only on items/in areas that . . . and not on items/areas of . . . (specify).

Client had difficulty answering questions, but cooperated to the best of her ability.
He tried to provide meaningful answers to specific questions, but no additional information was forthcoming.
She was frank with her answers, but could not give detailed information.

The client tried to have the examiner confirm one of a number of offered responses as the correct one.

She answered almost all questions with "I don't know."

He invariably responded with "I don't know" to questions, but on repetition of a question, produced a good/correct/scoreable response.

Client was initially hostile, but did become gradually less hostile/more forthcoming/sociable/friendly as the interview progressed.

Her anger/sense of outrage seemed to bubble along just below the surface throughout most of the interview.

Client was cautious, circumspect, and politic about the type and nature of the information offered.

For a Child:

When asked questions in mother's/caregiver's presence, child often/always/rarely glanced at/turned to her, hoping she would answer the question/seeking confirmation of answer/deferring to her superior knowledge.

Child was uncontrollable/destructive/untestable, acted out/had temper tantrums/was disruptive of testing, was unruly/distractible/difficult to evaluate/difficult to handle/stubborn.

Child counted on fingers/covered face with hands/hummed to self/looked about the room but was redirectable.

Child seemed to enjoy the opportunity to talk openly with the professional.

Child clapped/squealed with satisfaction/excitement/delight.

9

Presentation of Self

This chapter covers the **client's self-presentation to the evaluator**, as seen by the evaluator. These behaviors can also be seen as **interpersonal skill and impression management**.

9.1. PRESENCE/STYLE (↔ by degree)

See also Section 8.2, "Rapport/Relationship to Examiner."

withdrawn	*threatened*	*shy*	*friendly*	autonomous
isolating	distrustful	timid	inviting	direct
estranged	fearful	bashful	jocular	self-assured
distant	anxious	demure	warm	dominant
suspicious	distraught	passive	outgoing	surgent
guarded		reserved	jolly	businesslike
asocial	*vulnerable*	retiring	extraverted	assertive
introverted	weak	humble	chipper	
solitary	delicate	subdued	animated	stubborn
seclusive	would crumble	reticent	engaging	insistent
detached	fragile	introverted	charming	
aloof	low resilience	restrained		eccentric
dejected	threat-sensitive	composed		bizarre
		placid		dramatic
	awkward	mild-mannered		
	self-conscious	unassuming		
	tenuous	plaintive		
	frightened			

9.2. SELF-IMAGE/SELF-ESTEEM

The concepts of self-image/self-esteem include both components/functions relating to the interior self and ones relating to the social self. Aspects of the interior self include the following:

Self-concept, identity, ego boundaries.
Self-perception, self-consciousness, self-assessment, self-evaluation, self-monitoring, self-disclosure.
Self-determination, self-management, self-control, self-direction, self-efficacy, self-reinforcement.
Self-differentiation, self-discovery, self-knowledge, self-realization, self-actualization.

And aspects of the social self include the following:

Age and gender roles, gender identity, sexual identity.
Body image, appearance, body ego/boundaries, personal space, personal property.
Other aspects of the self in relation to others (self as child, parent, spouse/partner, friend, worker, etc.).

Be alert for the client's manifestations of these various aspects. In particular, watch for evidence of self-defeating/self-destructive behaviors, such as masochism, suicidal ideation/attempts, self-mutilation, and high-risk activities (specific coverage of these is provided in many other sections of this book). The following are descriptors that apply to a few particular components of self-image/self-esteem.

Confidence Levels

Expressed an exaggerated opinion of himself/herself, believes he/she is exceptionally capable despite evidence to the contrary, grandiose, self-exalting, boastful, vain, has "chutzpah," cocky, pompous, conceited.
(↔ *by degree*) Confident, accepting, congruent, self-respecting, modest, unassuming, humble, self-doubting, unrealistic, inadequate, pessimistic, self-deprecatory, self-accusing, self-abasing, described self as "a loser"/failure/misfit/unworthy/untalented.

Goals for Self

Hopeful, optimistic, eager, anticipates improvement, proactive, high aspirations, future orientation.
Has plans, plans are clear/comprehensive/realistic, has alternative approaches.
Plans are vague/unrealistic/poorly thought out, below reasonable expectations, pessimistic.
(↔ *by degree*) Presents self as a victim of her/his life, has no apparent interest in improving/motivation to improve her/his lot in life, is at least aware that improvements could be made, is willing to try to work on problems, is strongly motivated for change.

Pride (↔ *by degree*)

Dignity, good self-respect/esteem/regard/image, confidence, self-righteousness, vanity, ego, airs, arrogance, conceit, condescension, narcissism, paints the consequences of his/her actions in a very rosy color.

9.3. DEPENDENCY–SURGENCY

See also Section 9.2 above, as well as Sections 13.10, "Dependent Personality," and 13.16, "Narcissistic Personality."

(↔ *by degree*) "Spineless," meek, a follower, servile, dependent, clinging, whining/whiny, suppliant, tentative, docile, defers/deferential, inoffensive, passive, yielding, acquiescent, amenable, "wishy-washy," lacking in self-sufficiency, socially immature, compliant, assenting, consenting, cooperative, <normal>, self-confident, spunky, forceful, dominant, masterful, high-handed, autocratic, dictatorial, blustery, pugnacious, overbearing, pushy, self-centered, demanding.

9.4. SOCIAL SOPHISTICATION/MANNERS

Sophistication

The following groupings are arranged by increasing degree of sophistication.

Naive, unsophisticated, gullible, overly trusting, wide-eyed, suggestible, "Pollyanna"-like, "Little Orphan Annie"/"Charlie Brown," unschooled, backward, inept, culturally unsophisticated, medically/psychologically naive, naive attempts at manipulation, guileless, overused "Yes, Ma'am/Sir" and "No, Ma'am/Sir."

Socially inept/unskilled, limited ability to interact, "nerdy," simple, simplistic, immature, giddy, flighty.

Sophisticated, socially skilled, cultured, articulate, able to lobby/defend her/his interests, "street-smart," seductive.

Opportunistic, callous, predatory, "innocent"/blames others, denies, irresponsible, "finesses," manipulative, Machiavellian, sociopathic.

Manners ($\leftrightarrow$ *by degree*)

Polite, well-behaved, mannerly, graceful, poised, tactful, gracious, knows etiquette's rules, careless, thoughtless, blunt, pointed, tactless, offered outspoken criticisms, provocative, abrasive, offensive, vulgar, rude.

9.5. WARMTH–COLDNESS

See Section 8.2, "Rapport/Relationship with Examiner."

The following groupings are arranged by degree of decreasing warmth.

Overindulgent, soft-hearted, doting, overly affectionate, sweet, saccharine, oily, phony.

Responsive, warm-hearted, sympathetic, considerate, compassionate, intimate, gentle, tender, yielding, solicitous, thoughtful, fond, loving, benevolent, charitable, humane, forgiving, merciful, tolerant, devoted.

Friendly, affable, kindly, genteel, outgoing, convivial, companionable.

Reticent, taciturn, subdued, shy, inhibited, restrained, reluctant, aloof, uninterested, tough, remote, distant, cold, detached, indifferent, unresponsive.

Uncharitable, unfeeling, cold, callous, harsh, rough, severe, forbidding.

9.6. OTHER ASPECTS OF SELF-PRESENTATION

Self-Containment/Rigidity   *See Section 13.5, "Authoritarian Personality."*

Self-contained and in good charge of himself/herself, reserved, collected, matter of fact, static, mechanical, stereotyped, compulsive about neatness/order/planning, rigid, expressionless, stoic toward his/her illness/limitations.

Prim and proper, straight-laced, prudish, dour, austere, prissy, "stuffed shirt," self-righteous, puritanical, pious, sanctimonious, overreligious.

Childishness   *See also Section 13.14, "Inadequate Personality."*

Childish, immature, juvenile, silly, excessively attention-seeking, needy, pleading, begging, coaxing, manner suggestive of a much younger person/suggestive of a person much younger emotionally than physically, preoccupied with irrelevancies, feelings are easily hurt, easily upset.

The client seems to be suggestible to the whims and commands of his peers, who victimize him/ expose him to ridicule.
She tempts peers to take her money/books/possessions so that an adult/another will intervene on her behalf.
He is often teased/taunted/bullied.

Dullness/Inattention

Dull, "airhead," vapid, insipid, inattentive, forgetful, wistful, preoccupied, mind elsewhere, "space cadet," "spacey," "zombie-like," "burned out."

Worry/Anxiety

Worrisome, a "worry wart" or excessive worrier, easily threatened, feels inept, manifested anxiety throughout the interview around every topic.

Flamboyance/Histrionics   *See also Section 13.12, "Histrionic Personality."*

Flamboyant, exaggerated, dramatic, melodramatic, theatrical, thespian, histrionic, vivacious, bubbly, volatile, labile, pert, seductive, oversexualized, saucy, coy, titillating, suggestive, flirtatious, excessively girlish/boyish.

Antisocial Features   *See also Section 13.4, "Antisocial Personality."*

Arrogant, bragging, cocky, disdainful, tended to praise self excessively, mildly antisocial manner, cavalier, limited empathy, assumed/maintained an attitude of tolerant amusement.
Swaggering in order to impress interviewer with youthfulness/energy/toughness, "has a chip on his/her shoulder," uses embellishments to appear as a "bad actor" or powerful and dangerous person (e.g., uses vulgarity to shock, presents as a "tough cookie") or as possessing a high potential/many friends/etc., has a rapid-fire/smooth-talking style.

Unusual/Bizarre/Frightening Quality

A "character," individualistic, idiosyncratic, "marches to her/his own drummer," unusual ways of perceiving/behaving, eccentric, "oddball," does not fit in, outlandish, strange, odd, peculiar, bizarre, weird.
Menacing, frightening, imposing, intimidating, manipulating, "spooky," vaguely but intensely frightening, enjoys sadistic humor/is prankish.

Intellectualization

Intellectualizes all experiences, provides psychological jargon/"psychobabble"/labels when asked for descriptions of behaviors/symptoms, "reports" feelings.

Sense of Victimization

A "victim," recites life as a series of mishaps, melodramatically enumerates life's misfortunes, made a saga of his/her life in the telling, offered a woeful tirade/Jeremiad of woes/baleful stories/"Oliver Twist"-like story, presented self as a "born loser"/perpetual victim/outcast.
Presented self as frail and inadequate person of whom one should not expect much.

Guilt/Shame   *See also Section 10.6, "Guilt/Shame."*

Apologetic, described failures/mistakes/harm, apologized indirectly/simply/fully/appropriately/effusively.

Embarrassed, ashamed, self-blaming, self-reproaching, guilty, "worthless," became apprehensive when talking of behavior she/he now realizes was inappropriate.

Off-Task Behaviors

Clock-watched, offered/desired inappropriate bodily contacts, focused on examiner's office/speech/clothing/manner/role/appearance rather than the content of his/her/examiner's speech or the point of the interview.

Other Statements

There are no obvious behavioral stigmata that would set this client apart from other individuals of his age, social, or cultural group.

Her responses reflect wishful thinking rather than realistic plans.

He is dependent on institutional support and content to be hospitalized/taken care of.

Client put up a good front to cover ... (specify).

She made sure to tell me what she thought I should hear and know, and then it seemed that she felt satisfied.

He had his story to tell and went on without any assistance from me.

Client describes _____ (symptoms) that she labels as _____ (behaviors).

For a Child:

Child is pseudomature, uncommonly independent.

Child exhibits primitive, socially inappropriate, nonaggressive behavior.

SPEECH AND VERBAL INTERACTIONS
See Sections 7.4, "Speech Behavior," and 8.2, "Rapport/Relationship to Examiner."

PRESENTATION OF SELF

10

Emotional/Affective Symptoms and Disorders

10.1. GENERAL ASPECTS OF MOOD AND AFFECTS

See Section 3.5, "Affect/Mood," for questions.

"Mood" refers to pervasive and sustained emotional coloring of one's experience, a persistent emotional trend (like the climate). It is usually self-reported (but is sometimes inferred). "Affect" is of shorter duration, such as what the clinician observes during the interview, and is more variable and reactive (like the weather) to the subjects discussed. Note and document any differences between the two during the interview.

Give quotes/self-reports/verbatim descriptions of mood/affect/emotion. In addition, note or report the following:

Behavior reflecting emotional state: See sections on individual emotions below. In general, note tears, flushing, movements (tremor, etc.), respiratory changes and irregularities, voice changes, facial expression and coloring, wording, somatic expression of affects through . . . (specify).

EMOTIONS/ AFFECTS

129

Nature/source: Is the emotion reactive, endogenous, exogenous, characterological, life-long?

Degree: Is the client mildly, moderately, severely, or profoundly depressed (for example)?

Amount/Responsiveness/Range of Affect (↔ by degree)[1]

flat	blunted	constricted	normal	broad
affectless	apathetic	contained	integrated	deep
bland	inexpressive	low-intensity	euthymic	intense
unresponsive	unspontaneous	shallow	responsive	generalized
vacant stare	dispassionate	muted	normal range	pervasive
absent	detached	subdued	supple	
remote	unattached	"low-key"	adequate levels	
passive-appearing	uninvolved	restricted	of emotional	
expressionless	uncomplaining	uninflected	energy	

unvarying
unchanging

no/some/great difficulty in initiating, sustaining, or terminating emotional expression

Duration of Mood or Affect Changes (↔ by degree)

Mercurial/quicksilver, volatile, affective incontinence, dramatic, transient, unstable, fickle, rapid mood fluctuation, labile, fluctuates, plastic, changeable, mood swings, excitable, flexible, diurnal/seasonal mood cycles, short cycles (days), long cycles, shifts in tension, mobility of emotional state, appropriate, consistent, showed little/normal/much variation in emotions, frozen, permanent.

Appropriateness/Congruence of Affect or Mood and Behavior

The following groupings are sequenced by degree of increasing appropriateness/congruence.

Indifferent to problems, floated over his/her real problems and limitations, la belle indifférence.

Affect variable but unpredictable from the topic of conversation, modulations/shifts inconsistent and unrelated to content or affective significance of statements.

A range of emotions/feelings, appropriate emotions for the ideational content and circumstances, emotional reactions relevant to the thought content and situation, emotions seemed appropriate during the interview/examination.

Emotions highly appropriate to/congruent with situation and thought content/subject of discussion, face reflects emotions reported, all thoughts colored by emotional state.

Episodes of Mood Disorder

Is this an initial/single episode? Or are episodes repetitive, recurrent, irregular, cyclothymic, cyclical, seasonal, annual, anniversary reactions?

Is the disorder presently exacerbated, chronic, in remission?

Do recurrent episodes appear to be worsening over time?

Does the client have longer/shorter symptom-free periods?

Do periods of improvement not produce as much improvement as before? And does medication produce slower/less improvement?

Consider drawing a time-by-mood timeline. DSM-IV diagnoses of Bipolar I or II Disorder of Cyclothymic Disorder, or course specifiers of With Rapid Cycling, With/Without Full Interepisode Recovery, or With Seasonal Pattern, may be appropriate.

[1]Consider the possible effects of medications. (See Chapter 28, "Psychiatric Masquerade of Medical Conditions," especially Sections 28.4 and 28.5.)

EMOTIONS/ AFFECTS

10.2. ANGER

See also Section 8.2, "Rapport/Relationship to Examiner," for more behavioral aspects.

General Aspects

Look for the following:

Sources of anger.
Intensity.
Direction, target.
Handling/coping methods, impulse control, anger out/in.
Situational/state or personality/trait nature of anger.
Guilt over anger.

Hostility/Verbal Hostility (↔ by degree)

irritated	*temperamental*	*hostile*	*furious*
annoyed	whining	provoked	enraged
disgruntled	piqued	embittered	incensed
cranky	"pissed off"	exasperated	choleric
miffed	"burned up"	indignant	
displeased	"bugged"	simmering	threatens
"snippy"	smoldering	seething	shouts
"bothered"	ill-tempered	infuriated	yells
restive	bad-tempered		
	bellicose	insults	
grudging		swears	
resentful		curses	
sarcastic		foul-mouthed	
complaining			

Violence/Aggressive Behaviors   *See Section 12.20, "Impulse Control Disorders."*

10.3. ANXIETY/FEAR

See Sections 3.6, "Anxiety," for questions; see also Section 10.9, "Panic."

Autonomic Nervous System/Somatic Hyperactivity/Overarousal Facets

pallor or flushing	*Shortness Of Breath*	dizziness	*clamminess*
chest tightness	difficulty breathing	vertigo	sweaty palms
heart palpitations	chest pain	room spinning	cold sweats/chills
racing heartbeat/	choking/smothering	light-headedness	excessive perspiration
tachycardia	fast and deep	faintness	sweaty forehead
	respiration	syncope	dry mouth
diarrhea	air hunger	"wobbly"	
urgent urination	hyperventilation	"wobbly knees"	piloerection/
stomach	sneezing		"goose bumps"
"butterflies"	yawning	overall weakness	
stomach churned	sighing	unsteadiness	hot flashes
queasiness			
nausea	tingling	*paresthesias*	
dry heaves			
"lump in throat"	numbness		

EMOTIONS/
AFFECTS

Fight-or-flight response/arousal: All of the above, plus more acute hearing, spleen contracts, peripheral blood vessels dilate, bronchioles widen, pupils dilate, more coagulates and lymphocytes in blood, adrenaline secreted, stomach acid production decreases, loss of bladder/anal sphincter control, decreased salivation, etc.

Behavioral Facets

Motor Tension

Agitation, trembling, tightness, twitching, feeling shaky, tremulous, body swaying, rigid posture, stiff neck/back/muscles, muscle aches, sits on edge of chair, inhibited movements, restlessness, easy fatigability.

"Nervous Habits" (↔ by degree)

self-grooming	can't sit still	hair twirling	panicked
scratching	leg/arm swinging	combing fingers	rushed out
nail biting	rocking	through hair	vomited
	pacing	hair pulling	fainted
repetitive move-	stretching		
ments	body swaying	facial expressions	avoidance
fretful		of fear	behaviors
muscle tension	hands restrained/	worried look	avoidant
wringing hands	in pockets	tense face	withdraws
clutching hands	rigid arms	flashes of smiles	
tapping	shuffles feet	tears/crying	
fidgeting		wide-eyed	
yawning/sighing		brow grooves	
self-hugging		"deadpan"	
		avoids eye contact	
moistens lips			
coughing			
swallowing			
clears throat			
heavy breathing			

Speech/Voice   See also Section 7.4, "Speech Behavior."

Strained, quavery, tremor, stuttering, voice cracks, uncompleted/disconnected sentences.

Vigilance and Scanning

Easily startled, jumpy, oversensitive to stimuli, overreactive.
Lessened concentration, erratic, mind goes blank, unable to proceed, unable to function, immobilized, freezes.
Difficulty falling asleep or staying asleep, mind racing.

Affective Facets (↔ by degree)

imperturbable	calm	"nervous"	fearful	terrified
stolid	phlegmatic	uneasy	apprehensive	horrified
inhibited	steady	harried	frightened	rigid
	unemotional	irritable	alarmed	frozen
	stable	vulnerable	distraught	petrified
	composed	fragile		paralyzed

nonchalant	tense	"on edge"	
"cool"	edgy	frazzled	panicky
confident	unable to relax	flighty	panic attacks
sang froid	"uptight"		
	jittery		

Cognitive Facets

"A worrier," "a worry wart," apprehensive, worrisome, ruminates, thoughts of impending doom, exaggeration of the objective danger, anticipates dreadful occurrences/doom/catastrophe, "my world is caving in"/"getting out of hand," feels threatened by people or events commonly seen as of little or no concern, upset by fantasies/imagined scenarios/criticisms/attacks/hurts, dread, desire to escape, fear of losing control/dying/being attacked/losing consciousness/going crazy/ being rejected or abandoned.

Baffled, confused, jumbled thoughts, blurred thoughts, perplexed, lessened concentration, unable to recall/indecisive, forgetful, preoccupied, many errors, diminished initiative/productivity/creativity.

Overwhelmed/can't manage/can't get control/can't control thoughts.

Depersonalization, derealization, preoccupied with bodily sensations. *(See Section 12.11, "Depersonalization and Derealization," for descriptors.)*

High internal tension, feels inept/nervous, can't handle stress/pressure/demands, vulnerable, low self-confidence/efficacy, insecure, "fluttery," "quavery," "feels like I'll explode/my heart will burst through my chest."

Interpersonal Facets   *See also Chapter 9, "Presentation of Self."*

Thin-skinned, easily threatened/aroused to anxiousness, insecure, vulnerable, oversensitive, self-conscious, timid, timorous, uncertain what to say/how to act, dependent, clinging.

Avoids eye contact, withdraws, reduced involvement.

Blames others, hypercritical, self-deprecation.

Ill at ease, uneasy, social anxiety.

Other Facets

No depth of feeling when recounting events, erratic, guardedness, rigidity, confuses self, self-induced pressures, jumps from one subject/topic to another, low frustration tolerance, low stress tolerance, low tolerance for ambiguity, impulsive/acts out.

Accident proneness, susceptibility to minor illnesses.

For a Child:

Fears of animals, ghosts, demons, "the bogey man," darkness, getting lost, parental illness/disability/ death/loss, punishment, being embarrassed/humiliated.

10.4. CYCLOTHYMIA
See also Section 10.7, "Mania."

Cyclothymia runs a biphasic course, alternating manic and depressive patterns, often between the following:

Pessimism, brooding	Optimism, carefree attitudes
Unexplained tearfulness	Excessive punning, joking
Lethargy, decreased speaking	Eutonia, talkativeness

Hypersomnia	Decreased need for sleep
Introversion, self-absorption	Uninhibited people-seeking
Mental confusion, apathy	Sharpened and creative thinking
Shaky self-esteem, low self-confidence	Grandiose overconfidence
Unusually low productivity	Markedly high productivity, unusual working hours

This list is adapted from Akiskal et al. (1979). Used by permission.

10.5. DEPRESSION

See Section 3.11, "Depression," for questions. See also Sections 10.8, "Seasonal Affective Disorder," and 12.27, "PreMenstrual Dysphoric Disorder."

Affective Facets

Anhedonia   *See also Section 10.1, "General Aspects of Mood and Affects."*

Absence of pleasure, loss of pleasure in living, "nothing tastes good any more," joylessness, lack of satisfaction in previously valued activities/hobbies, loss of interests, no desire/energy to do anything, no fun in his/her life, indifference, "couldn't care less," apathy, boredom, lowered/no desires, nothing good to look forward to in life, indifference to praise/reward, emotional impoverishment, drabness, colorless, coldness, emptiness.

Dysphoria (↔ by degree)

wretched	*melancholy*	*sad*	moody
inconsolable	despondent	blue	plaintive
anguished	dejected	somber	
suffering	sorrowful	gloomy	
miserable	forlorn	beaten down	
desperate	bitter	glum	
pathetic	dysphoric	tearful	
in pain	morose	distraught	
	funereal	cheerless	
suicidal	despairing	dour	
self-desctructive	grave	disconsolate	
	profoundly sad		
	woeful	downcast	
	profoundly unhappy	down in the dumps	
	morbid	"down"	
	doleful	"wiped out"	
		troubled	
		dispirited	
		"bummed out"	
		downhearted	

Thoughts of Suicide   *See Sections 3.28, "Suicide and Self-Destructive Behavior," for questions; see Section 12.37, "Suicide," for descriptors.*

Irritability   *See "Social Facets," below, for descriptors.*

Behavioral Facets

Included here are the vegetative signs/physical malfunctioning.

Sleep Patterns   *See Section 12.35, "Sleep Disturbances," for descriptors.*

Eating

Appetite/hunger increase or decrease, anorexia, fewer/more frequent meals, fasting, selective hungers, "comfort foods," binges, weight increase/decrease.

Energy

Anergic, lowered energy, slowed down, listless, "needs to be pushed to get things done," "everything is an effort," easy fatigue, tired, feels "run down," mopes, muddles through, weakened, lethargic, deenergized, torpid, lassitude, "can't shake off the blues," energy is just adequate for life's tasks, inability to cope with routine responsibilities, weary, drained, exhausted.

Psychomotor Retardation/Acceleration   *See also Section 7.3, "Movement/Activity."*

Absence of/lessened spontaneous verbal/motor/emotional expressiveness, long reaction time to questions   [✓ indicate number of seconds], thoughts slowing/laborious/impoverished/racing.

Libido   *See Section 10.10, "Sexuality," for descriptors.*

✓ Remember that libido is sexual interest, not activity.

Bowel/Bladder Habit Changes

Increased frequency of urination, diarrhea/constipation, overconcern with elimination, chronic use or abuse of laxatives, sensations of abdominal distention or incomplete evacuation.

Substance Use

Overuse of prescription and over-the-counter medications (analgesics, laxatives, sleeping aids, vitamins), alcohol, caffeine.

Appearance/Presentation   *See also Section 7.1, "Physical Appearance."*

Sad/fixed/expressionless/unsmiling/downcast face, downward gaze, distracted look, blank stare, furrowed brow, smiled without warmth, "smiling depression."
(↔ *by degree*) Close to tears/tearful/teary, tears well up, weepy/weeps, cries, cries openly/fully, blubbers, sobs.
Dissipated, worn, drained, "a shell of a person," haphazard self-care, self-neglect.
Wrings hands, rubs forehead, shuffling gait.
Little inflection, flat/expressionless/monotonous voice.
Audible sighs.

Summary Statements

All appetites are muted.
Client has persistent physical symptoms that do not respond to medical treatment.   [✓ Note especially headaches, digestive disorders, and chronic and migratory pains.]

Cognitive Facets

Caring/Energy Investment (↔ by degree)

hopeless	*pessimistic*	cold	*bored*
helpless	suspicious	unconcerned	indifferent
unchangeable	disappointed	stoic	unspontaneous
cynical	disillusioned	phlegmatic	apathetic
defeated	cynical	ennui	matter-of-fact
futile	discouraged	weary	
negative	demoralized	humorless	
bleak	disenchanted	malaise	
feeling lost	defeatist	{weltschmertz}	
dreary			
nihilistic			
meaninglessness			
repetition/urging needed			

No plans for self, no future, nothing to look forward to in life, only an empty repetition of meaningless actions, loss of ambition, no goals/plans, resigned, futureless, no anticipation.

Mental Dullness

Inadequate, unable to cope, empty, exhausted
Slowed, ruminative, mulls over, indecisive, decreased concentration, trouble mobilizing thoughts
Confused, perplexed, "I'm not mentally here," worsened memory, spotty memory, vague, unclear
Excessive worrying, worrisome, frustrated

Self-Criticalness/Brooding (↔ by degree)   See also Section 10.6, "Guilt/Shame."

self-doubting	sorry	self-pitying
self-distrusting	regretful	"poor me"
self-deprecating	chagrined	ruined/wasted life
low self-esteem	embarrassed"	life is over
	ashamed	
self-blaming	humiliated	sarcastic/ironic
self-critical		suppressed rage
self-reproaching	vulnerable	self-condemning
fault-finding	threat-sensitive	self-hating
	criticism-sensitive	self-abusing
"inept"	rejection-sensitive	"a misfit"
"ineffectual"	overawed	"a freak"
"unproductive"	cowed	"of no value"
"inadequate"	intimidated	"a failure"
"inferior"	overwhelmed	"a loser"
		"a piece of shit"

Dysfunctional Cognitions

Clinicians such as Beck et al. (1961), Burns (1980), and Ellis (1976) have described the following types of dysfunctional cognitions:

Arbitrary inference: Drawing a negative conclusion not supported by the evidence.
Dichotomous thinking: Oversimplifying; black or white, good or bad, right or wrong, all or nothing.

Mind reading: Assuming one knows the other's thoughts (usually negative).
Magnification or minimization: Loss of proportion; exaggerating or minimizing the importance of an event.
Overgeneralizing: Basing a general conclusion on too few data or one incident; jumping to conclusions.
Personalization: Relating negative events to oneself without an empirical or rational basis.
Selective abstraction: Attending to only the negative aspect(s) of a situation and ignoring the other (positive) ones; mental filter; selective attention; disqualifying the positive.
Catastrophizing: Automatically assuming that the worst-case scenario will occur.
Telescoping of time and options.
Emotional reasoning: "Because I feel afraid, there must be danger."
"Fortune teller" error. Overprediction: The future will be repetitions of the past.
"Shoulding" on oneself or others; "should" statements. "Musterbation."

Summary Statements

Client demonstrated Aaron Beck's (Beck, Rush, et al., 1979) depressive triad of negative views of the self, world, and future.
Cyclic negative thought processes/dysfunctional cognitions were revealed.
Client's attributions are negative, stable/unstable, global/specific/situational, internal/external.
She/he dwelled on past failures, lost opportunities, what could never be, roads not taken, etc.
Alexithymia was evident.
He/she appeared to be feigning good spirits.

Social Facets

Interpersonal

reclusive	avoidant	envious	irritable	strained
inaccessible	distances	resentful	low frustration	relationships
asocial	self-absorbed	argumentative	tolerance	dependent
barricades self	withdraws	suspicious	bitter	passive
away	low social	feels scorned	demanding	unassertive
isolates	interest	feels abandoned	crabby	wary
hermit-like	subdued		easily irritated	distrustful
secludes	painfully shy		easily annoyed	
	separates from life/others		petulant	
	only watches		self-righteous	
	less talkative			

Support-Seeking   *See also Section 9.3, "Dependency/Surgency."*

Complains of life's unfairness, gossips, gripes, futilely indignant, sympathy-seeking, whiny, self-pitying, manipulative, emotionally hungry, seeks support only when in crisis, finds others always inadequately supportive or sympathetic.

Other Facets of Depression

Bear the following possibilities in mind:

Is client depressed because forced into dependency by disability/losses/injury?
Is depression worse during winter? *(See Section 10.8, "Seasonal Affective Disorder.")*
What do dexamethasone suppression test results indicate?
Is client self-defeating, self-victimizing? *(See Section 13.25, "Self-Defeating Personality.")*

EMOTIONS/
AFFECTS

Are there diurnal mood variations? Are depression's symptoms worse in the morning and lessen as day wears on?

Is there day–night reversal of activities?

Does client interpret deaths as desertions, yet is simply alone because she/he has outlived others?

Masked Depression

This subsection is adapted from Lopez-Ibor (1990). Used by permission.

Psychosomatic Symptoms

Gastrointestinal: Nausea, vomiting, gastralgia, meteorism, aerophagia, hiccups, constipation, diarrhea, ulcerative colitis, anorexia, bulimia.

Respiratory: Apnea, vasomotor rhinitis, asthma.

Genitourinary: Nervous bladder, impotency, premature ejaculation, hypersexuality, "frigidity," amenorrhea.

Cardiovascular: Tachycardia, palpitations, extra systoles, precordial pain, cardiac phobia.

Metabolic: Obesity, thinness.

Skin: Eczema, neurodermatitis, alopecia.

Psychological Symptoms and Disorders

Self-destructive behaviors, sexual deviations, alcoholism, addictions, gambling, phobias, obsessions, dysmorphophobia, kleptomania/theft, hypochondria, delusions, accident proneness.

Depression in Children (5–15 Years)

✓ **Note:** Children under 7 are usually unable to characterize internal mood states. Most symptoms are similar in children and adults, but some listed here are slightly different or in addition to adult ones.

Cognitions: Catastrophizing, assumption of personal responsibility for negative outcomes.

Lack of interest in playing/favorite activities, isolation, agitation, despair, hypersensibility, insecurity, boredom, temper tantrums, fugues, feelings of inferiority, nihilistic thoughts, suicidal impulses, obsessive thoughts, loneliness.

Irritability, difficulty getting out of bed in morning.

School problems: Learning difficulties, school refusal/"phobia," dyslexia, concentration difficulties.

Vegetative symptoms: Fatigue, asthenia, sleep disorders/terrors, appetite changes (very common at different ages), weeping, abdominal pains, alopecia aureata, tics, eczema, allergies, anorexia, bulimia, asthma.

Other: Fears of parents' dying, clinging, isolation in room, aggression, substance abuse.

Assessment Scales

Assessment scales for depression include the Hamilton Rating Scale for Depression (Hamilton, 1960), the Beck Depression Inventory (Beck et al., 1961), the Zung Self-Rating Depression Scale (Zung, 1965), and the Depression Adjective Checklist (Lubin, 1965).

EMBARRASSMENT   *See Section 10.6, "Guilt/Shame," just below.*

<u>SUICIDE</u> *See Sections 3.28, "Suicide and Self-Destructive Behavior," for questions and 12.37, "Suicide," for descriptors.*

10.6. GUILT/SHAME
See also Kohlberg's stages of moral development in Section 19.8.

General Descriptors

Apologetic, penitent, begging, pleading, repentant, sorry, chagrined, contrite, remorseful, burdened.

Guilty, responsible, guilt proneness, mortified, self-condemning, self-reproaching, has a punitive superego, transgressed superego boundaries, unacceptable impulses, fears of annihilation.

Embarrassed, humiliated, disgraced, reproached, depreciated, devalued, humbled, wishes to disappear/become invisible, avoids disclosure of flaws, hides inadequacies.

Ashamed, feels inferior, fears rejection/abandonment, fails to attain goal/measure up.

Guiltless, cold, hardened, cynical, unrepentant, conscienceless, shameless, unscrupulous, parasitic, incorrigible, predatory.

Assessment

The Mosher Guilt Scales (Mosher, 1968) assess sex guilt, morality/conscience guilt, and hostility guilt.

Distinctions between Shame and Guilt

The following distinctions are adapted by permission from Potter-Effron (1989).

Central trait	Shame	Guilt
Failure	Of being, of meeting goals, of whole self.	Of doing, of moral self.
Primary feelings	Inadequate, deficient, worthless, exposed, disgust, disgrace.	Bad, wicked, evil, remorseful.
Precipitating event	Unexpected, possibly trivial event.	Actual or contemplated violation of values.
Involvement of self	Total self-image involvement: "How could *I* have done that?"	Partial self-image involvement: "How could I have done *that*?"
Central fear	Of abandonment.	Of punishment.
Origins	Positive identification with parents.	Need to control aggressive impulse.
Primary defenses.	Desire to hide (withdrawal), denial, perfectionism, grandiosity, shamelessness.	Obsessive thinking, paranoid, intellectualization, seeking excessive punishment.
Positive functions	Awareness of limits of human condition, discovery of separate self, sense of modesty, identification with community, mastery, autonomy.	Sublimation, moral behavior, initiative, reparation.

10.7. MANIA

See Section 3.17, "Mania," for questions; see also Section 10.4, "Cyclothymia."

Affective Facets *(↔ by degree)*

cheerful	*high*	*hypomanic*	*exuberant*	*manic*	*ecstatic*
light-hearted	gay	happy	elated	laughing	exalted
positive	laughing	silly	ebullient	binges	rapturous
bright	buoyant	giddy		euphoric	
vivid	jovial	excessively	*irritability*	false joy	*panics*
intense	elevated	boisterous	anger	false elation	
		effervescent	rages		
labile	unstable	rapid		accelerating	
		fluctuations		course	

Behavioral Facets

(↔ by degree) Pressured speech, fast/rapid speaking, rapid-fire speech, hyperverbal, overtalkative, overabundant, loud, verbose, rhyming, punning, word play, hyperbole, overproductive, garrulous, tirades, singing.

(↔ by degree) Periods of hyperactivity/overactivity, paces, restless, speeded up, accelerated, quickened, fast, going fast, racing, frenzied, manic, anger, rages, assaultive.

Overconfident, exaggerated view of own abilities, starts many activities but does not finish or follow through with most.

Insomnia, decreased need for sleep, no acknowledgment of fatigue.

Incautious, frivolous, poor social judgment, fearless, engaging in reckless activities (e.g., dangerous driving, foolish business investments or buying sprees, impulsive spending, sexual indiscretions or acting out), greatly increased need for sexual activities, increased sexual drive/interests, hypersexual, disinhibited activities, increased smoking, telephoning.

Cognitive Facets *(↔ by degree)*   *See also the speech descriptors under "Behavioral Facets," above.*

expansive	overproductive	*flight of ideas*	loosened	delusions
exaggeration		illogical	associations	incoherent
grandiosity	idiosyncratic	racing thoughts	disjointed	bizarre
	associations	thought bom-	disorganized	
little or no	ideas of ref-	bardment	disoriented	hallucinatory
insight	erence		disconnected	experiences
		sexual/religious	thoughts	
limited concen-		preoccupa-	abrupt topic	
tration		tions	changes	
brief attention				
span				
distractible				

Social/Interpersonal Facets

(↔ by degree) Impatient, intolerant, irritable, oversensitive, touchy, insulting, uncooperative, resistive, negativistic, critical, provocative, suspicious, angry, easy/inappropriate anger, nasty, loud, abusive, crude, foul language, swears, curses, blasphemes, vulgar, bathroom language, obscene.

Suspicious, guarded, distrustful, believes that others collude against him/her, asserts that he/she was tricked into . . . , denies validity or reality of all criticisms.

(↔ by degree) Gregarious, likeable, dramatic, entertaining, pleasant, vivacious, seductive, cracks jokes, prankish, naive, infantile, silly, {*witzelsucht*}.

Entitled, self-important, grandiose, cocksure, self-confident, "chutzpah."

Dominating, controlling, boastful, challenging, surgent, conflicts with authority figures.

Delusions   *See Section 12.9, "Delusions."*

10.8. SEASONAL AFFECTIVE DISORDER

SAD can be bipolar or manic, but it presents primarily as depression. A milder form is called "winter blues" (Rosenthal, 1998).

The symptoms are worse or occur only in the fall/winter. The rate increases from south (1.4%) to north (9.7%) of the United States, but is affected by cloud cover and storms. SAD usually begins in a person's 30s; 75–80% of people with SAD are female. Light treatment to the eyes (10,000 lux for 30 minutes per day is common) controls serotonin levels. Symptoms include the following:

Lethargy, fatigue.

Ravenous appetite/weight gain/carbohydrate cravings.

Withdrawal from relationships.

Inability to concentrate, problems at work, inefficiency.

Anxiety and despair.

10.9. PANIC
See also Section 10.3, "Anxiety/Fear."

Fear of fear, rapid escalation of anxiety, loss of control over anxiety, intense fear/discomfort.

Feelings of impending/near "doom."

Unexpected/unpredictable/"out of the blue" onset.

Fears of loss of control/dying/going crazy/embarrassing self/doing something uncontrolled (loss of bladder control, falling down).

A cascade of symptoms.

10.10. SEXUALITY
See Section 3.23, "Sexual History," for questions; see also "Sexual Adjustment" under Section 6.4, "Adjustment History."

(↔ by degree) Disgusted, asexual, celibate, abstinent, apathetic, inhibited, ashamed, puritanical, prudish, prim, restrained, passive, hesitant, permissive, romantic, amorous, erotic, sensual, assertive, passionate, seductive, overactive, soliciting, compulsive, demanding, lustful, lewd, wanton, aggressive, assaultive.

Increased or decreased libido/desire, arousal, activity/relations, satisfaction.

Hypo-/hypersexuality.

Reluctance to initiate, slowness to respond.

Previously inhibited interests.

SHAME   *See Section 10.6, "Guilt/Shame."*

EMOTIONS/ AFFECTS

10.11. OTHER EMOTIONS/EMOTIONAL REACTIONS

Sense of Humor

($\leftrightarrow$ *by degree*) Spontaneously humorous, excellent/normal/adequate/diminished/absent/nonexistent sense of humor, humorless.

Mirth response is brief/flashes, grim little smile, he/she is capable of responding but not initiating humor.

"Stuffed shirt," takes self too seriously.

Cosmic/existential/absurdist, wry, deadpan, dry, ironic, tendentious, sarcastic, hostile, offensive, cynical.

Sophisticated, witty, gentle, mirthful, playful, jovial.

Jesting, impish, funny, entertaining, tells stories/jokes.

Teasing, flip, puns, wisecracks, mocks, silly, slapstick, off-color or offensive jokes, inappropriate remarks excused as "just kidding."

Grief/Bereavement

Normal Grief

Distress, sorrow, anguish, despair, heartache, pain, woe, suffering, affliction, troubles.

Preoccupied with loss/loved one/consequences/memories.

Easily made/becomes tearful, slowed thinking and responding with long latencies of response, stares into space.

Feels helpless/vulnerable/useless/lowered self-esteem.

Kübler-Ross (1969) has identified five stages of the normal reaction to loss: denial, anger, bargaining, depression, and acceptance.

Unresolved/Morbid/Pathological Grief

Partial denial of death, absence of grieving, pathological identification, hypochondriasis, chronic depression, chronic grieving, avoidance of cues to the deceased, isolation, reattachment.

Decreased immune system functioning, increased use of drugs and alcohol, depression, over-/misuse of medical care for grief.

A good starting point is Callahan et al.'s (1992) discussion of unresolved grief.

EMOTIONS/
AFFECTS

11

Cognition and Mental Status

This chapter contains descriptors for all the aspects of cognitive functioning assessed in a <u>Men</u>tal <u>S</u>tatus <u>E</u>xamination; the questions to elicit these behaviors and functions are provided in Chapter 2. Because there is no agreed-upon theory relating all these functions or skills, they are presented here in rough order of increasing complexity or demand on mental resources.

11.1. NO PATHOLOGICAL FINDINGS: SUMMARY STATEMENTS

The relevant DSM-IV code is V71.09, No Diagnosis or Condition on Axis I/No Diagnosis on Axis II.

Based on behavior observed during the interview, I believe . . .
In my professional judgment . . .

Examination is normal/benign.
The client is in <u>N</u>o <u>A</u>cute <u>D</u>istress/in <u>N</u>o <u>A</u>pparent <u>D</u>istress.
Examination was entirely <u>W</u>ithin <u>N</u>ormal <u>L</u>imits.
The client seems average/unremarkable/intact.
Nothing unusual was found.
No limitations in any of the domains assessed by these instruments/this examination.

No evidence/signs of a thought disorder, or a major affective/cognitive/behavioral disorder, was/
    were elicited.
No abnormalities of thought, affect, or behavior/no gross abnormalities/nothing bizarre/no cogni-
    tive slippage.
I did not find any unusual kinds of logic or strange associations.
No obvious indications of psychosis or organicity, no hallucinations in any field.
He/she experiences thoughts in a spontaneous and normal manner, and is lucid and coherent.
No indication of disordered mentation in the form of incoherent or incomprehensible speech.
Speech is relevant as to content and spontaneous as to delivery.

He/she is in full/partial/marginal/shaky remission.
I failed to elicit any symptomatic behaviors/indicants of previously described symptoms or disor-
    ders.
Based on current observations, there is no decompensation, deterioration, or exacerbation of past
    conditions.
I find no indication of notable decline of intellectual abilities.

No evidence of drug or alcohol abuse/legal record/psychiatric history of diagnosis or treatment.

11.2. LEVELS OF CONSCIOUSNESS

> See also Sections 2.3, "Rancho Los Amigos Cognitive Scale," and 2.4, "Glasgow Coma Scale."

The following groupings are sequenced by degree of increasing consciousness.

Coma, comatose, coma vigil, unarousable, unresponsive, obtunded.

   Stuporous, delirious, responsive only to persistent or noxious stimulation, postictal, twilight/
   dreamy state, drifts off, fluctuates, arousable/rousable, semicoma.

      Lethargic, reduced wakefulness, somnolent, only briefly responsive with a return to uncon-
      sciousness.

         Clouded consciousness, drowsy, falls asleep, responding requires heightened effort, less-
         ened ability to perform tasks, frequent hesitations, starting/startles, disoriented,
         groggy, "drugged," under the influence of medications that . . . (specify), in a daze.

            Alert, responds to questions, attentive, makes eye contact, interacts, asks ques-
            tions, converses, alert, lucid, intact, was spontaneously verbal.

11.3. ORIENTATION *(↔ by degree)*

See Section 2.5, "Orientation," for questions.

Incorrectly identified self by name, mistook/confused present location/correct time/objects/others, mistook/confused dates/persons/places, was off the mark by ___ years/months/days.

Appeared to be oriented only in the most simple sense/on basic measures, oriented to _____ but not to _____.

Fully oriented times three/to time, place, and person; times four/to time, place, person, and things.

11.4. ATTENTION

See Section 2.6, "Attention," for questions. See also Section 12.3, "Attention-Deficit/Hyperactivity Disorder."

The following groupings are sequenced by degree of increasing attentiveness.

Unaware, unable to attend, inattentive, unengaged, daydreams, autistic reverie, muses, pensive, "wool-gathering," ignored questions, attention could not be gained or held, attention limited by extraneous sounds/concurrent activities/fantasies/affects/memories.

Distractible, attention wandered, redirectable, attentive only to irrelevancies, responses were irrelevant, unable to reject interfering stimuli from environment/viscera/affects, guided by internal rather than external stimuli, easily overloaded by stimulation, needed much repetition, could not repeat familiar lists/phrases, attended only for brief intervals, fleeting attention, can't absorb details needed for responsible judgments beyond the routine.

Low attending skills, could not follow a three-stage command/written directions, cannot attend to coping/adaptive/purposeful tasks, could not spell words forward and backward, preoccupied, selective attention/inattention, showed lapses of attention.

Could focus on/select the relevant from among the irrelevant aspects of a situation, could maintain the focus/resist distraction, attention is sufficient for question responding/interview/psychotherapy/effective life management, showed freedom from distractibility, capable of prolonged attention but occasionally distracted, vigilant.

11.5. CONCENTRATION/TASK PERSISTENCE

See Section 2.7, "Concentration," for questions. See also Section 12.3, "Attention-Deficit/Hyperactivity Disorder."

General Descriptors

Unable to maintain concentration for more than several minutes/duration of the examination, defective when compared with peers, by report able to maintain concentration for several hours, had difficulty with tasks requiring vigilance.

For a Child:

Daydreams, has strong/weak subjects, doesn't complete assignments in class/homework, materials are disorganized/messy, forgets teacher's instructions, has to be reminded to sit still/pay attention. *(See also Section 8.3, "Response to the Methods of Evaluation . . . ")*

Interfering Factors

Concentration intact to direct questioning, but subtle recall deficits are evident when certain topics (e.g., symptoms or denied behaviors) are inquired into.

Performance anxiety, fear of failure, fear of being found wanting/inadequate, general anxiety, preoccupations with self or others.

Performance on Serial Sevens

Was able to subtract 7 from 100 ___ times/down to 2 accurately.

Did serial sevens down to ___ in ___ seconds with ___ errors, at which point I stopped her/him.

Was able to do serial sevens ___ times before making an error.

Self-corrected errors in the sequence.

Performed serial sevens with ___ initial errors, but subsequent subtractions were accurate based on the prior numbers.

Was unable to subtract serial sevens accurately/could sustain concentration only to the first plateau/on ___ trials, even with sincere effort.

Demonstrated adequate numerical reasoning, but made incorrect computations because of interfering anxiety.

Showed decrements/lessening/limitations of mental efficiency.

11.6. DEMENTIA

> *See also Sections 11.7, "Memory," 11.10, "Reasoning . . . ," and 11.13, "Social/Moral Judgment . . . "*

Reminders

✓ First, do not use "senility" to mean "dementia," because aging doesn't cause dementia. Aging is not a disease. At no age is dementia a normal state, and in many cases dementia is reversible while age isn't. "In the absence of disease there is no dementia." Differential diagnoses include depression, the "mindlessness" created by routine and passivity (Langer & Rodin, 1976), poor nutrition, drug interactions/toxicity, sleep deprivation, etc. *(See Sections 12.34, "Side Effects of Medications," and 28.6, "Organic Brain Syndrome/Dementia.")*

✓ Second, be alert for AIDS Dementia Complex. Onset is insidious, and ARC estimated to occur in up to 60% of People Living With AIDS. Greenwood (1991) and Mapou and Law (1994) provide a very good review of ADC. *(See also Section 12.2, which covers this topic.)*

Phases of Decline in Alzheimer's Disease: Global Deterioration Scale

The following table is adapted by permission from Reisberg (1983, 1985) and Reisberg et al. (1982).

GDS Stage	Clinical phase	Tentative diagnosis	Cognitive deficits	Personality changes
1	Normal	None	No complaints or objective evidence of memory deficits.	None
2	Forgetfulness	Normal aging	Complaints of memory deficits, such as forgetting names that were formerly well known or misplacing familiar objects, but without objective deficits in work or social situations.	Appropriate concern with mild forgetfulness.

GDS Stage	Clinical phase	Tentative diagnosis	Cognitive deficits	Personality changes
3	Early confusional	Compatible with incipient Alzheimer's disease	Increased cognitive decline and signs of confusion: gets lost going to a familiar place; family and coworkers notice forgetting of words/names; poor reading comprehension; inability to concentrate.	Denial of memory problems, but anxiety accompanies symptoms of forgetfulness and confusion.
4	Late confusional	Mild Alzheimer's disease	Decreased knowledge of current events; forgetting of one's personal history; decreased ability to handle finances or to travel.	Very obvious use of denial about memory problems. Flattening of affect and withdrawal from more challenging situations.
5	Early dementia	Moderate Alzheimer's disease	Moderately severe decline and intensified confusion: Inability to recall major current aspects of one's life, such as address, phone number, or the names of close family members/children; inability to recall major personal facts, like name of one's high school; some time disorientation (e.g., for date); may need assistance with choosing proper clothing.	
6	Middle dementia	Moderately severe Alzheimer's disease	Severe cognitive decline and confusion: Occasionally forgets name of spouse; largely unaware of all recent events and experiences and many past life events; unaware of surroundings; does not know season of year; can't distinguish familiar from unfamiliar persons.	Totally dependent on others for survival. Severe personality and emotional changes, such as delusions, obsessions, and high anxiety. Fails to follow through on intentions due to forgetfulness.
7	Late dementia	Severe Alzheimer's disease	Very severe decline and confusion: Loss of all verbal abilities; incontinent, need for assistance in eating and toileting; loss of basic psychomotor skills (e.g., inability to walk).	Unresponsive to all but the simplest communications. Total loss of social skills and personality.

11.7. MEMORY

See Section 2.10, "Memory," for questions, and 11.21, "Evaluation of Intellect and Cognitive Functions," for tests.

Indications of Defect (↔ *by degree*)

Forgetful, "spotty memory," "absent-minded," uncertain/expresses doubts, muddled, foggy, dreamy presentation, "spaced out," detached, confused, befuddled, confabulates, falsifies, perseverates, contaminations, diffusions.

MENTAL STATUS

Confuses time frames/sequences, nonsequential, overfocused on externals/situational issues, vague, hesitant, guesses/estimates/approximates, Ganser's syndrome, disjointed, gaps, skips over, skimpy/superficial history, contradictions, a poor historian/reporter of past events.
Can only recognize, sluggish recall, recalls only with much prompting/cueing, reproduces/reconstructs with much difficulty/inaccuracy.

Amnesias

Anterograde, retrograde, Total Global Amnesia, {*ictus amnésique*,} fugue, amnestic/amnesic disorder, Korsakoff's syndrome, Wernicke's syndrome.

Paramnesias

Fausse reconnaissance, retrospective falsification, confabulation, preknowledge of events/others' speech, *déjà vu*, *déjà entendu*, *déjà pensé*, *jamais vu*, hypermnesia, anomia, agnosia, prosopagnosia.

Impact of Memory Defect on Patient (↔ *by degree*)

Maximal/effective/poor/no use of compensatory mechanisms/coping skills, constricts lifestyle, ignores, denies.

Summary Statements about Memory Performance

Normal Memory

All components of memory are grossly intact.
The client is able to recount personal history normally.
His/her remote, recent, and immediate memories appear to be intact, as far as I can determine without independent verification of the historical facts.

As Historian

The client was un/able to give an account of his/her activities/life events in a chronological order.
Memory, as reflected in her/his ability to provide an intact, substantial, sequential, detailed, and logical history/narrative, was defective/quite poor/poor/adequate/normal/exceptional/unusual because . . . (specify).
Memory for events in relationship to time was vague/murky/chaotic.
He/she could not recall the time frames of school/work/family development/treatments.

Defective Memory

The client was un/able to recall three objects/words after 5/10 minutes of different/unrelated activities.
Memory was limited/deficient/defective/a problem in all time frames.
Memory is organically intact, but anxiety/depression interfere.
He appears defective/normal/exceptional in processes of registration, retention, and recall.
She seems defective/normal/exceptional in immediate/short-term retention/recent/recent past/remote memory.
Client shows the pattern of memory deficits typical of those with/with a history of _____ (specify diagnosis).
_____ memory is not affected/normal, but _____ memory is defective/exceptional.
Remote and recent memories appeared to be intact, but there was an emptiness and lack of color in client's descriptions of critical events.
Client did not offer a rich description of important events from memory.

Other Aspects of Memory

Types of Memory

Clinical: Recognition ("identify, select, pick, or find"), reproduction ("say, repeat, or copy"), recall (remember without cueing).

Types: Immediate, short-term/active/working, long-term, generic, eidetic, narrative, declarative/explicit vs. procedural/implicit, automatic vs. effortful, semantic vs. episodic, verbal (words, phrases, stories, associated word pairs), visual (colors, designs, pictures), spatial (positions of objects), episodic (contexts, situations, components, details, sequences, themes), practical/praxis (ability to demonstrate/pantomime how to open a can, brush one's teeth, butter bread, etc.).

Functions or processes: Acquisition, encoding, recoding, chunking, consolidation, rehearsal, transfer, storage, retention, decay, retrieval, reconstruction.[1]

Possible causes of forgetting: Decay, displacement, interference, retroactive and proactive inhibition, consolidation block theory, retrieval failure theory, explicit memory defect.

Factors affecting recall: Primacy, recency, vividness, frequency.

Methods for enhancing recall: Method of loci, mnemonics, elaborative rehearsal, priming, spatiotemporal markers, Tip-Of-the-Tongue phenomenon.

Characteristics of Senescent Forgetfulness

The following table is adapted by permission from Kral (1978).

Malignant	Benign
Shortened retention time.	Failures to recall are limited to relatively unimportant parts of an experience (e.g., a name or date).
Inability to recall an event of the recent past, including not only unimportant facts but the experience itself.	Details forgotten on one occasion may be recalled at another time.
Failure to recall accompanied by disorientation to place and time and, gradually, to person.	"Forgotten" data belong to remote as opposed to recent past.
Absent self-awareness of deficiencies.	Subjects are aware of shortcomings and may apologize or compensate.

11.8. INFORMATION

See Section 2.11, "Fund of Information," for questions.

Impoverished/deficient fund of information/general knowledge, unaware of current/practical/general information, doesn't know facts regarding his/her culture, fund of factual knowledge is low/spotty, unaware of many basic factual/measurement/historical/geographical concepts.

Summary Statements:

Limited education was apparent/demonstrated in low levels of the information typically acquired in grade school.

Considering his/her cultural background, level of formal education, and self-education, this client's information was ... (specify).

[1] I am indebted to Mustaq Khan, PhD, of London, Ontario, Canada, for several corrections in this section.

11.9. STREAM OF THOUGHT

This section covers speech as a reflection of cognition. See also Section 7.4, "Speech Behavior," and Section 11.10, just below.

Amount/Productivity (↔ *by degree*)

impoverished	laconic	*normal*	rapid	*flight of ideas*
paucity	slowed	spontaneous	overabundant	
restricted	hesitant	average	"logorrhea"	
decreased		abundant	copious	
unelaborated				
underproductive				
blocked				
slowed speed of cognitive processing				

Continuity/Coherence (↔ *by degree*)

incoherent	*loose*	*idiosyncratic*	disconnected	*clear*
incomprehensible	circumstantial	unusual	topic changes	realistic
clang associations	irrelevancies	associations	difficult to	rational
neologisms	tangential	personalized	follow	lucid
word salad	vague	meanings	fragmented	consistent
confabulations	derailed		flighty	coherent
{verbigerations}	rambling	conjectural	confusing	relevant
perseverative	garbled		disjointed	integrated
chaotic	confused	preoccupied		goal-directed
jabbers	sidetracked		baffling	logical
babbles	evasive		Byzantine	pertinent
prattles	distracted		perplexing	easy to
"rattles on"	digressive			follow
silly conclusions	drifting		mushy thinking	intact
	circumlocutions			sequential
	paraphrases		irrelevant	not pre-
	word substitutions			occupied
	nonsequential		incorrect	articulate
	jumbled		conclusions	
	illogical		unclear	
			imprecise	
	circular		indefinite	
	elliptical		poorly defined	
	circuitous			
	repetitive			

Coherence

The following groupings are sequenced by increasing degree of coherence:

No stepwise progressions, no logical sequences, lacking internal logic.

> Loosening of associations, connected associations by small and/or unusual similarities, needed to be refocused/redirected, failed to answer the questions asked.

> > Clear cause-and-effect thinking, responses cohered with/addressed the questions asked, common/realistic associations, coherent, to the point, linear.

Qualities of Thought Content

Personalized, idiosyncratic, carefully chosen, eccentric, odd, monothematic, overvalued ideas.
Sexual, earthy, erotic, scatological, pornographic, obscene, profane, blasphemous, vulgarities.
Bizarre themes, magical thinking, fabulized.
Trivial, platitudes, sentimental, oversimple, empty.

Preoccupations   *See above; see also Sections 12.9, "Delusions," 12.22, "Obsessions," and 12.25, "Paranoia."*

mental health
obsessions
compulsions
fears/phobias
symptoms

death and dying
suicide
homicide
dying
morbid thoughts
losses
tragedies

his/her plight
life situation
stressors
family/relatives
frustrations
disappointments
ambivalences

religion
piety
excessive prayer
blasphemous ideas
denigrating activities
irreligious practices/acts
fears/delusions about
    clergy/theology

relationships
injustices
violence
shame/embarrassment
regrets

escape
running away

sexuality

persecution
accusations
self-destruction
suicidal impulses

*somatic/hypochondriacal
    concerns*
current physical illness
mortal illnesses
popular diseases

Dissociation   (↔ *by degree*)   *See also Sections 12.11, "Depersonalization and Derealization," 13.12, "Histrionic Personality," and 13.7, "Borderline Personality."*

Daydreaming, fanciful story, trance, hysterical attack/episode, amnesia, fugue, somnambulism, automatic writing, out-of-body experience, extraterrestrial travel, previous lives lived.

Other Problems with Stream of Thought

Loss of goal, spontaneous but unproductive speech, condensations, overinclusive thinking, auto-echolalia, interpenetration of themes, loss of segmental set, cognitive slippage.

Summary Statements for Normal Thought Content

The client showed an average number of thoughts, which were neither speeded nor slowed/moved at a normal pace.
His/her thinking seems normal from the perspective of productivity, relevance, and coherence.
The client answered questions appropriately.
She presented her thoughts in an appropriately paced, understandable, and relevant fashion.
His thoughts were clear, coherent, well organized, and relevant to the subject at hand.
She reached the goal of her thought processes without introducing any irrelevant material.
His train of thought was goal-directed, relevant, and logical.

The client's stream of thought was coherent, focused, and without digressions, irrelevancies, disturbances of logic, or bizarreness.

There was no tangentiality, circumstantiality, or distractibility.

Speech was relevant, appropriate, and without evidence of unusual ideation.

The client showed no impairment reflective of disordered mentation.

There was a normal flow of ideas/continuity.

Her associations were well organized.

Speech showed good grammatical complexity.

The client showed no obsessions or phobias, ideas of reference, hallucinations, delusions, faulty perceptions, perceptual disturbance, misinterpretations of consensual reality, or psychotic distortions.

He is not preoccupied with obsessions, phobias, or suicide.

Her logic was easy to follow, although the responses were superficial.

He is very concerned about her health, but understandably and appropriately so.

Her thoughts about _____ (e.g., health problems) dominate her thinking but are not exclusive or preoccupying.

Summary Statements for Problematic Stream of Thought

The client will refer to topics in a symbolic or associational manner, which requires deciphering by the listener.

The client apparently does little analytic or discriminatory thinking.

He conversed in response to questions rather than speaking spontaneously.

Self-sufficient in providing responses, but volunteered little additional information.

Would not enlarge/expand on topics of interest; little/no elaboration of responses to my questions.

She showed word retrieval deficits/reported "forgetting"/had difficulty finding words/groped for words, would stop suddenly in middle of a sentence/speech.

He had great difficulty gathering thoughts rather than in finding words.

She substituted related words approximating the definitive/appropriate term.

Paraphrastic errors/dysnomias/unusual word and sentence formations/errors of syntax/constructional dyspraxia/malapropisms were evident.

The client demonstrated alexia/alexithymia.

When interrupted, he became confused and rambled.

11.10. REASONING/ABSTRACT THINKING/ CONCEPT FORMATION

See also Section 11.13, below; see Sections 2.12–2.15 and 2.17–2.18 for questions.

Level of Interpretation (↔ *by degree*)

Greatly defective, failed to grasp nature of question, overly concrete, it was not possible to find proverbs simple enough for him/her to interpret, no evidence of abstract thinking or even extended thought processes, "I've heard that one before" (without elaboration).

Distorted by thought disorder, showing personification/bizarre features/delusions.

Concrete (noted only surface features or appearance aspects of stimuli), offered only very specific examples, paraphrases, reasoned in a concrete manner, stimulus-bound associations.

Simplistic, difficulty with concept formation/judgment, abstraction, opposites/similarities/differences, comparative analogies, absurdities, proverbs.

Couldn't use appropriate/expected levels of abstraction in dealing with test materials, mixed up categories in hierarchies, poor abstract thinking and concept-handling ability, degree of generalization was overly broad/narrow, some difficulty with reasoning at an easy/moderately difficult/difficult level, offered unusual/idiosyncratic/antisocial interpretations.

Functional levels of interpretation, responded only in terms of the uses for the stimulus item or literal meanings.

Offered *popular* interpretations of proverbs, adequate reasoning skills, common sense.

Abstracted common properties of the stimuli (noted relationships between the stimuli/shared structural features), used principles, reasoned abstractly, offered similar proverbs/spontaneous rephrasings, comprehensive level of reasoning.

Overly abstract, attended only to selected/irrelevant aspects of stimuli, stylized, overly philosophical/obscure/arcane references, highly theoretical, Byzantine.

Summary Statements

Normal Abstraction

The client had common-sense/functional understanding of everyday objects.
She was able to respond with an abstract relationship between pairs of terms/items I presented to her.

He was able to form concepts well.
She handled ideas well and without concreteness.
He was able to identify opposites, similarities, differences, and absurdities.

Client was able to analyze the meaning of simple proverbs, all at appropriate levels of abstraction.
She could give me the deep meanings of the proverbs I offered.

Faulty Reasoning

The client engaged in faulty inductive/deductive inference/reasoning.
She reached conclusions based on false/faulty premises.
He made errors of logic and judgment/came to incorrect conclusions.
She was unable to relevantly support answers given.
His reasoning appears autistic/dereistic/idiosyncratic.
Non sequiturs/pars pro toto/trance logic/paleologic was/were evident.

11.11. ARITHMETIC

See also Section 17.5, "Math Ability"; see Section 2.16, "Calculation Abilities," for questions.

Overall ($\leftrightarrow$ *by degree*)

Anumerate, lacks practical/everyday/survival/basic mathematical skills, dyscalculia, skills approximately equivalent to those mastered in school grade ___.

Financial   *See Section 14.8, "Financial Skills."*

11.12. SOCIAL MATURITY

See also Section 11.13, just below.

Irresponsibility   *See also Section 13.16, "Antisocial Personality."*

Denies/lies about responsibilities, steals/destroys others' property, refuses to pay debts/for property destroyed, cheats, blames innocents, shows no guilt, offers no explanations, fakes guilt, offers only empty/"phony" apologies, falsely begs/pleads, not remorseful, "crocodile tears."
On the job he/she resists/doesn't cooperate with/ignores/defies rules/directions/deadlines, starts many tasks but does not complete any, manipulates coworkers into doing his/her work, "cons," needs close/continuous supervision, Absent WithOut Leave/slips away, tardy/takes too many/overlong rest periods/breaks/leaves early, intoxicated at work.

Self-Centeredness   *See also Section 13.16, "Narcissistic Personality."*

Manipulates, unrealistic/lacks/only immediate goals, selfish, uncaring, resents limits, self-indulgent, impulsive, arousal-seeking, acts out.

Financial Behavior   *See Section 14.8, "Financial Skills."*

Social Interaction   *See also Chapter 15, "Social/Community Functioning," and 16, "Couple and Family Relationships."*

Resistant to authorities (parents, supervisor, police, human service professionals), chooses/imitates inappropriate or pathological models, touches others without consent, touches self inappropriately, teases, threatens vaguely to leave/take revenge/destroy property/commit violence, threatens when confronted with own irresponsible behaviors, bullies/intimidates.
Has only limited contact with others so little opportunity to behave inappropriately,
Client never/rarely/often/usually plays/socializes with/relates to persons of her own age group.
He prefers to relate to things/paper/numbers/ideas/people.

Summary Statements

Child is as mature as same-age peers/is only pseudomature/has been "parentified" by his family/is overly mature.
When/as compared with others of same age/culture/education, she demonstrated . . . (specify).

11.13. SOCIAL/MORAL JUDGMENT AND KNOWLEDGE

See also Sections 11.10, 11.11, 11.12, 11.16, and 11.18. See Section 2.20, "Social Judgment," for questions.

Defective Understanding/Lack of "Common Sense"

Substantial defects in capacity to appreciate common/consensual reality.
Rational but not realistic thoughts.
Impaired ability to make reasonable and realistic life decisions.
Makes major decisions without sufficient information/impulsively/depending on hearsay/so as not to refuse a friend, impulsive, immature/infantile, awkward.
Makes decisional errors under even the mildest stress.

Seems guided by false beliefs.
Heedless/reckless/feckless/careless, irresponsible.

For a Child:

Excessive imagination, confuses wishes/fears/impulses with objective/consensual reality.

Normal Judgment/"Common Sense"

Has common-sense understandings, common-sensical.
Subscribes to usual explanations of people's motivations.
Has sought treatment for medical/psychological problems.

Learned from experience/feedback/others' mistakes/correction/instruction, is "street-smart."

Understands/anticipates the likely outcome of behavior and thinks/plans ahead.
Responsible, understands/anticipates the likely consequences of his/her behavior/actions.
Can plan ahead effectively.
Has strong/weak executive functions (decision making, social perception, flexibility of thinking/ judgment), generates good/poor alternatives/solutions/positions.

Propriety–Impropriety

Distinguishes socially acceptable from unacceptable behaviors and acts on this understanding.
Able to identify and control behaviors harmful to self and others/contrary to acceptable rules/ beyond the limits of the community.
Does not display outlandish or bizarre behaviors inappropriate to social interactions.

Acts contrary to acceptable behavior.
Judgment intact in terms of understanding (e.g., the demand characteristics of social settings) but not in terms of behaviors.
Does not comprehend the expected/usual consequences of his/her behaviors or the impact/ impression upon others.
Inadequately cognizant/aware of basic social conventions.

Victimization

Engages in actions harmful to self.
Has been taken advantage of repeatedly.
Not discriminating in choice of companions.
Makes blatantly defective and self-damaging choices.

Might unwittingly enter a situation of jeopardy or be unable to extricate self from one.
Requires close support/monitoring to avoid loss/damage/exploitation.
Easily misled and swindled/misused/taken advantage of.
Judgment insufficient for independent living/assisted living.
Has a lifelong history of ineffective coping.

Other Statements

The client has difficulty with performing the tasks supportive of/related to carrying out the deci- sions made.
Given the defective quality of her/his thinking/understanding, judgment has to be impaired.
Evaluation of client's judgment, as based on a comparison with premorbid state or with expected ability based on intellect/age/education/social experience, is . . . (specify).

11.14. TEST JUDGMENT: SUMMARY STATEMENTS

The client gave reasonable responses to hypothetical judgment questions.

He/she responded appropriately to imaginary situations requiring social judgment/knowledge of the norms/usual rules/customs and expectations of society.

Performance on the judgment questions asked/tests used was poor/adequate/good/normal/ expected/excellent, which suggests that in the external/social/"real" world this client would . . . (specify).

11.15. REALITY TESTING

See also Section 11.13, above.

Intact, functional, not distorted by psychodynamics/defenses/psychopathology, perceives the social world as most people do, understands cause–effect links as other people do, shares common attributions of causality, functional/adequate/good/extensive fund of knowledge/awareness of the external world.

Defective reality testing, repeatedly makes poor judgments, easily mislead and taken advantage of, misinterprets common-sense reality, cannot anticipate others' reactions to her/his behaviors, overresponds to stimuli/others' behavior, distorted/idiosyncratic interpretations of events and their meanings, acts as if the world was as she/he would like it to be, lives in a fantasy world.

11.16. INSIGHT

See Section 2.23, "Insight into Disorder," for questions.

Nil or Little

No insight, blindly uncritical of own behavior, denies presence of psychological problems/illness/ symptoms, aware of problem but blames others/circumstances/physical factors/something unknown or mysterious for problems, rebuts psychological or motivational interpretations of behavior, fights the system and does little or nothing to help self, fatalistic resignation.

Denies (despite the evidence) that current symptoms are important or that he/she needs help, feels no need to change attitude/behavior/feelings in some specific way, minimizes/denies/ obfuscates/evades staff evaluations/findings during discussion.

Does not know what to make of her/his situation.

Superficial, shallow, platitudinous, difficulty in acknowledging the presence of psychological problems, self-deceiving, unable to focus on issues, lacks objectivity.

Some

Understanding is more peripheral than central or visceral.

Unable to make use of correct insights, only flashes of insight.

Doesn't understand self too well.

Is aware of not functioning up to capacity/potential.

Seems to recognize some symptomatology but not to have any understanding of its mechanisms or processes.

Continues trying to make sense of own psychotic thinking.

Has some insight into behavior, but apparently is not able to respond appropriately or perceive satisfactory solutions to life situation.

Full

Believes he/she is ill, recognizes need for treatment, came to treatment voluntarily, labels own illness, takes medicines, attends therapy sessions, works in therapy, acknowledges psychological/physical/historical limitations present.

Accepts that her/his symptoms/problematic behaviors/failures in adaptation are at least in part due to irrational thought/feelings/internal states/defenses/personal history, can identify the emotional/cognitive antecedents and consequents of symptomatic behaviors, recognizes relation of symptomatic behavior (e.g., alcohol abuse) to emotional states, acknowledges its impact on life's duration/quality/satisfaction.

Open to new ideas/perspectives on self and others, self-aware, psychologically minded, accepts explanations offered by caregivers, can apply understanding to change actions/direction of his/her life, understands causes/dynamics/treatments/implications of illness.

Understands outcomes of behavior and is influenced by this awareness, is able to identify/distinguish/comprehend behaviors contrary to social values/socially nonacceptable/personally counterproductive.

For a Disability Report: [✓ Note applicant's perception of relationship between injury/illness and psychological conditions.]

11.17. MOTIVATION FOR CHANGE: SUMMARY STATEMENTS

See also Chapter 23, "Prognostic Statements," Section 11.16, "Insight," and the "Responses to Treatment" heading under Section 12.36, "Substance Abuse and Use."

Motivation is limited by low frustration tolerance/dependency/ambivalence/low initiative.
Motivation is needed for change/therapy/habilitation/rehabilitation/self-improvement.
Client is aware of problems but is not yet sufficiently motivated to take action.
Client is powerfully motivated for change, as seen in . . . (specify).

11.18. DECISION MAKING

See also Section 11.13, above; see Section 2.21, "Decision Making," for questions.

The following groupings are sequenced by degree of increasing decision-making ability.

Easily confused, easily overwhelmed in choice situations, lacks understanding of options, fails to evaluate choices.

Indecisive, flounders, dithers, procrastinates, ponders endlessly, avoids decision situations, reverses decisions, wishy-washy, vacillates, ambivalent, seeks/requires others to decide.

Unable to carry out choices verbalized, deficient in carrying out instructions/in finishing tasks started, can make only simple/work-related decisions.

Decisive, effective, follows through, tolerates frustration/ambiguity/delay/errors/peers/setbacks/changes/ambival ence.

Ambivalence

Mixed feelings, conflicted, at cross-purposes, "left hand doesn't know what right hand is doing," alternates, "I want and don't want it at the same time," indecisive, can't decide/make up mind, repetitive weighing of alternatives, seeking of other options, stuck.

11.19. ABILITY TO LEARN

The following groupings are sequenced by degree of increasing ability to learn.

> Does not learn new information/material with repeated exposures, does not generalize learning to new problems/settings, little/no effect on behaviors from reward or punishment, requires special educational efforts and procedures.

> > Easily grasps concepts and methods on first trial, generalizes from earlier situations, uses theoretical models, alters own behaviors in light of experience/changed situation/requests from others, curious, attentive.

11.20. OTHER SUMMARY STATEMENTS FOR MENTAL STATUS

> This client appears to have impaired mental control functions.
> He/she seems unable to shift cognitive sets/rigid/inflexible/unable to learn or plan ahead.
> Defective sequencing ability is evident.
> A dementing process may be present. *(See Section 11.6, "Dementia.")*

> Client has only fleeting contact with "reality"/is internally entertained.

> Cognitive functioning seems limited rather than faulty.
> He/she showed a good balance of self-esteem/confidence and self-criticism.
> Cognitive functioning is intact based on my casual officed-based testing.

> This client is precocious/very learned/brilliant.

> Problem-solving ability is lacking/defective/distorted/limited by intelligence/disorder.

> Considering this client's age and education . . .

For a Child:

> This child showed evidence of soft neurological signs (incoordination, poor balance, poor speech, delayed development, etc.).

11.21. EVALUATION OF INTELLECT AND COGNITIVE FUNCTIONS

> See also Chapter 2, "Mental Status Evaluation Questions/Tasks," Section 13.27, "Personality Assessment," and Section 12.3, "Attention-Deficit/Hyperactivity Disorder."

Keep in mind that there are more kinds of "intelligence" than are assessed by widely available tests. Gardner (1983) has suggested seven.

If you suspect the presence of a learning disability, mental retardation, or any physical condition that would affect school performance, consultation with or referral to a school psychologist or educational specialist who can utilize the many specialized instruments for evaluation and remediation is usually appropriate.

There are thousands of published instruments for evaluation of almost any aspect of mental functioning, and hundreds of these have good reliability and validity. The ones listed below are the most popular and are well-standardized instruments. (Note that in these lists, commonly used acronyms are indicated as usual by underlined letters. In addition, when a test is known by the name of its originator or another word, the word is underlined.)

Child Development/Adaptive Behaviors

Adaptive Behavior Inventory for Children
Adaptive Performance Instrument
American Association on Mental Deficiency Adaptive Behavior Scale
Battelle Developmental Inventory
Bayley Scales of Infant Development II
Birth to Three Developmental Scale
Brigance Diagnostic Inventory of Early Development—Revised
Burk's Behavior Rating Scales
Callier–Azusa Scales
Camelot Behavior Checklist
Child Behavior CheckList (Achenbach)
Child Behavior Rating Scale

Conners Parent Rating Scale—Revised
Conners Teacher Rating Scale—Revised
Denver Developmental Screening Inventory
Developmental Activities Screening Inventory—II
Developmental Assessment for Severely Handicapped
Developmental Indicators for Assessment of Learning—Revised
Developmental Profile II
Normative Adaptive Behavior Checklist
Vineland Adaptive Behavior Scale
Vineland Social Maturity Scale

Intelligence (Screening)

McCarthy Scales of Children's Abilities
Peabody Picture Vocabulary Test—Revised
Expressive One Word Picture Vocabulary Test—Revised

Quick Test
Slosson Intelligence Test—Revised
Kaufman Brief Intelligence Test

Intelligence (More Precise Evaluations)

Wechsler Preschool and Primary Scale of Intelligence—Revised
Wechsler Intelligence Scale for Children—III
Wechsler Adult Intelligence Scale—III
   ✓ **Note**: All Wechsler tests offer a Verbal Intelligence Quotient, a Performance Intelligence Quotient, and a Full Scale Intelligence Quotient.)
The Stanford–Binet Intelligence Scale—Edition IV

Cattell Infant Intelligence Scale
Leiter International Performance Scale

Kaufman Assessment Battery for Children
Raven Progressive Matrices

Speech and Language

Bankson Language Test, Second Edition
Early Language Milestone Scale—2
Goldman–Fristoe Test of Articulation

Sequenced Inventory of Communication Development—Revised
Test Of Language Development—Primary-3

Educational Readiness, Ability, and Achievement

California Achievement Tests, Forms C/D
Detroit Tests of Learning Aptitude— Primary 3
Detroit Tests of Learning Aptitude—4

Differential Ability Scales
Illinois Test of Psycholinguistic Ability
Iowa Test of Basic Skills, Forms G and H

Kaufman Test of Educational Achievement—Comprehensive
Peabody Individual Achievement Test—Revised
Wechsler Individual Achievement Test
Jastak Wide Range Achievement Test—3
Woodcock–Johnson Psycho-Educational Battery—Revised
Test Of Written Language—3

MENTAL
STATUS

Learning Disabilities

Beery Developmental Test of Visual–Motor Integration
Clinical Evaluation of Language Fundamentals–3

Vocational Guidance

Differential Aptitude Tests Strong Vocational Interest Blank
Edwards Personal Preference Schedule Kuder Occupational Interest Survey
Self-Directed Search Geist Picture Interest Inventory

Neuropsychological Functioning

Halstead–Reitan Neuropsychological Test Battery
Luria–Nebraska Neuropsychological Battery
Stroop Color–Word Test
Bender Visual Motor Gestalt Test (with the Canter Interference procedure)

Memory

Wechsler Memory Scale-III, and the Russell modification
The Wechsler subtests of Digit Span, Digit Symbol, and Information
Benton Visual Motor Retention Test–Revised
Graham–Kendall Memory for Designs Test
Wide Range Assessment of Memory and Learning
Rey Auditory Verbal Learning Test
Rey-Osterreth Complex Figure Test with Meyers's norms
Clock Test
Rivermead Behavioural Memory Test
Denman Neuropsychology Memory Scale

Motor Development

Brazelton Neonatal Behavioral Assessment Scale
Peabody Developmental Motor Scales
Bruininks–Oseretsky Test of Motor Proficiency

11.22. CLASSIFICATIONS OF INTELLIGENCE

See Chapter 21, "Diagnostic Statement/Impression," for DSM-IV diagnoses and codes for Mental Retardation and Borderline Intellectual Functioning.

IQ Categories for Adults *For DSM-IV diagnoses, see Section 21.9.*

WAIS-R/WISC-III	IQ score range	% of population included in each
Very superior	130 and above	2.2
Superior	120-129	6.7
High average	110–119	16.1
Average	90–109	50.0
Low average	80–89	16.1
Borderline	70–79	6.7
Mentally retarded (WAIS-R) Intellectually deficient (WISC-III)	69 and below	2.2

This table is based on Wechsler (1981) for the WAIS-R, Wechsler (1991) for the WISC-III, and the DSM-IV (American Psychiatric Association, 1994).

Validity of Scores: Summary Statements

The obtained test scores are believed to be valid indicators of/significantly underestimate current intellectual functioning.

The scores are consistent with developmental history and degree of functional loss but not with potential, because . . . (specify).

Notes

✓ Weigh the levels of adaptive behavior (Activities of Daily Living, needs for assistance), as well as the results of intelligence testing (and the standard errors of these scores), into your diagnosis.

✓ Consider the potential effects of education, depression, dementia, distracting anxiety, relationship with the examiner, intercurrent medical illnesses, etc., on intellectual functioning.

✓ After 3 years from the date of the evaluation, test data and findings should be treated with caution, and should be trusted even less when the subject is/was a child.

✓ Generally, IQ scores below 40 are not meaningful.

✓ Consider the possibility that current functioning represents a decline; if so, offer an estimate of premorbid intelligence based on current subtest results, earlier testing, changed levels of adaptive behavior, etc.

12

Abnormal Signs, Symptoms, and Syndromes

In this chapter you will find ways to report areas of psychopathology that are not purely emotional/affective symptoms and disorders (for those, see Chapter 10) or purely cognitive dysfunctions (for those, see Chapter 11). It is a somewhat heterogeneous collection containing some actual DSM-IV diagnoses (such as Autistic Disorder, Conduct Disorder, and Schizophrenia), as well as many symptoms (such as compulsions, denial, hallucinations, and paranoia).

You are likely to be asked to evaluate conditions that are not yet formal diagnoses but are more than isolated symptoms. Some of these syndromes are included here: battered woman syndrome, chronic fatigue syndrome, Fetal Alcohol Syndrome, chronic pain syndrome, Premenstrual Dysphoric, and rape trauma syndrome. Other sections in this chapter address topics of similar concern, such as the risk factors for homicide and suicide, the commonly encountered and confusing side effects of medications, sexual "addiction," and malingering.

The topics are presented in simple alphabetical order.

12.1. ABUSE, PHYSICAL

See also Sections 12.5, "Battered Woman Syndrome," 12.20, "Impulse Control Disorders," and 12.32, "Sexual Abuse, Child."

The relevant DSM-IV codes are complex. *(See "Problems Related to Abuse or Neglect" in Section 11.21, "V Codes, Etc.")*

Consider the following risk factors for abusing families (described by Nietzel & Himelein, 1987):

Parents' histories: Experienced abuse/neglect, lack of parental affection, large families, started family early.

Current family status: Socially isolated/lack of social support, marital discord/conflict, impulsivity of parents, parental illiteracy, parental mental retardation, stressful situation (poverty, poor housing, etc.).

Parental child-rearing practices: Rarely praising children, strict demands, ignorance of development/unrealistic expectations, low level of supervision of children, early toilet training, dislike of caretaking, parental disagreement over child-rearing practices.

ADULT CHILDREN OF ALCOHOLICS   *See Section 13.8, "Codependent Personality."*

ABNORMAL SYMPTOMS

AFFECTS   *See Chapter 12.20, "Emotional/Affective Symptoms and Disorders."*

AGGRESSION   *See Section 12.20, "Impulse Control Disorders."*

12.2. AIDS DEMENTIA COMPLEX

The relevant DSM-IV code is 294.9, Dementia Due to HIV Disease.

ADC can appear in up to 60% of People Living With AIDS, as well as in some who are only HIV+. The following material is adapted by permission from Greenwood (1991). More information can be found in Kalichman (1995, 1996), Grant and Martin (1994), and Wallack et al. (1995).

Cognitive Changes (↔ by degree)

Loss of memories, inability to concentrate, loses train of thought in midsentence, mild confusion, absentmindedness, verbal deficits across intellectual/memory/language tests, mental slowness, forgets to practice safer sex, agitation, inability to speak, loss of self-care functions, unaware of degree of illness/losses, seizures, indifference to surroundings, hypersomnolence, coma.

Motor Dysfunctions (↔ by degree)

Leg weaknesses, unsteady gait, poor coordination, handwriting difficulties, tremor, paraplegia, incontinence.

Other Changes

Headache, lethargy, reduced sexual drive, apathy, indifference, suicide risk, withdrawal (especially in previously gregarious personalities), cerebral atrophy/edema/areas of demyelination.

✓ The Centers for Disease Control operate the Divisions of HIV/AIDS Prevention at http://www.cdc.gov/nchstp/hiv_aids/dhap.htm which has enormous resources.

12.3. ATTENTION-DEFICIT/HYPERACTIVITY DISORDER

See Sections 2.6, "Attention," and 2.7, "Concentration," for questions and Sections 11.4, "Atttention," and 11.5, "Concentration/Task Persistence," for descriptors.

The relevant DSM-IV codes are 314.00, ADHD, Predominantly Inattentive Type; 314.01, ADHD, Predominantly Hyperactive–Impulsive Type or Combined Type.

ADHD can be seen as a concentration disorder. Also consider high lead levels, heavy metal poisoning, maternal drug/alcohol use, etc., as causes of impulsivity, distractibility, low frustration tolerance, etc. Barkley's works (1998 and, for adults, 1994) are the standard references.

Behavior

Restless, fidgets, wriggles, twists, squirms, "antsy," much out-of-seat/off-task behavior, does not sit through an interview or meal, always "on the go," prefers to run rather than walk, climbs on furniture, hops/skips/jumps rather than walking, fiddles with objects, taps/hits and makes noises, moves unnecessarily, disrupts shopping and family visits, acts "wild" in crowded settings, babysitters complain about his/her behavior.

Shifts from one incomplete task to another, does not finish what she/he starts, play is frenetic/nomadic, rushes/jumps from one topic of conversation to another, avoids conversing at any length.

Noncompliant, does not obey instructions, does not sit when told to, breaks school/game's rules, unable to follow a routine, resistant, "sassy"/"talks back," argumentative   [✓ and these are not due to oppositional patterns or failure to understand the instructions, so child should not be called defiant].

Does not play quietly, talks excessively, does everything in the noisiest way, makes odd noises.

Needs constant/continual/one-to-one supervision/monitoring/teaching, needs closeness and eye contact to understand instructions, fails to attend to details in schoolwork or other activities.

Impulsive, blurts out answers, reacts without considering, acts before thinking, limited self-regulatory functions.

Senseless/repetitive/eccentric behaviors, darts around aimlessly, destroys toys and property.

Ignores consequences of own behaviors and so engages in physically dangerous activities.

Adapts to changes in situation/routine/personnel poorly.

Poor fine motor skills, is disorganized with possessions, clumsy, low concern for accuracy/neatness/quality of work, disregards instructions.

Has difficulty only at specific times, behavior/mood deteriorates during course of day.

Cognitive Features

Attention

Easily distracted, self-distracting, lessened ability to sustain attention/concentration on school task/work/play, low attending skills, often stares into space, reports daydreaming.

Needs/asks for repetitions of instructions, gets confused, doesn't "listen" although hears normally, inattentive to significant details, misses announcements, needs excessive individual supervision.

Low short-term memory skills (two- or three-step instructions), fails to remember sequences, loses place when reading, poor self-monitoring.

Academic Difficulties

Problems with counting/telling time/recognizing letters, adds/substitutes/reverses letters/words/sounds, copies letters and words poorly, word-finding difficulties, stops in middle of a sentence or thought, confuses/reverses word order in sentences, mistakes similar-sounding words.

Performs below ability level, refractory to usual instructional approaches, may seem unresponsive to punishment or rewards.

Disorganized Work Habits

Difficulty organizing schoolwork, does not study/prepare/organize/protect own work/do problem's steps in sequence, does not complete assignments on time, starts work before receiving instructions, has great difficulty organizing goal-directed activities, poor at gathering materials and sequencing activities toward a goal, fails to finish tasks, is destructive of materials, loses things necessary for an activity (such as toys, pencils, keys, assignments, books, equipment), unprepared for school assignments, does not use study times.

Affects

Unpredictable and unrelated mood changes, often depressed/blue/sad/pessimistic/gloomy, has low self-esteem/image, feels worthless, feelings are easily hurt/offended, cries easily or frequently, easily angered/upset, gets overexcited, irritable, easily frustrated/low frustration tolerance, no patience, impulsive, excitable, explosive, temper outbursts, unpredictable behavior.

Social Characteristics

Interrupts/intrudes/"butts in," talks out in class, talks out of turn, shouts/blurts out answers/comments, makes disruptive noises, does not wait turn in group situations, grabs others' possessions, breaks all school behavior rules.

Fights with sibs/peers/teachers, violent, aggressive, destructive, plays "tough guy/girl," often involved in physically dangerous activities without considering possible risks/dangerous consequences, hits/punches/strikes/kicks/bites, cries/withdraws, verbal conflict/insults/harasses/teases, coerces/intimidates/manipulates/"bosses," provokes/disrupts other children's activities, betrays friends, peers avoid/reject him/her, has great difficulty keeping friends.

Tolerates only a minimum of questions about mood/behavior, reacts adversely if pressed, avoids talking about own problems.

Other Proposed Subtypes of ADHD

The following list is adapted by permission from Horacek (1992).

Poor perseverance: Normal performance until time of onset of severe subjective boredom; loss of interest, fatigue, irritability, even sleep.

Frequent omission errors: Frequent 1- to 2-second gaps in attention, unawareness of mistakes.

Impulsivity: High vigilance so no errors of omission, but fails to inhibit responses to nontarget stimulus; the "oops" error; aware of error after the fact.

Variability of attention: High variability in response time, stimuli noted "in the nick of time," difficulty processing sequential information.

Hyperactivity: Distracting effect appears immediately upon testing and persists; may do better or normally if allowed great activity level, which may be self-arousing.

Distractibility: Performance normal in an environment low in or free from distractions, but very poor in real-world settings.

Overfocused: "Absent-minded professor" who may be bright, divergent-thinking, creative, "right-brained." May overcome attentional deficits with high motivation and cognitive strategies such as reasoning and memory. May do well in difficult subjects, but poorly in less stimulating classes requiring concrete information and memorization.

Mixed: A combination of some of the above; possibly also emotional overreactivity, learning disorders, anxiety disorders, obsessive–compulsive traits, or motoric traits.

Developmental Pattern of People with ADHD

Infancy: Very frequent crying, sleep difficulties, restless sleep, overactivity, difficult to soothe.

Preschool: Inattentiveness, overactivity, temperamental/emotional, misconduct/aggression, rejection by peers.

Elementary school: Overactivity, impulsivity, inattention, fidgeting, poor school achievement, low self-esteem, slightly below-average IQ, much subtest scatter/variability, clumsiness, disorganization.

High school: Restlessness, poor grades, rebelliousness, difficulty studying, lying, defiance, alcohol/drug use, failure to graduate.

Post-high school: Restlessness, poor concentration, impulsivity, motor vehicle accidents, alcohol/drug abuse, antisocial personality patterns, low self-esteem, emotional/behavioral problems.

Assessment

For accuracy, assessment of ADHD should involve at least one of these scales. I am particularly impressed with the ADDES series.

ACTeRS   ADHD Comprehensive Teacher's Rating Scale, Second Edition (Ullman et al., 1991).

ADDES	Attention Deficit Disorder Evaluation Scale, Second Edition (McCarney, 1995).
ADHDT	Attention-Deficit/Hyperactivity Disorder Test (Gilliam, 1995).
Brown ADD Scales	Brown Attention Deficit Disorder Scales (Brown, 1996).
CPRS-R	Conners Parent Rating Scale–Revised (Conners, 1996).
TOVA and TOVA-A	Tests Of Variables of Attention (Greenberg & Waldman, 1993).

Characteristics of Adult ADHD

General

Chronic forgetfulness, tardiness, relying on a sibling or spouse to remind one of commitments or to bring order to one's affairs; interrupting others' conversations; impulsiveness; poor-quality decisions/decisions without appropriate planning; easy anger/irritability, low frustration tolerance, poor emotional control; periodic depressions; heedlessness of the effect of statements on others.

Work

Taking on too many projects to complete them, poor time management; frequent job changes; underachievement compared to peers or sibs (despite intelligence); intense interest followed by boredom (even after substantial financial commitment); inability to stick with long-term projects.

12.4. AUTISTIC DISORDER

The relevant DSM-IV code is 299.00.

Autistic Disorder must be distinguished from Rett's, Asperger's, and Childhood Disintegrative Disorders, as well as from Mental Retardation (although 80% of autistic children have IQs ≤ 70).

Aloneness

Fails to develop attachment, no social smile, does not seek comforting from others or seeks it in strange ways when distressed/upset/frightened, ignores people, avoids eye contact, looks "through" people.

Emotionally distant, no affection or interest when held, going limp/stiff when held, preoccupied so is neither receptive to nor defensive of touch, does not need caregiver, unaware of caregiver's absence.

Lacks social give and take/reciprocity/modulation/resonance/mutuality, marked lack of awareness of the existence of feelings in others (lacks a "theory of mind"), lacks parallel or social play, plays alone, ignores/withdraws from/does not return affection, uses others in mechanical way, no friendships, lacks understanding of social rules.

Relates to inanimate objects, carries objects, ritual behaviors (see below).

Communication

Muteness   [✔ 50% of autistic children are mute], lack of verbal spontaneity/sparse expressive speech, does not imitate or does it strangely/mechanically, echolalia (immediate or delayed).

Affirmation by repetition (repetition of the question asked as agreement), pronoun reversal (referring to self in second and third persons and by name), neologisms, extreme literalness or "metaphorical language" (e.g., using a specific "No" situation to mean all other "No" situations), part–whole confusion (e.g., "ketchup" to mean dinner).

ABNORMAL
SYMPTOMS

Rituals and Compulsions

Preservation of sameness: Change in any aspect of daily routine or surroundings leads to persistent crying or temper tantrum.

Stereotypic behaviors: Manipulating things, rocking, hand flapping, tiptoe walking, spinning, twirling, staring at spinning things like fans.

Unpredictable/bizarre behaviors: Lunging, darting, sudden stops, swaying, head rolling.

12.5. BATTERED WOMAN SYNDROME

See Sections 3.2 and 3.4 for questions about physical and sexual abuse, and 12.1 for physical abuse risk factors. See also Section 12.28, "PostTraumatic Stress Disorder."

The relevant DSM-IV code is V61.1, Physical Abuse of Adult/Sexual Abuse of Adult.

Battered woman syndrome is a form of PTSD and so it has the core elements of arousal, avoidance, and intrusive memories (Walker, 1984, 1991).

Client needs assessment of the lethality/danger, various means of protection, and an escape plan.

Characteristics

Denial or minimization of the details of the abuse.   [✔ Paralleling the abuser's sense of entitlement and his denial—of responsibility, of the fact that it is "abuse," of its severity/consequences, etc.]

Fear of accusations of being crazy/exaggerating/making it up, if she seeks help.

Caught up in a cycle of violence.

Low self-esteem (especially efficacy).

Putting the abuser's needs first even at great cost to herself, remaining in a psychologically and physically harmful situation, passive and dependent behavior.

Types of Partner Abuse

Nonviolent: Overly calm talking, sulked, withdrew/isolated/ignored/shunned, yelled/swore, insulted, called names, threatened abandonment of children/support/obligations.

Intimidation: Prevented movement/restrained freedom/space, interrupted activities.

Threats of violence: Driving dangerously, with weapons, toward children/pets/spouse/relatives.

Violence: Threw items, pushed, painful restraint, wrestled.

Assault: Slapped, kicked, bit, punched, choked, raped.

Attempted murder: Severe beating, out of control, used weapon.

Ten Risk Factors

Presence of two of these factors doubles the rate of families with no factors; with seven of these factors, the rate is 40 times greater. However, remember that abuse occurs in all kinds of relationships, so **always ask every client**.

The following list is adapted from Geller (1992).

1. Male is unemployed.
2. If employed, male has blue-collar occupation.
3. Male uses illicit drugs at least once a year.
4. He saw his father hit his mother.
5. He did not graduate from high school.

6. He is aged 18–30.
7. Male and female have different religious backgrounds.
8. They cohabit and are not married.
9. They use severe violence toward the children in home.
10. Total family income is below poverty line.

BULIMIA *See Sections 3.12, "Eating Disorders," for questions, and 12.12, "Eating Disorders," for descriptors.*

12.6. CHRONIC FATIGUE SYNDROME

Chronic fatigue syndrome is also called "chronic postviral fatigue syndrome" and "chronic Epstein–Barr virus syndrome." See Krupp et al. (1991) for an overview.

Persistent/interfering/debilitating fatigue, 50% or more decrease from premorbid activity level, easily and persistently fatigued after little exercise, abrupt onset of fatigue, not relieved by rest.
Mild/low-grade fever, tender/palpable lymph nodes, inflammation of mucous membranes, sore throat, cough, chronic headaches, joint pain/muscle pain, diffuse pains, weakness.
Irritability, confusion, poor concentration, depression, photophobia, sleep disturbances.

CHRONIC PAIN SYNDROME *See Section 12.24, "Pain Disorder/Chronic Pain Syndrome."*

12.7. COMPULSIONS

See also Sections 3.8, "Compulsions," and 3.18, "Obsessions," for questions; see also Section 12.22, "Obsessions," for descriptors.

The relevant DSM-IV code is 300.3, Obsessive–Compulsive Disorder.

Goodman et al. (1989) have created an instrument for assessing obsessions and compulsions, called the Yale–Brown Obsessive–Compulsive Scale.

Greist et al. (1986) suggest this classification for rituals:

Cleaning of real or imagined contamination by dirt or germs (e.g., handwashing).
Repeating a ritual behavior a certain number of times.
Completing a sequence of actions correctly. Restarting from beginning if interrupted.
Checking and rechecking, especially locks, items of potential danger (e.g., knives, stove).
Meticulousness about the exact and proper location of objects.
Hoarding, collecting, or sorting or stacking of nonuseful objects.
Avoiding of contamination by rituals (to make unnecessary the need to clean).

Summary Statements:

Client denied problems with common compulsions.
Client engages in rituals for meals/sleep/dressing, house cleaning/washing/defecation, school or work tasks/other mental tasks, etc.
Client feels compelled to repeatedly check the house/kitchen/windows/doors/locks/dangerous objects/children, etc.
Client feels compelled to repeatedly touch/rub, count, order, arrange/rearrange objects.

12.8. CONDUCT DISORDER

See also Sections 12.23, "Oppositional Defiant Disorder," and 13.4, "Antisocial Personality."

The relevant DSM-IV code is 312.8.

DSM-IV types: Childhood-Onset Type, Adolescent-Onset Type.

For parent training approaches see Patterson and Forgatch (1987) and Forgatch and Patterson (1989).

Aspects

Will cheat/lie in order to win/be seen as the winner, believes others are against him/her or that he/she is being treated unfairly, makes an effort on a task or toward others only if it serves his/her interests, selfishly accepts favors without any desire to return them.

Aggressive, violent, dangerous, assaults, fights with anyone, threatens, intimidates, bullies, lies/cheats/breaks any rules/steals, denies truth/blames others, swears offensively/vulgarisms.

Violence toward property: Vandalism, deliberate destruction of property known to belong to others, firesetting, stealing, shoplifting, burglary, theft, auto theft, joyriding, purse snatching, armed robbery.

Violence toward people: Extortion/blackmail, physical cruelty to animals or people, mugging, assault, initiating physical fights, using a weapon.

Running away, truancy, trading sex for money/goods/drugs, coerced sexual activities, substance use before age 13 and recurrent use after 13.

Callousness, toughness, low frustration tolerance, temper, recklessness.

✓ Prognosis is worsened by ADHD, parental rejection, harsh discipline, absence of a father, delinquent friends, parental substance abuse.

CYCLOTHYMIA   *See Section 10.4, "Cyclothymia," for descriptors.*

12.9. DELUSIONS

See Section 3.9, "Delusions," for questions; see also Sections 12.25, "Paranoia," and 12.30, "Schizophrenia," for descriptors.

Degree of Confidence/Organization/Expression

(↔ *by degree*) Faint suspiciousness, distrust, pervasive distortions, magical thinking, personalized meanings, ideas of reference, allusions to trickery and deceit, believes in _____ but not in _____, not of delusional force, convinced of truth of . . . , formed delusions/deluded, lives in a fantasy world.

Fragmented, poorly organized, well organized, systematized/extensive system of beliefs.

The delusions are. . . .
  fixed/trusted/doubted/rejected/denied.
  extensive/circumscribed/isolated/encapsulated.
  shared with others/family members.   [✓ Shared delusions can be described as *folie à deux* or *à trois*; DSM-IV offers Shared Psychotic Disorder.]
  rarely/often/continually expressed.
  elicited easily/with difficulty/only with exceptionally trusted others.

Contents of Delusions

grandiosity	*persecution*	poverty	suicide	*somatic disease*
megalomania	ideas of		homicide	hypochondriasis
omniscience	reference	*erotomanic*	approaching	infection[1]
omnipotence	being followed	*wishes*	death	distorted body
extraordinary	being	sexual identity		image
abilities	influenced	alleged lover	self-deprecation	foul odors[2]
self-importance	misidentific-	infidelity	self-accusation	disfigurement[3]
special relation-	ation	jealousy	guilt	
ship with	special	"lovesickness"	derogation	voodoo
famous person	identity	zooanthropic	shame	occult
or deity	alien control		sin	communication
special mission	thoughts known	*religion*	blamelessness	with dead
for gover-	to others	nihilistic	innocence	mind reading
ment/religion	being ridiculed	fears		mental telepathy
			neglect of	foreknowledge
			an urgent	psychokinesis
			responsibility	ExtraSensory
			caused harm to	Perception
			befall another	
			contaminated	
			others	
			accidentally	

✓ Distinguish delusions (demonstrably false, unshakeable, and idiosyncratic beliefs, not supported by the social reality of the client's culture or subculture; for examples, see above) from "overvalued ideas" (idiosyncratic or shared beliefs that greatly influence the person's actions and seem exaggerated to the observer—e.g., morbid jealousy, racial superiority); from "illusions" (false but reasonable interpretations of perceptions—e.g., percieving someone lurking in a shadow); from *pseudologica fantastica* (storytelling where the true and false, imaginary and real are mixed); and from "hallucinations" (perceptions without sensations or without an objective stimulus for the perception; see Section 12.16 "Hallucinations," for examples).

Types of Delusions in Different Syndromes/Disorders

In mania: Grandiosity.
In depression: Guilt, somatic concerns.
In dementia: Ideas secondary to a perceptual disturbance.
In paranoia: Jealousy, persecution.
In schizophrenia: Being controlled, sometimes persecution, bizarre/impossible ideas.

12.10. DENIAL

Denial can be either adaptive or maladaptive. Breznitz (1988) identified several kinds of denial, which are listed below and illustrated with sample client statements.

---

[1] For example, parasitosis.
[2] Bromosis.
[3] Dysmorphophobia. Distinguished from dissatisfaction with appearance.

ABNORMAL
SYMPTOMS

Type	Example
Denial of provided information	"I never knew that." "No one ever told me about it."
Denial of information about a threat	"No one ever told me there was anything to worry about." "I never saw the risk involved."
Denial of personal relevance	"That doesn't apply to me, only others." "I have nothing to worry about."
Denial of vulnerability	"Nothing bad will happen to me."
Denial of urgency	"There is no rush." "I can think about that later."
Denial of emotion	"I'm not afraid/angry/hurt/upset by it."
Denial of the emotion's relevance	"Yes, I'm scared, but there is no reason to feel that way."

Other types of denial: of a problem's importance; of one's ability to change; of the problem's persistence; of the rationality or necessity of change.

12.11. DEPERSONALIZATION AND DEREALIZATION
See Section 3.10, "Dissociative Experiences," for questions.

The relevant DSM-IV codes are 300.6, Depersonalization Disorder; 300.15, Dissociative Disorder NOS.

✓ **Note:** Most symptoms of depersonalization and derealization can also be symptoms of temporal lobe epilepsy.[4]

Reports observing self from a distance/corner of the room, feels as if outside one's body, body appears altered.
Self-estrangement, extreme feelings of unreality/detachment from self/environment/surroundings, floating in the sky, "dreaming"/living a dream, feels as if the world were not real, sometimes not part of the world, feels mechanical/robot-like.
Experienced thoughts as not his/her own, felt as if body and mind were not linked.

✓ **Note:** Episodes are pathological if they are more frequent and of longer duration; occur with other symptoms; and are *not* related to single/severe psychological trauma, fatigue, sleep times, drug and alcohol use, medical illness, etc.

DEPRESSION   *See Section 3.5, "Affect/Mood," for questions; see Sections 10.5, "Depression," and 12.37, "Suicide," for descriptors.*

DEPRESSION, MASKED   *See "Masked Depression" under Section 10.5, "Depression."*

DISSOCIATIVE IDENTITY DISORDER   *See Section 13.11, "Dissociative Identity Disorder"*

---

[4] I am grateful to Frank O. Volle, PhD, of Darien, CT, for this insight.

12.12. EATING DISORDERS
See Section 3.12, "Eating Disorders," for questions.

Anorexia

The relevant DSM-IV codes are 307.1, Anorexia Nervosa; 307.50, Eating Disorder NOS.

Physical Presentation

Cachexia/cachectic, emaciated, amenorrhea, bradycardia, hypothermia, edema, weight loss of at least 15% without disease.

Cognitive Aspects

"Food phobia," morbid fear of gaining weight/becoming fat, distorted and implacable attitudes toward food, avoidance of "fattening" foods, overvalued ideas of/dread of fatness, obsessional, preoccupied with food, obsession with thinness.

Dissatisfaction with bodily appearance, distorted body image (believes she/he is always too fat), denial of exhaustion/hunger/illness, fear of pubertal changes.

"Positive" view of family, enmeshment with a parent, mother anxious/overprotective/indulgent/ self-martyring/martyrizing, denial of family conflict.

Perfectionism, self-disciplined, overly controlled, pride in weight management/self-inflicted starvation, overly critical of others, does not reveal feelings.

Behavioral Aspects

Laxative/diuretic misuse/abuse, fasting/starvation/reduced food intake, overexercising.

Ritualized food habits (cutting food into very small pieces, chewing for long periods), eating only low- and no-fat/calorie foods.

Social Aspects

Shy, compliant, dependent.

Sexual immaturity/inexperience.

Less antisocial behavior than bulimics.

Mistrusting of professionals.

Bulimia

The relevant DSM-IV codes are 307.51, Bulimia Nervosa; 307.50, Eating Disorder NOS.

Physical Presentation

Insomnia, constipation, lanugo, premature aging, hair loss, dental problems (erosion due to acid vomitus), amenorrhea, dehydration, weight fluctuations, cardiovascular disorders, electrolyte imbalances.

Near-normal weights (sometimes obese), great body weight fluctuations ($\geq$20 lbs. $\geq$5 times).

Irregular menstrual periods, intense hunger.

Cognitive Aspects

Distorted/irrational body image, overconcern with body appearance/shape/weight, dissatisfaction with bodily appearance, fear of obesity [✓ and this does not decrease as weight drops].

Inability to think clearly, dichotomous thinking, overpersonalization, perfectionism, rationalization of eating/symptoms.

Low self-esteem; weight central to self-evaluation, feels powerlessness about weight, lifelong dieting, self-loathing, disgust over body size.

Awareness that eating pattern is abnormal, preoccupation with food, craving/urges/hungers.

Behavioral Aspects

Purchases large quantities of food that suddenly "disappear," makes such purchases/eating "on the
spur of the moment," other people's food "disappears."

Frequently eats large quantities/high-calorie foods yet does not gain weight.

Hyperactivity, overexercising.

Frequent weighing, attendance at weight control clinics.

Overuse of laxatives/diuretics/cathartic/thyroid preparations/appetite suppressants.

Junk food consumption, binge eating, vomiting, sneaking binges, severely restrictive diets/fasting.

Shoplifting, sexual acting out, suicide attempts.

Social Aspects

Eating alone due to embarrassment over amount eaten, frequent trips to bathroom (for purging).

High achievement, academic success.

Oversensitivity to criticism, fragility, vulnerability.

More antisocial behavior than anorectics.

Impulsive.

Perceives intense family conflict.

More trusting than anorectics of professionals who want to help.

More sexually experienced than anorectics, dramatic.

Affective Aspects

Mood swings, depression, masked anger, specific affective precipitants of binge.

Feeling disgusted with self/self-deprecation, depressed/guilty/other marked distress over binge eat-
ing/vomiting.

Other Aspects

These factors may or may not matter:

Diet's composition (various foods or only some such as sweets, salty, snacks, etc.).

Dissociative qualities ("numb," "spaced out").

Higher-than-usual levels of various psychopathologies and medical conditions.

✓ If symptoms are more intense, consider diagnosis of Bulimia Nervosa; if less intense, consider diagnosis of Eating Disorder NOS.

Binge Eating Disorder

DSM-IV offers Binge Eating Disorder as a diagnosis for further study.

Eats larger quantity than normal, eats rapidly, eats alone, irritation or self-disgust after overeating,
doesn't purge.

Obesity   *See also "Weight" under Section 7.21, "Physical Appearance."*

Factitious, obsessional concerns, ___% overweight, obese, chronic/stable, overweight for height/
build, compulsive dieting, escalating weight over time/diets.

Pica

Eats lead, paint flakes, antifreeze, dirt, worms/insects, feces, other nonfood items.

Additional Note

✓ People can have eating disorders and present as morbidly obese, overweight, average-weight, underweight, maintaining periodic control, or unable to control compulsive eating. They may present with obsession over body size, weight, and shape; grazing, bingeing, compulsive dieting, or starving; overexercising, vomiting, and/or laxative/diuretic abuse; use of food as reward or for comfort; use of diet pills, quick-loss schemes, and/or medical/surgical interventions; etc.

12.13. EPILEPSY

There are more than 20 forms of epilepsy, which is a syndrome that can be caused by many diseases. In epilepsy, the brain has a tendency to produce bursts of electrical energy that disrupt other brain functions. Seizures are a symptom of epilepsy. Most seizures are benign, but a prolonged seizure can evolve into *status epilepticus*, a condition that sometimes leads to brain damage and occasionally death.

Types of Seizures

Partial (one brain area).
Simple partial (one brain area/function, usually motor).
Complex partial (one area/function and changes in consciousness—e.g., hallucinations, memory distortions—but no loss of consciousness).
Generalized (whole brain/many functions).
Tonic–clonic seizures (formerly called grand mal) begin with a tonic phase of limb rigidity, no breathing, eyes rolling upward, incontinence, and clenched jaws. After 30–60 seconds, a clonic phase of shaking persists for a few minutes, followed by a recovery of consciousness. The postictal phase includes confusion, a desire to sleep, headache, and sore muscles. There may be a preictal phase with sensory distortions, a sudden cry, etc.
Absence seizures (formerly called petit mal) show vacant staring, no falling, and rapid recovery; they may occur many times each day.
Rarer types.
Myoclonic (symmetrical shock-like limb contraction and possible loss of consciousness).
Atonic (brief loss of muscle tone resulting in a fall or head dropping).
Tonic (back arching with or without loss of consciousness).
Status epilepticus (continual or prolonged seizures, possible mortality).
Jacksonian (progressive "march" from partial to generalized).
Temporal lobe (variety of partial complex).

EXPLOSIVE DISORDER   *See Section 12.20, "Impulse Control Disorders."*

EXTRAPYRAMIDAL SYMPTOMS   *See Section 12.34, "Side Effects of Medications."*

12.14. FETAL ALCOHOL SYNDROME

Look for the following:

Size: Low weight and height, microcephaly (smaller-than-average head size).
Deformities of heart, genitals, kidneys, nervous system.

Face: Small eye slits, droopy eyelids, flattened nasal bridge, short/upturned nose, thin upper lip, malformed ears, short jaw, narrow forehead.
Mental retardation [✓ variable; IQ scores lower with age], developmental delays.
Incoordination, impulsiveness, poor speech/hearing.

12.15. GAMBLING, PATHOLOGICAL

The relevant DSM-IV code is 312.31, Pathological Gambling.

The genders are equally affected by pathological gambling, although the course may be different. High rates of substance abuse and suicidality are often found. Recreational gambling has a very high frequency among teens and students, and may progress after a big win to pathological gambling.

Summary Statements:

His thoughts and speech are filled with stories of and plans for gambling.
Her gambling is compulsive—anxiety-controlling, depression-reducing, showing habituation, felt as an irresistible impulse, chronic and repetitive, concealed, demonstrating superstitions/special techniques/rituals, etc.
He shows the typical cognitive distortions of gamblers: overconfidence in his ability to predict the outcomes, irrational expectations of a "big win" to compensate for losses/start over fresh, illusions of control or prediction of the outcome of a bet, poor sense of probabilities, systematic cognitive biases, poor decision-making procedures.
Her emotional reactions include remorse, lessened ambition, or lessened motivation.
Gambling is used as a way to compensate for frustration or disappointment.
His gambling has been socially/occupationally/financially harmful, he has borrowed money to gamble or gambled until out of money.

The South Oaks Gambling Screen (Lesieur & Blume, 1987) is a reliable assessment device of 20 items. DSM-IV offers 10 criteria to distinguish recreational from pathological gambling.

12.16. HALLUCINATIONS

See Section 3.14 "Hallucinations," for questions, and 12.30, "Schizophrenia," for more descriptors.

Hallucinatory experiences are also common in temporal lobe epilepsy.[5]

Sensory Modalities: Examples

Visual: Unformed/lights/flashes, formed/people/animals/things, Lilliputianism. *(See Section 12.19, "Illusions.")*
Tactile (haptic): Electricity, sexual sensations, tickling.
Kinesthetic: Creeping, crawling, biting, gnawing, twisting, churning, pains.
Auditory: Noises or voices (see below).
Olfactory: Disgusting/repulsive/objectionable odors (e.g., of death or disease).[6]
Gustatory: Poisons, acid, foul tastes.
Visceral/somatic: Phantom limb, "hollow insides," "rotting insides."
Vestibular: Sensations of flying, falling, lightness.
Synesthesia: Blending sense impressions (e.g., "It smells red").

---

[5]I am grateful to Frank O. Volle, PhD, of Darien, CT, for this perspective.
[6]Olfactory hallucinations are common in temporal lobe epilepsy as auras.

Auditory Hallucinations

Contents

Noises: Whistling, ringing.
Daymares, flashbacks.
Idiosyncratic themes: Presence of another person, or a doubled self, *doppelganger* (replacement of another/self).

✓ In the case of voices, note whose they are (if this can be identified), whether they are male or female, what their ages are, and whether they are clear or muffled. Note also the content of utterances (disconnected words, client's own thoughts, remarks addressed to client, etc.); Schneider (1959) notes that audible thoughts, voices arguing, and voices commenting are diagnostically most important.

Nature

Informative, friendly, benign, comforting, helpful, socially focused.
Arguing, dialoguing/conversing among themselves, commenting on thoughts/behavior/motives, grandiose.
Condemning, malevolent, accusatory, persecutory, harassing, hateful, spiteful, berating, threatening.
Controlling, seductive, compelling, premonitory, hortatory/imperative/commanding.
Conquering, menacing, consuming, terrorizing, constant, relentless, isolating.

Attitudes toward Hallucinations

(↔ *by degree*) Ego-alien, frightening, terrifying, "bizarre," resisted/struggled against, engages in conversations/dialogue with imaginary interlocutor, comforting, familiar, ego-syntonic, accepted.
(↔ *by degree*) Convinced of their reality, vivid fantasy, "altered state," impossibility, "only a fantasy," doubting its reality/own perceptions, making various efforts to control/cope with it, "rare."

Circumstances of Occurrence

Hypnagogic, hypnopompic, with delirium, in withdrawal, flashbacks, spontaneously, unbidden, cultural/situational anxiety/external stimuli influence the hallucinatory experience, having an undiscoverable relationship to circumstances.

Comparison of Organically and Psychogenically Based Hallucinations

Organically based	*Psychologically based*
Sharply demarcated.	Fleeting and transient.
Vivid and well formed.	Vague, shadowy, misty.
Polychromic and/or polysonic.	Usually in shades of gray.
Hypermobility (e.g., bugs creep).	
Accompanied by terror, apprehension.	
Perseverative quality.	
Patient *acts* as though he/she really sees/hears/ feels.	Patient has an idea that he/she sees, feels, etc., but then does not act consistently.
	May be associated with patient's psychodynamics.

ABNORMAL
SYMPTOMS

Summary Statements

Hallucinations are denied by the patient, but she/he seems to be responding to internal/unseen stimuli.

They involve small/moderate/great distortion of consensual reality.

The hallucinations are suspected/dialogical/undoubted/denied.

12.17. HEADACHE

This is a complex topic. The following are brief descriptions of common types of headache.

Tension Type

This is the most common headache type. Characteristics are as follows: Steady ache on both sides of head (bilateral); pressing or tightening/squeezing quality; mild to moderate intensity; not worsened by physical activity; no or mild nausea/no vomiting; sensitivity to light (photophobia) and/or sound (phonophobia). Lasts from 30 minutes to 7 days, and is distracting but not usually disabling. Responds to analgesics. Usually caused by high muscle tightness.

Migraine Types

"Common migraine" (from the Greek *hemikrania*—"half the head") afflicts 6% of men and 18% of women (although the percentages are equal before puberty). Characteristics: Pounding/throbbing/pulsating ache on one side (unilateral) of the head (in 60% of patients); moderate or severe pain; nausea, with or without vomiting; sensitivity to light and sound; worsened by activity. "Classical migraine" (experienced by 20% of migraneurs) involves unique sensory disturbances ("aura," from the Greek for "a warning wind") before headache. Usually migraine attacks are occasional, but they sometimes occur as often as once or twice a week (though not daily). An attack can last from 4 to 72 hours and can be quite disabling. It may respond to medications but not usually to analgesics. Attacks are caused by decreased regional blood flow and overcompensating dilation of cerebral arteries.

Cluster Type

About 1% of individuals (85% male), suffer a series of severe headaches over several days or weeks and then none for weeks to years. These are characterized by brief (1–2 hours) but severe pain (often around one eye, which becomes inflamed and watery) and nasal congestion on the affected side. There is often an "alarm clock" pattern (a headache occurs during sleep or at the same time each day). Sufferers commonly have a history of heavy smoking and drinking, with alcohol as a trigger.

Rebound Type

This type occurs among those with tension or migraine headaches and is due to daily use or overuse of prescription or nonprescription pain relievers.

Other Types of Headaches

Mixed types are common.

Sinus headaches also show low-grade fever, drainage, and tenderness over the sinuses.

Posttraumatic or postconcussion headaches may result from motor vehicle accidents or blows to the head, and usually involve a constant, dull pain. They often last 1–3 months but 85% of those affected recover over 1 year.

Pain from the TemporoMandibular Joint, or from eyes or ears, may become a general head pain (cephalgia).

Treatment

✓ Keeping a headache diary will help a client determine whether factors such as food, change in weather, and/or mood have any relationship to her/his headache pattern.

✓ Martin (1993) is an excellent guide to the psychological treatment of headache.

12.18. HOMICIDE RISK FACTORS

See also Section 12.20, "Impulse Control Disorders."

Intense wish to kill, specified or named victim, command hallucinations, ambivalent wish to kill, nonspecific hostility.

Violent/destructive/antisocial behaviors, violent acts in unrelated settings, arrest/assault repeatedly in the same setting, carrying of weapons, chronic problems with the authorities, criminal record.

Attempts to kill by stabbing/strangling/shooting, physical abuse causing harm, slapping/pushing/ punching, unpredicted destruction of objects.

Young male, little education, psychotic patient with delusions, substance abuse history, character disorder diagnosis.

No home/family/friends, no institutional support or involvement, has home but no one can observe the patient, family not interested in patient.

HYPERACTIVITY   *See Section 12.3, "Attention-Deficit/Hyperactivity Disorder."*

12.19. ILLUSIONS

See Section 3.14, "Illusions," for questions.

Sense deceptions, deceptive sensations, visual/auditory/tactile distortions, speeded-up or slowed passage of time, macropsia, micropsia, Lilliputianism, gigantism.

INTERMITTENT EXPLOSIVE DISORDER   *See Section 12.20, below.*

12.20. IMPULSE CONTROL DISORDERS

See Section 3.16, "Impulse Control/Violence," for questions. For descriptors, see also Sections 10.2, "Anger," 12.18, "Homicide Risk Factors," 12.37, "Suicide," 13.3, "Aggressive Personality," 13.4, "Antisocial Personality," 13.5, "Authoritarian Personality," and 13.22, "Sadistic Personality."

Types of Impulse Control Disorders

Intermittent Explosive Disorder (DSM-IV code, 312.34).
Kleptomania (DSM-IV code, 312.32).

Pathological gambling (DSM-IV code, 312.31).
Pyromania (firesetting) (DSM-IV code, 312.33).
Self-damaging/self-mutilating behaviors.
Sexual impulsivity, "nymphomania," "satyriasis," "sexual addiction" *(see Section 12.33).*
Trichotillomania (DSM-IV code, 312.39).

Degree of Control *(↔ by degree)*

overcontrolled	*patient*	*volatile*	*impulsive*	*violent*
armored	tolerant	loses temper	may attack	explosive
inhibited	controlled	"short fuse"	"blows his/	aggressive
denied	thoughtful	low frustration	her top"	combative
overcautious	deliberate	tolerance	impetuous	assaultive
rigid		quicksilver	hot-headed	dangerous
		quick-tempered	flares up	
cool-headed		"flies off the	lashes out	
restrained		handle"	abrupt	
self-possessed		"riled up"	precipitous	
staid		easily offended	unpredictable	
		excitable	incontinent	
		irritable	reckless	
		easily irritated	outbursts	
			leaves situation	
			hasty	
			rash	

What Person Fears Doing

Embarrassing self, losing control, "wetting pants"/losing bladder control, fainting, harming self or others, homicidal ideation/threats/behavior, not being able to resist impulses to commit delinquent or illegal acts.

Reason's Influence

Acts without weighing alternatives, likely to act without consideration of alternatives/with little hesitation, unreflective, acts without examination, unmediated, "acts on spur of the moment," easily agitated, off-handed/ill-considered actions, self-centered actions, seeks immediate gratification of urges, heedless, willful, limited intellectual control over expression of impulses, poor planning.

Targets of Violence

Objects, property, self, family, strangers, women, children, animals, authority figures, peers, elderly/weaker persons, any available target, inside/outside the home.

Antisocial Behavior   *See also Section 13.4, "Antisocial Personality."*

Obstructiveness, irresponsibility, cheating, lying, stealing, crimes, arrests, fighting, forceful aggression.

Correlates of Serious Aggression

Tortures animals.
Commits hidden aggressive acts.

Fights with weaker opponents.
Pride in history of aggression.
Profitless damaging of property (especially one's own).
Apparently purposeless aggressive actions.
Careless of risk of self-harm when acting aggressively.
"Out of control" when aggressive.
Plans aggressive actions.

Other Variables to be Evaluated for Assessment of Violence

This list is based on work by Beck (1990).

History of violence before mental health diagnosis/treatment.
Mental status: Defective judgment, arousal level, psychosis, impaired consciousness.
Impulsiveness, as seen in history of driving violations, spending money, sexual/social relationships, risk-taking behavior, work history.
Use of intoxicants, history of drug/alcohol abuse.
Availability of weapons/victims.
Childhood exposure to violence/abuse/neglect, chaotic family, violent subculture.
Instability: Frequent moves, firings.
Ability to vent frustration/anger nonviolently: verbal skills, intellect, coping mechanisms, support system.
Need for external controls when internal ones are lacking/defective/easily overcome.

Characteristics of violent behaviors:
    Location, time, frequency, others present or alone, method, relationship with object of violence, lethality of method.
    Motives/benefits/perceptions, threats, precipitants.

Other behaviors: Postural tension (on chair's edge, gripping edge), voice (loud, strident), motor activity (restlessness, pacing, leaving), startle response (easily, full).

Factors Associated with Violence Recidivism

This list is based on work by Monahan (1981).

Criminal history: Recidivism increases with each prior criminal act. Risk of recidivism exceeds 50% with more than five prior offenses.
Age: Youth is highly associated with crime. Greater risk if a juvenile at first offense.
Gender: Males are much more violent.
Race: African-Americans are at higher risk.
SocioEconomic Status: Lower status and job instability.
Drug and alcohol abuse history.
Nonstable, nonsupportive family environment.
"Bad company" peers and associates.
Greater availability of victims: Either a broad range of victims, or repeated assaults on a narrow class of victims who remain available (e.g., girlfriends).
Access to weapons.
Access to alcohol.

INSIGHT   *See Section 11.16, "Insight," for descriptors.*

LATE LUTEAL PHASE DYSPHORIC DISORDER
See Section 12.27, "PreMenstrual Dysphoric Disorder."

12.21. MALINGERING
See also Section 13.13, "Hypochondriacal Personality."

The relevant DSM-IV code is V65.2.

According to Rogers (1997) and contrary to DSM-III-R, this condition is not rare, not easy to detect, and not a global response style; is not significantly correlated with psychopathy or criminality, or with the presence of other valid psychiatric symptoms; and is not easily detected on psychological testing.

Better criteria for malingering of mental disorders include the following:

1. Highly atypical symptom presentation (rare, blatant, absurd, contradictory, indiscriminate, rapidly changing). Rogers (1984) offers these: Client recounts symptoms of extreme severity, endorses a large number of symptoms, describes symptoms inconsistent with clinical formulations and diagnostic impressions, exhibits a "heightened" recall of psychological problems.
2. Noncorroboration of this presentation by interviews with collaterals, or by psychological or medical tests.
3. Exclusion of patients with diagnoses of borderline personality or factitious motivations.

Adams (1991) adds the following as markers of possible malingering:

4. Patient's being directly referred by an attorney.
5. Marked discrepancy between claimed disability and objective findings.
6. Lack of cooperation with either evaluation or recommendations.
7. Antisocial personality disorder or traits.

The following criteria for differential diagnosis of symptoms suggesting physical illness are suggested by Hyler and Spitzer (1978), the footnotes have been added.

Diagnosis	Can a known physical mechanism explain the symptom?	Are the symptoms linked to psychological causes?	Is the symptom under voluntary/conscious control?	Is there an obvious goal?
Conversion	Never	Always	Never	Sometimes
Malingering	Sometimes	Sometimes	Always	Always*
Psychosomatic disorders	Always	Always	Never	Sometimes
Factitious disorders	Sometimes	Always**	Always	Never (other than medical attention)***
Undiagnosed physical illness	Sometimes	Sometimes	Never	Never

*Such as money, avoiding responsibility, controlling others.
**Symptom amplification for unconscious needs.
***Or being seen as ill or injured.

Terms for similar presentations: Malingering, simulation, exaggeration, magnification of pain and disability, overevaluation, functional overlay, conversion hysteria, supratectorial factors, conscious embellishment/amplification.

Another excellent educational resource is Pankratz (1998).

MANIA   *See Section 10.7, "Mania," for descriptors.*

MULTIPLE PERSONALITY   *See Section 13.11, "Dissociative Identity Disorder," for descriptors.*

12.22. OBSESSIONS
See Section 3.18, "Obsessions," for questions. See also Sections 13.19, "Obsessive Personality," 3.8, "Compulsions," 12.7, "Compulsions," and 11.9, "Stream of Thought."

The relevant DSM-IV code is 300.3, Obsessive–Compulsive Disorder.

Monomania, monothematic thought trains, repetitive themes, egomania, megalomania, overvalued ideas (e.g., dysmorphophobia).
Contamination/cleaning: Touching or being touched, bodily excretions, clothing, dirt/trash/contaminants, animals, resulting illness of self or other.
Sexual: Erotomania, children/incest, homosexuality in heterosexuals, aggressive sexuality, "perversities."
Religious: Sacrilege, blasphemy, morality, right/wrong.
Somatic: Illness or disease, body parts.
Other: Colors, sounds, music, names, titles, numbers, phrases, memories, unpleasant images, impulses (hurt, blurt, harm, steal, cause disaster), not/saying certain things, not losing things, needing to remember, etc.

12.23. OPPOSITIONAL DEFIANT DISORDER
See also Sections 12.8, "Conduct Disorder," and 13.4, "Antisocial Personality."

The relevant DSM-IV code is 313.81.

Stubbornly resists others' ways of doing things, independent, stubborn, noncompliant.
Argumentativeness, talks back, "sasses," insubordinate, challenges, disputes.
Irritability, resentfulness, negativism, provokes others, mean, spiteful, rude.
Always places blame on others.
Temper outbursts or tantrums.

12.24. PAIN DISORDER/CHRONIC PAIN SYNDROME
See Section 3.20, "Pain, Chronic," for questions.

The relevant DSM-IV codes are 307.80, Pain Disorder Associated with Psychological Factors; 307.89, Pain Disorder Associated with Both Psychological Factors and a General Medical Condition.

Miller (1993) provides a good brief overview.

Pain Behaviors

Groans, flinches, winces, grimaces, grits teeth.

Slow and careful movements/body placements, assumes/maintains odd positions, needs to shift position/stand/walk/stretch frequently.

Takes multiple/ineffective medications.

Increased resting ("down"/"horizontal"/bed) time and decreased active ("up/vertical") time, appears fatigued, decreased sleep effectiveness.

Decreased or absent sexual activity/duration/frequency/interest.

Interference with appetite, and associated weight change.

Lessened concentration.

Mood

Restricted range and intensity of expression.

Irritability, "cranky," anger, threatening, low frustration tolerance.

Overly disrespectful/critical.

Depressed, demoralized, pessimistic, expressions of hopelessness re: change/improvement/return to work, intermittent depressions as reaction to pain's exacerbation.

Thought Content

Preoccupied with losses/accommodations/somatic conditions/treatments/pains/symptoms/health status and its implications, focus on small signs of progress, may create illusory correlations of pain/limitations/depression/symptoms with progress/change/bodily processes.

Ruminations concerning "Why me?"/causation/revenge/financial concerns.

Feels "like a cripple," "worthless," helpless, optimistically reports "learning to live with it/the pain" but without change.

Desperate for the situation to change but doubting the effectiveness of any intervention.

Has a sense of entitlement, focuses on the unfairness of the situation.

Inward focus on physical self that is not hypochondriacal but a reaction to chronic pain.

Suicidal ideation in the form of passive death wishes.

Feels/believes self harassed/unappreciated by current or former employer(s) or by worker's compensation boards/insurance companies/Social Security Disability, resentful of unfair way treated by helpgivers/insurance carriers.

Reports being "sick and tired" of pursuing insurance claims/being medically evaluated/filling out forms/"jumping through hoops" to obtain only what is rightly his/hers.

Social Aspects

Decreased social activities, withdrawal/isolation, decreased/absent recreation.

Adopts role of "patient": dependency, passivity, helplessness, avoidance/displacement of responsibility, medical/biological model of pain and recovery, seeks a "miracle cure" vs. accepts limitations and "tries another way," etc.

Wants to be believed more than relieved, concerned that her/his symptoms be accepted as authentic.

Assessment

For some clarity of the evaluation of the psychogenicity of pain, see Thomas Hackett's (1978) MADISON scale. He believes that pain is more likely to be psychological if the client shows the following: Multiplicity of varieties and locations, Authenticity or need to be believed, Denial of emotional problems or of the effects of emotions on pain, Interpersonal relationships affecting the pain, Singularity/uniqueness of the pain problem/this patient, "Only you can help me," and Nothing helps or changes the pain.

For more detailed documentation of the pain, use the McGill–Melzack Pain Questionnaire in Turk and Melzack (1992), Melzack and Wall (1983), Feuerstein and Skjei (1979), and Hase (1992).

12.25. PARANOIA

See Section 3.21, "Paranoia," for questions; see also Sections 12.9, "Delusions," and 13.20, "Paranoid Personality."

The relevant DSM-IV codes are 295.30, Schizophrenia, Paranoid Type; 301.0, Paranoid Personality Disorder.

The following groupings are sequenced by degree of increasing paranoia:

Not paranoid, denies any special powers or missions, feels that she/he is quite well treated by individuals and the community.

Believes self to be exceedingly virtuous, denies that he/she distrusts others, persistently naive about other's motives, believes self to be especially sensitive, overvalues own subjective knowledge.

Alert watchfulness, demonstrations of suspiciousness, distrust, belief that everything is not as it should be, paranoid trends, persecutory ideas, reports paranoid ideation, feels scrutinized, systematized delusions, reinforced delusions.

Pervasive suspiciousness about everyone/everyone's actions, inappropriate suspiciousness, expects people to seek retribution, views people as vindictive, sees self as victim of others/enemies/vendetta, partially supported delusions, likely story of persecution/evidence of persecution, on guard, hyperalert, vigilant, wary, spied on, plotted against, attempts made to harm, attacks, attacks foiled.

✓ Note whether the client demonstrates a paranoid mode of thinking/cognitive style (see Shapiro, 1965):

1. Suspiciousness.
2. Protective thinking (selective attention to confirm suspicions and blaming of others for own failures).
3. Hostility.
4. Paranoid illumination ("Now everything makes sense").
5. Delusions of influence, persecution, and grandiosity.

✓ Note also whether the person demonstrates Cameron's (Cameron & Rychlak, 1968) "pseudocommunity" of all those united in a plot against him/her.

12.26. PHOBIAS

See Section 3.22, "Phobias," for questions, and Section 10.3, "Anxiety/Fear," for descriptors.

The relevant DSM-IV codes are 300.29, Specific Phobia; 300.23, Social Phobia; or the codes for diagnoses involving Agoraphobia (which does not have a code number to itself).

Phobias involve persistent, recognized-as-unrealistic fears; high levels of circumscribed anxiety; and avoidance of the anxiety-arousing situations/animals/social settings/persons.

Types of phobias include traumatically learned phobia, animal phobias, "school phobia," social phobia, agoraphobia, acrophobia, algophobia, claustrophobia, xenophobia, and zoophobia. About 375 named phobias are listed in an appendix to the *Blakiston's Gould Medical Dictionary* (1972). "Homophobia" is more likely a part of a personality disorder. *(See Sections 13.5, "Authoritarian Personality," and 13.20, "Paranoid Personality.")*

12.27. PREMENSTRUAL DYSPHORIC DISORDER

DSM-IV offers PMDD as a diagnosis for further study. Be careful in using this diagnosis, as its rationale has mixed research support and is obviously gender-specific.

PMDD is a more severe form of PreMenstrual Syndrome. Disabling symptoms of PMS, occurring in the week before menses, have been described by Rubinow and Roy-Byrne (1984) and Severino and Moline (1989) and are summarized below.

Vegetative Aspects

Appetite/eating changes, anorexia, craves specific foods.
Sleep changes/hypersomnia/hyposomnia/insomnia, lethargy/fatigue, stays in bed/naps.

Affective Aspects

Depression, hopelessness.
Mood swings, feeling overwhelmed/stressed, sadness, suicidal ideation, crying.
Anxiety, tension, "on edge," restlessness, persistent anger/irritability, lability.
Decreased interest in activities.
In some cases, affectionate.
Excitement, well-being, burst of energy/activity.

Pains

Cramps, headache, mastalgia, joint/muscle pain, general aches and pain, muscle stiffness, backache.

Autonomic Nervous System Aspects

Nausea/vomiting, palpitations, sweating/cold sweats, "hot flashes/flushes," dizziness, fuzzy vision, numbness/tingling, heart pounding, chest pain, ringing in ears, feeling of suffocation.

Fluid Balance

Weight gain, "bloating," edema, breast tenderness/swelling.

Cognitive Aspects

Lessened concentration/distractibility, forgetfulness, confusion, lowered judgment, indecision.
Decreased efficiency, lowered school or work performance, accidents, motor incoordination, decreased orderliness.
Impulsivity.

Interpersonal Aspects

Distrust, oversensitivity to rejection, isolation, avoidance, loneliness.

Dermatological Aspects

Acne, greasy/dry hair.

12.28. POSTTRAUMATIC STRESS DISORDER/SYNDROME

The relevant DSM-IV code is 309.81.

Components and Symptom Clusters for Evaluation

Affective Symptoms

Emotional numbing, deadening, lack of emotional responsiveness to usual experiences, patterns of avoidance.

Cognitive Symptoms

Decreased concentration and memory functioning.
"Flashbacks," reexperiencing/reliving of the traumatic situation, intrusive memories.
Foreshortened future, believes will not have a family/career/normal lifespan.

Behavioral Symptoms

Avoidance of stimuli similar to or elements of the original traumatic situation because these cause experiences of recall.
Worsening of symptoms when in situations like the original.
Symptoms of increased arousal/secondary symptoms (easy startling, vigilance, sleep disturbance).
Impulsive behaviors.
Control loss leading to violence.

Social Symptoms

Fear of intimacy, general alienation.
Intolerance of authority.
"Survivor guilt," integrity problems (feelings of betrayal, responsibility for acts of omission/commission, personal responsibility and guilt).

Considerations for Veterans

Vietnam Veterans

Stressors/traumatic events could include receiving incoming fire, receiving sniper fire, having a unit on patrol ambushed, having a unit engage in a firefight, patrolling rivers, etc. Integrity problems may include feeling betrayed by the government or by how the war was fought.

World War II Veterans

Symptoms by decreasing frequency in World War II vets with "combat fatigue" were as follows (Archibald & Tuddenham, 1965):

Depression, restlessness, irritability, poor sexual adjustment, poor economic adjustment, excessive jumpiness/startle response, easily fatigued, waking during night, difficulty concentrating, sweaty hands/feet, severe headache, difficulty falling asleep, memory difficulties, momentary blackouts, dizziness, excessive smoking, abdominal discomfort, heart palpitations, combat dreams, pervasive disgust, shortness of breath, sighing and yawning, diarrhea, difficulty swallowing.

Key Features of PTSD

Pies (1993) has developed the TRAUMA model as a way of summarizing PTSD's key features:

Trauma or actual harm outside normal range.
Recurrent disturbing dreams, recollections.

ABNORMAL SYMPTOMS

Avoidance of troubling memories, Amnesia for key events of trauma.
Unwanted images, "flashbacks."
Markedly diminished interest.
Autonomic overactivity, Anger outbursts.

PREOCCUPATIONS

See Sections 11.9, "Stream of Thought," 12.9, "Delusions," and 12.22, "Obsessions," for content.

12.29. RAPE TRAUMA SYNDROME

The following is adapted by permission from Burgess and Holmstrom (1974).

Acute Phase

Impact

Shock/disbelief, controlled style or expression of high emotion (e.g., crying), anger, anxiety, restlessness, tenseness.

Somatic Reactions

Physical trauma such as bruising, muscle tension (headaches, fatigue), sleep disturbances (insomnia, crying out), startle reactions, gastrointestinal (stomach pains, appetite, nausea), genitourinary (discharge, itching, burning, pain, rectal bleeding/pain).

Affective Reactions

Fear of violence and death, humiliation/embarrassment, anger, revenge, self-blame.

Long-Term Phase

Changing residence/phone number, taking trips, visiting family for support, nightmares, traumatophobia (fear of cues for recall of rape—e.g., being indoors/outdoors, alone/crowds, people coming up behind victim, sexual behaviors).

Silent Rape Reaction

Reaction to a previous undisclosed rape–like delayed PTSD.

12.30. SCHIZOPHRENIA

See also Sections 11.9, "Stream of Thought," 12.9, "Delusions," and 12.16, "Hallucinations."

The relevant DSM-IV codes are as follows: 295.10, Schizophrenia, Disorganized Type; 295.20, Schizophrenia, Catatonic Type; 295.30, Schizophrenia, Paranoid Type; 295.60, Schizophrenia, Residual Type; 295.90, Schizophrenia, Undifferentiated Type.

"Schizophrenia" is so called because of the split between thoughts and feelings that is involved (note that it does not mean "split personality"). It includes what Eugen Bleuler (1911/1968) referred to as the "four A's": disorders of Association, Affect, Ambivalence, and Autism.

Schneiderian or First-Rank Symptoms

The following list is based on Schneider (1959).

Primary delusional perception (a common perception that takes on special significance and is elaborated in a delusional way).
Passive reception of a somatic sensation imposed from an outside agency.
Thought transmission, broadcasting, insertion, withdrawal, or interference.
Clouding.
"Made" (externally directed) impulses (delusions of somatic passivity).
"Made" volitional acts.
"Made" feelings or sensations.
Voices arguing with the subject in the third person, calling his/her name.
Voices making a continuous commentary on the subject's actions.
Voices speaking the subject's thoughts aloud (*écho de pensées*).

Positive versus Negative Symptom Patterns

Factor	Type I: Positive subtype (behaviors not usually found in normal persons)	Type II: Negative subtype (absence of behaviors usually found in normal persons)
Diagnosis:	Paranoid, Undifferentiated, Disorganized, Catatonic, Residual.	"Simple."
Symptoms:	Positive: Behavioral excesses. Hallucinations, delusions (q.v.). Thought disorder, incoherence. Bizarre or disorganized behavior.	Negative: Behavioral deficits. Alogia: Poverty of speech and thought processes, vagueness, blocking, great latency. Flattened affect, anhedonia. Asociality, withdrawal. Avolition, apathy. Attentional impairment. Psychomotor retardation, monotone.
Brain abnormalities:	Overactivity of dopamine in limbic system; normal CT scans.	Underactivity of dopamine in frontal cortex. Enlarged ventricles.
Intellectual impairment:	Minimal.	Significant.
Premorbid functioning:	Better.	Worse.
Onset:	Acute.	Insidious.
Gender:	More women.	More men.
Course:	Episodic, exacerbations, and remissions.	Chronic.
Response to treatment:	Favorable response to older neuroleptics.	Poor response to older neuroleptics.
Prognosis:	More likely to return to previous level of functioning.	Less likely to return to previous level of functioning.
Social functioning:	Normal social functioning between remissions and exacerbations.	Poor social functioning in social, vocational, educational, relationship areas.

SCHNEIDERIAN SYMPTOMS   *See Section 12.30, "Schizophrenia," for descriptors.*

12.31. SCHOOL REFUSAL/"PHOBIA"

School "phobia" is not truly a phobia, as the child is not (usually) afraid of school (a bad teacher, a bully, etc.—always ask), but is fearful of abandonment by or harm coming to the caregiver.

The following comparison of two types of school "phobia" is adapted by permission from Kennedy (1965):

Early onset	*Late onset*
Present case is the first episode.	Present case is second, third, etc.
Monday onset, following illness previous Thursday or Friday.	Monday onset not too common.
Acute onset.	Incipient onset.
More common in lower grades.	More common in upper grades.
Expresses concerns about death.	Absence of death theme.
Mother/caregiver is ill or child believes she is.	Health not an issue.
Good parental communication.	Poor parental communication.
Parents well adjusted.	Mother neurotic, father character-disordered.
Parents competitive in household management.	Father uninterested in children, household.
Parents easily understand dynamics of refusal.	Parents difficult to work with.

SEASONAL AFFECTIVE DISORDER   *See Section 10.8, "Seasonal Affective Disorder," for descriptors.*

12.32. SEXUAL ABUSE, CHILD
See Section 3.4, "Abuse (Sexual) of Child or Adult," for questions.

The relevant DSM-IV code is V61.21, or 995.53 if the focus of clinical attention is on the victim.

Physical Aspects

Genital or anal area pain/swelling/itching/bleeding, bruises, torn/stained/bloody underwear, frequent urinary tract infections, painful urination, vaginal or penile discharge, symptoms of Sexually Transmitted Diseases, pregnancy.

Behavioral Aspects

Unexplained changes in eating habits, sleeping habits (nightmares and insomnia), difficulties in sitting or walking, excessive masturbation, indiscriminate hugging/kissing/seductive behaviors with children and adults.

Affective Aspects

Excessive, and especially sudden, fearfulness about particular persons or places.

Social Aspects

At home/play: Clinging, withdrawal, regression, poor peer relations.
At school: Refusal to attend, absences, drop in grades, refusal to attend or participate in physical education, arriving early or leaving late.

Cognitive Aspects

Premature knowledge of sexual behaviors, changes in fantasy play to themes of sexuality or harm.

✓ You know that all suspected child abuse (sexual or physical) must be reported. The Child Help USA Hotline is (800) 4 A CHILD. Your state or local number is _____ (fill in).

12.33. SEXUAL IMPULSIVITY/"ADDICTION"/"COMPULSION"

The following characteristics have been described by Barth and Kinder (1987):

Preoccupation with sex.
Feel driven to seek out sexual encounters.
Have sexual encounters even with the risk of disease/arrest/shame/embarrassment.
Feel regret/depression/suicidal ideation afterwards.
Childhood history of restrictiveness (leading to acting out) or neglect/abuse (leading to seeking gratification as escape).

12.34. SIDE EFFECTS OF MEDICATIONS

The most easily available source of information is the *PDR Guide to Drug Interactions, Side Effects, Indications, Contraindications,* in its latest edition. The following material is based on the work of Bernstein (1989), except where noted.

Behavioral Effects

Fatigue, lethargy, weakness, psychomotor retardation, excessive sedation.
Drowsiness, sleepiness, oversleeping.
Insomnia, nightmares.

Cognitive Effects

Confusion, delirium, internal tension.

Neuromuscular Effects

Akinesias, akathesias, dystonias, Tardive Dyskinesia. *(See Tardive Dyskinesia below.)*
Reduction of the seizure threshold.

Parkinsonian Effects

Reduced arm accessory movements, cogwheel rigidity.
Mask-like facial expressions, "woodenness."
Shuffling gait.
Resting tremors, restlessness, bradykinesia.
Involuntary muscle movements: lip smacking, tongue rolling/thrusting, jaw clenching, drooling/excessive salivation, tics, tremors, dyskinesias, oculogyric crises, torsion spasms.

Other Bodily Reactions

Blurred vision, other visual problems.
Dryness of mouth, decreased sweating, difficulty voiding/urinary retention, constipation.
Cardiac rhythm changes, postural hypotension, pallor/flushing, impaired temperature regulation (risk of heatstroke), agranulocytosis.
Itching, eczema, uticaria.
Weight gain.
Irregular menstruation, difficulty with erection/"impotence," delayed ejaculation, decreased sexual drive, breast enlargement.
Photosensitivity.
Liver problems.

Neuroleptic Malignant Syndrome

NMS is a potentially life-threatening, fairly rare reaction to just about any neuroleptic medication (it affects 1% or fewer of those taking such drugs). Pelonero et al. (1998) provide a comprehensive review on diagnosis and treatment.

Severe Parkinsonian rigidity with high fever, Autonomic Nervous System instability (flushing/pallor, unstable blood pressure, diaphoresis, tachycardia), elevated consciousness, altered Creatine PhosphoKinase, increased white blood cell count.

Tardive Dyskinesia

TD usually occurs after 3–6 months, but it can begin after up to 6 years of treatment. Although it is often irreversible, many recover.

Irregular/spastic/choreiform or slow/writhing/athetoid movements, usually involving mouth (chewing, swallowing, licking, sucking, tongue movements, blinking, grimaces) and sometimes fingers.

Acute Dystonic Reaction

Spasms of the neck/trunk/muscles of the eyes (usually occurring within the first few days of neuroleptic medication), torticollis, retrocollis, hip rocking, oculogyric crisis, laryngeal spasm.

12.35. SLEEP DISTURBANCES

See Section 3.25, "Sleep," for questions.

The relevant DSM-IV code for most is 307.4x.

✓ Avoid the use of the term "insomnia" alone, as it has multiple meanings and so is vague.

Types of Sleep Disturbances

Difficulty Falling Asleep: Initial insomnia, sleep latency.
Sleep Continuity Disturbance: Interrupted/broken/fragmented sleep, middle insomnia.
Early Morning Awakening: Terminal insomnia   [✓ frequent in depression].

The sleep and arousal disorders are classified by the Association of Sleep Disorder Centers (1979) as follows:

I. Dysomnias (disturbances in the amount, timing, or quality of sleep).
   A. Primary insomnia: Microsleeps, sleep state misperceptions, sleep stress, asomnia.
   B. Primary hypersomnia.

    C. Narcolepsy: Cataplexy, sleep paralysis, hypnagogic or hypnopompic hallucinations.
    D. Breathing-related sleep disorder—sleep apnea: Obstructive/central/mixed.
    E. Circadian rhythm sleep disorder—sleep–wake schedule disorder: Jet lag type, shift-work type, delayed sleep phase type, advanced sleep phase type, non-24-hour sleep–wake syndrome, reversal of day–night pattern.

II. Parasomnias (dysfunctions associated with arousal and sleep stage transitions).

    A. Nightmare disorder: Dream anxiety disorder.
    B. Sleep terror disorder: Sleep paralysis, confusional arousals/sleep drunkenness, sleep starts.
    C. Sleepwalking disorder: Somnambulism.

Sleep Patterns

Night Terrors

Pavor nocturnus in children, expression of terror with distorted features, sitting up or jumping from bed, profuse sweating, reported by others and not recalled by client in morning, sudden screaming/thrashing/calling out, sleep not interrupted (or if awakened client cannot recall scream or reason for scream), still asleep/cannot be awakened or have terror shortened by others, if awakens does not recognize others/location, hallucinates dream objects, terror may last up to 20 minutes, peaceful sleep upon end of terror.

Nightmares

Frightening/often paranoid quality, awakening follows, only moaning or small movements, no sweating, no hallucinations, is awake when others arrive and can recall dream, can recognize others and surroundings, may stay awake and review dream, maximum duration 1–2 minutes, fairly well recalled in morning.

Vivid Dreams

"Almost real," well-organized contents, of neutral mood, felt as very different from usual dreaming, concerning persons and events from dreamer's remote past.

Other Patterns

Apnea: Central, upper airway, mixed.
Nocturnal jerking/myoclonus/"restless leg syndrome"/itching/crawling symptoms, somnambulism.
Hypnagogic/hypnopompic hallucinations.
Lucid dreaming.
Somniloquy, somnirexia, nocturnal vocalizations.
Bruxism/clenching/grinding teeth.
Incontinence, bedwetting/enuresis, urinary urgency.

Other Aspects of Sleep Disturbance

Poor sleep architecture: Extended time to fall asleep, wakes with headache, choking, etc.
Sleep deprivation/debt, daytime sleepiness/drowsiness, tiredness/fatigue, repeated or extensive daytime napping, wakes unrefreshed.
Total sleep time decreased/increased/unaffected/normal/underestimated.
"Lark" pattern (morning alertness with evening ineffectiveness) or "owl" pattern (the opposite).

Etiological Considerations

Disorders: Depression, chronic illness, pain, drug/alcohol use to sleep.

Poor sleep hygiene: Irregular bedtimes/locations, consumption of meals/stimulants/alcohol/tobacco/medications too near bedtime, strenuous exercise near bedtime, disruptive noise or light, effortful attempts to go to sleep.

Disruptions due to bed partner/small children/need to use the bathroom, transmeridianal travel, being away from home, changed family demands.

<u>SOMATIZATION DISORDER</u>   *See Section 13.13, "Hypochondriacal Personality."*

The relevant DSM-IV code is 300.81. (This disorder used to be called "Briquet's syndrome.")

12.36. SUBSTANCE ABUSE AND USE

See Sections 3.26, "Substance Abuse: Drugs and Alcohol," and 3.27, "Substance Use: Tobacco and Caffeine," for questions.

This section concentrates on drug and alcohol abuse. The phrase "<u>A</u>lcohol and <u>O</u>ther <u>D</u>rugs" may replace "substance abuse."

DSM-IV has about 100 codes and labels for these disorders. *(See Chapter 21, "Diagnostic Statement/Impression.")*

Signs of Intoxication

Smell of alcohol on breath, slurred speech, slowed movements and responses, discoordination, unusual pupil size, elevated pulse/blood pressure, sweating, tremor, fever, tinnitus.

Agitation, irritability, flat or exaggerated affect or expression, psychomotor activity, rage, violence, dozing off or prolonged sleep.

Ataxia, opthalmoplegia, nystagmus, peripheral neuropathy, cerebellar signs, seizures.

Disorientation, "quiet global confusion," delirium.

Impairment of short-term memory, lessened concentration, loosened associations, confabulation, amnesia for rage episode.

Perceptual distortions (visual and tactile), hallucinations (usually auditory, of command or derogatory type, often haptic).

Delusions (usually paranoid and transient). *(See Sections 12.9, "Delusions," and 12.16, "Hallucinations.")*

Symptoms of Problem Drinking/Drug Use

Tolerance.

Withdrawal (a substance-specific syndrome).

Use to control withdrawal symptoms.

Preoccupation with drinking/use, spends time buying/selling/taking/talking about drugs/alcohol.

Continued use despite physical/medical disorder or social problem made worse by use.

Consumption pattern: Impulsive, gulping, in inappropriate circumstances, solitary, secret/hidden supply, use of drugs and alcohol together.

Guilt over drinking/use.

Rationalizations: Medicine, health benefits, relaxation, social ease, etc.

Periodic attempts at abstinence/cutting down.

Social avoidance/isolation, frequent intoxication/impairment when expected to fulfill social or occupational obligations.

Missing appointments/work/recreation/etc. in order to drink/use.
Daily use, morning tremor, morning drinking/use.
Use to point of intoxication/unconsciousness, loss of control.
Arrests for: Driving While Intoxicated, Driving Under the Influence, public intoxication, violence.

Stages in the Progression of Alcoholism

Jellinek (1960) and others have described a disease model reflecting a sequence/"pathological pattern of use," which is widely accepted but often does not fit the individual's history.

Prodromal phase: Periodic excessive drinking, drinking to reduce tension/forget stressors, increased tolerance, furtive drinking, guilt, urgency, blackouts.
Crucial phase: Loss of control over drinking, repeated efforts at control (promises, geographical escapes, scheduling, change to "only beer"), excuses for drinking, remorse, use of alibis, rationalizations, grandiose/aggressive behavior, avoidance of family/friends, work/financial difficulties, loss of interests, tremors, morning drinking, decreased tolerance, deterioration and illness, can stop for days, "benders."
Chronic/compulsive phase: Defeat, impaired thinking, drinking with inferiors, obsession with drinking, inability to initiate actions, neglect, drinking despite serious consequences, Delirium Tremens, hospitalizations, nonbeverage alcohol.
Rehabilitation phase: Learns of disease model, meets former addicts, stops drinking, medical aspects attended to, does personal stock taking, group therapy, improved appearance, appreciates possibilities of different future, regular habits, realistic thinking/recognition of rationalizations, return of self-esteem, new interests, new friends, contentment in sobriety, economic stability.

Stages-of-Change Model

The simple but powerful stages-of-change model for addictive behaviors is beginning to supplant the disease model because of its heurism. For more information, see Prochaska et al. (1992). The five stages of change are as follows:

Precontemplation: No intention to change behavior; no awareness of need to change.
Contemplation: Awareness that a problem exists and thinking seriously about overcoming the problem.
Preparation: Intention to change, with some small behavioral actions in preparation.
Action: Overt behavioral change (e.g., abstinence).
Maintenance: Working to prevent relapse and maintain the change.

Temperamental Risk Factors

High activity level, disinhibition, impulsivity, short attention span, lack of persistence, high emotionality, low soothability, high sociability.

Sex Differences in Drinking

Most of the following is based on work by Lawson et al. (1984). Note that females of lower SocioEconomic Status may have patterns more like males; females of middle and upper SESs may show patterns like those below. Middle- and upper-SES women have traditionally been more protected against public disgrace but more punished within the family than those of lower SES have been.

Less likely than men to get into trouble with the law.
Risk factors: Difficulty participating in traditional female sex roles, frustrations in the family and with children.

More likely than men to suffer physical illness from drinking and at an earlier stage in the disorder, and to die of cirrhosis.

Blood alcohol levels from the same intake vary with menstrual cycle times.

Begin drinking and having problems later than men do.

Move more rapidly through stages of abusive drinking than do men.

More likely than men to cite a specific stressor or traumatic event that led to abusive drinking.

More solitary drinking/more at home, due to greater social disapproval of female drinking.

More depressions/guilt/anxieties and fewer sociopathic behaviors than men.

More consequences in the family (men have more consequences in the workplace).

More likely than men to have a model of abusive drinking in the family (e.g., spouse).

Points in a Cost–Benefit Analysis Approach

The following table is adapted by permission from Horvath (1995). See Miller and Rollnick (1991) for use of this material in "motivational interviewing."

Benefits/motivators	*Costs/demotivators*
Reduction of negative emotions (anxiety, guilt, depression, helplessness, worthlessness).	Reduced productivity
	Impaired relationships.
	Impaired health.
Submission to social pressure of friends to consume/not be abandoned or criticized.	Diminished self-respect.
	Unstable moods and emotions.
	Legal risk.
Ability to ignore irresolvable interpersonal conflict.	Financial costs.
	Diminished sexual enjoyment.
Enhancement of positive emotional states.	Impaired cognitive functioning.
Prevention of intolerable withdrawal symptoms.	Impaired sleep and rest.
Avoidance of pain, pressures, problems.	Impaired response to obligations.
Hope to improve sexual performance.	Guilt.
Elimination or reduction of cravings so as not to "go crazy."	Uncomfortable cravings.
	Dishonesty (or temptation thereto).
Opportunity to test self-control.	Association with dealers, other addicts.
Pleasures.	Diminished sense of self-control.
Improved socializing.	Reduced energy, endurance, ability.
Elimination or reduction of sense of separateness because will always have this habit: "the bottle."	Reduced available time.
	Unhealthy appearance.
	Impaired driving.
Belonging to a social group.	
Need to feel normal, not "a wreck" or "falling apart."	
Time filling, pastimes.	
A way to get going.	
Expansion of consciousness.	

Factors Indicating Poor Prognosis

Person has no sobriety support system, lives in a high-risk area, has low self-esteem/efficacy expectations, has a history of physical/sexual/emotional abuse.

Responses to Treatment

Identification as an Alcoholic/Addict

The following groupings are sequenced by degree of increasing identification.

Denial: Does not admit to any intemperate use/drinking problem/bingeing/alcoholism, brags about sprees, "not addicted," does not appreciate the need for treatment, grandiose/superior/arrogant, seeks/exaggerates/manufactures differences between self and other addicts, complacent about own patterns of use, hostile to "accusations" of addiction, only external motivators.

Minimizes consequences of drinking/use, too easily/glibly admits his/her alcoholism/addiction, self-medicates with . . . (specify substances), acknowledges the negative consequences of his/ her use but fails to recognize using as self-defeating, verbally identifies as an alcoholic/addict but shows no changed behaviors such as improved social skills, resists/denies alternative problem solutions that would support freedom from addiction, is unconcerned/too little concerned with failure of previous treatments for substance abuse, hopeless of change, seeks only to avoid problems from addiction/use or to please other people and not to change own symptomatic behaviors, fearful of facing the outside world, verbalizes motivation but seems insincere, "just going through the motions," "treatment-wise," uses defensive anger/blaming/projecting.

Identifies self as "an alcoholic"/"in recovery," has made sobriety her/his first priority, demonstrates insightful identification as an addict/cross-addict through change in identification/ lifestyle/relationships/behaviors, is open and receptive to/understands the concepts presented, shares honestly her/his complete chemical history, is dealing with the issues from a dysfunctional childhood, knows she/he is powerless over alcoholism/addiction and cannot recover without help and support from others, explains progress of the disease and the impact on her/his life, grieves over her/his losses, expresses regret/anger, feels cheated/ abandoned, has released a lot of emotion/cried, reports hope, demonstrates hope through new behaviors, has prepared an aftercare plan including a daily plan/home group meetings, plans to attend ___ meetings per week for a total of ___ meetings/weeks/days, understands Adult Child Of Alcoholic concepts.

Able to offer support/be appropriately confrontative, is keeping sobriety as his/her top priority, willing to/does whatever is necessary, has a positive and optimistic attitude toward the future, spiritual commitment as an asset in a continued struggle, understands and practices relapse prevention techniques, has resisted/avoided high-temptation situations, recognizes and has plans for preventing Hungry, Angry, Lonely, and Tired cues to drinking, has dealt with the central issues of addiction/anger/denial/ grief, has a functioning and non-alcohol-centered support network/role models, has stable life in terms of finances/relationships/legal aspects, appreciates the need for and uses meetings/sponsor, leads a recovering lifestyle.

Spouse's/Partner's Response   *See also Section 13.8, "Codependent Personality."*

Participates, willing to examine self, becoming involved in her/his own recovery, supportive, blaming/angry/resentful, untrusting, needing to be convinced, uncooperative, codependent.

Alcoholics Anonymous and Other Treatments: Summary Statements

This client has a history of previous chemical dependency treatments, going back to _____ (specify date). The longest period of sobriety afterward was _____.

Client denies need for/denigrates/rejects/grudgingly admits need for/is proud of membership in AA/other Twelve-Step group (specify).

Client attends Twelve-Step meetings never/occasionally/regularly/daily; he knows name of/is a sponsor.

She attended rehabilitation programs with only short-term/time-limited/progressively greater/ excellent success at abstinence/control.

He has been exposed to/learned about/understood/applied/changed because of disease concept of addiction/identity as an alcoholic/cross-addiction/codependency/etc.

Other Summary Statements

Concerning her insight, she treats her alcoholism with indifference and resignation; she feels hope-less and defeated so that she continues to abuse alcohol as a lifestyle.

He rationalized about his drinking in an illogical manner suggesting its value to him. For example, he uses it to sleep, control the "shakes," and loosen up. He also reports that being drunk saved his life in an auto accident.

This clinically frustrating patient has been approached, encouraged, or lectured by most of the staff to little effect.

He is addicted only to one of several drugs used.

When she came to sobriety . . .

12.37. SUICIDE

See Section 3.26, "Suicide and Self-Destructive Behavior," for questions; see also Section 12.20, "Impulse Control Disorders."

Degree of Suicidal Ideation and Behavior

The following groupings are sequenced by degree of increasing suicidality.

"Impossible," highly unlikely, improbable, against strongly held religious beliefs or philosophy of life, "never" considered, rejected, wishes to live, reasons for living exceed reasons for dying, no thoughts of giving up or harming self.

Passive death wishes/escape wishes, "subintentioned/subintended death" (Shneidman, 1980), "chronic suicide" (Menninger, 1967), "wish to die," would leave life/death to chance, wishes without plan, tired of living.

Considered and abandoned, only flimsy rationales for refusing suicide, not currently con-sidered, fleeting thoughts of suicide, passive suicide attempt, would avoid steps necessary to save or maintain life, suicidal "flashes," whims.

Thoughts/ideation/wishes to end life, expressed ambivalence, debating, inclination, wonders if he/she will make it through this, raises questions of life after death.

Verbalizations, recollections of others' suicides, makes plans, discusses methods/ means, states intent, used as a threat, thoughts of self-mutilation, asks others to help kill her/him, reunion wishes/fantasies.

Behaviors, gestures, rehearsals, nonlethal/low-lethality/nondangerous method, acts of self-mutilation, symbolic/ineffective/harmless attempts, command hallu-cinations with suicidal intent.

Attempt(s), deliberateness, action planning, method/means selected/ac-quired, high-lethality method, gives away possessions, arranges affairs, wrote note, told others of intent, made "good-bye" calls.

Persistent/continuous/continual efforts, unrelenting preoccupation.

Risk Factors for Suicide

Thorough reviews of the risk factors for subpopulations are valuable and have been done for adults (Maris et al., 1992), adolescents (Lewinsohn et al., 1996), and the elderly (McIntosh, 1995).

Psychiatric Status

Having a psychiatric disorder/diagnosis raises rate 8–10 times, and having depression raises the rate 80–100 times (and severe depression raises it 500 times), all for males.

Among psychiatric patients, the rates of suicide for males and female are about equal, because the rate for females rises greatly.

Psychological Symptoms

  Depressive symptoms, such as vegetative symptoms, hopelessness/helplessness, anhedonia, sense of lessened worth/guilt over fault, increased irritability.
  Cycling of mood within an episode of depression.
  Extreme anxiety or panic.
  Psychosis (especially hallucinated commands to commit suicide), psychotic symptoms acute rather than chronic, remission of psychotic episode but continuing depression.
  Severe sleep disturbances (highly correlated) with suicide.
  Confusion and disorganization of thoughts, no sense of control over ideations/etc.
  Loss of affective reactivity.
  Acceptance that painful situation is inalterable/final/irresolvable/incurable/permanent.
  Consistent pattern of leaving life crises rather than facing them.
  Recent angry/enraged/violent behavior.
  Morbid preoccupation with death/suicide.

Demographics

  European-American: Three times (3 ×) more adult and 2 × more adolescent completers than African-Americans and other minorities, but rates are more equal in urban centers.[7] Most completers are white, U.S.-born men aged 45–60.
  Male: 3–4 × as many male attempters, 70% male completers, 30% female completers. This difference is due mainly due to the lethality of the means selected.
  Lowest-SES groups have highest rates.
  Age: Young adult (15–24; 50% of attempters are under 30) or geriatric (twice average rate for those 75–84, 4 × for white males age 85).
  Medical/dental/mental health professionals, lawyers, etc., seem to have high rates.
  Protestants higher than Jews or Catholics.
  Divorced status (4–5 × greater). Divorced people are also more likely to make repeated attempts or to have made an attempt shortly before present one (within 6 months).
  Never-married or widowed status (single is 2 × greater). Married people with children have lowest rates.
  History of suicide in the family.

Feasible Plan of Action

  Availability of means/method/opportunity/resources (e.g., weapons).
  Highly lethal method selected.

---

[7]I am grateful to Robert W. Moffie, PhD, of Los Angeles, CA, for correction and clarification of this issue.

Specific/detailed plan, has made preparations (means, privacy).
Has made final arrangements (a will/funeral/burial), put life's affairs in order, given away favorite possessions.
Feels capable/competent/courageous of taking action.
Little imminence of rescue.
Written a suicide note.
Concealed/denied ideation to interviewer.
Clearly determinable time of suicide attempt.

Prior Suicidal Behaviors

✓ **Note:** Although 50–60% of completers have one previous attempt, only 10–20% of attempters complete suicide.

Current ideation of longer duration, higher frequency, greater acceptance.
Multiple attempts, multiple threats/statements.
Recent attempts.
High-lethality/painful/violent method in past attempt.
Attempts with little chance of discovery.
Intended to die in earlier attempts.
Attempts on anniversaries of significant events.

Social Isolation

No friends nearby, living alone or with other than family members, few or no family members available.
Highly dependent personality.
Family instability/early rejection, loved ones all rejecting/punitive/unsupportive, no warm/close/interdependent relationships.
Loss of sense of continuity with past or present.
Partner also suicidal, partner self-absorbed/competitive.
No therapeutic alliance with therapist.

Stressors

Sudden onset of stress.
Irrevocable losses: Serious medical illness or disability, chronic illness, failing health (especially in the previously robust).
Failure to perform major life role behavior (unemployment, failing grades, etc.) resulting in humiliations.
Self-evaluation excessively based upon performance in standard gender roles.
Recent loss of persons/positions/possessions, without replacement.
Anniversary of death or loss.

Other Risk-Increasing Variables

High level of psychological pain, absence of "secondary gain" (e.g., message sending), beginning of recovery from depression, recent psychiatric hospital discharge, lack of plans for the future, few or weak deterrents, refusal or inability to cooperate with treatment, prior inpatient psychiatric treatment.

Impulsiveness, agitation, history of criminal behavior, considering homicide as well as suicide, motivation based on revenge/attention getting, history of life-risking "accidents"/accident proneness.

Discussing own funeral/how friends will feel later, suicide attempt modeled on one reported in the media, suicide of friends/coworkers/colleagues.

Hypochondriasis.
Organic brain syndrome.
Alcoholism: Current alcohol intoxication, or long history of alcohol abuse without current drinking.
Depression with low level of 5-HIAA/high level of cortisol/high ratio of adrenaline to noradrenaline.
Death of mother, especially within last 3 years.

For a Child or Adolescent: Causes of suicide and rationales differ with developmental age. Risk factors include the following:

Girls make 3 × more attempts; boys are more likely to complete suicide.
Older adolescents/young adults (15–24) more at risk.
Greater risk in rural areas.
Native Americans at highest risk; African-American and European-American about equal.
Earlier attempts.
Strained family relationships (in 75% of attempters).
Substance abuse in family or adolescent.
Stressors such as loss of a significant other, recent suicide of peer or family member ("social contagion"), legal difficulties, unwanted pregnancy, recent changes of school, withdrawal, birth of a sibling.

Coping with the Aftermath of Suicide

According to Lukas and Seiden (1990), whose book is recommended, survivors ask continuing questions about the cause, their role, and ways the suicide might have been prevented. Common coping methods include the following:

The long good-bye: Unending mourning and fixation.
Scapegoating: Blaming a few others, displacing rage from the suicider.
Guilt as punishment: Assumption of responsibility and self-blame.
Cutting off: Strangling all feelings, including pleasure.
Physical problems: Somatizing and focusing on these.
Running: Endless moves and changes.
Suicide: Following the suicider in death.

Psychological Autopsy

The following outline for conducting a "psychological autopsy" on a person who has committed suicide is based on that of Shneidman et al. (1970). Ebert (1987) offers another, very complete set of guidelines.

Demographic data.
Details of death: Cause or method, laboratory studies, coroner's report, police report, etc.
Brief social history: The usual, including medical illnesses, educational, employment, and military history, psychotherapy, previous suicide attempts, and suicide notes/other writings.
"Death history" of victim's family: Suicides, fatal illnesses, age at death.
Personality and lifestyle of victim.
Typical reactions to stress: Periods of disequilibrium, mood, mental status.
Stresses: Pressures, surprises, tensions, or anticipations of trouble during last year.
Role of drugs and alcohol in lifestyle and in victim's death.

Nature of interpersonal relationships: Include relation with physician/clinician.
Fantasies, dreams, thoughts, premonitions, or fears of death/accident/suicide.
Recent changes in the victim's habits, hobbies, eating, sexual patterns, or other life routines.
Information about the victim's "life side"—successes, plans, upswings.
Assessment of the role of the victim in his/her demise, presuicidal behavior.
Rating of lethality of method(s) used.
Reactions of informants to the victim's death.
Comments, unusual features.

Ways of Classifying Suicidal Behavior

Anomic, egoistic, altruistic suicides (Durkheim, 1897/1966).
Indirect Self-Destructive Behavior (Farberow, 1980), "parasuicide" (Farberow, 1980), "sub-intended death" (Shneidman, 1980).
Death seeker, death initiator, death Ignorer, death darer, courts death (Shneidman, 1980).

Assessment

More formal assessment measures include scales of ideation (Beck, Kovacs, et al., 1979; Reynolds, 1987), intent (Beck et al., 1974), and hopelessness (Beck, 1987).

THOUGHT CONTINUITY, CONTENT, AND OTHER ASPECTS
See Section 11.9, "Stream of Thought," for descriptors.

VIOLENCE   *See Sections 12.18, "Homicide Risk Factors," and 12.20, "Impulse Control Disorders," for descriptors.*

13

Personality Patterns

For each syndrome, personality disorder, character type, or behavior pattern included in this chapter, there are listed descriptive words and phrases organized into clusters. No validity claims are made for the clusters or their contents; these are simply descriptors that are commonly used in reports and in research studies. Because the clusters and concepts overlap, do review similar types. The chapter concludes with two sections on the assessment and diagnosis of personality, and two sections on other dimensions of personality (traits related to developmental stages, and cognitive or thinking styles).

13.1. A AND B PERSONALITY TYPES

Type A

Time Urgency

Impatient, hurries, under pressure, prompt and often early for appointments, watches clock, walks/talks/eats rapidly, does multiple activities simultaneously (multitasks), lives in the future/always planning, feels that "there's never enough time."

Hates delays, irritable/restless with others' pace, high impatience at having to wait for someone, rage at having to wait in line, detests wasting time, drives over the speed limit, evades red lights, is "hard on equipment," always underestimates the time a job will take.

Hostility/Struggle for Control

Competitive, "must win," makes bets, finds competitive aspect of all activities, plays as hard as works, detests losing, plays to win even against children/friends, sets higher goals for self, challenging, hard-driving.

Constant struggle for control/avoiding helplessness, helplessness is feared/denied, sees the world as threatening, cycles of desperate efforts to control environment, followed by profound abandonment of efforts, reluctant to share power/control/delegate.

Dominates conversations, emphasizes words in speech, finishes others' speeches, interrupts speakers, dislikes small talk.

Aggressive, high and inhibited need for power.

Self-Destructive Behaviors

Gorging on high-fat foods, overuse of stimulants, low levels of exercise, high alcohol intake, smoking, no time for self-care.

Works during vacations, overplans vacation's activities, works in bed, inability to relax/be unproductive, fails to notice beauty/scenery/"smell the flowers," overschedules self, overcommitted, guilt over relaxing, always works more than 8 hours a day.

Sits on edge of chairs, makes fists, clenches jaws, taps fingers, jiggles legs, rapid blinks, never still.

Continual emergency reaction.

Cognitions

Measures everything in numbers/dollars, attributes success to own speed, concerned with getting and having rather than being.

Perfectionistic, demands continual self-improvement, demands excellence in every area, always seeking to improve efficiency, underestimates own achievements, underestimates time and effort needed, disappointment/self-doubt.

Negative, cynical, critical, ruthless in self-reproach/self-examining.

"Workaholic" Traits

Ambitious, gets higher grades/income.

Overworking, takes on more and more work, pursues more challenging tasks, recreation only with friends from work, better communication at work than at home, organized hobbies, work as substitute for intimate contacts, reading is all work-related, works late more than peers do, when awakened thoughts go to work, lives by deadlines and quotas, creates unnecessary deadlines.

Type B

Relaxes readily, focuses on quality of life, paces self, easy-going, "one day at a time."

Less ambitious, lower incomes/grades.

Less irritable.

ADULT CHILDREN OF ALCOHOLICS/ADDICTS   *See Section 13.8, "Codependent Personality."*

Ackerman (1987) provides a bibliography of 700 references to ACOAs in the clinical and empirical literature. In general, there has been little empirical support for the validity for a pattern of characteristics in ACOAs or in grandchildren of alcoholics/addicts. (See, e.g., Logue et al., 1992, and Sher, 1991.)

13.2. "ADDICTIVE" PERSONALITY

Not in DSM-IV.

There has been little research support for the concept of an "addictive" personality, perhaps because a particular substance's use creates the traits seen. Some general traits include the following:

Dissatisfaction with life.

Extreme dependence, resentment of authority, flagrant selfishness, insistence on immediate gratification.

13.3. AGGRESSIVE PERSONALITY

See also Sections 12.20, "Impulse Control Disorders," 13.4, "Antisocial Personality," 13.5, "Authoritarian Personality," and 13.22, "Sadistic Personality."

Not in DSM-IV.

Cardinal Features

Aggression, low self-restraint.

Behaviors

Vicious, brutal, pugnacious, temperamental.

Reckless, unflinching, fearless, undeterred by pain/danger/punishment.

Interpersonal Aspects

Intimidating, dominating, surgent, obstinate, controlling.
Humiliating, abusive, derisive, cold-blooded, persecutes, malicious.

Cognitions

Opinionated, close-minded, prejudiced, bigoted, "authoritarian."

Self-Image

Proud of independence, hard-headed, tough, power-oriented, powerful.

13.4. ANTISOCIAL PERSONALITY

See also Sections 12.20, "Impulse Control Disorders," 13.3, "Aggressive Personality," 13.5, "Authorotarian Personality," and 13.22, "Sadistic Personality."

The relevant DSM-IV codes are as follows:

For those over age 18: 301.7, Antisocial Personality Disorder.
For those under age 18: 312.8, Conduct Disorder.

Those over age 18 who engage in criminal behavior without "psychological" motivation should be diagnosed as showing Adult Antisocial Behavior (DSM-IV code V71.01).

Cardinal Features

Classic criteria can be found in Cleckley's famous book *The Mask of Sanity* (1976) and Hare (1980).

Predatory attitude and behavior toward others, long-standing indifference to and repetitive violation of others' rights, parasitic lifestyle, repetitive socially destructive behaviors.
Absence of delusions or other signs of irrational thinking, anxiety or other neurotic symptoms, suicide attempts, or a life plan or ordered way of living.

Social Aspects

Irresponsibility

Untrustworthy, evades responsibility, unreliable, rejects obligations, ruthless.
Wandered from place to place without a home for a long time, told a lot of lies, used an alias, trouble because failed to pay her/his bills, multiple financial irresponsibilities.
Multiple marriages/divorces, marital instability, frequent marriages, suddenly left/hit/unfaithful to spouse, irresponsible parenting, seriously hurt/neglected a child.
Cavalier, acting wild, slept around with people he/she didn't know very well, earned money by pandering/procuring/pimping/having sex with another person.

Selfishness

Unique and self-serving ideas of "right and wrong," lies easily, frequent lying other than to avoid negative consequences, does not believe her/his behaviors/crimes will be or should be punished, uses guilt inductions on others.
Feels or believes self to be harassed/misused/victimized, resents, distrusts, suspicious, justifies behavior with lies and manipulation, argues about "who's in charge," revengeful, petty, superficial relationships.
A chronic pattern of infringement on the rights of others, violates social codes by lies or deceits,

chronic speeder and drunk driver, reckless, indifferent to the rights of others, breaks rules, rebellious.
Ingratitude, arrogance.

Behaviors

General

Impulsivity, impetuous, spur-of-the-moment, short-sighted, incautious, imprudent, lack of long-term plans.
History of drug/alcohol/telephone/etc. overuse/abuse [✓ but not the cause of antisocial behaviors].

Illegal or Immoral Activities

Lying, stealing, swindling, cheating, commission of/involvement in minor or serious illegal/delinquent acts.
Has conned/manipulated/cheated people out of their money/possessions, predatory, often victimizes the easiest/weakest members of society, "white-collar" criminal.
From an early age: Criminal arrests/convictions, diagnosed as antisocial personality, served time, poor probation/parole risk, many types of offenses (including felonies).
Initiates physical fights, used a weapon in a fight, tortured animals, physically cruel to other people.
Has deliberately destroyed others' property, steals/vandalize/"messes up" property, firesetting.
Has forced someone into sexual activity with him/her, promiscuity.

For a Child: See also Section 12.8, "Conduct Disorder."

Starting fights, vandalism, tortured/abused ("played tricks on") animals/pets, early and extensive drug/alcohol use, behavior difficulties, theft, incorrigibility, running away overnight, bad associates, impulsivity, recklessness/irresponsibility, slovenly appearance, lack of guilt, pathological lying.
Trouble with the police/juvenile or school authorities, truancy/plays a lot of hooky, has been a discipline problem/expelled/suspended from school.

Cognitions

See especially Samenow (1980).

Does not believe she/he will be blamed/caught/punished, low planning, lack of consideration of alternatives or consequences, projects blame, rationalizes, Machievellianism, ends justify any means, does not profit from experience of punishment, low insight.
Average or above-average intelligence.

Affects

Lacking in remorse/guilt/regret, insensitive, lacks compassion, hardened, callous, cold-blooded, emotionally detached, low motivation to change, shallow affects, no deep or lasting emotions.
Irritability, aggressiveness, short-tempered, "bottled-up" anger, intolerance of delayed gratifications, easily provoked to violence, low frustration tolerance.
Deficient emotional arousal, stimulation seeking, thrill seeking, easily bored.

Vocational Aspects

Unstable employment: Fired, ran away, quit a job impulsively/without another to start, didn't work because he/she "just didn't want to," court-martialed/demoted, missed a lot of work or was late a lot and so got into trouble.
Lack of career or other long-term plans.

ANXIOUS PERSONALITY   *See Section 13.17, " 'Nervous' Personality."*

<u>ATTENTION DEFICIT/HYPERACTIVITY DISORDER</u>
See Section 12.3, "Attention-Deficit/Hyperactivity Disorder."

13.5. AUTHORITARIAN PERSONALITY

For descriptors, see also Sections 12.20, "Impulse Control Disorders," 13.4, "Antisocial Personality," and 13.22, "Sadistic Personality" for contrast.

Not in DSM-IV.

See Adorno et al. (1950), Milgram (1974), and Miller (1986) for detailed discussions of the authoritarian personality.

Cognitions

Rigid adherence to middle-class/bourgeois/conventional values.
Commitment to severe punishment for deviation from conventional values.
Reactionary/ultraconservative, moral ideology overrides all other concerns.
Prejudiced against minorities/etc., outsiders seen as dangerous/dehumanized ("subhuman," "animals," "undeserving").

Social Aspects

Blind obedience, conformity, no questioning or criticism of authority, exaggerated need to submit to those above, harshness to those below.
Uses official/"clean" vocabulary.
Power and dominance are the most central dimensions of relationships, views people as either weak or strong, glorifies toughness/denies tenderness, values stern discipline.
Idealizes parents, father seen as stern/harshly punitive/demanding of absolute obedience.

13.6. AVOIDANT PERSONALITY

The relevant DSM-IV code is 301.82, Avoidant Personality Disorder.

Cardinal Features

Oversensitive and vacillating, discomfort in all social situations, watchful for any hint of disapproval.

Cognitions

Belief that others know of his/her anxiety and are constantly watching for his/her mistakes.

Interpersonal Aspects

Yearns for closeness/warmth/affection/acceptance but fears rejection/disapproval in relationships.
Fears "goofing up"/gaffes/social errors/gaucheries/*faux pas* and so "making a fool of myself," fears crying/blushing/embarrassment.
Wary, distrustful, vigilant for offenses/threats/ridicule/abuse/humiliation, hypersensitive/keen sensitivity to potential for rejection or humiliation by others, expects not to be loved, needs constant reassurance/guarantee of uncritical affection.
Withdrawing, guarded, private, lonely, shy/reticent/timid, compliant.

Affects

Anguished, intensely ambivalent, anxious, "bored."

Self-Image

Devalues own accomplishments, angry and depressed at self for social difficulties, sees self as rejected/basically defective/flawed/odd/inadequate.

Other

Vicious cycle as follows: Low self-esteem, fear of rejection, shallow or awkward attempts at social relating, hypersensitivity to lack of enthusiasm/disapproval, concludes/confirms low worth, feels rejection, withdraws, fears of relationships, loneliness, yearning, trying again, rejection, etc.

Extensive reliance on fantasizing for gratification of needs for contact and anger discharge.

Alden (1992) is a fine starting point for cognitive–interpersonal treatment of the avoidant personality.

13.7. BORDERLINE PERSONALITY

The relevant DSM-IV code is 301.83, Borderline Personality Disorder.

These people often present a mixed picture with elements of other personality disorders present; they often also have mood disorder diagnoses.

Cardinal Features

Instability in all aspects of living/personality functioning/mood/social relating, lack of personality consistency/cohesiveness, "cuts loose"/abrupt shifts of affect/relationships.

Interpersonal Aspects

Close/demanding/dependent/intense relationships, disillusionment when intensity is not reciprocated, terror of abandonment.

Unstable relationships, inexplicable changes in attitude/feelings toward others, capricious, "ups and downs," vacillating reactions, dependence–independence cycles, intense dislike of isolation and loneliness so engages in a series of transient/stormy/brief relationships, superficiality of relationships based on alternating idealization and deflation.

Impaired object relations, lacks internalized soothing/holding function so relies on others.

Affects

Labile, mercurial, brittle, erratic, unpredictable, rapid/short-lived but intense mood swings, low tolerance for affects, tenuous/shifting controls.

Anger barely hidden/under the surface, pessimism, argumentativeness, irritable, easily annoyed, sarcastic, intense and sudden rages or depressions, sudden dramatic and unexpected outbursts, rage over failure of others to provide soothing, rage at intimates.

Spells of emptiness/boredom/dejection/apathy, numbness.

Areas of seemingly unalterable and crushing negativity, worthlessness/badness/blame/fault assumption, feelings of unlovability.

Identity

Lack of individuation, identity diffusion/shakiness, shifts of identity/gender identity/career choices/long-term goals, frequent "Who am I?" questions, instability of self-esteem/self-image, uncertain values/loyalties, "incompetence," "imposter."

Fragmentation of self, splitting, nebulous/multiple identities/personalities, "parts"/"voices"/nick-names, threats to right to survive from parts of self. *(See Section 13.11, "Dissociative Identity Disorder.")*

Behaviors

Impulsivity/poor judgment, lapses of judgment.
Manipulative suicide threats/gestures or attempts/overdosing.
Self-destructive/mutilating/damaging behaviors.
Running up huge bills/shoplifting, gambling sprees, eating binges, sexual acting out.
Addictive traits and patterns, drug misuse/abuse, reckless driving.
Ambivalence, indecision, procrastination.

✓ **Note:** According to Morey and Ochoa (1989), overdiagnosis/misdiagnosis of borderline personality is more likely with less experienced, female, psychodynamically oriented, nonpsychologist clinicians, and with poorer, European-American, female patients.

✓ Miller (1994) offers a brief but powerful description of borderline personality alternative from a patient's perspective.

13.8. CODEPENDENT PERSONALITY

See also Section 10.3, "Anxiety/Fear," Section 10.5, "Depression," and the sections in this chapter on many other personality patterns (especially borderline personality).

The relevant DSM-IV code is likely to be 301.6, Dependent Personality Disorder, but dependent and codependent personality are not identical.

Interpersonal Aspects

General Descriptors

Overresponsible.
Self-sacrificing, unassertive, does not pursue own rights, adapts rather than changing a bad situation.
Submission to others for predictability/security.
Oversensitive to others' difficulties.
Puts up a front, hides "true self."

Roles Adopted

Rescuer: Protecting/covering for the addicted underfunctioning person by making excuses for absences or social mistakes.
Caretaker: Minimizing negative consequences of addicted person's negligence through over-responsibility and overfunctioning. *(Also see "Other Features," below.)*
Joiner: Rationalizing or participating/assisting in addicted person's chemical dependency.
Hero: Protecting the family's public image, drawing attention away from the addiction with enor-mous/"superhuman"/self-sacrificing efforts.
Complainer: Blaming all the family's problems on the addicted person with no hope of change.
Adjuster: Avoiding discussion of the addiction in hopes it will disappear, hiding concern and confu-sion with apathy.

For a Child:

Overachieving: Trying to give the family something to be proud of.
Entertaining: Never taking anything seriously in order to relieve tension, "class clown."

Withdrawing: Escaping to friends' homes or spending time alone.
Rebelling: Acting out anger, causing trouble to draw attention away from family problems.

Family Characteristics

Extreme family loyalty.
Family rules: "Don't talk, don't trust, don't feel."
Distorted family image: Happy, no problems, see only the good.
Overdeveloped sense of responsibility and concern for others.
Control is valued, lack of control is terrifying; order, stability, routine, regularity, peace, not chaos.
Only superficial relationships, no intimate ones.

Other Features

Caretaking: Undeserved loyalty, unappreciated/excessive devotion, excessive caretaking/dependency (especially when stressed), overreliable/overresponsible (to compensate for the addict's irresponsibility), anticipates and participates in satisfying others' needs ("enabling"), need to control people and situations, rigidity.
Dependency: Longing for love/approval, tolerates abuse, always meeting others' needs before one's own.
Denial: Ignores/rationalizes/minimizes problem, denies increased substance abuse.
Loss of daily structure: Missing appointments, having meals at irregular times, not getting to bed or up on time.
Fails to complete tasks/follow through/make plans, easily overwhelmed with tasks, reactive rather than proactive.
Crisis orientation, not long-term: Good in crisis situation/beginnings and endings, but not in middles.

Self-Image

Low self-esteem, self-blame for any problems/other's substance use, guilt, extreme/unproductive self-criticism/flagellation, assumption of blame due to inconsistency of parental behaviors, insecurity, fear/belief in one's unlovability/insanity/badness/dirtiness, rejects compliments.
Sense of powerlessness.
Shame at addiction, secretive, very reluctant to ask for help.
Acts the way he/she believes is "normal," doesn't know what are normal behaviors/emotional responses, anxious over not feeling/acting sufficiently "normal" or feeling different from anyone else.
Adopts extreme role models and standards acceptable to a group with low self-esteem.

Affects

Depression, negativity, uncontrollable mood swings, no fun in life, dulled feeling, anhedonia, enjoyment only at someone else's expense/vicariously.
Seriousness, life as series of problems and crises to be solved, worry is normal.
Frequent resentments and anger, "got a raw deal from life."
Numerous fears/anxieties, fear of anger (own and addicted person's) because it will end the relationship, indecision, fears of being hurt/abandoned/rejected.

Cognitions

Obsessive thinking, overreliance on analytical thinking, perfectionism.
Delusions/irrational beliefs (especially that love conquers all—or at least substance abuse).

Dishonest/lies/denial, unaware of dishonesty, "(The addicted person's behavior) is not the 'real' person."
Low memory of childhood.

Behaviors

Physical/sexual/psychological abuse and neglect.
"Addictive" behaviors (eating disorders, substance abuse) to cope with own frustrations/pain.
Compulsions as attempts to control.
Acting out to get attention or approval.

Other

Health problems: Stress-related disorders, lack of personal care.
Lack of attention in childhood ("stroke-starved") leads to denial of own needs.

For a Child:

Premature adulthood and responsibilities, struggle with adult problems as child, loss of childhood.
Impact of addiction varies with developmental stage of child living in addictive household:
   Bonding stage: World is not safe.
   Exploratory/separation stage: Sense of being either engulfed or abandoned; passivity; no right to say "No."
   Latency stage: Failure to learn rules, what is normal, problem-solving skills; living with lies, denial, and anxiety.

Characteristics of Codependents

Schaef (1986) describes the following:

External referencing: Distrusts own perceptions, lacks boundaries, believes one cannot survive without a relationship/addicted to relationships, fears abandonment, believes in the perfect union.
Caretaking: Becomes indispensable, becomes a martyr.
Self-centeredness: Personalizes all events, assumes responsibility for others' behaviors.
Overcontrolling: Increases control efforts when chaos increases, attempts to control everything and everyone, controls without caring for those controlled, believes that with more effort she/he can fix the addict/family.
Feelings: Unaware of feelings, distorts emotional experiences/accepts only "nice" feelings, fearfulness.
Dishonesty: Manages all impressions made, omits/lies about the truth, rigidity.
Gullibility: Is a bad judge of character, unwilling to confront, overtrusting, accepts what fits the way he/she wishes things were.

Cermak (1991) offers these criteria:

Changing who one is to please others.
Feeling responsible for meeting other people's needs at the expense of one's own.
Low self-esteem.
Being driven by compulsions.
Denial.

Critical reviews of these codependency characteristics are provided by Morgan (1991) and O'Brien and Gaborit (1992).

Other Criteria

Continued investment of self-esteem in the ability to influence/control feelings and behavior, both in oneself and in others, in the face of serious adverse consequences.

Assumption of responsibility for meeting others' needs, to the exclusion of acknowledging one's own needs.

Anxiety and boundary distortions around intimacy and separation.

Enmeshment in relationships with personality-disordered, chemically dependent, and impulse-disordered individuals.

Exhibits at least three of the following:

Excessive reliance on denial.
Depression.
Compulsions.
Substance abuse.
Stress-related medical illnesses.

Constriction of emotions (with or without dramatic outbursts).
Hypervigilance.
Anxiety.
Recurrent victim of physical or sexual abuse.

Has remained in a primary relationship with an active substance abuser for at least 2 years without seeking outside support.

13.9. COMPULSIVE PERSONALITY

See also Section 13.19, "Obsessive Personality."

The relevant DSM-IV codes are 300.3, Obsessive–Compulsive Disorder, and 301.4, Obsessive–Compulsive Personality Disorder.

✓ **Note:** DSM-IV does not differentiate between Obsessive and Compulsive Personality Disorders. But because the writer of reports is dealing with the unique individual, "obsessive" and "compulsive" *are* separated here, to allow emphasis on aspects of the clinical core.

Cardinal Feature

Repetitious behaviors or else irresistible anxiety.

Behaviors

Highly regulated/organized lifestyle.

Cognitions

See Shapiro (1965).

Rumination prevents task completion, hypercareful, doubting, indecisive, poor decision making/follow-through, poor time management.

Excessively moralistic concerns, scrupulousness, intense self-evaluation/scrutiny, "black or white" judgments, need for immediate closure.

Perfectionistic approach, overattention to detail and avoidance of error, neatness, meticulous, a "fanatic."

Officious; concern with form over content, procedures/regulations more than the goals, letter of the law not the spirit, orderly task procedures rather than the outcome; sees the world in terms of schedule/rules/regulations, work as yet undone/burden.

Affects

Satisfaction in elaborate planning and arranging, only mild/brief pleasure with the completion of projects, a "work, not pleasure" orientation.

Joyless, solemn, controls most emotions, unrelaxed, occasional intense righteous indignation, perceived lack of control of environment leads to intense depression, great need/effort to control tension/anxiety.

Self-Image

Industrious, reliable, efficient, loyal, prudent/careful.

Interpersonal Aspects

Demands that others do things his/her way.
Is seen as somber/formal/cold/grim.
Respectful, conventional, follows the proprieties, polite, correct.
Shows reaction formation in positive/socially acceptable presentation of self.

13.10. DEPENDENT PERSONALITY

See also Section 13.25, "Self-Defeating Personality," and 13.8, "Codependent Personality."

The relevant DSM-IV code is 301.6, Dependent Personality Disorder.

✓ **Note:** Be sensitive to gender bias in using this diagnosis. Many studies (e.g., Broverman et al., 1970) have demonstrated gender bias in diagnosing various personality disorders: Clinicians of all stripes equate healthy males with healthy adults, but see females as dependent, self-dramatizing, vain, demanding, and overreacting to minor events—all of which resemble society's view of "normal" women. Moreover, R. E. Kaplan (1983) stresses that biases exist in the DSM definitions of how dependency is expressed. Examples not taken into account by DSM include male dependency on females to maintain their houses or raise their children; the impairment of function that may be seen in a male employed outside the home who is never home when the children return from school; or the impaired occupational functioning that may be seen in a female not employed outside the home. A final caution: Do not assume sexual masochism in those with dependent traits, or confuse such masochism with dependent personality.

✓ Although the majority of people diagnosed in practice as dependent personalities are female, in objective testing four women for every three men are so diagnosed (Millon, 1986).

Cardinal Feature

Unnecessary dependency upon others for many life functions.

Interpersonal Aspects

Conciliatory, placates, deferring, uncompetitive, "niceifier," unwilling to make critical comments.

Dependent, allows others to assume responsibility for self, childlike, immature, reliance on others to solve problems or achieve goals, to decide on employment/friendships/child management/vacations/clothing/purchases, absence of independent decision making, avoids external demands and responsibilities, low self-reliance, low autonomy, exaggerated and unnecessary help-seeking behaviors.

Submissive, dominated, secondary status, self-defeating, abused, unable to make demands on others, passive, docile, compliant.

Abused, neglected, insulted, belittled, berated, "imprisoned," exploited, tolerates partner's abusive affairs/beatings/drunkenness.

Self-sacrificing, subordinates own needs so as to maintain protective relationships/fulfill core role/identity, anxiously watchful and agitated.

Overdevoted, superloyal, attached, overloving, "love slob" sacrificing anything for "love," willing to tolerate more negatives in a relationship than the evaluator would.

Gullible, too trusting, easily persuaded, naive, unsuspicious, "Pollyanna," overhopeful of change.

Vicious cycle of dependency, abuse, separation/desertion, proof of helplessness and worthlessness, emotional devastation, avoidance of taking self-respecting or independent actions, lessened self-esteem, greater dependency.

Behaviors

General ineffectiveness in autonomy but not incompetence (may demonstrate exceptional skill in some areas).

Lacking in skills/motivation for independent life, ill equipped to assume mature roles.

Mood

Hidden depression and angers, whiny/tantrums/complains.

Tries to keep emotions under tight control.

Separation leads to depression/terror of abandonment.

Cognitions

Believes in magical solutions to problems.

Belief in salvation through love (*Amor omnia vincit*).

Unimaginative/cognitively constricted.

Guilt proneness, assumes blame.

Unwilling to take risks for satisfaction.

Preoccupied with fears of desertion.

Reluctant to make decisions.

Fails to identify own needs.

Self-Image

Self-derogating, belittling, martyr-like, self-sacrificing, low self-confidence, "inferiority complex," "stupid," untalented, unworthy, humble, self-effacing, self-deprecating, inadequate, inept, fragile.

Hidden strengths, denies/undervalues own skills, needs great encouragement.

13.11. DISSOCIATIVE IDENTITY DISORDER

See also Sections 12.11, "Depersonalization and Derealization," and 13.7, "Borderline Personality."

The relevant DSM-IV code is 300.14, Dissociative Identity Disorder.

✓ **Note:** Most studies have found extensive overlap with the symptoms of borderline personality. Ross et al. (1990) have suggested that the crucial differentiator is some form of amnesia or blank spell in DID or MPD. Good references are Ross (1989) and Putnam (1989, 1991, 1997).

Characteristics of Separate Selves

One central self/primary/host personality: Depressed, anxious, compulsively good, "masochistic," moralistic, seeks treatment.

Other personalities/Alters: Semiautonomous, numerous [3 to 100, mean = 15], some good and some bad, some believe that the host cannot handle memories/pain, some convinced that host must be punished/should die, may have mutual or unidirectional amnesias for one another and for host (odd names/characterological titles).

Common "roles" of alters: child, protector, persecutor, an opposite-sex person, a perfect person.

Transitions: Sudden/unexpected, precipitated by stress or some regular pattern of social/environmental cues, often accompanied by headaches/feelings of weakness/amnesia/blackouts.

Presenting Symptoms

Coons and Milstein (1986) mention the following symptoms of DID/MPD, listed here in descending order of frequency:

Amnesia, depression, history of childhood sexual abuse, fugue, suicide attempts, auditory hallucinations, history of drug abuse, history of childhood physical abuse, sexual dysfunction, headaches, child personalities, history of alcohol abuse, history of any type of conversion disorder, history of rape.

These are also common:

Problems with showing anger/frustration/defiance, problems with trust/safety/betrayal/suspicion, assumes that she/he will be disbelieved.

Confusion about location/time/person, responding to more than one name, marked and rapid shifts in personality, forgetting recent events, losing track of time, intense and sincere denial of responsibility when confronted, hearing of voices.

Extreme or odd variations in skills (e.g., handwriting), food preferences, artistic abilities, responses to discipline.

Self-injurious behaviors, somatic complaints or "conversion" symptoms such as sleepwalking, sudden blindness, loss of sensation.

The following characteristics of a history of sexual and/or physical abuse are frequently seen:

Believes self responsible for abuse suffered, believes deserved abuse because of badness/anger/imperfection, believes abuse will/does continue although impossible. (DID/MPD as a form of coping with victimization.)

13.12. HISTRIONIC PERSONALITY

The relevant DSM-IV code is 301.50, Histrionic Personality Disorder.

✓ Current usage does not support "hysteric," and histrionic personalities are not all females. *(See also the caution concerning sexism in Section 13.10, "Dependent Personality.")*

Cardinal Feature

Attention seeking through self-dramatization and exaggerated emotion.

Affects

Exaggerated, labile/vivid/shallow affect, easily "overcome" with emotions, easily enthused/disappointed/angered, excitable, theatrical/flamboyant/intensely expressed reactions, overly dramatic behaviors, creates dramatic effects/seems to be acting out a role, exaggerated and unconvincing emotionality.

Behaviors

Overreacts to minor annoyances, inappropriate.
Affectations/affected, overdetermined.
Repeated/impulsive/dramatic/manipulative suicide gestures/attempts.
Creative/imaginative/artistic, stylish, sensitive.
Stylized/caricatured "femininity"/"masculinity."

Cognitions

See Shapiro (1965).

Forgetting, repression, unreflective, self-distracting/distractible.
Lives in a nonfactual world of experience/impressionistic perception/recollection, global/diffuse, lacking in sharpness, nonanalytical.
Impressionable, susceptible to the vivid/striking or forcefully presented.
Magical solutions to problematical situations, hunches, "women's intuition," childlike, does not adapt to change well.
Superficial and stereotyped insights, "psychobabble."

Interpersonal Aspects

Exhibitionistic, dominates conversation, trivializes topics, lengthy dramatic stories, self-dramatizing, bragging, facades, "life of the party"/center of attention, fickle, wants to please, excessive needs for attention/praise/approval/gratification.
Romantic outlook: Fantasies of rescue and victory; nostalgia, sentimentalism, idealization of partner; world of "villains and heroes"; makes poor social relationship choices and decisions, poor judgments about partners/friends/spouses; stormy relationships with little real or durable enjoyment.
Vain, initially seen by others as warm and affectionate, guileless, vivid. Later seen as selfish, narcissistic, shallow/superficial and insincere, ungenuine, inconsiderate, self-pitying, shows astonishment at little understanding of the implications of her/his behavior or its consequences/effects on others/destructiveness.
Oppressively demanding, taking without giving, egocentric, vain, petulant, easily bored, requires excessive external stimulation, attention-seeking, help seeking, manipulates for reassurances, manipulative, asserts "a woman's right to change her mind"/masculine prerogatives.
Helpless, dependent, suggestible, uncritical, unassertive, sees assertion as rude or nasty, seen as fragile.
Impetuous, period of wild acting out, irresponsibility, chemical abuse/"bar hopping," "bed hopping"/sexual promiscuity/casual sexuality, low/poor impulse control/judgment/insight, thoughtless judgments.
Self-centered, feels hurt/deserted/betrayed in all relationships, brief and superficial contrition, sees self as sensitive and vulnerable, unsubstantial sense of self, absence of political or other convictions.
Coy, seductive, flirtatious, sexually provocative, blushes, easily embarrassed, giggles, naive, lacking in accurate sexual knowledge, seductive for help rather than sex, seems preoccupied with sex, immature, self-dramatizing/sexy/flamboyant/dramatic clothing/hairstyle/makeup, looks/dresses like a teenager/prostitute/"slut"/"tramp"/"boy toy"/"macho man."

Self-Image

Charming, gregarious, stimulating, playful, sensitive to others/feelings, selective incompetencies in areas of low importance (e.g., numbers, specifics).

Somatic Complaints

Vague, changeable, movable, "women's problems," complains of aging/appearance changes/loss of sexual skills or performances, "faints" at the sight of blood, swoons, "the vapors," feigns illness, always wrong weight, *la belle indifférence*   [✓ infrequent—about 30%].

13.13. HYPOCHONDRIACAL PERSONALITY

See also Section 17.21, "Malingering."

The relevant DSM-IV codes are 300.7, Hypochondriasis; 300.81, Somatization Disorder.

General Characteristics

Data do not suggest a more frequent presentation of hypochondriacal personality in the elderly or in females. Tyrer et al. (1990) have described the following characteristics:

Preoccupation with maintenance of health through dietary restriction/"healthy" medications/vitamins.
Distorted perception of minor symptoms so that they are elevated to major and life-threatening diseases. Never feels completely well.
Demands medical consultations for investigation/treatment/reassurance, seeks alternative health care providers when these are unproductive.
Rigid and persistent beliefs about health and lifestyles.
"Familiar face," "crock" (treated by a "quack"), "frequent flier," "thick-chart patient."
Dependent hostility (expecting both care and failure).
Multiple and changing complaints, unusual/singular somatic complaints that are described in affect-laden terms, strange aches and pains, chronic, unvarying fatigue.
Hypersensitivity to all medications, many foods, etc.
Joyless/unfulfilling lifestyle/overresponsible.

Spectrum of Somatic Presentation

The following table, classifying somatic presentations according to their basis in medical, psychiatric, or legal causes, is adapted by permission from Nadelson (1986).

	Medical	*Psychiatric*	*Legal*
Specific diagnostic category	Infection, trauma, cancer, metabolic disease, etc.	"Psychosomatic" or "psychological factors affecting physical condition." Repetitive somatization, psychogenic pain, hypochondriasis, conversion disorder	Factitious disorder Munchausen syndrome Malingering
Psychological forces as mechanism	No psychic factors involved in symptom production	Unconscious production of symptoms and signs	Conscious production of signs and symptoms

13.14. INADEQUATE PERSONALITY

Not in DSM-IV.

Cardinal Feature

Underresponsive in all life functions, immature, vulnerable, preoccupied.

Interpersonal Aspects

Underproductive/ineffective in all areas (conversational initiatives, qualities of emotions, depth of
relationships, etc.), socially inept/gauche, painfully shy.
Victimized/abused, taken advantage of/gullible.
Passive and unaware.
Involvement in melodramatic situations, overseriousness/subservient to authority figures.

Self-Image

Intense feelings of inadequacy and inferiority, self-consciousness (often painfully so).

Affects

Anxious/insecure.
Weepy sentimentalism.

Other

Undifferentiated, primitive defenses, unable to use intelligence to address problems.

13.15. MANIPULATIVE PERSONALITY

See also Sections 13.4, "Antisocial Personality," and 13.16, "Narcissistic Personality."

Not in DSM-IV.

Cardinal Feature

Unprincipled and deceitful in dealing with others who have something he/she wants.

Behaviors

Externalizes all blame, takes no responsibility for unfavorable outcomes.
Repeated, impulsive, dramatic, self-serving suicide gestures/attempts.
Evasive/indirect responses to questions, dishonest, untruthful.

Self-Image

Grandiose ideas about self.

Social Aspects

Likeable, attractive, engaging, center of attention, socially capable/effective/charming/graceful, tells
tall tales, flip, glib, fast, witticisms, attempts to con, puns/word plays, overabundant ideas.
Imposter, narcissistic.
Connives, cheats, deceptive, fraudulent, Machiavellian, unethical, unprincipled, unscrupulous, cavalier.
Showy acts of devotion, disloyal, untrustworthy, unfaithful, unscrupulous.

MULTIPLE PERSONALITY DISORDER   *See Section 13.11, "Dissociative Identity Disorder."*

13.16. NARCISSISTIC PERSONALITY
See also Section 13.15, "Manipulative Personality."

The relevant DSM-IV code is 301.81, Narcissistic Personality Disorder.

Cardinal Feature

Self-centeredness.

Associated Features

Exhibitionism, craves adoration.

Self-Image

Grandiose self, fantasies of self-importance/uniqueness/entitlement/"specialness," easy loss of self-esteem, "a fraud/fake," times of intense self-doubt/self-consciousness.

Fantasies of continuous conquests/successes/power/admiration/beauty/love, brags of his/her talents and achievements, predicts great success for self, believes self entitled to and deserving of a high salary/honors/etc., overvalues all of his/her own achievements.

Interpersonal Aspects

Entitled, confident, self-assured, expects to be treated as a sterling success/gifted person or at least better than others, feels special and preeminent, hides behind a mask of intellectual or other superiority, exaggerated self-esteem easily reinforced by small evidences of accomplishment and easily damaged by tiny slights and oversights.

Compliment hunger, demanding of affection/sympathy/flattery/favors, insatiably requires acclaim for momentary good feelings, attention-getting behaviors.

Fragile self-esteem, loss of self-esteem when disapproved, crushed/inflamed by life's wounds, responds to criticism with rage/despair/apparent cool nonchalance, compulsive checking on others' regard, may ruminate for a long time over nonthreatening social situations and interactions, extensive brooding.

Relationships seen entirely in terms of what others can give rather than as exchanges, exploitative, lack of objectivity, arrogant, socially insensitive, resents any failure to immediately and totally gratify her/his needs, shallow relationships, finds it easy to revoke commitments she's/he's made, no deep or abiding relationships, flouts social rules, alternates between idealization of and arrogant contempt for friends, long history of erratic relationships, takes others for granted, drives people away, conversations so self-centered that others lose interest, understanding of social conventions is distorted by egocentrism.

Striking lack of empathy, indifferent to rights of others, neglectful, thoughtless, tactless, selfish, ungrateful, unappreciative.

Oppositional/argues with authorities/instructions/examiner/supervisor, insistence on having his/her own way, little attention paid to work tasks, lies to protect ego/privileges/position, rationalizes, self-deceives, distorts facts.

Grandiose, cocky, intimidating, belligerent, resentful, pretentious, sarcastic, cavalier, boorish, bumptious, obnoxious, self-indulgent.

Affects

Nonchalant/imperturbable/insouciant/optimistic unless ego threats/damage occur, chronic unfocused depression, absence of expressions of warmth.

Cognitions

Envy, solipsism, preoccupation with own performance's value.

Approval-Seeking Styles

The following table is put together by permission with statements from Goleman (1988).

Normal self-interest	*Self-defeating narcissism*
Appreciates praise but does not require it to maintain self-esteem.	Insatiable cravings for adulation; praise leads to momentary good feelings about self.
May be hurt temporarily by criticism.	Is inflamed or crushed by criticism, broods at length.
After a failure, feels unhappy but not worthless.	Failure sets off feelings of shame, enduring mortification and worthlessness.
Feels "special" or especially talented, but only to a degree or in some areas.	Feels far superior to everyone and superior in many ways, demands recognition for that superiority.
Feels good about self despite criticism.	Requires continual bolstering from others to have a sense of well-being.
Takes life's setbacks in stride, although upset temporarily.	Reacts with hurt, depression, or rage over prolonged periods.
Self-esteem is fairly steady in face of rejection, disapproval, and attacks.	Reacts to rejection, etc., with keen rage or deep depression and severe loss of self-esteem.
Does not feel hurt if no special treatment is received.	Feels entitled to special treatment; rules do not apply to him/her as to ordinary others.
Is sensitive to the feelings of others.	Is insensitive to others' feelings and needs, exploits others.

13.17. "NERVOUS" PERSONALITY
See Section 10.3, "Anxiety/Fear."

"High-strung," worrier, "worry-wart," anxiety-ridden, "bad nerves," excitable, easily upset, unstable, moody, skittish, temperamental, low stress/frustration tolerance, "cracks up," "falls apart."
Picky, chronically dissatisfied, carping, fault finding.
Avoids/dislikes crowds, socially anxious, shy, sensitive, "thin-skinned," low self-esteem, hard on self and others.

13.18. NORMAL/HEALTHY PERSONALITY

The relevant DSM-IV code is V71.09, No Diagnosis or Condition on Axis I/No Diagnosis on Axis II.

As alternatives to relying on the absence of pathology, here are several options for describing a healthy or highly functional personality—in other words, criteria for positive mental health.

Frisch (1992) offers these 17 areas of life function as assessed by his Quality of Life Inventory:

Health.	Realistic self-regard.	Having a philosophy of life.
Work.	Recreation.	Learning.
Creativity.	Social service to others.	Civic action.
Love relationship.	Friendships.	Relationships with children.
Community.	Relationships with relatives.	Having a home.

Having a stable and adequate standard of living.
Neighborhood safety/aesthetics/naturalness/people.

Freud's famous formula for normality was "*Arbeiten und leben*" (to be able to work and love).

Jahoda (1958) mentions the following:

Awareness, acceptance, and correctness of self-concept.
Mastery of the environment and adequacy in meeting demands of life.
Integration and unity of personality, whole-hearted pursuit of one's goals.
Autonomy and self-reliance.
Perception of reality and social sensitivity.
Continued growth toward self-actualization.

Shoben (1956) describes these characteristics:

Aptitude for capitalizing on past experience.
Self-control.
Ability to envisage ideals.
Social reliability (predictability).
Capacity to act independently while still acknowledging the need for relationships (interdependence).

Mosak and Shulman (1988) suggests that normality can have various meanings in various contexts:

The common, the usual, the frequent.
As I think others act: Referential.
As a therapist acts: Therapist as referent.
Me: Taking oneself on faith.
As I used to be: My premorbid condition.
Conformity to social rules and norms, the normative: Being a good student (i.e., no trouble to the educational establishment), a good kid (quiet and undemanding).
Mediocrity/mediocre: Nothing in excess, the mean.
Square, boring, straight, "Dullsville."
Perfection.
The absence of symptoms.

Finally, W. C. Menninger (1967) offers these criteria for emotional maturity:

The ability to deal constructively with reality.
The capacity to adapt to change.
A relative freedom from symptoms produced by tensions and anxieties.
The capacity to find more satisfaction in giving than in receiving.
The capacity to relate to other people in a consistent manner, with mutual satisfaction and helpfulness.
The capacity to sublimate—to direct one's instinctive hostile energy into creative and constructive outlets.
The capacity to love.

PERSONALITY
PATTERNS

13.19. OBSESSIVE PERSONALITY

See Section 13.9, "Compulsive Personality," especially the "Note" there. See also Sections 12.7, "Compulsions," 12.22, "Obsessions," and 13.1, "A and B Personality Types."

The relevant DSM-IV codes are 301.4, Obsessive–Compulsive Personality Disorder, and 300.3, Obsessive–Compulsive Disorder.

Cardinal Features

Overideational, worries, overconscientiousness.

Cognitions

See Shapiro (1965).

Ruminates, doubting, balances pro and con, overdeliberateness, "thinks too much," distrusts own judgments, discounts/rejects new ideas or data, flounders, dithers, ponders endlessly, indecisive, avoids decision situations, reverses decisions, wishy-washy, vacillates.

Must never be irresponsible/careless/unappreciative/bad/imperfect/flawed,[1] overresponsibility, fears making any mistake, overconscientious.

Overdependence on intellect and logic ("lives in head"), overconfidence in own willpower, intolerant of affects.

Preoccupation with trivial details, overconcern with technical details, compelled attention to details, "can't see the forest for the trees," "rearranges the deck chairs on the *Titanic*," a "fanatic," a stickler for details, gives unnecessary warnings and reminders.

Preoccupation with the mechanics of efficiency, such as list making/organizing/schedule making/revising/following rules; fears of loss of control.

Perfectionism, demandingness, rigidity, inflexibility, "never good enough," concern with doing things the one right way, judgmental, moralistic, controlled by "tyranny of the shoulds" (Horney), "musterbates" (Ellis).

Religious concerns, scrupulosity, seeking repeated reassurance from spiritual guides, repetition of religious rituals because of their possible invalidation, sense of sinfulness and guilt.

Attention rigidly and narrowly focused on own interests/technical indicators/details, novel stimuli rejected as distractions.

Behaviors

Procrastinates, dawdles, delays, avoids, denies, ineffective, important tasks done last, mistakes the immediate for the important.

Exquisite care of belongings/"preciousness," meticulous, preserves worthless items.

Tense activity, effortful, burdened, driven, suffers under deadlines, pressured, racing thoughts.

Mild rituals, ritualistic interests, repeated "incantations," magical thinking (e.g., one's specialness, innocence, virtue).

Affects

Isolation of affect, loss of spontaneity, stiff and formal in relating, incapable of genuine/intense pleasure in anything, ambivalences, mixed feelings, depression.

Terrified of being embarrassed/humiliated, fears being found inadequate/wanting/making a mistake.

Terror of the unknown/uncontrollable/unpredictable.

Detects/discovers feelings through own behaviors (e.g., "I'm crying so I must be sad").

---

[1]This was suggested by Marcia L. Whisman, ACSW, of St. Louis, MO.

Interpersonal Aspects

Proper, careful, dutiful, stilted, dogmatic, opinionated, inflexible.
Uncomfortable on vacations or unstructured times, forgets to "smell the flowers."
Demanding and controlling but resists others' control.

13.20. PARANOID PERSONALITY
See Section 17.25, "Paranoia."

The relevant DSM-IV code is 301.0, Paranoid Personality Disorder.

Cardinal Features

Distrust and vigilance.

Interpersonal Aspects

Distrusts, un-/mistrustful of others, overcautious, suspiciousness, unwarranted distrust, expects mistreatment and treachery, distrusts motives of others, suspects manipulations, distrusts previous "allies," questions loyalty of others, believes others are trying to put him/her at a disadvantage/plotting against/laughing at/commenting on him/her.
Skeptical/cynical view of others.
Vigilant, sensitive to deception/betrayal/deprecation/"putdowns," listens for insulting/questioning references, hypersensitivity to criticism.
Guarded, defensive, reinforced expectations lead to isolation/enhancing distrust.
Hostile, belligerent, oppositional, confrontational, argumentative, stubborn, quick to take offense, easily offended, desire to vanquish/humiliate/deprecate, makes disparaging remarks.
Revenge fantasies, preoccupied with/desires to get even, carries grudges, schemes.
Desires to remain independent, no close relationships, refusal to confide, aloof, distant, isolated, withdrawn, retreats, secretive, terror of being controlled, continuous and extreme defense of autonomy, dread of passive surrender, a loner unless in total control of other/group, jealous of others' status.
Made indirect references/hinted/ideas of reference, knowing looks/winks/oblique references, power themes in all conversations.
Difficult, rigid, oppositional, deflects criticism onto others, recognizes no faults in self, denies responsibility or blame, blames others for all negative outcomes and frustrations, externalizes blame, never forgives or forgets, "chip on shoulder."
Carping, hypercritical, fault-finding.
Arrogant, prideful, overbearing, boastful, sensational plans, grandiosity, inflated appraisal of own worth/contacts/power/knowledge, takes a superior posture, disgusted by others' weakness.
Attention is narrowly focused on searching for confirmation/clues, novel stimuli are interpreted for real meanings, immune to contrary/corrective evidence.

Cognitions

See Shapiro (1965).

Projects onto others what is unacceptable about self, distorts the significance of actions and facts, loss of a sense of proportion.
Rigid and repetitive searching for confirmation of suspicions/ideas of reference/personalized meanings, attends only to conforming evidence/clues, belief in own convictions of underlying truth, magnifies minor social events into confirmations of the evil intentions of others and their lying,

exaggerating distortions resulting in delusions, flimsy or unfounded reasons produce intense suspicion, sensitive to slights.

Vigilant for signs of trickery/exploitation/abuse, hypervigilant, constant scanning for treachery, resentful, hypersensitive, hyperalert, oversensitive to any changes/the unexpected/anything out of the ordinary, fears of surprises.

Affects

Shallow emotional responses, cold and humorless, absence of tender or sentimental feelings, unemotional, restricted, enigmatic and fixed smile/smug, humorless.

Edgy, rarely relaxes, on guard, tense, anxious, worried, threatened, motor tension, touchy, irascible, jealous/envious of the progress of others.

Self-Image

Bitter, feels mistreated/taken advantage of/tricked/pushed around/overlooked/abused/threatened, collects injustices, suspects being "framed/set up."

Grandiose/self-important.

Sees self as objective, unemotional, rational, careful.

Delusional System   *See also Section 12.9, "Delusions."*

Belief in unusual or irrational ways of knowing (e.g., reading the future, magical thinking, ExtraSensory Perception).

Delusions of power/status/knowledge/contacts.

Creates a "pseudocommunity" (Cameron & Rychlak, 1968) of persons for and against her/him, schemes, etc.

Other

Auditory hallucinations/voices that command, mock, or threaten.

Litigious tendencies.

PASSIVE PERSONALITY   *See Section 13.10, "Dependent Personality."*

13.21. PASSIVE–AGGRESSIVE PERSONALITY

DSM-IV offers Passive–Aggressive Personality Disorder (Negativistic Personality Disorder) as a diagnosis for further study. ICD-10 includes no such diagnosis.

Cardinal Features

Intentional ineffectiveness and unacknowledged hostility.

Interpersonal Aspects

Superficially submissive.

Indirect control of others without taking responsibility for actions or anger, denies/refuses open statements of resistance/maintains own "good intentions."

Cannot say a direct "No," indirectly expressed resistance to demands of others for performance, thwarts/frustrates authority/spouse/partners/relatives.

Intentional but unconscious passivity to hide aggression, denial of/confusion over own role in conflict, gives mixed signals ("Go away and come close"), hostile defiance alternating with contrition.

Overcritical, "left-handed" compliments, subtle attacks, blames, insults, complains to others/ "bitches," critical of boss/all authorities/those with power/control over him/her, carping/fault-finding as defense against intimacy/commitment, unnecessary and prolonged argumentativeness.

Autocratic/tyrannical, demanding, manipulative, harassing, ruminates, troubled/conflictual relationships.

Affects

Denial of most emotions (especially anger, hurt, resentment), hostile motives, deeply and persistently ambivalent, sullen, envious, resentful.

Vocational/Academic Aspects

Intentional inefficiency that covertly conveys hostility, veiled hostility, resents control/demands.

Qualifies obedience with: tardiness, dawdling, sloppiness, stubbornness, sabotage, "accidental" errors, procrastination, forgetfulness, incompleteness, withholding of critical information/responses/replies, leisurely work pace, fails to meet deadlines.

Not lazy or dissatisfied with job, but spotty employment record/no promotions despite ability.

PSYCHOPATHIC PERSONALITY   *See Section 13.4, "Antisocial Personality."*

13.22. SADISTIC PERSONALITY

See also Sections 12.20, "Impulse Control Disorders," 13.3, "Aggressive Personality," 13.4, "Antisocial Personality," and 13.5, "Authoritarian Personality."

Not in DSM-IV.

Cardinal Feature

Cruelty.

Behaviors

Demeaning, aggressive/dominating behavior pattern, embarrasses/humiliates/demeans others.

Brutal, enjoys making others suffer, has lied to make others suffer, intimidates/frightens/terrorizes others to gain own wants, restricts others' autonomy, uses power in harsh manner for discipline or mistreatment, uses threats/force/physical cruelty to dominate others, quickly escalates level of violence to reestablish dominance, fascinated by violence/injury/torture/weapons/martial arts.

Dynamics

According to Goldberg (1995), crucial features of the personality include shame (self-contempt), which is the most common; contempt for others (projected defects); rationalization (of the cruel behaviors); justification (based on one's superiority); the inability or unwillingness to examine one's dark side (fearing the unacknowledged parts of oneself); and magical thinking.

✓ **Note:** According to Weinberg et al. (1984), *consensual* sadomasochistic activities have these characteristics:

1. Agreement about which partner is dominant/submissive ("top/bottom").
2. Shared awareness that they are play-acting ("in scene," "subspace," with costume, bondage equipment/"toys").

3. Informed, voluntary, explicit consent (agreed-upon "safe word" to stop, discussion of and respect for "bottom's" limits).
4. A sexual context.
5. Shared awareness that this behavior is sadomasochistic, "kinky," "BDSM," unusual, etc.

13.23. SCHIZOID PERSONALITY

The relevant DSM-IV code is 301.20, Schizoid Personality Disorder.

Cardinal Features

Social remoteness, emotional constriction.

Social Aspects

Solitary, aloof, social isolation, no close friends, "loner," withdrawn, unobtrusive, "fades into the background," remote, indifferent to others' praise/feelings/criticism, complacent.
Solitary interests, daydreams, self-absorption, may seem "not with it," inaccessible.
Limited social skills, lacking in social understanding, maladroit, says inappropriae things and immediately apologizes, unresponsive, unable to form attachments, peripheral roles, rarely dates or only passively, attends to only the formal and external aspects of relationships.
Normal or below-average work performance and achievement unless work does not require social contact.

Cognitions

Circuitous thinking, preoccupied with abstract/theoretical ideas, vague and obscure thought processes, unconventional cognitive approach, cryptic.
Intellectualizes, mechanical, impoverished/barren/sterile cognitions.
Vague and indecisive, absent-minded.
Excessive compulsive fantasizing, fantasies are sources of gratification and motivation, hostile flavor to fantasies.

Behaviors

Lethargic, low vitality, lack of spontaneity, sluggish.

Affects

Emotional coldness, limited capacity to relate emotionally, flat, impassive, blunted affect, emotional remoteness, absence of warm emotions toward others, no deep feelings for another, unfeeling, only weak/shallow emotions, weak erotic needs, cold/stark affects.

13.24. SCHIZOTYPAL PERSONALITY

The relevant DSM-IV code is 301.22, Schizotypal Personality Disorder.

Cardinal Features

The interpersonal difficulties of the schizoid, plus eccentricities or oddness of thinking/behavior and/or perception.

Behaviors

Idiosyncratic, odd, curious, bizarre, undoing of "evil" thoughts/"misdeeds."
Odd speech with vague/fuzzy/odd/idiosyncratic expressions.
Odd clothing or personal style.

Cognitions

Magical thinking, superstitiousness, clairvoyance, telepathy, precognition, recurrent illusions, sometimes paranoid ideation and style.
Autistic, ruminative, metaphorical; poorly separates personal and objective, fantasy and common realities; dissociations/depersonalizations/derealizations; sees life as empty and lacking in meaning.

Affects

Chronic discomfort, negative affects.

Interpersonal Aspects

Suspicious, tense, wary, aloof, withdrawn, tentative relationships, gauche, eccentric, peripheral, clandestine, dull, uninvolved, apathetic, unresponsive or obliquely reciprocating.

13.25. SELF-DEFEATING PERSONALITY

See also Section 13.10, "Dependent Personality."

Not in DSM-IV.

✓ **Note:** Beware of gender bias in the application of this diagnosis. (*See the caution concerning sexism in Section 13.10.*)

Cardinal Features

Chooses situations that will cause him/her to suffer mistreatment, failure, or disappointment.

Interpersonal Aspects

Excessive and unsolicited self-sacrifice, sacrifice induces guilt in others and then avoidance, provokes rejection by others and then feels hurt or humiliated, responds to success with depression/guilt/self-harming behaviors.
Avoids pleasurable or success experiences, does not perform success-producing tasks despite possessing the ability.
Rejects or does not pursue relationships with seemingly caring or needed/helpful individuals (e.g., a therapist), undermines self, seeks hurt/humiliation, "snatches defeat from the jaws of victory," chooses unavailable partners, sees those who treat her/him well as boring or unattractive, selects relationships with abusive persons, possibly sexually stimulated in relationships with exploitative or insensitive partners, "masochistic," incites anger/abuse/rejection.

SOCIOPATHIC PERSONALITY   *See Section 13.4, "Antisocial Personality."*

TESTS OF PERSONALITY   *See Section 13.27, "Personality Assessment."*

TYPE A AND TYPE B PERSONALITIES   *See Section 13.1, "A and B Personality Types."*

13.26. INTERPERSONAL DIAGNOSES OF PERSONALITY

The DSM's categories are rather indifferent to the social context in which an individual's maladaptive behavior occurs. McLemore and Benjamin (1979) argue that personality diagnoses ought to be rigorous descriptions of the interpersonal and social behaviors of interest. A number of models for making interpersonal diagnoses of personality have been developed:

1. The Structural Analysis of Social Behavior (Benjamin, 1996) incorporates the most relevant interpersonal dimensions: friendliness–hostility (affiliation) and control–autonomy giving (interdependence). The SASB is designed not only to categorize interactions in psychotherapy, but to chart changes in a patient's intrapsychic functioning.
2. Transactional Analysis, as formulated by Eric Berne (1964) and others, is a well-worked-out paradigm. *(See Section 26.8, "Transactional Analysis.")*
3. Schutz's Fundamental Interpersonal Relations Orientation–Behavior describes relationships and personality. See Schutz (1958).
4. Leary (1957) developed an interpersonal model that deserves more attention than it has received.

For other aspects of the evaluation of personality, see Chapter 26.

13.27. PERSONALITY ASSESSMENT
For assessment of intellect and cognitions, see Section 11.21.

Millon's Model

Millon's perspective and diagnostic schema (see Millon & Everly, 1985) are becoming more popular. They focus on reinforcement: What **types** of reinforcement (positive or enhancing/pursuit of pleasure vs. negative or relieving/avoidance of pain) does a personality typically seek? What are the usual **sources** of this reinforcement (self/independent vs. others/dependent vs. vacillating/ambivalent vs. no one/detached)? And what instrumental processes or **strategies** (active/modifies environment vs. passive/accommodates to environment) does the person employ?

These three dimensions result in eight categories of **normal** personalities (defined as those who seek positive types of reinforcement) and eight categories of **abnormal** personalities (those who seek negative types of reinforcement):

	Self	*Others*	*Vacillating*	*Detached*	
Active	Forceful	Sociable	Sensitive	Inhibited	} Normal
Passive	Confident	Cooperative	Respectful	Introversive	
Active	Antisocial	Histrionic	Passive/aggressive	Avoidant	} Abnormal
Passive	Narcissistic	Dependent	Obsessive/compulsive	Schizoid	

Source of reinforcement

The Five-Factor Model of Personality

Norman (1963) originated this simple and well-supported model. Costa and McCrae (1987) have given the five robust factors of personality the names listed below, and provided the dichotomous descriptors that follow (each factor is thought of as a continuum). Listed below these descriptors are applicable subscales from the well-validated NEO Personality Inventory–

Revised (Costa & McCrae, 1992), and terms from other sources that apply to one pole or the other of the continuum.

Neuroticism: Worrying–calm, nervous–at ease, high-strung–relaxed, insecure–secure, vulnerable–hardy.
Subscales: Anxiety, Anger–Hostility, Depression, Self-Consciousness, Vulnerability, Impulsiveness.
Other terms: Emotionality, temperamental, negative affectivity, hypochondriacal. Opposites: Ego strength, steady, cool, poised, self-confident.

Extraversion: Sociable–retiring, fun-loving–sober, affectionate–reserved, talkative–quiet, joiner–loner.
Subscales: Warmth, Gregariousness, Assertiveness, Activity, Excitement Seeking, Positive Emotions.
Other terms: Sociability, surgency, leader-like, dominance, capacity for status, social prescience, need for power, not withdrawn, frank and open, adventurous, sociable. Opposites: Reserved, not outgoing, secretive, cautious, reclusive.

Openness: Original–conventional, creative–uncreative, independent–conforming, untraditional–traditional.
Subscales: Fantasy, Aesthetics, Feelings, Actions, Values, Ideas.
Other terms: Open to new experiences, interested in experience for its own sake, eager for variety, daring, imaginative, intellectance, culturedness, unusual ideas, highly tolerant of uncertainty and what others think/do/say, broad-mindedness. Opposites: Concrete, practical, narrow interests.

Agreeableness: Good-natured–irritable, courteous–rude, lenient–critical, flexible–stubborn, sympathetic–callous.
Subscales: Trust, Straightforwardness, Altruism, Compliance, Modesty, Tendermindedness.
Other terms: Cooperative, interpersonally supportive, need for affiliation, need for love, friendly compliance, not jealous, mild and gentle, cooperative. Extreme forms: Dependent and self-effacing. Opposites: Grumpy, unpleasant, disagreeable, headstrong, negativistic.

Conscientiousness: Reliable–undependable, careful–careless, hard-working–lazy, punctual–late, persevering–quitting.
Subscales: Competence, Order, Dutifulness, Achievement Striving, Self-Disciplined, Deliberative.
Other terms: Thorough, ambitious, achievement-oriented, responsible, prudent, will to achieve, constrained, work ethic, fussy and tidy, scrupulous. Opposites: Undirected, lazy, fickle, unscrupulous, undependable.

A sixth personality factor may be intelligence.

Goldberg (1992) offers 50 bipolar rating scales (10 for each factor), or 100 well-established human traits that are subsumed under the five factors.

Objectively Scored Tests

Commonly used acronyms are indicated by the underlined letters. In addition, when a test is known by the name of its originator or another word, the word is underlined.

For Clinical Populations

Minnesota Multiphasic Personality Inventory, MMPI–Adolescent, and MMPI-2
Millon Clinical Multiaxial Inventory-II

Personality Assessment Inventory
Millon Adolescent Clinical Inventory

For Nonclinical Populations

<u>C</u>alifornia <u>P</u>ersonality <u>I</u>nventory–<u>R</u>evised
<u>NEO</u> <u>P</u>ersonality <u>I</u>nventory–<u>R</u>evised
<u>P</u>ersonality <u>I</u>nventory for <u>C</u>hildren

<u>C</u>hildren's <u>P</u>ersonality <u>Q</u>uestionnaire
<u>O</u>mnibus Personality Inventory
<u>S</u>ixteen <u>P</u>ersonality <u>F</u>actor Test (16PF)

Projective Tests

<u>C</u>hildren's <u>A</u>pperception <u>T</u>est
<u>H</u>ouse–<u>T</u>ree–<u>P</u>erson (drawings)
<u>R</u>orschach or <u>H</u>oltzman Inkblots
<u>T</u>hematic <u>A</u>pperception <u>T</u>est

<u>D</u>raw-<u>A</u>-<u>P</u>erson, Draw-A-Family
<u>K</u>oppitz Human <u>F</u>igure <u>D</u>rawing Test
<u>R</u>otter Incomplete Sentences Blank
Three Wishes

13.28. PERSONALITY TRAITS RELATED TO PSYCHODYNAMIC DEVELOPMENTAL STAGES

Psychoanalytic thinkers have formulated theories of personality/character traits corresponding to developmental stages. The theories of developmental stage fixations and regressions are too complex to be presented here, but the following table briefly summarizes the main stages, the themes and personality traits associated with them, subtypes of some stages, and some psychiatric syndromes linked with fixation in each stage.

Stage	*Theme*	*Derivative traits and features*
Oral	Dependency	Need for immediate gratification. Preoccupied with giving/getting, dependency/independence, aloneness/attachment, being passive or active. Hostile dependency: Petulance, deference, depression, rage. Self-esteem dependent on others/"supplies." Curious, open to novelty, seeking of "input." Optimistic resulting from overindulgence, or pessimistic resulting from frustration of needs. Magical thinking, grandiosity, compensatory behaviors. *Subtypes:* Oral-receptive/erotic, Oral-biting/sadistic. *Syndromes:* depression, grandiose mania.
Anal	Control	Anal triad of orderliness, stinginess, and stubbornness. Demands to perform, control, master, be autonomous. Cleanliness, rigidity, righteousness, reduced empathy *or* acting out, impulsivity, argumentativeness, impatience. Interpersonally objective, controlling *or* impulsive, manipulative. Self-esteem is lowered by buildup of anger, resentments. *Subtypes:* Anal-expulsive/sadistic (doing the opposite of what others want/request); anal-retentive/erotic (passively resisting). *Syndromes:* Obsessive–compulsive's overcontrol or acting out; psychopathic dyscontrol.

PERSONALITY PATTERNS

Stage	Theme	Derivative traits and features
Phallic	Assertion	Assertion seen only in inappropriate overt anger *or* seen in passivity and denied. Reckless, resolute, self-assured, narcissistic, excessive pride/vanity. *(See Section 13.16, "Narcissistic Personality.")* Self-esteem affected by failure, impotence, inaccessible goals. *Syndromes:* Narcissistic exhibitionism, passive–aggressive style.
Oedipal	Competition	Conflicts over loyalty; sexual acting out, guilt over disloyalty. Ambivalence prevents commitment, even involvement. Excessive competition, rivalry, or denial of these. *Syndromes:* Paranoid, critical stance *or* hysteric, agreeable, suggestible style (both denying competition).

13.29. COGNITIVE OR THINKING STYLES

The well-researched personality variables of cognitive or thinking styles have received less attention recently, but are still very powerful in understanding the interactions of personality and cognition: how someone processes information, draws conclusion, and chooses actions in school, on the job, and in relationships. For more information, see Sternberg and Grigorenko (1997).

Field-dependent vs. field-independent (psychological differentiation) (Herman Witkin).
Impulsive vs. reflective (or cognitive tempo) (Jerome Kagan).
Cognitively complex vs. fewer dimensions of a stimulus used (George Kelly).
Internal vs. external locus of control (Julian Rotter).
Global vs. analytical or scanning vs. focusing.
Sharpeners vs. levelers or splitters vs. levelers.
Abstract vs. concrete.
Constricted vs. flexible control.

C. The Person in the Environment

The larger world that the client lives in and how well or poorly he or she functions in it is of concern. Therefore, this subdivision offers ways to describe his or her performance of the basic Activities of Daily Living, his or her involvement in society and community, the extent and qualities of intimate relationships, his or her competence in vocational and academic skills, and other more specialized areas of evaluation.

14

Activities of Daily Living

✓ **Note**: If there are deficits in ADLs or there has been a change generally, indicate the reasons for this situation. And, as applicable, describe behaviors or deficits that limit independent living.

14.1. LIVING SITUATION/LEVEL OF SUPPORT NEEDED

(‹ › *by degree*) Lives independently in own home/apartment, uses community's support services (e.g., soup kitchen, food bank/community pantry, "Meals on Wheels," homemaker services), lives with spouse/children/partner/parental family/relatives/friends/roommate, occupies single/sleeping room with/without cooking facilities, lives in monitored individual apartment, attends partial/day hospital/sheltered workshop/day activities center, lives in residential drug/alcohol treatment program, in rehabilitation facility, in a Community Living Arrangement/Community Rehabilitative Residence/group home/supervised group apartment, in a boarding home, in a custodial/domiciliary care facility, in a personal care home/nursing home, in a Skilled Care Facility, in an Acute Care Facility, in a private/community/state/city/Department of Veterans Affairs hospital, in an Intensive Care Unit.

14.2. QUALITY OF PERFORMANCE

Each area of ADL performance can be evaluated as to its safety, independence, appropriateness, and effectiveness.

> Has a history of accidents/is accident-prone, performance of ADLs is unsafe/self- and other-endangering (e.g., gets lost, burns food).
> Is aware/unaware of the large hazards of life and can/cannot avoid them.
> (↔ *by degree*) Makes it worse, disorganized, ineffective, needs to be redone, unacceptable, sloppy, casual, neat, orderly, fussy, fastidious, meticulous, obsessive.

14.3. ASSISTANCE LEVEL REQUIRED

> (↔ *by degree*) Incapable/unable, needs 1:1/hands-on assistance, limited by physical/medical conditions rather than psychiatric ones, only simple tasks, helps spouse/partner/family with chores, participates, needs to be reminded/prompted/monitored/supervised, does with help, finishes unassisted, initiates/independent/autonomous.
> ADLs done by spouse/partner by tradition/agreement/default/because of physical limitations.
> ADLs performed by children/relatives/landlady/live-in friend/paid helpers/publicly provided aides.

14.4. SELF-CARE SKILLS

Eating and Toileting

> Feeding: (↔ *by degree*) Cannot feed self, assists with own feeding, feeds self.
> Eating: Eats ir-/regularly, appetite in-/appropriate, food preferences, good/poor balance/nourishment, restrictions, allergies.
> Toileting: Problems with elimination/urination/using toilet, uses laxatives/stool softeners/etc., incontinence (stress, night/day).

Grooming   *See also Sections 7.1, "Physical Appearance," and 7.2, "Clothing/Attire."*

> Bathing: Bathes ir-/regularly, attends to basic hygiene, uses makeup/shaves, gets haircuts, trims nails.
> Dressing: (↔ *by degree*) Dons and doffs clothing, dresses self, dresses appropriately for weather/occasion, does laundry, buys clothing.

Health Care

> Exercise: (↔ *by degree*) No activity, stretching, regular exercise, aerobic movements.
> Sleep: (↔ *by degree*) Sleeps well, has occasional difficulty, has significant problems. (*See Section 12.35, "Sleep Disturbances."*)
> Medications: Takes prescribed medications without prompting, with reminders/prompts/urging/seldom/irregularly/refuses, misuses/takes other's medications, takes many unnecessary over-the-counter medications.

14.5. COOKING

> (↔ *by degree*) Must have all meals prepared and served, eats all meals out, eats only snacks/fast foods/prepared foods/takeout/carryout, prepares boxed or canned foods (e.g., canned soup and sandwiches), no/simple preparation, top-of-stove/light cooking (fries, boils), full menu,

nutritionally balanced, uses all kitchen appliances, coordinates foods' types and preparation times, bakes, entertains.

14.6. HOUSE CARE/CHORES/DOMESTIC SKILLS

Cleaning

Food cleanup: Sets the table, clears table, washes, dries, puts away, silverware, does pots, uses dishwasher correctly, cleans up kitchen.

Neatens up house: Runs sweeper/vacuum, straightens up bedroom, takes out trash, dusts, mops, cleans bathroom.

House is immaculate/neat/clean/functional/cluttered/disorganized/chaotic/in disrepair/dangerous.

Clothing Care

Laundry: Recognizes dirty, collects, separates, washes/runs washer, dries, folds, irons, puts away.
Sews/repairs/replaces.

Other

Maintenance: (↔ *by degree*) Recognizes malfunctioning appliances, recognizes emergencies, calls for help/repair persons, shovels snow, mows lawn, can turn off electricity and water supplies, changes light bulbs, does minor repairs, changes faucets/switches, does major repairs.

Decoration: (↔ *by degree*) Chooses bed covers, chooses and hangs curtains/slipcovers, paints, wallpapers, remodels.

Plant/pet care: (↔ *by degree*) Cares for plants, fish, cat, dog.

14.7. CHILD CARE

(↔ *by degree*) Abuses, exploits, neglects, feeds regularly/appropriately/healthily, bathes regularly/safely, changes diapers and clothes, dresses child appropriately for weather and setting, performs routines (bedtimes, up and off to school, mealtimes), is affectionate with, actively interacts with, does not leave alone, babysits, defends, amuses/entertains, teaches, disciplines effectively, advocates for.

14.8. FINANCIAL SKILLS
See also Section 17.5, "Math Ability."

(↔ *by degree*) Counts, makes change, has receptive and expressive recognition of denominations of coins/metal money/currency/checks, handles all finances on a cash basis, can perform arithmetic calculations sufficient to allow over-the-counter purchase, buys money orders, has checking account (writes checks, deposits checks, able to do routine banking), saves money for large purchases, has credit card, manages all financial resources.

Squanders resources, impulsive/inappropriate/useless/wasteful purchases, easily duped into situations leading to financial risks/difficulty, not able to manage own finances, mathematically/intellectually/emotionally incompetent, not financially competent, able to handle small sums but not larger sums/own purchases/checking account/bill paying/saving/investing.

14.9. SHOPPING

($\leftrightarrow$ *by degree*) Unable to shop alone, can for snacks/toiletries/own clothes/simple foods/prepared foods/full menu foods/presents, can run errands for self/others, shops as entertainment, waits for and recognizes bargains/sales, makes major purchases effectively.

Is able to estimate the costs of common foods/items, knows which store sells which kinds of merchandise, can separate needs from wants/can control impulse shopping, is a wise consumer.

14.10. TRANSPORTATION

($\leftrightarrow$ *by degree*) Does not travel at all, needs companion, uses special bus/paratransit/"jitney"/taxi/ regular buses/mass transit, gets about by walking/bicycling/hitchhiking, driven by family/friends/ spouse/etc., drives with companion, drives alone, vacations independently.

14.11. HAZARD RECOGNITION AND COPING

Traveling

Wanders away from home.
Gets lost; does not recognize route home, streets, or house numbers.
Travels through dangerous places unaware of risks.
Fails to look for approaching traffic.
Does not respond to stop or direction signs when walking.

Fire

Overuses electrical outlets or extension cords, does not replace frayed/loose wires.
Smokes in bed or reclining chair, careless with matches/candles.
Heats home with oven, lets food burn.
Searches for gas leak with a flame.

Home Care

Cannot state what to do about a leaking faucet or pipe.
Cannot keep thermostat at a regular setting.
Leaves doors or windows open inappropriately.
Mixes or misuses cleaning products.
Fails to clean up broken glass or other risks safely.
Fails to care for pets/plants, causes suffering or death.

Food Preparation

Does not eat healthily (only snacks, meals too small or too few, fails to follow prescribed diet rules).
Does not store food safe from deterioration, will consume spoiled food.
Fails to set proper cooking temperatures, fails to monitor cooking progress on stove/oven/ toaster/microwave.
Leaves refrigerator/oven open, water running, items cooking.

Clothing

Wears loose or otherwise dangerous clothing.
Clothing inappropriate for weather or season.

Illness/Injury

Does not recognize signs of serious illness or injury and respond appropriately (cleaning wound/burn, bandage, taking medications, seeking help).

Does not take medications appropriately or as prescribed, takes wrong doses, wrong schedule.

Does not recognize side effects of medications.

Hazard Recognition: Summary Statements

Cannot be left unattended because simply cannot respond appropriately to environment.

Appears to be completely unaware of dangers, risks, and demands of situation.

14.12. SUMMARY STATEMENTS

Level of personal independence is adequate, given SocioEconomic Status and lifestyle.

The client has adapted well to reduced circumstances.

She is intellectually and psychologically capable of performing ADLs but does not, due to physical limitations/primarily due to physical/medical circumstances.

He is not able to care for his own needs, and so requires ___ support services. *(See also Chapter 22, "Recommendations.")*

She is functional in her current lifestyle/supportive situation, but in a more independent setting (i.e., living independently/alone), she appears to lack adequate self-direction and other resources for maintenance/continued functioning.

For a Child:

He goes to bed by himself and does not need a night light.

She does not go into parents' bed during night.

Child can sleep over at friend's house or visit for a day.

15

Social/Community Functioning

This chapter covers **social and community activities** only. Descriptors for **interpersonal behavior in the interview** can be found in Chapters 8 and 9, and for **couple and family relationships** in Chapter 16.

✓ **Note**: If social relating has been reduced in any area, try to indicate why this has happened.

15.1. LIFESTYLE

Location

Rural, farm/ranch, suburban, urban, small/medium/large city, commuter, inner city.

Qualities (↔ *by degree*)

nomadic	*unstable*	*solitary*	low variety	*low activity*	comfortable
vagrant	limited by	vegetative	low stress	no productive	independent
wanders	poverty	homebound	low intensity	activities	autonomous
migratory	survival	reclusive	low demand	low ambition	ambitious
roams	marginal		minimal	unproductive	
street person			mundane	indolent	comfortable
panhandles			circumscribed	recumbent	satisfied
			constricted		
parasitic			limited		
predatory			regressed		
symbiotic			centers around TV		
chaotic			routine		
			simple		
			monotonous regularity		

15.2. INVOLVEMENT IN SOCIAL/COMMUNITY ACTIVITIES

The following groupings are sequenced by increasing degree of involvement.

Hermit, recluse, isolated, withdrawn, aloof, avoidant, no interest in social relationships, uninterested in people and relating, no social activities, keeps to self.

Goes only to medical appointments/etc., no outside interests or functioning in any organizations, talks on phone, visited but does not visit, gardening/bird watching/other solitary pursuits, hunts/fishes alone, attends sporting events as spectator.

Window-shops, church attendance only on major holidays, visits/goes out with/drinks with friends, drops in on nearby friends, writes to or calls friends, hangs out with/loafs with/visits family/neighbors, eats out with others, regular "coffee klatch"/"breakfast club"/"night out," interested/participates in community groups, small outings (church, bingo, bowling, senior center, movies), friends help if he/she is sick, gets along selectively/appropriately with friends/family/authorities/public, shops in a variety of stores for all needs.

Gregarious, actively participates in church/religious group/social club weekly or more often, has out-of-town guests, goes to movies/sports events, visits museums, participates in musical and other cultural activities, votes in elections.

Attends adult school or classes, active in the community, plans life goals/self-improvement, plays team sports, visits out of town alone, does volunteer work, fully participates in society.

✓ **Note**: If client reports "attends church/temple/synagogue/mosque" or "plays cards," inquire what she/he does there, what the name of the clergyperson is, or which games are played. This will enable you to assess level of interests, demands (active or passive, skill or chance), satisfactions, and the quality and intensity of her/his social performance.

For a Child:

✓ Because a child's social activities are usually dependent on a caregiver's efforts, question carefully to separate out child's interests, skills, and performance.

15.3. CONFLICTUAL COMMUNITY RELATING

Problems at Work   *See also Chapter 17, "Vocational/Academic Skills."*

Warnings, close supervision/monitoring, reprimands, suspensions, firings, fighting with peers, given "cold shoulder," teases/provokes, threatening/disruptive behaviors.

Legal Aspects

Police contacts, warnings, tickets, summary offenses, arrests (indicate for what, when, with whom, and consequences), misdemeanor/felony, trials, convictions, probation, jail/prison time, parole.
History of fighting/drunkenness, Driving Under the Influence/Driving While Intoxicated.
Evictions, bankruptcies.
Conflicts with neighbors, agency personnel, landlords, store clerks.
Child/spouse/relative/animal abuse, Protection From Abuse orders.

SOCIAL FUNCTIONING

16

Couple and Family Relationships

DSM diagnoses are almost exclusively about individuals, not intimate relationships, situations, or interactions. Yet current understandings of disorders emphasize interactions, stressors and diatheses, family therapy, systems thinking, etc. Therefore this chapter lists several ways to evaluate couple and family relationships and interactional processes, and I would be grateful for your suggestions of more and better ways.

✓ You can record much useful information about couples and families on a genogram. *(See Section 6.6, "Family Genogram/Family Tree/Pedigree.")*

16.1. ASPECTS OF COUPLE RELATIONSHIPS

For questions and descriptors pertaining to sexual aspects of couple relationships, see Sections 3.23, "Sexual History," 6.4, "Adjustment History," and 10.10, "Sexuality." See also Sections 12.1, "Abuse, Physical," and 12.5, "Battered Woman Syndrome."

Dating Intensity (↔ *by degree*)

Never, seldom/rarely, only periodic/special events/holidays, group/car date/dyadic, "gets together with," interested in more dates but ..., frequently, dates compulsively/promiscuous, many dating partners, has many/only brief relationships, "dating" same person for many years, exclusive relationship/"going steady," serial monogamy, progressively better relationships, has a single committed long-term relationship.

Other Qualities

Physical/verbal/emotional abuse, abusing spouse/partner, abused spouse/partner, neglecting, exploitative, punishing, parasitic, repeatedly unfaithful, avoidant, "leaky," fragile, distant, boring, stale, stalemate, "truce," unhappy, mismatched, ill-considered, hasty, unhealthy, unsupportive, limiting, unsatisfying, symbiotic, stable, functional, adequate, satisfying, rewarding, intimate, enhancing, loving, fulfilling.

16.2. FAMILY INTERVIEWING METHOD

Questions to Ask Each Member

"What are the main problems in your family?"
"What do you have to do in this family to . . .
    be alone/maintain your privacy?"
    get others to stop bugging you?"
    get attention, appreciation, physical contact, love?"
    be listened to?"
    get the family together?"
"When do you feel . . .
    tense, depressed, upset, worthless?"
    best, freest, most worthwhile, proudest, optimistic, loving, loved?"
    you have to conceal your feelings/fake it?"
"How do you show your feelings of . . .
    anger, disappointment, frustration, sadness, tension?"
    affection, love, appreciation?"
"Whom do you depend on?"
    "Whom can you count on to . . . ?"
    "Who helps with . . . ?"
"What big changes/problems have happened in this family?"
"What are you working on yourself?"

Questions to Ask the Family as a Group

"Plan something you can all do together."
"What are your family's biggest goals/plans/fears?"
"What are the strengths in this family?"
    "Who has athletic skills? Manual skills? Academic skills?"
    "Best sense of humor? Smartest? Most faith?"
"Besides you all, who else is part of this family?" (Relatives, friends, boarders, pets, etc.?)
"When do you all get together?"
"Who's the boss of this family?"
"Who calls the shots in what areas?"

16.3. INTAKE ASSESSMENT OF FAMILIES

✓ Evaluate both current and previous marriages.

Presenting Problem, Chief Complaint/Concern, Referral Reason

These are listed in alphabetical order.

Abuse/violence/neglect (spouse/partner, child; sexual, physical).
Adolescent adjustment problem.
Chemical abuse (parent, child).
Child behavior problem/parenting problem.
Child custody.
Divorce mediation.
Enrichment (marital, family, personal, relationship).
Health/medical/nutritional/physical conditions.
Legal difficulties (child, parent, other; civil, criminal, misdemeanor, felony).
Marital/couple conflict.
Parenting (skill enhancement).
"Poor communication."
School problem (behavior, academic, peer).
Separation/breakup, spouse/partner absence, divorce.
Sexual dysfunction/patterns/conflicts.
Time management/conflict/absence.   [✓ Ask about each member's daily schedule.]
Truancy/runaway.
Other: Cultural problems, religion, job/financial problems, education, peer problems, relatives.

Who?

Ask these questions:

"Who is seeking treatment? Why?"
"Who is involved in the problem?"
"Who currently resides in the household?"

Perceptions of Problem and Circumstances

Ask:

"What is _____'s (the referrer's) perception of the problem?"
"Why is help being sought now?" (Possible precipitants: changes, births, illnesses, deaths, re-/ marriages, divorces, moves, job changes, departures, other transitions.)
"What is each family member's perception of . . .
    the problem?"
    the major tasks/changes desired/facing the family now?"
    the time frame for improvement?"
    who has the problem (i.e., is the Identified Patient)?"

Previous Solutions

Find out about the following:

Efforts/attempts, outcome, ineffective attempts to maintain homeostasis.
Previous treatment of whom, for what, when; intervention, outcome.

Developmental Issues

Learn about individual development issues for children and adults.

History of adults' relationship:
    How met, courtship, each family's attitude.
    Relationship to grandparents, other relatives.
    Beginning expectations, satisfaction/fulfillment levels.
    Children's birth, blended family (if applicable).

Family stage/life cycle: Courtship, early marriage, child bearing, child rearing, parents of teenagers, launching, middle years, retirement, transitions.

Legal and Social Status

Ascertain the following:

Adults' current status—describe as:
Never married, "single," living together, People of Opposite Sex Sharing Living Quarters, paramours, "live-ins," roommates, boyfriend/girlfriend, common-law marriage, married, "commuter marriage," separated/living apart, estranged, divorced, remarried, marriage of convenience/outward appearance of a marriage.
Previous relationships/cohabitations/marriages: For each, note duration, satisfaction, reasons ended/termination reasons, age and date at termination.
Number, names, ages, and genders of children.
Relationship with spouse/partner, ex-spouse/partner (if applicable), children.
Adultery/extramarital relations/satellite relationships, expectations of exclusivity/monogamy.
Whether an adult is in process of divorcing/ex-spouse-to-be/"pre-ex."

Other: Summary Statements

_____ (name) is ignored by, distanced, never/rarely visited, only fought with, only contacted by phone, estranged, struggling to individuate from family of origin.
_____ (name) feels he/she gets much/some/no support from spouse/partner in parenting/child management/child raising/child care, doing chores, handling finances, dealing with relatives, doing home maintenance, supporting household.
Child rearing is viewed as unsuccessful/overwhelming/stressful/difficult at times.
A high priority/high risk/danger/matter of great seriousness is _____ (specify).
_____ is an emergency/crisis/critical need, recurrent crisis/problem requiring only ordinary procedures, past crisis/chronic crisis.

16.4. A COMPETENCY-BASED MODEL

Marsh (1992a, 1992b) offers a very positive model for viewing families—one that emphasizes health, competencies, coping strategies, strengths, skills, resources, problem solving, empowerment, and ecology. Her model poses professionals not as therapists but as active enablers, collaborators, advocates, and strengtheners of the family system and network, using reframing, positives, and skill development.

16.5. SYSTEMIC FAMILY EVALUATIONS

Theoretical Constructs to Guide Evaluation

Structure/coupling: Involvement, enmeshed vs. disengaged (Minuchin, 1974), isolation, individuation, power structure.
Boundaries: Rigidity vs. flexibility, closed vs. open, generational boundaries.
Coalitions: Schism, skew (Lidz & Fleck, 1985), pivotal members, dyads, triangles, labels, identifications, mappings, alliances, interfaces, relationship of spouses.
Style: Closed (traditional/authoritarian) vs. open (collaborative/democratic), random (individualistic/permissive) vs. synchronous (perfectionistic/consentient); note family image vs. actual behaviors on these style criteria.

Dynamics:
  How problem works, who is involved, who is served by the problem.
  Motivators, demotivators.
  Strengths.
  Disablement: Who is blocked from which targets, collective failings.
Subsystems:
  Couple system, sibling system, intergenerational system.
  Boundaries, patterns, alliances, ethnic influences, "shoulds," conflict and cooperation,
    cutoffs.
  Other subsystems: Friends, work, school, church, professionals, agencies.
  Support systems: Relatives, friends, etc.
Other aspects:
  Family lifestyles, themes, myths (security, success, taboos, secrets).
  Pseudomutuality (Wynne, 1988).
  Scapegoating (Ackerman, 1982): Scapegoat, persecutor, family healer.
  Paradoxes, double binds (Bateson, 1972).
  Discordance, disturbance, disruption.
  Centripetal and centrifugal family interaction patterns (Beavers, 1990).

Summary

Formulate hypotheses re: maintenance of symptoms, functional analysis, payoffs, tradeoffs,
homeostasis.

16.6. ASPECTS OF CHILD REARING/RAISING

Parental Restrictiveness

Limits: Overprotection/excessive restriction, overpermissiveness/indulgence, unrealistic demands.
Strictness/leniency re: feeding, mobility, interruption by children, table manners, neatness, cleanli-
    ness, bedtime, noise, radio and TV, chores, obedience/compliance, aggression.
Restrictiveness regarding sexuality (nudity, modesty, masturbation, sex play).
Aggression: Encouraged to fight back/defend self, toward parents/sibs/peers, inhibited, redirected.
Parental differences: High/low ratio of maternal to paternal discipline, mother/father views other
    parent as overly strict, conflicts over discipline.
Problematic discipline: Lack of discipline, inconsistent discipline, harsh/overly severe discipline,
    fear/hatred of parent, decreased initiative/spontaneity, unstable values.

Parental Acceptance

Warmth: Sympathetic/rejecting response to crying, open/muted/no demonstrations of affection,
    fun/no fun in child care, great/little/no warmth of bond, playtime initiated by mother/father/no
    one.
Use of praise: For table manners, for obedience, for nice play/amount of play, no use of praise.
Other: Positive/negative feelings when pregnancy discovered.

Parent–Child Misfit

Thomas and Chess (1977; Thomas et al., 1968) have described "parent–child misfit," which
results when there is a mismatch between the temperament variables of children and the
expectations of their mothers/caregivers. Particularly well described are the characteristics of
"difficult babies": irregular eating/sleeping/elimination, mainly negative moods, much crying,

irritability, and poor adjustment to change (this last may be manifested in illness, as well as further disturbances in sleep and eating).

16.7. MEASURES ASSESSING COUPLE AND FAMILY FUNCTIONING

Couple Functioning

There are many scales for assessing couple relationships, so evaluate your needs in your setting.

Assessment of Marriage Problems

An old and well-researched scale of marriage problems has been updated by Swenson et al. (1992a). It lists 43 areas of possible conflict (each rated as occurring at one of five levels of frequency), clustered into six factor-analyzed subscales covering these areas:

1. Problem solving, decision making, and the goals of marriage.
2. Child rearing and home labor.
3. Relatives and in-laws.
4. Personal care and appearance.
5. Money management.
6. Outside friendships and dissatisfactions with the expression of affection in the marriage.

Assessment of Love and Affection

Swenson et al. (1992b) offer a recent revision of a scale that has been well researched and that seems to address all the measurable meanings of love and affection in marriage. There are six factor-analyzed subscales covering the following areas:

1. Verbal expressions of affection to and from the loved one.
2. Self-disclosure of intimate personal facts to and by the loved one.
3. Toleration of loved one's bothersome aspects.
4. Moral support, encouragement, and expressions of interest shown and received.
5. Feelings felt but not expressed overtly.
6. Material evidence of affection, as seen in gifts, chores performed, financial support, favors done by and for the loved one.

Other Assessment Methods

Other approaches to assessing couples include the following:

Life chronology, timeline (Satir, 1967; Toman, 1993).
Structured family interview (Watzlawick, 1977).
Genogram. *(See Section 6.6, "Family Genogram/Family Tree/Pedigree.")*
Life cycles of marriages/relationships.

There are many other scales for assessing couples. I happen to like Stuart and Jacobson's (1991) Couple's Pre-Counseling Inventory. Many useful questionnaires and problem lists can be found in Lasswell and Brock (1989). Karpel (1994) offers outstanding comprehensive and practical guidance in couple evaluation.

RELATIONSHIPS

Family Functioning

A very complete source for assessment instruments and approaches for assessing the whole family is a book by Grotevant and Carlson (1989). L'Abate's (1994) textbook covers family evaluation methods, rationales, and report writing.

Kinston's (1988) Family Health Scales are an interesting "attempt to capture formally the intuitive assessment made by clinicians." The goal is formalizing the clinician's judgments, not mathematical measurement. Evaluations are made at the family level, the network-of-relations level, and the level of individual functioning. An outline of the sections and subscales will suggest its richness.

Family Character:
 Affective Life: Family atmosphere, nature of relationships, emotional expression, emotional responsiveness.
 Communication: Overall patterns, continuity, expression of messages, reception of messages.
 Boundaries: Family cohesion, family roles, intergenerational boundary, sexual identity, individual autonomy.
 Alliances: Family structures, marital relations, parental coalition, parent–child relationships, sibling relationships.
Family Competence:
 Conflict Resolution.
 Problem Solving.
 Family Life-Cycle Tasks (e.g., child management).
Family Relationship with the Environment:
 Family Stability.
 Community.
 Extended Family.
 Relationship with the Interviewer/Treater.
Family Process:
 Family Interaction.
 Interaction between Family and Environment.

17

Vocational/Academic Skills

This chapter covers much of the information you may need for **disability reports**, as well as other evaluations of vocational and academic functioning.

VOCATION/
ACADEMICS

17.1. BASIC WORK SKILLS

Energy Level (↔ *by degree*)

Sickly, low, adequate/normal, healthy, vital, vigorous, impressive, excessive, driven.

Motor Skills (↔ *by degree*)

Poor coordination, good/adequate/normal dexterity, dextrous, excellent coordination. Eye/hand, cross-body, fingers, etc.

Appearance (↔ *by degree*)

Shows minimal/unacceptable regard for personal attire or cleanliness, disheveled and sloppy/wears dirty clothes, needs a bath or shave, adheres to standards of nonoffensive personal cleanliness, is cleanly but inappropriately dressed, appears typical of his/her community's workers in grooming/cleanliness/attire choice.

Concentration (↔ *by degree*)   *See also Section 11.5, "Concentration/Task Persistence."*

Deficiencies of attention/persistence, low frustration tolerance, occasionally distracted, can focus and maintain attention.

Motivation to Work *(↔ by degree)*

Refuses, apathetic, indifferent, is minimally motivated/compliant without complaint/positive/eager, willing to work at tasks seen as monotonous or unpleasant.

Memory *(↔ by degree)*

Is unable to retain individual instructions for simplest of tasks, requires constant/hands-on/one-on-one supervision/continual reminders/coaching to perform routine tasks, requires reinforcement to retain information from day to day, requires little or no direction after initial instruction or orientation, remembers locations/work procedures/instructions/rules, able to learn job duties/procedures from oral instructions/demonstrations/written directions, carries out short/simple/detailed/multistep instructions.

Mistakes *(↔ by degree)*

Makes an un-/acceptable number of errors that must be corrected by client/coworkers/supervisors, does not notice exceptions/failures, has low/poor/adequate/high inspection skills, monitors own quality, conceptualizes the problem, corrects situation/alters own behavior, quality/accuracy/waste/scrap decreases with repetition/training/supervision.

Productivity *(↔ by degree)*

Minimal/below expected/equal to ___% of average competitive worker's rate/quantity of work, increased production/productivity by ___% over original measured rate, quantity/productivity increases with practice/repetition/training/supervision, shows acceptance of competitive work norms, able to compete.

Attendance *(↔ by degree)*

Unreliable/inadequate/minimal/spotty/deficient, has unusual/large number of unexcused absences per month/calls in sick, seldom/generally punctual for arrival/breaks/lunch hours, performs without excessive tardiness/rest periods/time off/absences/interruptions from psychological symptoms, dependable, responsible.

Communication *(↔ by degree)*

Seldom communicates beyond the minimum and often misunderstands directions, is misunderstood by peers/supervisors, can comprehend some nonconcrete aspects of work situation, communication is usually understood by others, communications are clear and work-relevant, uses telephone properly, has the ability to ask questions or seek assistance as needed.

Response to Supervision *(↔ by degree)*

Rebels against supervision, resists supervision, does not seek supervision when needed, personalizes supervisor–worker relationship, is oppositional to requests of supervisor, often withdraws/refuses offers of interaction, is difficult to get along/work with, requires firm supervision, asks for unnecessary help/requests excessive supervision, interacts with the general public/coworkers/supervisors without behavioral extremes/appropriately, reports appropriately to supervisor, improves work methods/organization under supervision, works in small/large groups, is helpful to supervisor and peers.

Emotional Responsiveness *(↔ by degree)*

Tends to become emotional/angry/hurt/anxious when corrected/criticized/cannot have own way and is unable to continue work, argues, responds angrily or inappropriately to comments but with counseling or encouragement can remain at work site, verbally denies problems but . . . , maintains composure and attention to task, takes corrective action, responds appropriately by adjusting behavior or work habits, reacts appropriately to conflict/authorities/peers/coworkers, maintains even temperament.

Adaptability *(↔ by degree)*

"Set in her/his ways," exhibits serious adjustment problems when work environment changes, is unable to cope with job's pressures, displays inappropriate or disruptive behavior only briefly after work changes and is able to return to task with supervisory encouragement, generally adapts to/copes with/tolerates work changes/schedules/deadlines/interruptions/pressures, accepts instructions/criticism/authority/supervision/feedback/rules, relies on own resources, learns from mistakes/instruction/supervision.

Hazard Awareness

Oblivious to/aware of hazards and able to take precautions, seems to be "accident-prone" beyond usual frequency of accidents, has an "accident" whenever eligible for promotion or transfer.

Decision Making *(↔ by degree)*

Cannot make simple decisions to carry out a job, indecisive, confused by choices and criteria, cannot organize himself/herself/prioritize work/arrange materials, becomes paralyzed by decisions, makes correct routine decisions, makes up own mind, effectively sequences steps in a procedure.

Pacing/Scheduling *(↔ by degree)*

Cannot conform to a schedule/tolerate a full workday/perform within a schedule/sustain a routine, shows an uneven/unsteady work pace throughout workday, shows necessary/expected/ normal/required stamina, maintains motivation, completes assignments, finishes what she/he starts, continues despite obstacles/opposition/frustrations, works in a time-conscious manner.

Conscientiousness *(↔ by degree)*

Maintains/cares for tools/supplies/equipment, sometimes does not repair/adjust/replace/service as needed, wastes materials or damages equipment, is not a conscientious worker, irresponsible.

Travel to Work *(↔ by degree)*

Drives to work, travels independently by public transportation or makes own arrangements to get to job site, travel arrangements are unreliable, will not use available travel options.

Relationship to Peers/Coworkers *(↔ by degree)*

Avoidant, distant, shy, self-conscious, nervous, conflictual, domineering, submissive, competitive, suspicious, attention-seeking, clowning, immature, provocative, inappropriate, dependent, troublemaker, ridiculing, teasing, <normal>, friendly.

VOCATION/ ACADEMICS

Maladaptive or Odd Behaviors

Too introverted/withdrawn, loud/domineering, manipulative/takes advantage of peers, limits conversation to "yes" or "no" answers, will not look at person he/she is addressing, gossips, will not start a conversation, seeks unwanted/ill-timed/inappropriate physical contacts, has attention-getting odd behaviors/offensive personal hygiene, confuses actual and imagined abilities, makes excessive or unrealistic complaints.

17.2. VOCATIONAL HISTORY

Ask about the following:

Has client ever been employed/"worked"/had a wage-earning job outside the home? If so, number/duration/kind of jobs?

Is client currently employed/unemployed/laid off/underemployed/retired? If employed, is employment marginal/labor pool/temporary/seasonal/part-time/full-time?

Is employment history regular/irregular/interrupted/sporadic? Number and reasons for firings? Problems with absenteeism, conflict with customers/peers/coworkers/supervisors?

Any job trials, work attempts, job coaches, job-finding clubs, work-hardening programs?

Have any background factors (e.g., medical, home, school) kept client from benefiting from formal education?

Does client have a history of low productivity/achievement/progress throughout life?

17.3. VOCATIONAL COMPETENCE/RECOMMENDATIONS

Overall Competence: Summary Statements

Normal

This client is capable of performing substantial gainful employment at all levels.
There are no psychological barriers to employment.
She can perform in a competitive work setting/in the open labor market.

Somewhat Limited

He is intellectually limited, but not to the extent that would preclude appropriate employment.
She is able to relate to coworkers and supervisors, handle the stresses and demands of gainful employment within her intellectual/physical limitations.
This person could understand, retain, and follow instructions within the implied limitations of his borderline intellectual functioning/mild/moderate mental retardation.
The client is able to understand, retain, and follow only simple, basic instructions.
She would be able/unable to meet the quality standards and production norms in work commensurate with her intellectual level.
He can perform activities commensurate with his residual physical/functional capabilities/capacity.

Significantly Limited

He can function only in a stable setting/sheltered program/very adapted and supportive setting.
The client requires appropriate prevocational experiences/work adjustment training/work-hardening program/diagnostic work study/evaluation of vocational potential.
This person can/can't tolerate pressures of workplace, is un-/used to the regularities and demands of the world of work.
No Residual Functional Capacity for Substantial Gainful Activity.

The cumulative impact of the diagnoses presents a very significant deterrent/obstacle to employment/productivity/substantial gainful activity.

Setting and Tasks Needed

The following groupings are sequenced by degree of increasing demand on the client.

Nonstressful/unpressured/noncompetitive setting, simple/basic/repetitive/routine/noncomplex/slow-paced/unpaced/nonspeeded tasks that do not require facility in academics.

Solitary/nonsocial tasks, working alone/no contact with the public.

Closely supervised.

Sheltered/highly supportive, stable.

Part-time/flexible hours, full-time, overtime.

Employment Level *(↔ by degree)*

Unskilled/helper/laborer, semiskilled, skilled, professional, managerial, self-employed.

Supervision *(↔ by degree)*

Requires continual redirection, repetition of instructions, working under close and supportive supervision, instruction only, monitoring only, occasional overview, can work independently.

Ambition *(↔ by degree)*

Avoidant, lethargic, indolent, listless, lackadaisical, self-satisfied, content, eager, persistent, hopeful, enterprising, greedy, opportunistic, pretentious, unrealistic.

Self-Confidence *(↔ by degree)*

Grandiose, impractical/unrealistic, overconfident, reasonably self-assured, marginal/low opinion of own abilities, highly/unproductively self-critical.

Job Seeking/Hunting

The following groupings are sequenced by degree of increasing effort on the client's part.

Has no actual or realistic history of seeking, efforts have been episodic/half-hearted, efforts have been determined but initiative is now exhausted.

Poor/low/inadequate knowledge of vocational and educational resources.

Employment is seen as too/highly/moderately/mildly stressful.

Has job-finding skills/interviewing skills, can identify obstacles to successful completion of training/skill development/employment, has a feasible vocational goal/time frame for actions.

Obstacles to Success: Summary Statements

This client is academically so deficient that he/she cannot find or hold a job.

Engages in excessive off-task behaviors.
She invents excuses for lateness/absences/mistakes/inattention, is irresponsible.
He avoids some essential tasks.
She engages in inappropriate or disruptive behaviors, agitates intentionally.

She does not work effectively when under any/normal/expected pressure.
He responds to criticism with anger/anxiety/hurt/withdrawal.

She uses/overuses offensive language.
He puts worst foot forward.

The client does not appear disabled, but is not employable because . . . (specify).

17.4. WRITTEN LANGUAGE SKILLS/ABILITY
See also Section 18.4, "Reading Materials."

Reading Comprehension

Test client with a paragraph from a magazine on a current topic and ask about its meanings.

(↔ *by degree*) Alexic, illiterate, functionally illiterate, lacks basic/survival reading skills.

(↔ *by degree*) Names letters, says simple words, reads out loud/silently, only small sight reading vocabulary, reads signs/directions/labels/instructions/recipes, low/normal comprehension, deciphered word meanings, slow reader, basic functional literacy, no reading for pleasure, usual skills, literate, avid, scholarly.

Worked hard, asked for assistance, recognized errors, used word attack skills to successfully identify/decipher several words on a reading test.

Summary Statements:

His/her reading is limited to a small group of memorized words.
He/she has rudimentary phonetic abilities, but cannot identify unfamiliar or phonetically irregular words.

His/her poor reading skills prohibit responding to/guidance by written instructions.
Reading skills are adequate for basic literacy and utilization of written texts for getting directions.

Spelling/Writing

Spelling: (↔ *by degree*) Agraphic, letter–sound relationships are absent/poor/need strengthening.
Spelling skills are poor/good/excellent, shows/demonstrates a solid grasp of underlying phonetic principles.
Writing from dictation: Reversals, inversions, omissions, substitutions, additions, confused attack on letters, labored writing, reckless.
Handwriting: Good/poor quality, problems with upper-/lower-case letters, inversions, reversals, confused one letter with another, degree of effort required, awkward handgrip position/use of the page, size of letters.

Statements of Implications for Vocational/Academic Functioning

Relationship of client's skill level to expected school/work achievement is . . . (specify).
Areas of educational strength/weakness/handicap and need for intervention suggest . . . (specify).

17.5. MATH ABILITY
See also Section 14.8, "Financial Skills."

The following groupings are sequenced by degree of increasing skill.

Anumerate, can say the digits, knows the sequence, holds up the correct number of fingers when asked for a number, counts items, knows which number is larger.

Can do simple tasks of counting and measurement but not computation beyond addition and subtraction.

Can do simple addition and subtraction of single-digit/double-digit numbers but only when borrowing is not involved.

Ability limited to simple computation in orally presented arithmetic problems, can do problems requiring addition/subtraction/multiplication/division.

Can solve problems when regrouping is required.

Can do correctly problems involving decimals/fractions/measurements. Understands prices, counts change, makes change, possesses basic survival math (measurements, portions, percentages, fractions, weights, etc.), knows basic business math/consumer's math, is fully numerate.

17.6. REHABILITATION ASSESSMENT

The articles by Brodwin et al. (1992a, 1992b) are useful starting places, as they offer sample reports (initial evaluation, medical, background, progress) and job analyses (job description, duties, physical demands, etc.) in terms of the job's stressors.

17.7. SPECIAL CONSIDERATIONS FOR DISABILITY REPORTS

✓ If a client has an attorney and is not working, record this fact.

✓ Note also that in a disability report, you should not state unequivocally that the client is or is not "disabled." This is usually an administrative decision and is based on criteria beyond just your findings.

VOCATION/ ACADEMICS

18

Recreational Functioning

18.1. ENTERTAINMENT: TV/RADIO/TAPES/RECORDS/MUSIC

(↔ *by degree*) Avoids, dislikes, confused/overstimulated by, just as background/passive listener, aware of news/weather, selective/chooses/plans for particular programs, "Must see my stories/soaps," recalls, actively tapes/records/purchases recordings, attends musical events regularly, plays musical instrument.

18.2. HOBBIES

(↔ *by degree*) No hobbies, does puzzles/letter games/board games, (cards, checkers, Monopoly), does crafts/needlecrafts, tinkers, paints by numbers/in water/oil/acrylics, builds models, takes photographs, hunts/fishes, gardens, reads, collects, repairs, plans, travels, builds.
Cares for pets (feeds, exercises, cleans up after, grooms, teaches, consults veterinarian, etc.).

For a Child:

Plays with toys/dolls/miniatures, builds models (airplanes, cars, etc.), has/maintains collections.

18.3. SPORTS

Specify the sport(s) with which the client is involved.

(↔ *by degree*) Watches on TV, attends/spectates, reads about, discusses, participates in, Special Olympics, bowling league, plays on sports team, has individual sport(s), regularly participates in sport, competitive player.
Exercises regularly, walks, jogs, aerobics, health club, golfs, swims, lifts weights, other.

18.4. READING MATERIALS

See also Section 17.4, "Written Language Skills/Ability."

Newspapers (↔ *by degree*)

Headlines only, comics, horoscopes, simple stories, advertisements/prices, classifieds, news, columnists, editorials, news analyses, arts sections, reviews.

Magazines (↔ *by degree*)

Word-finding magazines, children's books/magazines, comic books, adventure, gossip, supermarket, women's, men's, newsweeklies/current events, crosswords, science fiction, special interest (e.g., war, detective, biker, guns, wrestling, hobby, trade, technical, professional, literary, arts).

Books (↔ *by degree*)

Romances, short stories, mysteries, novels, Westerns, horror, adventure, science fiction, contemporary literature, poetry, biographies, self-help, nonfiction, texts, classics.

18.5. QUALITY OF PARTICIPATION/PERFORMANCE

(↔ *by degree*) No recreational activities, nothing for relaxation/fun, very few pleasurable activities, moderate interest in recreation, active and satisfying recreational life, recreation integrated into work and social lives.

(↔ *by degree*) Discontinues, has many unfinished projects, completes but only at a very low quality, takes much longer than usual/previously, is very slow, forgets, neglects/distracted from activities, finishes only the simplest/quickest, usually completes, always finishes, compulsively completes.

For a Child:

(↔ *by degree*) Autistic movements/manipulation, watches/participates passively only, stereotyped actions built into toys, has imaginary playmates, takes active part in play/sporting activities, creative, makes own toys, involves others.

RECREATION

19

Other Specialized Evaluations

This chapter covers a variety of other dimensions of functioning that clinicians are often asked to evaluate.

19.1. COMPETENCE TO MANAGE FUNDS/ FINANCIAL COMPETENCE

See also Section 14.8, "Financial Skills," and 14.9, "Shopping."

✓ **Note:** "Incapacitated" is currently preferred to "incompetent," as it focuses on receiving and evaluating information, which is more capable of accurate evaluation.

Standards/Criteria

Ability to manage own property/likelihood of dissipating own property.
Likelihood of becoming the victim of designing persons.
Ability to make or communicate decisions about the use and management of entitlements.

Components of Financial Competence Assessment

Psychological evaluation/Mental Status Evaluation/data base of testing of orientation, memory, judgment, reading ability, emotional disturbance, intelligence. Determine answers to these questions:

Is this person oriented to time, place, person, common items?

Does he/she have adequate memory functions, social judgment, test judgment, control of emotions?

Is his/her overall/general intelligence adequate for money management?

Can he/she make simple mathematical calculations?

Psychological/psychiatric evaluation of quality of reality contact (delusions, hallucinations, thought disorder, disordered thought processes, etc.).

Assessment of person's factual knowledge of the source and extent of her/his assets, understanding of financial terms and concepts, recognition of currency, change-making ability, values/costs of several common items, simple/basic arithmetic.

Evaluation of person's functional ability/behavior, such as observed/historical ability to conduct transactions/conserve assets, competent performance of financial management/responsibilities, perception of situations of potential exploitation.

Summary Statements

On the basis of the present evaluation, this person is therefore considered . . .

incapacitated in all financial areas.

able to manage only small amounts of money.

able/not able to manage his/her property, likely/unlikely to dissipate/squander his/her property.

able/unable to avoid exploitation, manage welfare/etc. benefits, and make long-range financial decisions autonomously, responsibly, and effectively.

likely/unlikely to fall victim to/become the victim of designing persons, be duped/gulled.

able/unable to make or communicate responsible decisions about the use and management of his/her entitlements and assets.

likely/unlikely to hoard funds rather than make necessary purchases.

If benefits are awarded, this person would use the money for drugs/alcohol/gambling or disorganized/impulsive purchases, and therefore he/she may/will/should not be the best recipient of funds for his/her management.

19.2. COMPETENCE TO MAKE A WILL/ TESTAMENTARY COMPETENCE

The individual must understand (1) the nature and extent of her/his property; (2) the identity and relationships of the usual beneficiaries; and (3) the nature and (4) effects of making a will. The book by Melton et al. (1997) covers testamentary competence in detail.

19.3. COPING ABILITY/STRESS TOLERANCE

See also Section 6.4, "Adjustment History."

Types and Dimensions

Instrumental, affective, and escape coping.

Frustration tolerance, ability to delay gratifications, tolerance for ambiguity/uncertainty/conflict/low information/structure, hardiness.

OTHER EVALUATIONS

Coping Skills *(↔ by degree)*

Inept, incompetent, "can't cope," unadaptable, rigid, inflexible, stubborn.

Has developed specific psychological skills: anger management, assertiveness, rational self-talk, has developed self-soothing techniques.

Uses social support system/friendships/informal consultants.

Resourceful, skilled, "survivor," courageous, realistic, adaptable, flexible, adjusts, conforms, bends, resourceful, "just down on his/her luck," valiant, proud.

Assets/Strengths and Liabilities/Weaknesses

See also Sections 26.3, "Format for Psychodynamic Evaluations: Developmental Model," and 26.4, "Format for Psychodynamic Evaluations: Structural Model."

Assess the following in the client:

Assets, strengths, resources, qualifications, reserves, possessions, skills, abilities, aptitudes, capabilities, knowledge, dexterity, talents, prowesses, proficiencies, competencies, experience, expertise.

Vigor, drive, spirit, courage, determination, valor.

Liabilities, weaknesses, areas of skill deficit, absence of needed capabilities, lack of experience, challenges, etc.

19.4. IMPAIRMENT'S EFFECTS ON A PERSON

(↔ by degree) Has become psychotic, suicidal, decompensated, devastated, catastrophic reaction, regressed, denial of event or its consequences, overwhelmed, maladaptive, deteriorating, depressed, adjustment disorder, prolonged/delayed mourning, saddened, marginal functioning, adjusting to disability/losses, adequate/fair functioning, functional, adapting, assimilating, accepting, accommodating, using psychological coping mechanisms, compensating, has devised compensatory/prosthetic/mnemonic/coping devices, successful, overcompensating, mature, is challenged, is growing.

Summary Statement:

The cumulative impact/effect of this client's emotional and physical impairments results in no/insignificant/mild/significant/moderate/severe/crippling limitations.

19.5. CULTURALLY SENSITIVE FORMULATIONS

Culture may include ethnicity, race, religion, social class, gender, age, and similar categories. We all know that culture can affect behaviors, personality, self-image, symptoms, complaints, response to treatment, and other clinical data. These interactions are very complex, usually underestimated, and poorly understood. To add to the complexity, some aspects of culture may affect some clinically interesting phenomena in different ways and to different degrees.

Our ethical guidelines require us to have "cultural sensitivity (i.e. awareness of cultural variables that may affect assessment and treatment) and cultural competence (i.e. translation of this awareness into behavior leading to effective assessment and treatment of the particular multicultural group . . .)" (Paniagua, 1998). It is impossible to know well all of the cultures we encounter as clinicians, but we must learn what we can, and we should be constantly aware of our assumptions, expectations, stereotypes, and ethnocentrisms.

DSM-IV (American Psychiatric Association, 1994) offers some guidance. First, what little is known is indicated in the DSM-IV's descriptions of many disorders, under "Specific Culture, Age, and Gender Features." Second, DSM-IV's Appendix I contains a "Glossary of Culture-Bound Syndromes," as well as an extremely useful "Outline for Cultural Formulation," which is adapted (by permission of the American Psychiatric Association) and expanded below. Please consider this only a beginning, and just one formulation of factors to be considered.

1. The client's cultural identity:
   a. Ethnic or cultural reference group as seen in his/her preferred self-descriptions.
   b. Degree of involvement with the culture of origin and host culture.
   c. Language abilities and preferences, ability to switch between standard English and the language used with family and friends, preference of idioms, etc.
   d. Other aspects of communication, such as interpersonal distance and eye contact.
   e. Other behaviors, such as clothing choices, food preferences, and religious practices.
2. The individual's cultural explanation for the illness:
   a. The "idioms of distress through which the symptoms . . . are communicated (e.g., 'nerves,' possessing spirits, somatic complaints, inexplicable misfortune)."
   b. The "meaning and perceived severity of . . . symptoms in relation to norms of the cultural reference group."
   c. The explanatory models of causation offered by the culture.
   d. Expectations about the course and outcome of the disorder.
   e. The use of any culture-bound syndrome diagnoses (see the "Glossary" in Appendix I of DSM-IV).
3. "Cultural factors related to psychosocial environment and levels of functioning." These include culturally relevant interpretations of the following:
   a. Social stressors of all kinds and sources. These may include traumatic experiences of losses, deaths, torture, dislocation, separation, flight, etc., due to war, disaster, persecution, or other experiences unfamiliar to you as the clinician. Attend to racial and ethnic prejudice, victimization, oppression, and rejection.
   b. Supports of all kinds, including ones the clinician may not use. DSM-IV suggests investigating the "role of religion and kin networks in providing emotional, instrumental, and informational support." Also investigate individual coping strategies, defenses, and attitudes toward helpers.
   c. The resulting levels of functioning and disability, again within the client's culture's expectations. Also, inquire into the client's history of higher and lower functioning.
4. "Cultural elements of the relationship between the individual and the clinician":
   a. Differences in social status.
   b. Racial, ethnic, religious, and other differences.
   c. Any "problems that these differences may cause in diagnosis and treatment (e.g., difficulty in communicating in the individual's first language, in eliciting symptoms or understanding their cultural significance, in negotiating an appropriate relationship or level of intimacy, in determining whether a behavior is normative or pathological)."
   d. The patient's current preferences for and past experiences with professional and culturally sanctioned sources of care and about expectations for treatment.

The best and most readily available introductory books in this area are those by Sue and Sue (1999) and Paniagua (1998). The one by Okpaku (1998) contains many more advanced chapters, and Tseng and Streltzer (1997) provide much information on patterns specific to groups.

OTHER
EVALUATIONS

19.6. THE REFUGEE PROCESS

This material is adapted by permission from Gonsalves (1992).

Phases of the Process

Preflight: Mounting anxiety, sense of abandonment, "victim of fate," "no one cares."
Flight: Traumatizing experiences, varying in intensity, duration, and number; returning as intrusive memories, often on anniversary dates.
Resettlement: Complex; a lifetime process of coping with different language, traditions, etc.

Stages of Resettlement

Early Arrival

From 1 week to 6 months after their arrival in the new country: Refugees learn the surroundings/"lay of the land," remain involved with their homeland, and experience disorientation, low energy, sadness/loss, anger, guilt, relief, and excitement. Examiners should be alert to possible PTSD symptoms.

Destabilization

From 6 months to 3 years after arrival: Refugees acquire survival tools, develop a support group, and learn the language/social customs/culture due to economic pressures. They may experience great stress and pain, hostile withdrawal from the new culture, resistance to the new culture, or uncritical compliance with the new culture. They generally view the old country as better, feel lonely, and show denial.

Exploration and Restabilization

From 3 to 5 years after arrival: Refugees usually develop more flexible culture-learning methods, and often experience marital conflict and adjustment. They may also resist further adaptation, remain linked to other refugees, experience anger at their lowered status, fear of failure, and isolation, and/or undergo premature culture or identity closure.

Return to Normal Life

From 5 to 7 years after arrival: Refugees generally maintain flexible cultural accommodation while retaining some old values, develop realistic expectations for new generations, develop a positive identity, and expect these personality changes to last. They may also show delayed grief reactions, and experience rigidity and intergenerational conflict.

Decompensation

Some refugees may decompensate at any time from 1 week to 7 years after arrival, as they struggle to meet survival needs, modify identity, enter the new culture, continue family commitments, and connect to the past, present, and future. They may experience psychosis, identity disorders, depression, and existential crises.

19.7. RELIGIOUS AND SPIRITUAL CONCERNS

The relevant DSM-IV code is V62.89, Religious or Spiritual Problem.

✓ Note: Distinguishing a religious crisis from a manic episode, delusions from personalized beliefs or overvalued ideas, or obsessive scrupulousness from piety can be very difficult.

Different religious traditions raise different spiritual issues, so please use your knowledge to modify these points for the evaluation of religious and spiritual concerns.

History

As about the following:

Role of religion during childhood, adolescence, adulthood; church attendance, praying, holidays.
Spiritual concerns during these periods: Existential concerns, search for life-guiding values, spiritual health.
Past and present religious denominations, affiliation/membership, involvement in activities, etc.
Frequency of religious observance—describe as:
    Only in crises, holidays/with family, routine, daily.
Attitude/devotion/commitment—describe as:
    Compulsive, pious, observant, routine, agnostic, hostile, atheistic.
Perception of Higher Power/God/prophets.

Concerns about Morality

Conflicts among moral or ethical behavior of self or others, values, religious training.
Excessive or minimal guilt, feelings of being punished, need to atone, inability to feel forgiven.
Confusion about sin/evil, right vs. wrong.

Concerns Related to the Loss or Questioning of Faith

Differences/conflicts/problems with a church/organization, teachings, clergy, scripture/sacred texts/prayers (e.g., hypocrisy).
Doubts because of injustice/suffering/illness/deaths/unfulfilled prayers.
Anger, fears, or distrust of Higher Power.
Doubts because of loss of control/illness/losses/despite religious conformity or sinlessness.
Difficulty believing in or getting closer to a Higher Power.
Conflicts between concepts of a Higher Power as judgmental and demanding vs. accepting, loving, and forgiving.

Concerns Related to Conversion from or Marriage into a Different Faith

Difficulties with initiation procedures into new faith.
Being considered apostate/unchurched/lost/dead by family/members of former faith.
Questions about arrangements of marriage, handling of ceremonies/holidays, religious training of children.

Concerns about Death and Suicide

Fears about dying (e.g., unfinished spiritual business, arrangements for funeral/burial).
Beliefs about what happens after death (e.g., reunion with decedents/never-ending sleep/darkness, judgment after death, an afterlife in Heaven or Hell, reincarnation, etc.).
Religious beliefs against suicide.

Religious Experiences

Responses to prayer or effects of praying.
A vocation/call.
Special revelations.

OTHER EVALUATIONS

Demonic possession, being the Messiah/a Prophet/etc.
Abandonment by God.

Other Concerns

Demand for a therapist of client's faith.

19.8. DEVELOPMENTAL STAGES

Erikson's (1963) "eight stages of man" are highly psychosocial and hopeful. Each stage presents
a challenge to the ego to learn new adaptive skills or suffer limitations on ego identity.

Psychosexual stage	Crisis/conflict	Strength, virtue
Oral–sensory	Basic trust vs. mistrust	Drive, hope
Muscular–anal	Autonomy vs. shame, doubt	Self-control, will
Locomotor–genital	Initiative vs. guilt	Direction, purpose
Latency	Industry vs. inferiority	Method, competence
Puberty and adolescence	Identity vs. role confusion	Devotion, fidelity
Young adulthood	Intimacy vs. isolation	Affection, love
Adulthood	Generativity vs. stagnation	Production, care
Maturity	Ego integrity vs. despair	Renunciation, wisdom

Mahler's (1975) stages: Normal autism, normal symbiosis, separation–individuation (subphases: differentiation, practicing, rapprochement, individuality, and emotional object constancy). Splitting, reintegration vs. fragmentation.

Piaget's stages (see Gruber & Von Eiche, 1977): Sensorimotor, preoperational, concrete operations, formal operations. Assimilation, accommodation, conservation.

Freud's stages: Oral, anal, phallic, latency, genital. (See also Section 13.28, "Personality Traits . . .")

Maslow's (1962) hierarchy of needs: Physiological, safety, belongingness/social, esteem, cognitive, aesthetic, self-actualization, peak experiences.

Sullivan's Stages (see Perry, 1953): Infancy, childhood, juvenile, preadolescent, early adolescent, late adolescent.

In Kohlberg's (1984) stages of the development of moral reasoning, morality is defined as follows at each stage:

Premoral level	1	Obedience to avoid punishment.
	2	Gains reward. Instrumental purpose and exchange.
Conventional level	3	Gains approval and avoids disapproval of others. Interpersonal accord and conformity.
	4	Defined by rigid codes of "law and order." Social accord and system maintenance.
Principled level	5	Defined by a "social contract" agreed upon for the public good. Utility and individual rights.
	6	Personal moral code based on universal, abstract ethical principles.

19.9. STAGES IN THE FORMATION OF HOMOSEXUAL IDENTITY

The following is partly quoted and partly adapted (by permission) from Cass (1979).

Confusion: Conscious awareness that homosexuality has relevance to oneself: "My behavior may be called homosexual. Does this mean that I am a homosexual?" → turmoil, alienation, searching → denial of personal relevance, antihomosexual stance, or inhibition of homosexual behaviors → foreclosure.

Comparison: "I may be homosexual" → "I'm different, I don't belong to society at large," "I do not want to be different."

Tolerance: "I am probably a homosexual."

Acceptance: "I am a homosexual."

Pride: "Gay is good," "Gay and proud."

Activism: Confrontation activities, disclosure as a strategy. "How dare you presume I'm heterosexual?" Also, "them and us"—"Homosexual is good, heterosexual is bad."

Synthesis: "There are some heterosexual others who accept (my) homosexual identity as I do." At this stage homosexual identity is no longer "seen as *the* identity, it is now given the status of being merely one aspect of self."

D. Completing the Report

The chapters in this last subdivison of Part II flow logically. They start with a pulling together of your findings and observations, so that you can offer a diagnosis that is a professional shorthand version of your conclusions. From these two summaries of your understanding of the client, you are in a position to make meaningful recommendations for treatment or other services. Then you can offer a statement of expected outcomes—a prognosis. The last chapter addresses the issues of closing the report and contains the standard language.

20

Summary of Findings
and Conclusions

20.1. OVERVIEW

The summary of findings and conclusions is the place to offer your integration of history, findings, or observations, and your understanding of the client's functioning in the areas most relevant to the referrer's or reader's needs. If there is a referral question, it is likely to be answered here. However, for referral questions seeking a disposition, the recommendations may be a more appropriate heading for such an answer. (See Chapter 22, "Recommendations.") A summary is the appropriate place to review the episode of therapy you have conducted or the conclusions you have drawn from an evaluation you have conducted.

Because there will always be readers who need or want to read only a brief summary, be sure to include the information or conclusions with the most important implications for the client.

20.2. BEGINNING THE SUMMARY

Open the summary with one of these phrases or a similar version:

In summary/In short/To summarize . . .
In my professional opinion, and with a reasonable degree of professional/medical certainty . . .

Then give a brief description of the client's demographics:

(Name of client)/this (age), (gender), (any other decision-related factors such as marital status or parental status) client/patient/consumer/etc. . . .

SUMMARY
OF FINDINGS

See the "Attributions" heading in "Getting Oriented to the *Clinician's Thesaurus*" for other terms to use (besides the three given above) in referring to a client.

20.3. SUMMARY OF PREVIOUS INFORMATION

Condense the background information and history (see Chapter 6) and the referral reasons (see Chapter 5) into a few sentences or a short paragraph.

20.4. RELEVANT FINDINGS AND/OR CONCLUSIONS

In a separate paragraph, or as part of the summary of previous information, offer only the most referral-relevant three or four major findings or conclusions. For treatment summaries, offer the most important themes of the therapy process, with an eye to assisting the client's next therapist. For other situations, tailor the list of your findings to your understanding of the report's audience.

For testing reports, findings should be organized by topic (integrating the results of different tests)—such as cognitive functioning, emotional controls, interpersonal relations, etc., depending on the referral questions. A reliability statement is also needed (see Section 4.6, "Reliability Statements").

If the psychological symptoms presented may be due to a medical condition, see Chapter 28, "Psychiatric Masquerade of Medical Conditions."

20.5. DIAGNOSTIC STATEMENT

Generally a diagnostic statement is in a separate section of a report, following the summary of findings and conclusions. However, if the diagnosis is simple or does not alter current treatments or previous diagnoses, it can be included in this summary section. For more on diagnoses, see Chapter 21, "Diagnostic Statement/Impression."

20.6. CONSULTATIONS AND FURTHER EVALUATIONS

Record the following about all outside consultations performed on the client: reasons/need; type of evaluation; name of consultant; date(s) performed; conclusions and recommendations; and, if not apparent, the locations and dates of the original copies of those consultations (so that they can be requested by others).

If your suggestions for further evaluations are simple or routine, they can be included here; if they are more complex, describe them more fully in the recommendations section of your report (see Chapter 22, "Recommendations").

20.7. SUMMARIZING TREATMENT

Services Rendered

Record the types of services rendered (consultation, assessment, evaluation, treatment, etc.), as well as the number of sessions and the dates of the first and last sessions.

Termination

Note the source of the decision to terminate (client, therapist, client and therapist together, agency, other), as well as the reason(s) for termination. Descriptors for termination reasons include:

Refused services, excessive/unexplained no-shows, little/no progress, planned pause in treatment, successful completion of program/achievement of goals, transfer to another therapist or service provider because . . . (specify), referred elsewhere, no longer eligible for services because . . . (specify), other (specify).

Outcome Summary Statements

Treatment has been a complete/partial/minimal success.
Some/the majority of/nearly all goals were exceeded/achieved/not achieved.

This patient has followed a productive hospital course.
He is in good remission due to medications/is in good chemical remission.
She has received maximum benefit from treatment/hospitalization/services.

Treatment received has had no success/been ineffective in removing/reducing symptoms.
Treatment has had a negative outcome for this patient.
This patient's condition has shown adverse reactions/worsened/stayed the same/shown no improvement.

Disposition

Describe the disposition of the case as appropriate (inactive, closed, transfer, aftercare, referral).

21

Diagnostic Statement/ Impression

Although they are not as tightly tied to treatment in the mental health field as in medicine, diagnoses are a kind of professional shorthand for integrating many kinds of data. In most cases, your diagnosis should follow from and sum up the data you have reported earlier. A diagnosis also orients your reader to the recommendations and treatment planning that follow it.

Generally offer only the most important one or two diagnoses, unless diagnosis was the reason for the referral, you are in training, or your setting's culture requires a fuller listing. You should include all five axes of a DSM-IV (or ICD-10) diagnosis and any "rule-outs" or other qualifications (see Section 21.1, "Qualifiers for Diagnosis"). Offer a "diagnostic impression" if you are not qualified to offer a DSM-IV diagnosis or if you are quite uncertain.

DIAGNOSIS

21.1. QUALIFIERS FOR DIAGNOSIS

A diagnosis may be described or qualified with one of the following terms:

> Initial, deferred, principal, additional/comorbid, Rule Out ..., admitting, tentative, working, final, discharge, in remission, quiescent.

DSM-IV offers these qualifiers: If the criteria are currently met for a diagnosis, Mild, Moderate, or Severe; or if the criteria are no longer met, In Partial Remission, In Full Remission, or Prior History. Not Otherwise Specified is used when not all the criteria are met.

21.2. ICD-10

The current international reference for mental disorder diagnoses is the *International Classification of Diseases,* 10th Revision, Chapter V: Mental and Behavioral Disorders (World Health Organization, 1993). It has been adopted in most countries except the United States, where DSM-IV and its ICD-9-Clinical Modification codes are used. In about 2002, a version called ICD-10-CM will become the standard for use by insurance companies and statisticians in the United States. More information about this is available from the American Psychiatric Press (see the next section). In anticipation of this, ICD-10 codes are given in the right-hand column in sections of this chapter from 21.4 on.

21.3. DSM-IV

The current U.S. reference for mental disorder diagnoses is the *Diagnostic and Statistical Manual of Mental Disorders,* Fourth Edition (American Psychiatric Association, 1994). DSM-IV is available from the American Psychiatric Press, Inc., Order Department, 1400 K Street N.W., Washington, DC 20005, or (800) 368-5777. It is available in hardcover, paperback, and computer disk formats. Call the American Psychiatric Press for information; its catalog is also a good resource.

The DSM-IV system is **multiaxial**. The five axes are as follows:

Axis I: Clinical Disorders (but not Personality Disorders) and Other Conditions That May Be a Focus of Clinical Attention (most V codes) *(see Section 21.21).*
Axis II: Personality Disorders (long-standing patterns, in adults) and Mental Retardation.
Axis III: General Medical Conditions.
Axis IV: Psychosocial and Environmental Problems. *(See Section 21.22.)*
Axis V: Global Assessment of Functioning Scale. *(See Section 21.23.)*

DIAGNOSIS

Proposed additional axes:

Global Assessment of Relational Functioning Scale.
Social and Occupational Functioning Assessment Scale.
Defensive Functioning Scale (defense or coping mechanisms used). *(See Section 26.3, "Format for Psychodynamic Evaluations: Developmental Model," and 26.4, "Format for Psychodynamic Evaluations: Structural Model.")*

Selected DSM-IV codes and diagnoses are presented in the remainder of this chapter. They are reprinted with permission from the *Diagnostic and Statistical Manual of Mental Disorders*, fourth edition. Copyright 1994 by the American Psychiatric Association. Note that "DSM" and DSM-IV" are also copyrighted by the American Psychiatric Association.

The diagnostic categories are given below **in order of frequency of use**; diagnoses within each category are listed **in numerical order**. (Note that there are occasional slight differences between the categories as defined below and as defined by DSM-IV.) DSM-IV code numbers are given in the left-hand column. The diagnoses themselves are given in the middle column (name changes from the preceding edition, DSM-III-R, are given as tips—in square brackets, with check marks). Again, ICD-10 code numbers are provided in the right-hand column. (Instances where ICD-10's method of coding a diagnosis differs from DSM-IV's are noted as tips—in **square brackets, with check marks**—in the middle column, following the DSM-IV diagnosis name.)

This is **almost a complete listing** and is presented only for convenient reference by the knowledgeable clinician. If there is any uncertainty about a choice of diagnosis, DSM-IV or ICD-10 should be consulted.[1]

21.4. ANXIETY DISORDERS

See Section 21.12 for codes for Substance-Induced Anxiety Disorders.

DSM-IV		ICD-10
300.00	Anxiety Disorder Not Otherwise Specified	F41.9
300.01	Panic Disorder Without Agoraphobia	F41.0
300.02	Generalized Anxiety Disorder	F41.1
300.21	Panic Disorder With Agoraphobia	F40.01
300.22	Agoraphobia Without History of Panic Disorder	F40.00
300.23	Social Phobia. Specify if: Generalized	F40.1
300.29	Specific Phobia	F40.2
	[✓ Simple Phobia, in DSM-III-R]. Specify type: Animal/Natural Environment/Blood–Injection–Injury/Situational/Other	
300.3	Obsessive–Compulsive Disorder. Specify if: With Poor Insight	F42.8
	[✓ ICD-10 offers these: Mostly Obsessions = F42, Mostly Compulsions = F42.1, Mixed = F42.2, Unspecified = F42.9]	
308.3	Acute Stress Disorder	F43.0
309.81	Posttraumatic Stress Disorder. Specify if Acute/Chronic or With Delayed Onset	F43.1
293.84	Anxiety Disorder Due to (Indicate the General Medical Condition). Specify if With: Generalized Anxiety/With Panic Attacks/With Obsessive–Compulsive Symptoms	F06.4

---

[1]Morrison (1995b) is by far the best guide to making diagnoses and using DSM-IV to best advantage. His precise language, realistic vignettes, and clinical wisdom make learning easy, pleasurable, and satisfying.

Mixed Anxiety–Depressive Disorder is a diagnosis proposed for further study. See Appendix B of DSM-IV.

21.5. MOOD DISORDERS

See Section 21.12 for codes for Substance-Induced Mood Disorders.

Readers familiar with DSM-III-R should note that DSM-IV has introduced changes in the conceptualization of the bipolar disorders. A careful study of the manual is recommended.

For diagnoses below with code numbers ending in "x," use the last digit to code current state as follows: 1, Mild; 2, Moderate; 3, Severe Without Psychotic Features; 4, Severe With Psychotic Features (specify: Mood-Congruent/Mood-Incongruent); 5, In Partial Remission; 6, In Full Remission; 0, Unspecified.

Note also that the following specifiers can apply to various mood disorders:

Chronic.
With Catatonic Features.
With Melancholic Features.
With Atypical Features.
With Postpartum Onset.
With/Without Full Interepisode Recovery.
With Seasonal Pattern.[2]
With Rapid Cycling.

For tables indicating which of these apply to which disorders, again, consult DSM-IV itself.

DSM-IV		ICD-10
293.83	Mood Disorder Due to (Indicate the General Medical Condition)	F06.xx
296.0x	Bipolar I Disorder, Single Manic Episode. Specify if: Mixed	F30.x
296.2x	Major Depressive Disorder, Single Episode	F32.x
296.3x	Major Depressive Recurrent	F33.x
296.40	Bipolar I Disorder, Most Recent Episode Hypomanic	F31.0
296.4x	Bipolar I Disorder, Most Recent Episode Manic	F31.x
296.5x	Bipolar I Disorder, Most Recent Episode Depressed	F31.x
296.6x	Bipolar I Disorder, Most Recent Episode Mixed	F31.6
296.7	Bipolar I Disorder, Most Recent Episode Unspecified	F31.9
296.80	Bipolar Disorder NOS	F31.9
296.89	Bipolar II Disorder. Specify current or most recent episode: Hypomanic/Depressed	F31.8
296.90	Mood Disorder NOS	F39
300.4	Dysthymic Disorder. Specify if: Early/Late Onset, With Atypical Features	F34.1
301.13	Cyclothymic Disorder	F34
311	Depressive Disorder NOS	F32.9
V62.82	Bereavement	

Premenstrual Dysphoric Disorder, Recurrent Brief Depressive Disorder, and Minor Depressive Disorder are diagnoses proposed for further study. See Appendix B of DSM-IV.

---

[2]When this specifier is applied, consider Seasonal Affective Disorder, which is not (yet) an accepted DSM diagnosis. (However, *see Section 10.8.*)

21.6. ADJUSTMENT DISORDERS

DSM-IV		ICD-10
309.0	Adjustment Disorder With Depressed Mood [✓ ICD-10 has F43.20 for Brief and F43.21 for Prolonged Depressions]	
309.24	Adjustment Disorder With Anxiety	F43.28
309.28	Adjustment Disorder With Mixed Anxiety and Depressed Mood	F43.22
309.3	Adjustment Disorder With Disturbance of Conduct	F43.24
309.4	Adjustment Disorder With Mixed Disturbance of Emotions and Conduct	F43.25
309.9	Adjustment Disorder, Unspecified	F43.9

For all Adjustment Disorders, specify Acute/Chronic.

21.7. PERSONALITY DISORDERS

Code all of these (except V71.01 and 310.1) on Axis II.

DSM-IV		ICD-10
301.0	Paranoid Personality Disorder	F60.0
301.20	Schizoid Personality Disorder	F60.1
301.22	Schizotypal Personality Disorder	F21
301.4	Obsessive–Compulsive Personality Disorder	F60.5
301.50	Histrionic Personality Disorder	F60.4
301.6	Dependent Personality Disorder	F60.7
301.7	Antisocial Personality Disorder	F60.2
301.81	Narcissistic Personality Disorder	F60.8
301.82	Avoidant Personality Disorder	F60.6
301.83	Borderline Personality Disorder	F60.31
301.90	Personality Disorder NOS	F60.9
V71.01	Adult Antisocial Behavior	Z72.8
310.1	Personality Change Due to (Indicate the General Medical Condition)	F07.0

Passive–Aggressive Personality Disorder (Negativistic Personality Disorder) and Depressive Personality Disorder are diagnoses proposed for further study. See Appendix B of DSM-IV.

21.8. IMPULSE-CONTROL DISORDERS

DSM-IV		ICD-10
312.30	Impulse-Control Disorder NOS	F63.9
312.31	Pathological Gambling	F63.0
312.32	Kleptomania	F63.2
312.33	Pyromania	F63.1
312.34	Intermittent Explosive Disorder	F63.8
312.39	Trichotillomania	F63.3
V71.01	Adult Antisocial Behavior	Z72.8

DIAGNOSIS

21.9. CHILDHOOD DISORDERS

Mental Retardation

All of these are coded on Axis II.

DSM-IV		ICD-10
V62.89	Borderline Intellectual Functioning (not Mental Retardation)	R41.8
317	Mild Mental Retardation	F70.9
318.0	Moderate Mental Retardation	F71.9
318.1	Severe Mental Retardation	F72.9
318.2	Profound Mental Retardation	F73.9
319	Mental Retardation, Severity Unspecified	F79.9

IQ equivalents for these categories are as follows:

Borderline Intellectual Functioning (not Mental Retardation)	71–84
Mild Mental Retardation	50–55 to approximately 70
Moderate Mental Retardation	35–40 to 50–55
Severe Mental Retardation	20–25 to 35–40
Profound Mental Retardation	Less than 20–25
Mental Retardation, Severity Unspecified	Not testable

Pervasive Developmental Disorders

DSM-IV		ICD-10
299.00	Autistic Disorder	F84.0
299.10	Childhood Disintegrative Disorder	F84.3
299.80	Rett's Disorder	F84.2
299.80	Pervasive Developmental Disorder NOS	F84.9
299.80	Asperger's Disorder	F84.5

Learning Disorders

DSM-IV		ICD-10
315.00	Reading Disorder	F81.0
	[✔ In ICD-10 Spelling is F81.1]	
315.1	Mathematics Disorder	F81.2
315.2	Disorder of Written Expression	F81.8
315.9	Learning Disorder NOS	F81.9

Communication Disorders

DSM-IV		ICD-10
307.0	Stuttering	F98.5
307.9	Communication Disorder NOS	F80.9
313.23	Selective Mutism	F94.0
	[✔ Elective Mutism in DSM-III-R]	
315.31	Expressive Language Disorder	F80.1
315.32	Mixed Receptive–Expressive Language Disorder	F80.2
315.39	Phonological Disorder	F80.0
	[✔ Developmental Articulation Disorder in DSM-III-R]	

DIAGNOSIS

Attention-Deficit and Disruptive Behavior Disorders

DSM-IV		ICD-10
314.00	Attention-Deficit/Hyperactivity Disorder, Predominantly Inattentive Type	F98.8
314.01	Attention-Deficit Hyperactivity Disorder, Predominantly Hyperactive–Impulsive Type, or Combined Type	F90.0
314.9	Attention-Deficit/Hyperactivity Disorder, NOS	F90.9
312.xx	Conduct Disorder. Specify type: Childhood-Onset is 312.81, Adolescent-Onset Type is 312.82, Unspecified is 312.89	F91.8
312.9	Disruptive Behavior Disorder NOS	F91.9
313.81	Oppositional Defiant Disorder	F91.3
V71.02	Child or Adolescent Antisocial Behavior	Z72.8

Other Disorders

DSM-IV		ICD-10
307.20	Tic Disorder NOS	F95.9
307.21	Transient Tic Disorder. Specify if: Single Episode/Recurrent	F95.0
307.22	Chronic Motor or Vocal Tic Disorder	F95.1
307.23	Tourette's Disorder	F95.2
307.3	Stereotypic Movement Disorder. Specify if: With Self-Injurious Behavior	F98.4
315.4	Developmental Coordination Disorder	F82
309.21	Separation Anxiety Disorder. Specify if: Early Onset	F93
313.89	Reactive Attachment Disorder of Infancy or Early Childhood. Specify type: Inhibited [✓ ICD-10 has F94.1 for Inhibited, F94.2 for Disinhibited]	F94.x
313.9	Disorder of Infancy, Childhood, or Adolescence NOS	F98.9

21.10. EATING AND ELIMINATION DISORDERS

In DSM-IV, the first three of these disorders have their own section; the others are grouped with the disorders of infancy/childhood/adolescence.

DSM-IV		ICD-10
307.1	Anorexia Nervosa. Specify type: Restricting/Binge-Eating/ Purging Type	F50.0
307.50	Eating Disorder NOS	F50.9
307.51	Bulimia Nervosa. Specify type: Purging/Nonpurging Type	F50.2
307.52	Pica	F98.3
307.53	Rumination Disorder	F98.2
307.59	Feeding Disorder of Infancy or Early Childhood	F98.2
307.6	Enuresis (Not Due to a General Medical Condition). Specify: Nocturnal Only/Diurnal Only/Nocturnal and Diurnal	F98.0
307.7	Encopresis, Without Constipation and Overflow Incontinence	F98.1
787.6	Encopresis, With Constipation and Overflow	R15

Binge-Eating Disorder is a diagnosis proposed for further study. See Appendix B of DSM-IV.

DIAGNOSIS

21.11. "ORGANIC" COGNITIVE CONDITIONS

DSM-IV no longer uses the term "organic" for these conditions, but the descriptor is still widely used in practice.

For Dementia of the Alzheimer's Type With Early Onset and for Vascular Dementia, use the last digit to code predominant features as follows: 1, With Delirium; 2, With Delusions; 3, With Depressed Mood; 0, Uncomplicated. For all Dementia, specify if: With Behavioral Disturbance.

DSM-IV		ICD-10
290.0	Dementia of the Alzheimer's Type, With Late Onset, Uncomplicated	F00.xx
290.10	Dementia Due to Pick's Disease/Creutzfeldt–Jakob Disease	F02.1
290.1x	Dementia of the Alzheimer's Type, With Early Onset	F00.xx
290.20	Dementia of the Alzheimer's Type, With Late Onset, With Delusions	F00.01
290.21	Dementia of the Alzheimer's Type, With Late Onset, With Depressed Mood	F00.13
290.4x	Vascular Dementia [✓ Multi-Infarct Dementia in DSM-III-R]	F01.xx
293.0	Delirium Due to (Indicate the General Medical Condition)	F05.0
293.9	Mental Disorder NOS Due to (Indicate the General Medical Condition)	F09
294.0	Amnestic Disorder Due to (Indicate the General Medical Condition). Specify if: Transient/Chronic	F04
294.1	Dementia Due to (Indicate the General Medical Condition)	
294.8	Amnestic Disorder NOS	R41.3
294.8	Dementia NOS	F03
294.9	Cognitive Disorder NOS	F06.9
294.1	Dementia Due to HIV Disease	
780.09	Delirium NOS	F05.9

Postconcussional Disorder and Mild Neurocognitive Disorder are diagnoses proposed for further study. See Appendix B of DSM-IV.

21.12. SUBSTANCE-RELATED DISORDERS/ ALCOHOL AND OTHER DRUGS

Possible specifiers for Substance Dependence diagnoses (see below) include: With/Without Physiological Dependence, Early Full or Partial Remission, Sustained Full or Partial Remission, On Agonist Therapy, In a Controlled Environment, With Onset During Intoxication/During Withdrawal. See the manual for the appropriate application of these.

Alcohol Related Disorders

DSM-IV		ICD-10
291.0	Alcohol Intoxication/Withdrawal Delirium	F10.03/ F10.4
291.1	Alcohol-Induced Persisting Amnestic Disorder	F10.6
291.2	Alcohol-Induced Persisting Dementia	F10.73
291.3	Alcohol-Induced Psychotic Disorder, With Hallucinations	F10.52
291.5	Alcohol-Induced Psychotic Disorder, With Delusions	F10.51

291.8	Alcohol Withdrawal. Specify if: With Perceptual Disturbances	F10.3
291.8	Alcohol-Induced Mood Disorder/Anxiety Disorder/Sexual Dysfunction/Sleep Disorder	F10.8
291.9	Alcohol-Related Disorder NOS	F10.9
303.00	Alcohol Intoxication	F10.0
303.90	Alcohol Dependence	F10.2x
305.00	Alcohol Abuse	F10.1

Amphetamine-Related Disorders

DSM-IV		ICD-10
292.0	Amphetamine Withdrawal	F15.3
292.11	Amphetamine-Induced Psychotic Disorder, With Delusions	F15.51
292.12	Amphetamine-Induced Psychotic Disorder, With Hallucinations	F15.52
292.81	Amphetamine Intoxication Delirium	F15.03
292.84	Amphetamine-Induced Mood Disorder	F15.8
292.89	Amphetamine-Induced Anxiety Disorder/Sexual Dysfunction/Sleep Disorder	F15.8
292.89	Amphetamine Intoxication. Specify if: With Perceptual Disturbances	F15.00/F15.04
292.9	Amphetamine-Related Disorder NOS	F15.9
304.40	Amphetamine Dependence	F15.2x
305.70	Amphetamine Abuse	F15.1

Caffeine-Related Disorders

DSM-IV		ICD-10
292.89	Caffeine-Induced Anxiety/Sleep Disorder	F15.8
292.9	Caffeine-Related Disorder NOS	F15.9
305.90	Caffeine Intoxication	F15.00

Caffeine Withdrawal is a diagnosis proposed for further study. See Appendix B of DSM-IV.

Cannabis-Related Disorders

DSM-IV		ICD-10
292.11	Cannabis-Induced Psychotic Disorder, With Delusions	F12.51
292.12	Cannabis-Induced Psychotic Disorder, With Hallucinations	F12.52
292.81	Cannabis Intoxication Delirium	F12.03
292.89	Cannabis-Induced Anxiety Disorder	F12.8
292.89	Cannabis Intoxication. Specify if: With Perceptual Disturbances	F12.00/F12.04
292.9	Cannabis-Related Disorder NOS	F12.9
304.30	Cannabis Dependence	F12.2X
305.20	Cannabis Abuse	F12.1

Cocaine-Related Disorders

DSM-IV		ICD-10
292.0	Cocaine Withdrawal	F14.3
292.11	Cocaine-Induced Psychotic Disorder, With Delusions	F14.51
292.12	Cocaine-Induced Psychotic Disorder, With Hallucinations	F14.52

DIAGNOSIS

292.81	Cocaine Intoxication Delirium	F14.03
292.84	Cocaine-Induced Mood Disorder	F14.8
292.89	Cocaine-Induced Anxiety Disorder/Sexual Dysfunction/ Sleep Disorder	F14.8
292.89	Cocaine Intoxication. Specify if: With Perceptual Disturbances	F14.00
292.9	Cocaine-Related Disorder NOS	F14.9
304.20	Cocaine Dependence	F14.2x
305.60	Cocaine Abuse	F14.1

Hallucinogen-Related Disorders

DSM-IV		ICD-10
292.11	Hallucinogen-Induced Psychotic Disorder, With Delusions	F16.51
292.12	Hallucinogen-Induced Psychotic Disorder, With Hallucinations	F16.52
292.81	Hallucinogen Intoxication Delirium	F16.03
292.84	Hallucinogen-Induced Mood Disorder	F16.8
292.89	Hallucinogen-Induced Anxiety Disorder	F16.8
292.89	Hallucinogen Intoxication	F16.00
292.89	Hallucinogen Persisting Perception Disorder (Flashbacks)	F16.70
292.9	Hallucinogen-Related Disorder NOS	F16.9
304.50	Hallucinogen Dependence	F16.2x
305.30	Hallucinogen Abuse	F16.1

Inhalant-Related Disorders

DSM-IV		ICD-10
292.11	Inhalant-Induced Psychotic Disorder, With Delusions	F18.51
292.12	Inhalant-Induced Psychotic Disorder, With Hallucinations	F18.52
292.81	Inhalant Intoxication Delirium	F18.03
292.82	Inhalant-Induced Persisting Dementia	F18.73
292.84	Inhalant-Induced Mood Disorder	F18.8
292.89	Inhalant-Induced Anxiety Disorder	F18.8
292.89	Inhalant Intoxication	F18.00
292.9	Inhalant-Related Disorder NOS	F18.9
304.60	Inhalant Dependence	F18.2x
305.90	Inhalant Abuse	F18.1

Nicotine-Related Disorders

DSM-IV		ICD-10
292.0	Nicotine Withdrawal	F17.3
292.9	Nicotine-Related Disorder NOS	F17.9
305.10	Nicotine Dependence	F17.2x

Opioid-Related Disorders

DSM-IV		ICD-10
292.0	Opioid Withdrawal	F11.3
292.11	Opioid-Induced Psychotic Disorder, With Delusions	F11.51
292.12	Opioid-Induced Psychotic Disorder, With Hallucinations	F11.52
292.81	Opioid Intoxication Delirium	F11.03
292.84	Opioid-Induced Mood Disorder	F11.8

292.89	Opioid-Induced Sexual Dysfunction/Sleep Disorder	F11.8
292.89	Opioid Intoxication. Specify if: With Perceptual Disturbances	F11.00/ F11.04
292.9	Opioid-Related Disorder NOS	F11.9
304.00	Opioid Dependence	F11.2x
305.50	Opioid Abuse	F11.1

Phencyclidine- (or Phencyclidine-Like-)Related Disorders

DSM-IV		ICD-10
292.11	Phencyclidine-Induced Psychotic Disorder, With Delusions	F19.51
292.12	Phencyclidine-Induced Psychotic Disorder, With Hallucinations	F19.52
292.81	Phencyclidine Intoxication Delirium	F19.03
292.84	Phencyclidine-Induced Mood Disorder	F19.8
292.89	Phencyclidine-Induced Anxiety Disorder	F19.8
292.89	Phencyclidine Intoxication. Specify if: With Perceptual Disturbances	F19.00/ F19.04
292.9	Phencyclidine-Related Disorder NOS	F19.9
304.90	Phencyclidine Dependence	F19.2x
305.90	Phencyclidine Abuse	F19.1

Sedative-, Hypnotic-, or Anxiolytic-Related Disorders

DSM-IV		ICD-10
292.0	Sedative-, Hypnotic-, or Anxiolytic Withdrawal. Specify if: With Perceptual Disturbances	F13.3
292.11	Sedative-, Hypnotic-, or Anxiolytic-Induced Psychotic Disorder, With Delusions	F13.51
292.12	Sedative-, Hypnotic-, or Anxiolytic-Induced Psychotic Disorder, With Hallucinations	F13.52
292.81	Sedative, Hypnotic, or Anxiolytic Intoxication/Withdrawal Delirium	F13.03/ F13.4
292.82	Sedative-, Hypnotic-, or Anxiolytic-Induced Persisting Dementia	F13.73
292.84	Sedative-, Hypnotic-, or Anxiolytic-Induced Mood Disorder	F13.8
292.83	Sedative-, Hypnotic-, or Anxiolytic-Induced Persisting Amnestic Disorder	F13.6
292.89	Sedative-, Hypnotic-, or Anxiolytic-Induced Anxiety Disorder/ Sexual Dysfunction/Sleep Disorder	F13.8
292.89	Sedative, Hypnotic, or Anxiolytic Intoxication	F13.00
292.9	Sedative-, Hypnotic-, or Anxiolytic-Related Disorder NOS	F13.9
304.10	Sedative, Hypnotic, or Anxiolytic Dependence	F13.2x
305.40	Sedative, Hypnotic, or Anxiolytic Abuse	F13.1

Other

DSM-IV		ICD-10
304.80	Polysubstance Dependence	F19.2x
292.0	Other (or Unknown) Substance Withdrawal. Specify if: With Perceptual Disturbances	F19.04
292.11	Other (or Unknown) Substance-Induced Psychotic Disorder With Delusions	F19.51

292.12	Other (or Unknown) Substance-Induced Psychotic Disorder, With Hallucinations	F19.52
292.81	Other (or Unknown) Substance-Induced Delirium	F19.03
292.82	Other (or Unknown) Substance-Induced Persisting Dementia	F19.73
292.83	Other (or Unknown) Substance-Induced Persisting Amnestic Disorder	F19.6
292.84	Other (or Unknown) Substance-Induced Mood Disorder	F19.8
292.89	Other (or Unknown) Substance-Induced/Anxiety/Sexual Dysfunction/Sleep Disorder	F19.08
292.89	Other (or Unknown) Substance Intoxication. Specify if: With Perceptual Disturbances	F19.00/ F19.04
292.9	Other (or Unknown) Substance-Related Disorder NOS	F19.9
304.90	Other (or Unknown) Substance Dependence	F19.2x
305.90	Other (or Unknown) Substance Abuse	F19.1

21.13. PSYCHOTIC DISORDERS

See Section 21.12 for codes for Substance-Induced Psychotic Disorders.

For all subtypes of Schizophrenia, use these longitudinal course specifiers: Episodic with Interepisodal Residual Symptoms, Episodic with No Interepisodal Residual Symptoms, Single Episode in Partial Remission, Single Episode in Full Remission, Other or Unspecified Pattern. For the first three of these specifiers, also specify if: With Prominent Negative Symptoms.

DSM-IV		ICD-10
293.81	Psychotic Disorder Due to (Indicate the General Medical Condition), With Delusions	F06.2
293.82	Psychotic Disorder Due to (Indicate the General Medical Condition), With Hallucinations	F06.0
293.98	Catatonic Disorder Due to (Indicate the General Medical Condition)	F20.2x
295.10	Schizophrenia, Disorganized Type [✓ ICD-10 for Hebephrenic Schizophrenia is F20.1]	F20.1x
295.20	Schizophrenia, Catatonic Type	F20.2x
295.30	Schizophrenia, Paranoid Type	F20.0x
295.40	Schizophreniform Disorder. Specify if: With/Without Good Prognostic Features	F20.8
295.60	Schizophrenia, Residual Type	F20.3x
295.70	Schizoaffective Disorder. Specify type: Bipolar/Depressive Type [✓ ICD-10 for Bipolar is F21.0, for Depressive is F21.1]	
295.90	Schizophrenia, Undifferentiated Type	
297.1	Delusional Disorder. Specify Type: Erotomanic/Grandiose/ Jealous/Persecutory/Somatic/Mixed/Unspecified Type	F22.0
297.3	Shared Psychotic Disorder	F24
298.8	Brief Psychotic Disorder. Specify if: With/Without Marked Stressors, With Postpartum Onset [✓ ICD-10 for With Marked Stressors is F23.81, for Without is F23.80]	
298.9	Psychotic Disorder NOS	

Postpsychotic Depressive Disorder of Schizophrenia and Simple Deteriorative Disorder (Simple Schizophrenia) are diagnoses proposed for further study. See Appendix B of DSM-IV.

21.14. SLEEP DISORDERS

See Section 21.12 for codes for Substance-Induced Sleep Disorders.

Dyssomnias

DSM-IV		ICD-10
307.42	Primary Insomnia. Specify if: Recurrent	F51.0
307.44	Primary Hypersomnia. Specify if: Recurrent	F51.1
307.45	Circadian Rhythm Sleep Disorder [✓ Sleep–Wake Schedule Disorder in DSM-III-R]. Specify type: Delayed Sleep Phase/Jet Lag/Shift Work/Unspecified Type	F51.2
307.47	Dyssomnia NOS	F51.9
347	Narcolepsy	G47.4
780.59	Breathing-Related Sleep Disorder	G47.3

Parasomnias

DSM-IV		ICD-10
307.46	Sleep Terror Disorder	F51.4
307.46	Sleepwalking Disorder	F51.3
307.47	Nightmare Disorder	F51.5
307.47	Parasomnia NOS	F51.8

Other

DSM-IV		ICD-10
307.42	Insomnia Related to (Indicate the Axis I or II Disorder)	F51.0
307.44	Hypersomnia Related to (Indicate the Axis I or II Disorder)	F51.1
307.52	Sleep Disorder Due to (Indicate the General Medical Condition), Insomnia Type	G47.0
307.54	Sleep Disorder Due to (Indicate the General Medical Condition), Hypersomnia Type	G47.1
307.59	Sleep Disorder Due to (Indicate the General Medical Condition), Parasomnia Type	G47.8
307.59	Sleep Disorder Due to (Indicate the General Medical Condition), Mixed Type	G47.8

21.15. SOMATOFORM DISORDERS

DSM-IV		ICD-10
300.11	Conversion Disorder. Specify type: With Motor Symptom or Deficit/With Seizures or Convulsions/With Sensory Symptom or Deficit/With Mixed Presentation [✓ In ICD-10 the four subtypes are F44.4 through F44.7, respectively]	
300.7	Hypochondriasis. Specify if: With Poor Insight	F45.2
300.7	Body Dysmorphic Disorder	F45.2
300.82	Somatoform Disorder NOS	F45.9
300.81	Somatization Disorder	F45.0

300.81	Undifferentiated Somatoform Disorder	F45.1
307.80	Pain Disorder Associated With Psychological Factors. Specify if: Acute/Chronic	F45.4
307.89	Pain Disorder Associated With Psychological Factors and a General Medical Condition. Specify if: Acute/Chronic	F45.4

21.16. PSYCHOLOGICAL FACTORS AFFECTING MEDICAL CONDITION

DSM-IV		ICD-10
316	[Specified Psychological Factor] Affecting [Indicate the General Medical Condition]	F54

DSM-IV asks you to substitute one of the following for [Specified Psychological Factor]: Mental Disorder, Psychological Symptoms, Personality Traits or Coping Style, Maladaptive Health Behaviors, Stress-Related Physiological Response, and Other or Unspecified Psychological Factors.

21.17. DISSOCIATIVE DISORDERS

DSM-IV		ICD-10
300.12	Dissociative Amnesia [✓ Psychogenic Amnesia in DSM-III-R]	F44
300.13	Dissociative Fugue [✓ Psychogenic Fugue in DSM-III-R]	F44.1
300.14	Dissociative Identity Disorder [✓ Multiple Personality Disorder in DSM-III-R]	F44.81
300.15	Dissociative Disorder NOS	F44.9
300.6	Depersonalization Disorder	F48.1

Dissociative Trance Disorder is a diagnosis proposed for further study. See Appendix B of DSM-IV.

21.18. SEXUAL DYSFUNCTIONS AND DISORDERS

See Section 21.12 for codes for Substance-Induced Sexual Dysfunctions.

Sexual Dysfunctions

Specify type: Lifelong/Acquired/Generalized/Situational Type, Due to Psychological Factors/Due to Combined Factors.

DSM-IV		ICD-10
302.70	Sexual Dysfunction NOS	F52.9
302.71	Hypoactive Sexual Desire Disorder	F52.0
302.72	Female Sexual Arousal/Male Erectile Disorder	F52.2
302.73	Female Orgasmic Disorder	F52.3
302.74	Male Orgasmic disorder	F52.3
302.75	Premature Ejaculation	F52.4
302.76	Dyspareunia (Not Due to a General Medical Condition)	F52.6

DIAGNOSIS

302.79	Sexual Aversion Disorder [✓ ICD-10 for Lack of Enjoyment is F52.11, for Excessive Sexual Drive is F52.7]	F52.10
306.51	Vaginismus (Not Due to a General Medical Condition)	F52.5
607.84	Male Erectile Disorder Due to (Indicate the General Medical Condition)	N48.4
608.89	Male Dyspareunia Due to (Indicate the General Medical Condition)	N50.8
608.89	Male Hypoactive Sexual Desire Due to (Indicate the General Medical Condition)	N50.8
608.89	Other Male Sexual Dysfunction Due to (Indicate the General Medical Condition)	N50.8
621.0	Female Dyspareunia Due to (Indicate the General Medical Condition)	N94.1
621.8	Female Hypoactive Sexual Desire Due to (Indicate the General Medical Condition)	N94.8
621.8	Other Female Sexual Dysfunction Due to (Indicate the General Medical Condition)	N94.8

Paraphilias

DSM-IV		ICD-10
302.2	Pedophilia. Specify if: Sexually Attracted to Males/Females/ Both, Limited to Incest, Exclusive/Nonexclusive Type	F65.4
302.3	Transvestic Fetishism. Specify if: With Gender Dysphoria	F65.1
302.4	Exhibitionism	F65.2
302.81	Fetishism	F65.0
302.82	Voyeurism	F65.3
302.83	Sexual Masochism	F65.5
302.84	Sexual Sadism	F65.5
302.89	Frotteurism	F65.8
302.9	Paraphilia NOS	F65.9
302.9	Sexual Disorder NOS	F52.9

Gender Identity Disorders

DSM-IV		ICD-10
302.6	Gender Identity Disorder in Children	F64.2
302.85	Gender Identity Disorder in Adolescents or Adults. Specify if: Sexually Attracted to Males/Females/Both/Neither	F64.0
302.6	Gender Identity Disorder NOS	F64.9
302.9	Sexual Disorder NOS	F52.9

21.19. FACTITIOUS DISORDERS

DSM-IV		ICD-10
300.16	Factitious Disorder With Predominantly Psychological Signs and Symptoms	F68.1
300.19	Factitious Disorder With Predominantly Physical Signs and Symptoms	F68.1

| 300.19 | Factitious Disorder With Combined Psychological and Physical Signs and Symptoms | F68.1 |
| 300.19 | Factitious Disorder NOS | F68.1 |

Factitious Disorder by Proxy is a diagnosis proposed for further study. See Appendix B of DSM-IV.

21.20. MEDICATION-INDUCED MOVEMENT DISORDERS

DSM-IV		ICD-10
332.1	Neuroleptic-Induced Parkinsonism	G21.0
333.1	Medication-Induced Postural Tremor	G21.1
333.7	Neuroleptic-Induced Acute Dystonia	G24.0
333.82	Neuroleptic-Induced Tardive Dyskinesia	G24.0
333.9	Medication-Induced Movement Disorder NOS	G21.9
333.92	Neuroleptic Malignant Syndrome	G21.0
333.99	Neuroleptic-Induced Acute Akathisia	G21.1
995.2	Adverse Effects of Medication NOS	T88.7

21.21. V CODES, ETC.

In DSM-IV, "V codes" are assigned to conditions that are not themselves attributable to a mental disorder but that may be a focus of attention or treatment. This section covers most V codes, as well as some additional numerical codes.

Relational Problems   *See also Chapter 21, "Couple and Family Relationships."*

DSM-IV		ICD-10
V61.1	Partner Relational Problem	Z63.0
V61.20	Parent–Child Relational Problem	Z63.8
V61.8	Sibling Relational Problem	F93.3
V61.9	Relational Problem Related to a Mental Disorder or General Medical Condition	Z63.7
V62.81	Relational Problem NOS	Z63.9

Problems Related to Abuse or Neglect

DSM-IV		ICD-10
V61.21	Physical Abuse of Child (Use 995.54 if focus of attention is on victim)	T74.1
V61.21	Sexual Abuse of Child (Use 995.53 if focus of attention is on victim)	T74.2
V61.21	Neglect of Child (Use 995.52 if focus of attention is on victim)	T74.0
V61.1	Physical Abuse of Adult (Use V61.12 if focus of clinical attention is on perpetrator and abuse is of partner, V62.83 if focus of attention is on perpetrator and abuse is not by partner, or 995.81 if focus in on victim)	T74.1
V61.1	Sexual Abuse of Adult (Use V61.12 if focus of clinical attention is on perpetrator and abuse is of partner, V62.83 if focus of attention is on perpetrator and abuse is not by partner, or 995.83 if focus in on victim)	T74.2

Additional Conditions That May Be a Focus of Clinical Attention

DSM-IV		ICD-10
V15.81	Noncompliance with Treatment	Z91.1
V62.2	Occupational Problem	Z56.7
V62.3	Academic Problem	Z55.8
V62.4	Acculturation Problem	Z60.3
V62.82	Bereavement	Z63.4
V62.89	Phase of Life Problem	Z60.0
V62.89	Religious or Spiritual Problem	Z71.8
V65.2	Malingering	Z76.5
V71.09	No Diagnosis or Condition on Axis I/No Diagnosis on Axis II	Z03.2
300.9	Unspecified Mental Disorder (nonpsychotic)	Z99
313.82	Identity Problem	F93.8
780.9	Age-Related Cognitive Decline	R41.8
799.9	Diagnosis or Condition Deferred on Axis I/Diagnosis Deferred on Axis II	

[✓ In ICD-10 Axis I is R69, Axis II is R46.8]

21.22. AXIS IV: PSYCHOSOCIAL AND ENVIRONMENTAL PROBLEMS

Consider the last year's time period and list all problems seen as relevant to clinical presentation. DSM-IV Axis IV categories (reprinted by permission of the American Psychiatric Association) include the following:

Problems with primary support group.
Problems related to the social environment.
Educational problems.
Occupational problems.
Housing problems.
Economic problems.
Problems with access to health care services.
Problems related to interaction with the legal system/crime.
Other psychosocial and environmental problems.

21.23. AXIS V: GLOBAL ASSESSMENT OF FUNCTIONING SCALE

This is an abbreviated version and does not list examples. It is adapted by permission from DSM-IV.

Ratings are made for current level of psychological/social/physical functioning and for highest level in past year.

91–100	Superior functioning in a wide range of areas; no symptoms.
81–90	No or minimal symptoms; generally good functioning in all areas; no more than everyday problems or concerns.
71–80	Transient, slight symptoms that are reasonable responses to stressful situations; no more than slight impairment in social, occupational, or school functioning

61–70	Mild symptoms, or some difficulty in social, occupational, or school functioning.
51–60	Moderate symptoms, or moderate difficulties in social, occupational, or school functioning.
41–50	Serious symptoms, or any serious impairment in social, occupational, or school functioning.
31–40	Serious difficulties in thought or communication, or major impairment in several areas of functioning.
21–30	Behavior influenced by psychotic symptoms, or serious impairment in communication or judgment, or inability to function in almost all areas.
11–20	Dangerous symptoms, or gross impairment in communication.
1–10	Persistent danger to self or others, or persistent inability to maintain hygiene.
0	Inadequate information.

DIAGNOSIS

22

Recommendations

Making recommendations is usually the chief aim of report construction. If treatment is appropriate, its indicators and urgency must be presented to justify it. Selecting treatments from the hundreds of interventions available requires extensive knowledge of the structure and method of each intervention, its demands on client and therapist, and its likely outcomes. While treatment to client matching is beyond this book's scope, the sections here provide a large checklist of services to address the client's needs.

22.1. NEED FOR TREATMENT

Your description of the need for treatment should include the justifications/reasons/clinical rationales/indications for, the medical necessity (if any) of, and the risks and benefits of each proposed treatment choice/option/alternative.

Indication(s) for Hospitalization/Intensification of Treatment Efforts: Summary Statements

This patient, with a history of severe and/or prolonged psychiatric illness, is showing significant decompensation.

His disorder remains severe or persistent, despite appropriate outpatient treatment.

She is exhibiting suicidal ideation/threats/gestures/attempts, or is (considered) a physical danger to herself.

There is severe loss of appetite/weight, and/or sleep disturbance, considered to be detrimental to physical health.

He is seriously threatening to or acting in a physically destructive manner toward others or property.

She is demonstrating bizarre, antisocial, or risky behaviors that will progress unless she is hospitalized.

There is evidence of cognitive disorders, dementia, or organic brain syndrome requiring psychiatric, neuropsychological, or medical evaluation, which can only be provided in an inpatient setting.

I am/Dr. _____ is starting or modifying psychopharmacological treatments that require continuous monitoring and evaluation because of the type of medication or the presence of other medical conditions or complications.

The patient's substance abuse is of such intensity and persistence that hospitalization is required to control or prevent the severe physical and psychiatric consequences of withdrawal.

Precautions are needed to prevent assault/risky sexual behaviors/elopement/homicide/suicide.

Urgency

The following groupings are sequenced by degree of decreasing urgency.

Emergency, act without delay, immediate intervention required to preserve life or health.

Critical/serious disruption of functioning, act today/within 24 hours.

Patient is suffering, treatment/evaluation is needed, act soon.

Routine intake/evaluation/referral.

Wait for _____ (specify).

Estimate of Treatability

Although currently out of fashion, the issue of treatability is often worth considering, especially when resources are limited. In estimating treatability, weigh these characteristics of the patient:

Motivators/pain; demotivators/anxieties/avoidances.
Support needed and availability.
Barriers (financial, logistical, cultural, intellectual).
Openness to new experiences, intimacy of therapy, strong affect, new perspectives.
Psychological-mindedness, willingness to work, ego strength.
Probability of remaining in treatment.

22.2. TREATMENTS OF CHOICE

Although it is clear from meta-analyses that psychotherapy benefits most clients, it is also well documented that very few therapists have used research on the effectiveness of methods of therapy to guide their practices. There do appear to be important differences between treatments (see, e.g., Roth & Fonagy, 1996, and Nathan & Gorman, 1998). Of the perhaps 400 kinds or "brand-name" therapies, however, only a few dozen have been properly evaluated for effectiveness for any kind of outcomes, and fewer have been empirically supported (in medicine this is called "evidence-based practice").

You can find the most current version of the list of Empirically Supported Treatments at the Society for Scientific Clinical Psychology's World Wide Web site (http://www.sscp.psych.ndsu.nodak.edu.), which includes treatment manuals and resources for training. The following problems are addressed: Bulimia Nervosa, chronic headache, pain associated with rheumatic disease, coping with stressors, depression, discordant couples, enuresis, Generalized Anxiety Disorder, Obsessive–Compulsive Disorder, Panic Disorder, Social Phobia, Specific Phobia, and children with oppositional behavior. Probably the best published manuals are in the Treatment Manuals for Practitioners series, published by The Guilford Press (http://www.guilford.com);

those in the TherapyWorks series, published by the Psychological Corporation (http://www.psychcorp.com/sub/featured/fptw.htm), and those in the Best Practices for Therapy series, published by New Harbinger (http://www.newharbinger.com and then click on Best Practices).

Two books contain much useful guidance to clinical research on what is effective for whom: those by Roth and Fonagy (1996) and Nathan and Gorman (1998). The treatments listed there and below are almost exclusively behavioral and cognitive. This should not be interpreted as indicating that only these work, but that only these have been properly investigated. Many common therapies do not generate empirically testable or falsifiable hypotheses. Also, therapist variables such as competence in and adherence to the techniques of a treatment, personality, allegiance, and similarity to the client have all been shown to be important determinants of outcome. We really need more research to answer the question framed by Gordon Paul in 1966 as follows: "Which treatment, administered by whom, for what diagnosis/problem, in what kind of person, has what outcome?"

For those who wish to pursue a scientifically informed approach to therapy, the table below summarizes what core methods or techniques have been found effective for which diagnoses. Note that medications are mentioned for many diagnoses, but have not been demonstrated to be effective in some cases (e.g., childhood depressions).

Diagnosis	*Treatments of choice*
Fears, phobias, anxieties	Systematic desensitization, flooding, reinforced practice, modeling. Medications: Antianxiety drugs, antidepressants for phobias.
Compulsions	Participant modeling, with imaginal exposure; *in vivo* exposure, response prevention/interruption.
Major depression	Cognitive therapy, especially Beck's version (Beck, Rush, et al., 1979); interpersonal psychotherapy. Medications: Tricyclics, MonoAmine Oxidase Inhibitors, Selective Serotonin Reuptake Inhibitors. ElectroConvulsive Therapy.
Bipolar disorders	Cognitive therapies. Mood stabilizers and antidepressants.
Sexual dysfunctions	Masters and Johnson's (1970) techniques and variations.
Addictions	Veterans' groups, various Twelve-Step programs. Relapse prevention, harm reduction, motivational interviewing. Medications.
Overeating	Stimulus control methods, structured exercise, self-help groups.
Smoking	Combinations of nicotine substitutes, aversion therapies (e.g., satiation), contracting, relapse prevention, booster sessions, group contracts, and support.
Borderline personality	Cognitive-behavioral and combination therapies.
Eating disorders	Behavioral rehearsal, scheduling and modeling of proper eating, cognitive change of body image, cognitive and cognitive-behavioral techniques.
Schizophrenia	Neuroleptics, compliance-increasing efforts. Reduction of family/emotional/precipitating stress through family therapy and education. Day/partial hospitals, supportive living situations, brief hospitalizations.

22.3. TREATMENT OPTIONS/CASE DISPOSITION

See also Chapter 25, "Treatment Planning and Treatment Plan Formats."

General Statements

Continue current treatment(s).
Add further/concurrent treatments (specify).
Refer/transfer patient to a different hospital/program/therapist (specify).
Discharge; follow up with _____ (specify).

Carry out further evaluations/diagnostic studies: physical/medical, intellectual, personality, neuro-psychological, custody, family, forensic, speech/language, audiological, educational/academic, occupational/vocational/rehabilitative (specify).

Counseling or Psychotherapy   *See Chapter 25 for goals and methods.*

Medication Statement

Administer (name[s], either trade or generic) at a starting dosage of _____ for a duration of _____, and then increasing/decreasing/tapering to _____ for a duration of _____, with instructions regarding dosage, side and main/therapeutic effects, dealing with problems, etc. supervised/administered by patient/family/clinic staff/school nurse/visiting nurse.

Other Statements

Refer patient to a nutritional education program and recommend dietary change.
Refer patient to an exercise education program/exercise program.
Refer patient to recreation counseling, have him/her change social/recreational/etc. activities to _____ (specify), increase activities outside the home/family, take on volunteer activities such as _____ (specify).

22.4. TYPES OF THERAPIES/SERVICES

Types of therapies and services are listed alphabetically, both to reflect the fact there is no accepted hierarchy and to encourage consideration of the many options available.

Aftercare services, case management and monitoring, liaison.
Behavior modification methods[1]: Contingency management, contingency contracting, stimulus control, convert sensitization, time out, token economy, modeling, self-control methods, covert aversion therapy, Stress Inoculation Training, etc.
Behavior therapies: Systematic desensitization, flooding, implosion, Eye Movement Desensitization and Reprocessing.
Behavior referral: Self-control training, anger management, parenting skills/child management training, Parent Effectiveness Training, assertiveness training, antivictimization program.
Bibliotherapy and patient education.
Body–mind awareness: Primal (scream), Rolfing, bioenergetics, Autogenic Training, ges-

---

[1]Kratochwill and Bergan (1990) provide excellent guidance to the implementation of behavioral programs as a consultant. The book by Bellack and Hersen (1985) is a simple guide to about 150 methods with definitions, explanations, and resources. I particularly like the quality of the tools from Research Press, P.O. Box 9177, Champaign, IL 61826; (217) 352-3273.

talt, Rebirthing, Functional Integration, biofeedback, the Alexander method, structure patterning, Do'in, shiatsu, aromatherapy, reflexology, iridology, many kinds of yogas, martial arts training programs, tai chi, attunement therapies, Therapeutic Touch, etc.

Case management, intensive and tailored to programs.

Consciousness development: Arica, Living Love, Erhard Seminar Training, Transcendental Meditation, Silva Mind Control, zen, Buddha's Middle Way, Gurdjieff's method, etc.

Crisis intervention and management.

Expressive therapies: Art, music, dance/movement, poetry writing.

Family support, staff monitoring and ongoing evaluation, continual availability, respite care, in-home/mobile therapy, and other support services.

Psychological growth: Transactional Analysis, psychoanalysis, encounter/marathon/Open Encounter groups, Morita therapy, Reality Therapy, Psychosynthesis, Narrative therapy.

Relationship and communication: Sex therapy, Marriage Encounter, Relationship Enhancement, the Power therapies,

Residential services: Foster care, "group homes," community living arrangements, community residential services, "halfway house," structured/supportive living arrangement, transitional services, protective services, domiciliary care, etc.

Schooling: Local college/general studies/evening classes, vocational/trade/schools.

Skill-building groups: Toastmasters International, parenting skills/child management training, PET, anger management, assertiveness training, dating skills, antivictimization program, etc.

Support groups:

Grief counseling, victim support services, Mothers Against Drunk Driving, Parents of Murdered Children, Compassionate Friends (parents of children who died), Candlelighters (children with cancer), Make Today Count (those with fatal illnesses).

Encore (women with breast cancer), Reach for Recovery (women who have had breast cancer surgery).

Parents Anonymous (child abusers), Sojourn (battered women), Daughters and Sons United (sexually abused children).

Resolve (infertility), Adoptees Liberty Movement Association (adult adoptees and birth parents), Tough Love (parents of difficult adolescents), Single Parent Network, Neonate Support Group (parents).

Recovery (people with nervous and mental problems), Take Off Pounds Sensibly, HELP (herpes), Mutual Friends (ex-Jehovah's Witnesses), Dignity (gay and lesbian Catholics), etc.

Twelve-Step programs for many addictive behaviors: Alcohol/Cocaine/Narcotics/Families/Overeaters/Gamblers Anonymous, Al-Anon, Alateen.

Work adjustment training, work hardening program, work placement, internship program. *(See Chapter 17, "Vocational/Academic Skills.")*

✓ **Note**: You may want to create and insert here a reference list of additional or specific services, and their providers, available in your community or system.

For a Child:

Special education, language stimulation classroom, services for Socially and Emotionally Disturbed, Learning Support, Life Skills, services for learning-impaired, in-home/itinerant teacher.

Counseling, medical/psychiatric/medication evaluation/consultation, play and expressive therapy, child management skills training, parent–staff conference, social skills training (remedial/adaptive/for acceptance), etc.

23

Prognostic Statements

This Chapter's Sections:	Page

23.1. GENERAL PROGNOSTIC STATEMENT

This is a general format for a prognostic statement, with blanks to be filled in using the options below:

> The prognosis for this client's _____ (type of outcome) is _____ (prognosis descriptor). The course is/is expected to be _____ (course descriptor), because the client is/appears to be _____ (client descriptor).

Types of Outcomes

Improvement, full/partial recovery.
Employment (competitive/supportive/partial/sheltered workshop), return to original job/alternative work placement at _____ level.
Community/family/structured/institutional placement, or other.

Prognosis Descriptors (↔ by degree)

Excellent/good/uncertain because ... (specify)/variable/unknown/guarded/poor/precarious/negative/grave/terminal.

Course Descriptors (↔ by degree)

Benign, acute, waxing and waning, stepwise, fluctuating, with remissions and exacerbations, steady, chronic, static, unchanging with or without treatment, declining, worsening rapidly, fulminating, unrelenting despite our best efforts, malignant.

Client Descriptors (↔ by degree)

Recuperating, convalescent, making good progress, reaching a steady state, hard to treat, refractory to treatment, suffering from a virulent form of the disorder, intractable, failing despite all appropriate treatment.

23.2. OTHER STATEMENTS

This client's eventual prognosis for success in later life will be a function of how well the situational demands match his/her individual profile of abilities.

The severity and chronicity of her/his symptoms indicate a poor prognosis.

His/her course so far has been downhill, and his/her prognosis therefore must be considered negative unless . . . (specify).

This outcome/result of treatment is expected only if (specified) services are received, and progress is expected to be slow and difficult with many reversals.

The probable duration of treatment is _____ with these goals of therapy . . . (specify).

The client needs the structure of various social agencies with which she/he is involved.

24

Closing Statements

24.1. VALUE OF THE INFORMATION

I hope this information will be useful to you as you consider this case's/person's/client's needs, and will aid you in your tasks/evaluation/treatment/decisions.
I hope this information will be sufficient for you to judge this patient's situation.
In the hope that these data will prove of assistance . . .

24.2. THANKING THE REFERRER

Thank you for the opportunity/privilege of being able to evaluate your patient/this most interesting/challenging/pleasant patient/person/man/woman.
We appreciate your sending _____ to us/inviting us to assist in the care of _____/asking us to see _____.
Thanks again for the opportunity to participate in _____'s care.
Thanks for the chance to help take care of _____ with you.
I consider it a privilege to have been able to care for this patient.

It goes almost without saying that I appreciate your trust in allowing me to assist in the care of this patient.
My colleagues and I appreciate . . . (specify).
As always, thank you very much for your kind referrals.

24.3. CONTINUED AVAILABILITY

I trust that this is the information you desire/require, but if it is not . . .
Please feel free to contact me if I can supplement the information in this report/if other questions or issues arise.

Please let me know if you have any other thoughts about this person's condition(s).

If there are further questions I may address as a result of/on the basis of my examination of this individual, please contact me at your convenience.

I will make myself/am available for further information/consultation regarding this client's needs.

If I can be of further benefit to you with this case, do not hesitate to contact me.

If I can be of any further assistance with reference to this patient's treatment or problem or any patient's treatment, it certainly will be my pleasure to assist you.

If clarification is needed, I can best be reached on _____ (days) from _____ to _____ (times) at _____ (phone number).

Should additional examination/evaluation/testing/clarification/information/treatment be needed, I am/am not willing to provide it.

I am/am not willing to perform additional examinations/evaluations on this person.

I will see this client again in _____. I am certainly available sooner should problems arise.

I remain available to this patient to provide care should it be needed.

The client requires no further/active follow-up from our standpoint, but he/she is aware that he/she can contact us should further problems arise.

I am returning her/him to your care regarding . . . (specify).

As always, I shall keep you informed of my further contacts with/interactions with/treatment of your patient via/by means of copies of my progress notes, with the patient's full consent.

24.4. SIGNATURE, ETC.

Always sign a report with your personal signature, degree, and title, preceded by "Yours truly/ Sincerely/Respectfully." Add any of these statements as appropriate:

I authorize that my name may be mechanically affixed to this report.

Dictated but not read, to facilitate mailing to you.

Typed and mailed in the doctor's absence.

Part III

Useful Resources

25

Treatment Planning
and Treatment Plan Formats

Treatment plans are simply one step in the process of treatment: Do a comprehensive evaluation; plan treatment thoughtfully; do the treatment consistently, compassionately, and conscientiously; write complete progress notes; evaluate your efforts and outcomes; and write a closing summary.

25.1. THE FLOW AND NATURE OF TREATMENT PLANNING

The sequence of clinical **practice** suggests that a clinician goes from the initial assessment of the client to the interventions needed, provides them, and achieves the benefits. However, the sequence of clinical **thinking** goes from assessment to goals; only then, looking at both, does the clinician generate the means likely to achieve the desired outcomes. The following discussion follows this second path—how the clinician thinks about treatments.

Treatment planning begins with **assessment** of the client's presenting problem/Chief Complaint, presenting symptoms, mental status, risks, history (especially of treatment), and expec-

Much of this chapter is adapted from my book *The Paper Office* (2nd ed.). Copyright 1997 by Edward L. Zuckerman. Adapted by permission.

tations of treatment and outcomes. This leads to **diagnosis making**. Do all of this with the client, ask about all areas of functioning, and prioritize problems jointly and realistically.

The planning process then continues with a consideration of **outcomes**—goals, objectives, and benefits. Ask, "If we wish to achieve this goal by this date, what steps need to be taken before then?" Select and prioritize goals.

Now planning can proceed to **treatment design and selection**—the choice of interventions, efforts, methods, and means. Consider the resources available and the limitations imposed by reality, time, finances, etc. *See Section 22.2, "Treatments of Choice."*

25.2. SOME ADVICE ON WRITING TREATMENT PLANS

- Spending the time to develop a plan jointly with the client requires the kind of thoughtful, comprehensive, insightful efforts that will ensure successful therapy, so it is not a waste of therapy time but rather a productive focusing of it. A preliminary step could be to list, with the client, the major problems and related effects of these problems on his/her life. Review all the areas of functioning. Then inquire about expectations of treatment and of change for this problem list. Some see goal setting as the client's job, while selecting and implementing the means are the contributions of the therapist/professional.
- Berg and Miller (1992) offer these criteria for "well-formed treatment goals":
    They must be important to the client.
    They should be small.
    They should be concrete, behavioral, and specific.
    They should focus on the presence rather than the absence of something.
    They must focus on the first small steps, on what to do first, on a beginning rather than an end.
    They should be realistic and achievable within the context of the client's life.
    They should be perceived as requiring "hard work" (like Jay Haley's Prescribed Ordeal Therapy; see Haley, 1984).
- A symptom does not have to be absent completely, or for months, in order for a client to demonstrate recovery. It only has to be not significantly interfering with or limiting life functions.
- Treatment planning should logically include the ending of treatment and the client's proceeding with her/his life trajectory, which may have been interrupted by the disorder. Therefore, an integral aspect of treatment planning is preparation for ending treatment. Managed Care Organizations may ask what steps have been taken or will be taken to prepare the patient or family for discharge from treatment.
- Let your writings reflect options, rationales, and decisions at each stage of treatment, so that you can review and revise from a solid basis, communicate with peers and patients, evaluate and learn from your outcomes, and protect yourself from malpractice accusations.
- In writing plans, you may find yourself struggling between writing a plan that is too specific and will require continual revisions, and a plan that is too general and is an empty exercise because it offers no guidance for treatment. The overly precise plan requires either following it rigidly or constantly revising it in light of the vicissitudes of actual clinical practice.
- A caution for writing treatment plans: Avoid jargon, especially words understood only by professionals of a particular orientation. MCO reviewers are usually nurses or counselors untrained in more specific techniques and suspicious of ones with idiosyncratic and obscure terminology. Use common language translations of theory or focus elsewhere.

- I see writing treatment plans as an ethical as well as a clinical responsibility for us as therapists. If we don't write our plans down, our human nature will convince us that we intended to get to wherever we ended up. Treatment plans keep us honest.
- Much research comparing novices and experts points to the novices' lack of the large internal list of options that experts have developed. Novice treatment planners find it very difficult to design goals and generate methods. Experts may have a parallel difficulty: articulating what has become a "second-nature" understanding of goals and methods. These difficulties have led to the popularity of books and software on treatment planning, but with a little mental effort any clinician can generate perfectly satisfactory plan statements. For more details on how the contents of this book can be of assistance, see the relevant parts of the sections on MCO plans and outcomes, below.

25.3. VARIOUS FORMATS FOR TREATMENT PLANS

The Tabular Model

Each clinician, agency, funder, and monitor seems to have a different preferred format for treatment plans. Many of them use a page turned sideways and divided into columns. If you wish to use this approach offered below are four commonly used headings for the columns (and some optional others). For each column heading, I have supplied a series of terms used to express a similar idea. From these, you can choose headings that best fit your way of practicing and your setting.

The first column is the "Goal" column. Alternative terms:

Problem, Aim,[1] Mission, Behaviors to Be Changed, Long-Term Goal, Diagnosis-Related Symptoms.

The second is the "Outcome" column. Alternative terms:

Objective, Subgoal, Outcome Sought/Desired/Expected,[2] Output, Observable Indicators of Improvement,[3] Symptom-Related Goals, Focus of Treatment, Short-Term Goal, Discharge Level of Problem Behavior, Performance, Operationalization.

The third is the "Intervention" column. Alternative terms:

Resources to be Employed. Methods, Treatments, Means, Strategies, Tactics, Efforts, Inputs.

This column should answer these questions: Who is going to do what, where, how often and for how long, with whom, and supervised by whom when?

The last column is the "Time Frame" column.[4] Alternative terms:

Date of Evaluation, Date of Initiation, Target Date, Completion Date, Expected Number of Sessions to Achieve Objective, Date of Review/Reevaluation/Progress Evaluation.

Other columns may include the following:

Intensity, Frequency, Duration of Treatment.
Client's Strengths or Assets, Degree of Involvement.
Liabilities, Resistances/Barriers to Change (in the client or elsewhere).

---

[1]This term is used by Makover (1996).

[2]Goal Attainment Scaling is built on addressing the expected outcomes. See Kiresuk and Sherman (1968).

[3]This excellent phrasing was introduced, as far as I know, by Levenstein (1994).

[4]If you can, write the target for this column in terms of treatment sessions, because clients may miss meetings during a specified time period. Similarly, it is preferable to offer a review date rather than an achievement/completion date.

Priorities, Sequence of Objectives
Documentation of Involvement (of client, providers, payors, family, others).

Wilson's Social Work Model

From social work (Wilson, 1980) this model describes:

The ideal means of meeting the needs of this patient.
What you can do realistically to meet these needs.
The client's willingness and ability to carry out these treatment plans.
Progress made or not made since the plan was written.
What you will now do differently.

The Analytical Thinking Model

Using this model (also described by Wilson, 1980) to think about a client can be a productive exercise.

1. Review in your mind everything you know about the case.
2. Make a list of the 10–15 key facts of the case.
3. Imagine what feelings the client might have about his/her situation.
   a. At whom or what might the feelings be directed?
   b. Why might he/she feel that way?
   c. What would be the behavioral manifestations of those feelings?
4. Who are the client's "significant others"?
5. Develop a treatment plan:
   a. List all the possible outcomes of treatment (whether realistic or not).
   b. Label each as realistic or not.
   c. For each realistic goal, list the subgoals or objectives to be achieved, and put them in any necessary sequence.
   d. State the exact treatment techniques that would accomplish the subgoals.
   e. Rank the goals in a time sequence so you know where to start.
   f. Estimate the time needed to achieve each goal.

Write a summary of the main thoughts of steps 2 through 4, and discard all the material except this and the lists developed in step 5.

A Children's Residential Agency Model

Identifying information: Name, date of birth, date of admission, agency, primary worker.
Data and needs.
   1. Education.
   2. Medical/physical.
   3. Contacts: legal, family, etc.
   4. Personal development (goals).
      a. Personal hygiene.
      b. Peer relationships.
      c. Adult relationships.
      d. Group relationships.
      e. Specialized treatments/therapies/support.
      f. Specific events.
Treatment/program adjustments (to methods).
   1. Major incidents.
   2. Routine adjustments.
   3. Level changes (levels of programming).

4. Attitude and motivation.
5. Target summary (and changes in targets).
Family.

Multimodal Therapy Model

Arnold A. Lazarus (1976, 1981) has developed a model of assessment in which treatments of choice (those whose effectiveness for a specific problem has been supported by empirical research) are matched to each problem, analyzed at each of seven levels. The acronym for the levels is BASIC ID. There are no limitations on the methods of treatment that can be used, and so it can fit any paradigm. Proper diagnosis/problem specification is crucial to this model.

Assessment area/Problematic behaviors	*Interventions*
<u>B</u>ehavior:	
<u>A</u>ffect:	
<u>S</u>ensation:	
<u>I</u>magery (fantasies, expectations):	
<u>C</u>ognition (beliefs):	
<u>I</u>nterpersonal relations:	
<u>D</u>rugs (included here are all medical conditions):	

The Levels-of-Functioning Model

Kennedy (1992) offers an inventive, different approach to planning interventions. Using Axis V of DSM-IV (see Section 21.23), he has built numerous master treatment plans around levels of functioning in the areas of psychological impairment, social skills, dangerousness, <u>A</u>ctivities of <u>D</u>aily <u>L</u>iving/occupational skills, substance abuse, etc.

The "Seven P's of Problem Formulation" Model

No consensus exists on how to understand the causation and dynamics of a "problem," but most clinicians accept a biopsychosocial paradigm. Sperry et al. (1992) offer a well-thought-out (although elaborate) approach, which focuses on "seven dimensions for articulating and explaining the nature and origins of the patient's presentation" and then their "subsequent treatment." It is reprinted here (by permission) to expand your thinking about a client's life and dynamics.

1. *Presentation*: Nature and severity of symptoms, history, course of illness, and diagnosis.
   a. <u>C</u>hief <u>C</u>omplaint/<u>C</u>oncern.
   b. History of past treatment.
   c. Problem list: Separate the short-term, "acute, non-characterological, or fairly circumscribed or those that may be time limited" from the long-term, "less focal, more characterological skills deficits, or chronic symptoms, behaviors or issues."
   d. DSM diagnosis: All five axes, traits/defenses, and "rule-outs."
   e. Prognostic index/capacity for treatment: Ratings are made in 10 areas (symptom severity and focality; defensive style; social supports; psychological-mindedness; explanatory style; past treatment compliance, both general and in therapy; motivation for treatment; and information style), and then a prognostic statement is made.
2. *Predispositions*: "All the factors which render an individual vulnerable to a disorder." These include physical predispositions (if any), as well as "psychological predisposers which contribute to the present problem(s) social predisposers." These are all diatheses.
3. *Precipitants*: Stressors of all biopsychosocial kinds.

TREATMENT PLANS

4. *Pattern*: The person's "pattern and level of functioning in all three spheres (biological, psychological, social/interpersonal), if germane" in terms of "the predictable and consistent style or manner in which a person thinks, feels, acts, copes, and defends the self both in stressful and non-stressful circumstances." The individual's capacity for treatment would be included here.

5. *Perpetuants*: "Processes by which an individual's pattern is reinforced and confirmed by both the individual and the individual's environment."

6. *Plan* (of treatment):

   a. Patient's expectations for current treatment, both outcome and method. Take note of the patient's formulation—the individual's explanation for her/his symptoms or disorder.

   b. Treatment outcome goals: Short- and long-term in biological, psychological, and social areas.

   c. Rationale for the treatment plan: Setting, format, duration, frequency, treatment strategy, and somatic treatment.

7. *Prognosis:* Forecast of the individual's capacity and response to treatment.

25.4. A TREATMENT PLAN FORMAT FOR MANAGED CARE ORGANIZATIONS

The need for treatment plans, separate from their value, is largely created by the demands of MCOs. Therefore, a generic MCO treatment plan is used as the basis for the presentation in this section. Form 2 is adapted from a form in my book *The Paper Office*, 2nd ed. (Zuckerman, 1997). You may photocopy and adapt it for your work with clients without obtaining written permission but may not use it for teaching, writing, or any commercial venture without written permission. A more comprehensive version and more guidance on treatment plans can be found in *The Paper Office*. For space considerations, this version eliminates the lines you will need to enter your findings, and it limits the number of responses in each instance to three.

Authorization: The Report's Purpose When an MCO Is the Reader

Treatment plans are submitted to obtain reimbursement (payment after delivery) for mental health services. A form such as Form 2 documents the need for mental health services and the plans to deliver them. On the basis of these statements, an MCO can decide to authorize or deny payment for the services of providers. This form is completed at intake and, if treatment is initially authorized, again toward the expiration of the (small) number of authorized sessions ("concurrent review"). This micromanagement is still the most common format, despite its costs to all involved. See also the comments below under "III. A. Progress in current treatment to date."

For simplicity, again, the presentation here is confined to the end product—a plan written in a format suitable for and required by MCOs, as illustrated in Form 2. The meanings and rationale of each heading in this form from II. onward are discussed below, and advice is offered.

II. Case formulation/overview

A. Presenting problem(s)/chief complaint/chief concern

The client comes in with a "complaint" (his/her formulation) or distress (psychic pain), and the clinician inquires, tests, weighs evidence, and reinterprets this into a "diagnosis" (in a medi-

Individualized Behavioral/Mental Health Treatment Plan

This is for ❏ Preauthorization for initial certification ❏ Concurrent review for reauthorization of care

I. Identification of client(s) and provider(s)

II. Case formulation/overview

A. Presenting problem(s)/Chief complaint/Chief concern/Reasons for referral or seeking treatment/crisis(es)

Problem	Severity[1]	Duration
1.		
2.		
3.		

B. History of presenting problem(s) and current situation (precipitants, motivations, stressors and resources/coping skills, comorbid conditions, living conditions, relevant demographics):

C. Previous treatments:

Name	Location/phone	Type of services and dates

D. Brief summary of mental status evaluation results:

(cont.)

---

[1]Code for rating the severity of disruption or decreased performance of life routines and personal effectiveness: Mi = Mild, Mod = Moderate, S = Severe, VS = Very severe, or use GAF ratings from Axis V of DSM-IV.

E. Functional limitations and impairments (descriptions and ratings of severity of limitation):

    1. Self-care and ADLs—severity[1]:

    2. Academic/Occupational—severity[1]:

    3. Intimate relationships/marriage/children/family of origin—severity[1]:

    4. Social relationships—severity[1]:

    5. Other areas—severity[1]:

F. Strengths:

    1.

    2.

    3.

G. Diagnoses: ❏ DSM-IV or ❏ ICD-9-CM or ❏ ICD-10-CM

Title	Code #
Axis I:	
Axis II:	
Axis III:	
Axis IV:	

Axis V: _____   Current GAF: _____   Highest GAF in past year: _____

H. Current assessment of knowable risks:

    1. *Self-neglect or damage:* ❏ None ❏ Poor self care ❏ Significant self-neglect ❏ Self-abuse
    Specifics:

    2. *Suicide:* ❏ No evidence ❏ Ideation only ❏ Plan ❏ Intent without means ❏ Intent with means

    3. *Homicide:* ❏ No evidence ❏ Ideation only ❏ Plan ❏ Intent without means ❏ Intent with means

    4. *Impulse control:* ❏ Sufficient ❏ Inconsistent ❏ Minimal ❏ Explosive

    5. *Treatment compliance:* ❏ Fully compliant ❏ Variable ❏ Passive noncompliance ❏ Resistive

    6. *Substance use:* ❏ None/normal use ❏ Abusing ❏ Unstable remission ❏ Dependence

    7. *Physical or sexual abuse:* ❏ No evidence ❏ Yes ❏ Not reportable ❏ Date reported: _____

(cont.)

8. *Child or elder abuse or neglect*: ❑ No evidence ❑ Yes ❑ Not reportable ❑ Date reported: _____
   If yes, client is ❑ Victim ❑ Perpetrator ❑ Both ❑ Neither, but abuse exists in family

9. *If risk(s) exists*: Client ❑ can ❑ cannot meaningfully agree to a contract not to harm ❑ self ❑ others ❑ both

I.   **Recommended level of care:**

III. **Treatment concerns**

A. **Progress in current treatment to date**—gains made and current level of severity of problems, reasons for continuing treatment: ❑ No treatment yet

B. **Treatment plan**—a recommended program of coordinated liaisons, consultations, evaluations and treatment services:

1. Based on the current clinical evaluation, these **additional consultations or evaluations** are necessary:

Concern or question	Consultant
a.	
b.	
c.	

2. **Treatment's objectives** and **goals:** Significant improvement is to be expected, with treatment specified, for:
   Problem: _____

   • Behaviors to be changed:

   • Interventions (who does what, how often, with what resources; modality, frequency, duration):

   • Observable indicators of improvement (behaviors, reports):   • Expected number of visits to achieve each indicator:

   • Discharge level of problem behaviors: • Review date:

   [✔ Item 2 is repeated for each additional problem.]

3. **Case manager's additions.**   Name: _____   Date of consultation: _____

Problem	Suggested treatments and resources
a.	
b.	
c.	

(cont.)

4. **Other current treating professionals:**

Name	Location/phone	Treatments provided

5. **My signature** means that I have participated in the formulation of my treatment plan, that I understand and approve of it, and that I accept the responsibility to fully carry out my parts of the plan.

Client: _____ Date: _____

Service provider: _____ Date: _____

6. **Additional comments**, plans, or information:

IV. Administration

Authorization #	Date	No. of sessions	Start date	Date of progress review	Date billed

cal model), a "concern" (in a patient-centered approach), or a "problem" (in common language and MCO terms).

- *For questions to ask, see Chapters 2, "Mental Status Examination Questions/Tasks," and 3, "Questions about Signs, Symptoms, and Behaviors."*
- *For referral reasons in children, see Chapter 5, "Referral Reasons."*

B. History of presenting problem(s) and current situation

Mental health clinicians usually subscribe to an interacting biopsychosocial model for comprehensiveness, and to a "diathesis (vulnerability) plus stressor (demand for change) equals symptomatic behavior" model to explain abnormal behaviors. All the elements needing clinical attention are conceived of as either stressors, diatheses, or abnormal behaviors. In turn, behaviors may become new stressors.

As a clinician, you can focus on symptoms, complaints, problems, goals, functioning level, behavioral excesses and deficits, recovery by stressor reduction, growth and learning to cope, alteration of family dynamics/homeostasis, crisis management, etc. How you understand the problem—its cause, dynamics, and goals—depends on your paradigm and training.

C. Previous treatments

MCOs want to know about previous treatment so that they may exclude payment for the treatment of preexisting conditions, since as *in loco* insurers, they believe that a previous insurer should be responsible for the payment for services when disorders continue to exist or have reappeared.

Previous treaters are vitally important to you as a clinician for two reasons: (1) Misdiagnosing or mistreating a condition of which you were not aware but should have been (because all good clinicians always get old records) is a major source of malpractice vulnerability; and (2) you should learn what has and has not worked in the past, in order to make your own treatment more effective.

MCOs sometimes ask for previous psychological testing done (despite their almost universal unwillingness to pay for it): dates, tests given, reasons, and results. They are also likely to ask for intellectual and academic testing done on child patients.

D. Brief summary of mental status evaluation results

Conducting MSEs is a traditional skill area of clinicians, and you should strive to be a sophisticated evaluator. Here, write a summary of your abnormal findings and disregard all normal findings.

- *Chapter 2 presents the world's largest collection of MSE questions.*
- *Chapter 11 offers thousands of descriptors.*
- *Section 2.24 offers a form for recording your findings (Form 1).*

E. Functional limitations and impairments

Which areas of function to evaluate and how to label them are controversial topics. For individual clients, you might add or substitute "Affective functioning" (e.g., emotional paralysis from continuing grieving or depression with suicidal preoccupations), "Physical functioning" (e.g., chronic fatigue, dizziness, and incontinence resulting in isolation), or combinations of these areas.

The areas of functioning listed in Form 2 are the only ones of concern to MCOs and are given there in order of MCO's interest. If the client has discontinued working, returning her/him to employment is the most valuable service you can provide in the eyes of MCO personnel (who, after all, work for the client's employer).

- *For ADL evaluation, see Chapter 14.*
- *For relationships in society, see Chapter 15.*
- *For couple and family relationships, see Chapter 16.*
- *For the criteria for work or school functioning, see Chapter 17.*

Legal problems can go under "Social" or "Occupational"; leisure/recreational losses under Other, etc. Do not obsess over the best choice of category for each limitation; it doesn't matter to anyone else. Similarly, the titles of the categories themselves don't matter greatly ("Work," "Vocational," "Occupational," "Employment," and "Military" are functional equivalents).

MCOs are almost uninterested in some clinical areas, such as sexual dysfunctions, traumatic early experiences, and eating disorders, unless they can be shown to have a significant impact on work functioning. MCOs generally interpret learning disorders and other academic dysfunctions as educational/school problems rather than health problems, and refuse to pay for their assessment or treatment. Only lip service is paid to spiritual/religious, cultural/ethnic, and recreational aspects.

A key principle of MCO work is that therapy's goal is just to restore the client to an immediately previous level of functioning. Therapy with any aim higher than recovery to this level (perhaps healthier functioning, understanding, personality change, prevention of relapse, or even reduced costs of further treatment) is simply not the financial responsibility of the MCO.

I suggest a simple rating scale for severity of impairments. The GAF numbers provide both anchors for judgments and the illusion of precision.

- *See Section 21.23, "Axis V: Global Assessment of Functioning Scales," for the anchoring statements.*

F. Strengths

We clinicians focus to a great (indeed, excessive) extent on deficits and defects, and yet nothing can be built on a vacuum. MCOs, Joint Commission on Accreditation of Healthcare Organizations, and others rightly demand that we consider the client's resources as a foundation for growth and as a font of ideas about previous successes which might be inspirational or repeatable. Therapies such as the "solution-focused approach" and the "miracle cure" deliberately utilize these successes, and you may find that a thorough inquiry into resources makes your job easier.

- *Section 19.3 may help you assess coping ability.*

G. Diagnoses

We all know that diagnosis, impairment, and treatment are not tightly related in the mental health area; we don't treat a diagnosis, but a client with patterns and pains. However, the shorthand of a diagnostic label conveys important information about what is and is not present to the professionally educated. Because of their medical origins, MCOs demand diagnoses based on certain widely acknowledged standards, even when other aspects are the foci of intervention and the diagnoses fail to address interactive or interpersonal aspects.

MCOs are also reluctant to pay for treatment of Axis II diagnoses, because they seem to believe that therapy for personality disorders is ineffective. Nevertheless, make sure to record any Axis II conditions present. You are not paid by the number of diagnoses, and great precision is not required these days. However, you must be correct, so careful differential diagnosing *is* required. Morrison (1995b) will teach all you need to know.

- *Chapter 21 contains all the common diagnoses and almost all of their DSM-IV and ICD-10 titles and codes. Generally, MCOs prefer the DSM-IV and government agencies prefer ICD-10's diagnostic standards.*

H. Current assessment of knowable risks

For their finality, impacts, and legal consequences, homicide and suicide are risks of greatest concern to both clinicians and MCOs. Of only slightly less concern to MCOs are substance abuse and dependence.

- *Section 12.37 will help you evaluate suicide potential.*
- *Sections 13.3 and 12.20 may help you evaluate potential for violence.*

Form 2 offers simple checkoffs, but if you suspect that any of these risks are of significance or you are unsure and anxious, please elaborate on your concerns in a narrative. From a malpractice point of view, demonstrating that you were professionally thoughtful before a tragic incident is more important than accurately predicting it (which you generally cannot do).

I. Recommended level of care

Each MCO has guidelines for deciding on the intensity of services that are "medically necessary" for a client, based on the facts of the case as you and the client present them. The MCO creates a list of these levels-of-care options, based on legal, clinical, and professional guidelines; the resources available in the community; and, most importantly, the internal decision-making standards of the MCO. The point of including this heading is to prod you as the report writer to consider whether the services you can offer (such as outpatient group therapy) are appropriate for this client's level of functioning and history of benefit from previous treatment. Also, recommending an unavailable service will not usually bring about its availability.

Here is one such list of levels of care, in order of decreasing intensity:

Emergency/immediate admission to inpatient psychiatric service.
Routine admission to inpatient psychiatric unit.
Residential treatment facility.
Drug/alcohol detoxification service.
Inpatient chemical dependency program.
Group or supported housing, recovery home/halfway house.
Day/partial hospital/treatment program.
Structured intensive outpatient therapy program.
Outpatient therapy (individual and/or group).
Community resource other than the above.
In-house Employee Assistance Program.
Referral to Primary Care Physician/medical plan.

- *Chapter 22, "Recommendations," has a long list of therapeutic services from which to select.*

III. Treatment concerns

A. Progress in current treatment to date

This item is completed when you seek reauthorization for a continuation of your services. These Concurrent Reviews function like progress reports. They do not *have* to be positive to justify services, but should be thoughtful. If the client has returned to a previous level of functioning, continued services will usually be deemed unnecessary, generally without regard to the stability of the recovery. If little or no progress has been demonstrated, you should consider adding treatments (medications, family meetings, drug and alcohol evaluation, psychoeducational community groups) or changing your approach. This is both a financial consideration and an ethical one in the face of no progress after sincere efforts.

For completing this form as a Concurrent Review, you could revise section III based on progress or the lack of it, while the rest of the form would remain the same as the initial evaluation version.

B. Treatment plan

1. ADDITIONAL CONSULTATIONS OR EVALUATIONS

Although these questions are often missing from MCOs' forms, it is logical and clinically justifiable to ask them: What else do we need to know, and how can we find this out?

MCOs have gutted the assessment function, with the rationale that the treater learns all that is necessary to guide treatment by doing treatment. This is not necessarily the case. Although testing can be overused, it can still be valuable to know what kind of personality a depressed person has or what other problems are not being currently demonstrated to you during therapy. It is even more clear that treating a person with dementia for depression, no matter how effective the methods, is unlikely to result in significant improvement. I recommend that all therapists learn how to use and interpret at least a few screening tests and whatever instruments they intend to use for outcome assessment.

2. TREATMENT'S OBJECTIVES AND GOALS

To conserve space, only one problem is shown on Form 2. As indicated there, you should repeat this format as many times as necessary, based on your conceptualization of the case. Only a few problems should be listed, in order for you and your client to remain focused. Select ones tightly related to the diagnosis and the limitations of function, and present them in order of priority.

An MCO's reviewers are not consulting clinicians, lack the training and licensure to prescribe treatments, and do not want to know exactly what you are doing during the therapeutic hour. Like anyone at a distance, they cannot judge a plan's appropriateness for an individual client they have not seen. They look mainly for cohesiveness (given the diagnosis, is the proposed intervention a common and appropriate one?), comprehensiveness (have all the usual concerns for this kind of problem been considered?), and articulation (based on how you describe the plan, do you seem to understand the treatment methods and goals?)

Behaviors to be changed

This is essentially a restatement of the problem in terms of the behaviors demonstrating its dynamics—its signs and symptoms or behavioral manifestations. If you can't specify the behaviors, you may need to do a more thorough investigation and interview of the client.

Interventions

You can specify interventions by asking yourself questions like these: What approaches have been shown to work for this problem? (See Section 22.2, "Treatments of Choice.") What are you trained to do with these kinds of problems? (If you lack skill in these areas, do not try to fake it. Get training or refer the client.) What techniques address the symptoms presented? How are these implemented? (How often? For how long? With what tools?) What will you expect your patient to do? Generic, goalless, unfocused treatment is unethical. Avoid experimental or contraindicated techniques for MCO treatment plans.

Offer descriptors of the mode of therapy (individual, group, family, etc.), the orientation or modality (cognitive, interpersonal, psychodynamic, structural, etc.), and specific techniques ("hot seat," "covert sensitization," "relapse prevention"). Indicate the clinical focus of these, such as "traumatic experiences in marriage" or "depressogenic thought patterns."

MCOs seem fond of interventions with low or no costs to them. Try to include (where appropriate) community support groups, psychoeducational efforts by others, bibliotherapy, etc.

Goals

You may have noticed that there is no heading "Goals" on Form 2. That is deliberate. Instead, the form offers "Observable indicators of improvement" and "Discharge level of problem behavior," both of which are more easily understood and stated than the more popular "Goals." However, for generalizability, I use the word "goal" in the discussion to follow.

Goals are usually understood as long-term destinations, and objectives are the steps needed to reach those goals. But because there is no agreement in the field over the exact meaning of objectives, you need not be precise in differentiating them from goals. Objectives are usually more behavioral and concrete than goals. Objectives are also shorter-term and more easily measurable. They are usually described in terms of the client's performance ("The client will be able to . . . "). However, distinguishing short- from long-term goals or changes makes little sense when treatment will be limited to 10–12 sessions. Much effort has been spent in distinguishing goals from objectives, describing the actions of therapy as methods, and devising ways of articulating measurable outcomes. We clinicians have usually been more anxious and precise than is necessary. Take a problem, consider how it might change with therapy, and then state some goals. Most frequently, symptom reduction is all that is sought.

Some clinicians see the choosing the goals of treatment as the client's responsibility (with some assistance) and the selecting of methods as the clinician's contribution. Surely careful and sensitive negotiation and conscious agreement on these is productive.

Observable indicators of improvement

Being able to assess change is absolutely crucial. Write desired outcomes in behavioral language. This means what a camera would see (actions and expressions), not the invisible emotions, cognitive processes, history, and intentions. Consider the manifestations of these, and not your well-trained formulations and shorthands for them.

Avoid vague terms like "increase," as any small change might qualify. Also avoid very broad terms like "communication skills" or "depression," because the client and reviewer will not be able to know what counts as change. Tie each indicator of change (objective or step toward the goal or longer-range outcome) to the presenting limitations of function. Make these observable objectives measurable or at least quantifiable. Frequency, duration, intensity, and latency are the classic dimensions for describing symptomatic behaviors. This objectification allows impartial evaluation.

Avoid steps of change that are too difficult (so as not to reinforce failure, anxiety, or low confidence) or too easy (so as to make reaching them irrelevant and unmotivating) to achieve.

Because you cannot observe the client in her/his life circumstances, accept and use "client reports" of the new behaviors, as necessary. It would be best if you could get confirmation of changes from someone else who observes the client frequently (this person, you, and the client would then create a "triadic" assessment).

TREATMENT PLANS

Expected number of visits to achieve each indicator

Without good empirical support, MCOs are greatly prejudiced toward brief interventions. This currently often means four to eight sessions. Try to select goals that have a chance of being achieved in that time, given the methods you know. Do not overpromise and underdeliver, hoping for an extension of sessions. That is false, unethical, and risky for the patient. If you cannot in good conscience work within these time frames and method limitations, get out of a MCO-dependent practice (see Ackley, 1997).

You may notice that no time frames or dates are offered, because sessions may be missed or other issues may arise. Besides, payment is based on services rendered, not calendar time.

Discharge level of problem behavior

This is another way of saying "long-term goals," but is essentially the criterion of recovery of function. There is no specific mention here of dates for evaluation of progress or more formal reevaluations of the client's status, which would normally be part of the treatment plan. These functions are dealt with under "IV. Administrative."

3. CASE MANAGER'S ADDITIONS

Many clinicians are afraid of or resent the "interference" of MCO reviewers. This section suggests that you are attempting to use the MCO's reviewers as consultants. Often their experience and training can result in an improved plan and better treatment.

4. OTHER CURRENT TREATING PROFESSIONALS

You need this information to coordinate treatment; to prevent the loss of information crucial to your or another's treatment of the client (e.g., side effects of medications); perhaps to receive medical oversight to treat a client; to indicate supervision; to reduce duplication of services; to obtain backup in an emergency; to consult in regard to problems; etc.

MCOs ask about other therapists providing care so that duplication of services (or at least payments) can be prevented. They often ask whether other members of the family are receiving treatment, what their diagnoses are, etc. Even seeking this information, much less providing it, may put you in a confidentiality bind unless *you* are seeing the family members.

5. MY SIGNATURE MEANS . . .

Fully informed consent has largely replaced "paternalism" in health care. Treatment is seen more these days as a contractual arrangement between a client and a professional than as a process taking place between a passive patient and an active expert. If treatment is a shared adventure, both parties must know about and voluntarily agree to it.

It may be very therapeutically productive to share the planning with the client and not to treat this document as simply a burden required for payment.

MCOs have generally refused to pay for treatments provided by unlicensed or supervised professionals, so there is no line here for "Supervisor."

6. ADDITIONAL COMMENTS, PLANS, OR INFORMATION

This is self-explanatory and is included mainly for you to remind yourself, or the reviewer who will see this form, of any other less tidy details.

IV. Administration

This final area on Form 2 allows you to keep track of the MCO's needs; it is also provided for your own administrative clarity.

25.5. DOMAINS OF FUNCTIONING AS TREATMENT TARGETS FOR HOSPITALIZED PATIENTS

Allen et al. (1992) offer eight domains of functioning to be assessed and targeted in treatment plans for rather severely impaired hospitalized patients. The list below is reprinted with permission.

1. Self-concept and identity.
   - Low self-esteem/self-confidence.
   - Unclear/unstable identity/sense of self.
   - Uncertain masculine/feminine identity.
   - Self-concept and identity disrupted by dissociation.

2. Interpersonal relationships.
   - Excessive interpersonal isolation.
   - Unstable relationships.
   - Hypersensitivity to rejection and perceived abandonment.
   - Inability to function autonomously.
   - Excessive dependency.
   - Continual perception of victimization/abuse/exploitation.
   - Extreme distrust of others.
   - Extreme hostility in interactions with others.
   - Oppositionalism/indirect opposition to demands.
   - Dishonest behavior.
   - Extreme self-centeredness/arrogance.
   - Hypersensitivity to criticism.
   - Deficient social skills.

3. Thinking and cognition.
   - Impaired contact with reality.
   - Disorganized thinking.
   - Failure of accommodation to cognitive deficits.
   - Flashbacks with confusion of past and present.

4. Emotional functioning.
   - Depressed mood.
   - Suicidal intentions/preoccupation.
   - Mood-related withdrawal from people/activities.
   - Hyperactivity/euphoria.
   - Tension/fearfulness/panic.
   - Excessive and unrealistic guilt feelings.
   - Mood swings.

5. Impulse regulation/addiction.
   - Impulsivity.
   - Substance abuse (specify).
   - Self-injurious behavior.
   - Violence.

TREATMENT PLANS

Flight/elopement.
Inhibition/overcontrol.

6. Adaptive skills.
Impairment in ADLs.
Impairment in academic/vocational skills.
Poor medication compliance.

7. Family.
Lack of age-appropriate autonomy.
Alienation from family.
Marital difficulties.
Parenting problems.
Poor family alliance with treatment team.

8. Other (including medical).

25.6. TREATMENT PLAN COMPONENTS FOR SUBSTANCE ABUSERS

See also "Responses to Treatment" under Section 12.36, "Substance Abuse and Use."

Lewis (1990) makes the very rational and yet often overlooked point that diverse people can be dependent on alcohol or other drugs in different ways for different needs, and that effective treatment design and implementation must take these differences into account. The lists below of goals and methods are derived from statements from the literature and are designed to be comprehensive but not exhaustive.

Goals for Substance Abusers

Abstinence: Obtain and maintain sobriety, live a chemical-free life, cope with life without chemicals.
Controlled drinking: Follow patterns of use that have reduced harm.

Stabilize one's health, finances, vocation/school, employment, living arrangements.
Complete a physical examination as prescribed, and follow up the findings as indicated by medical staff.
Enhance health and fitness.
Resolve and avoid legal problems.
Develop sober leisure skills.

Stabilize one's intimate relationships, marriage, family.
Include significant others such as spouse/partner, children, relatives, friends, etc., in the recovery program as prescribed.
Improve social skills, assertiveness, emotional expression, communication.
Improve social support, friendships, social pursuits.

Deal/cope with/resolve emotional problems/feelings such as rejection, depression, unresolved grief/mourning, shame, guilt, abandonment.
Improve coping skills, stress management skills, relaxation abilities, self-control.
Understand the nature and processes of addiction and recovery.
Enhance self-esteem, confidence.
Accept responsibility for the consequences of one's behavior.
Improve problem-solving ability, setting of priorities, persistence, frustration tolerance.

Be an active participant in the treatment program by attending/participating in:
    Scheduled education classes about chemical dependency and the process of recovery.
    Scheduled counseling, psychotherapy and educational groups.
    Recreational activities to expand pleasures of physical activity, healthy competition,
        skill acquisition, socializing, interest areas, etc.
    AA/NA/CA/SA/etc. groups to develop a sober support fellowship in the community.
    The design and carrying out of a discharge plan that includes plans for employment, a
        place to live, sobriety.

Become a sponsor, substance educator, role model.

Methods

Education

Learn about the following (alternate phrasings can include be exposed to, understand,
    appreciate, apply, and change):
    The disease concept of addiction.
    The consequences of accepting one's identity as an alcoholic/drug user.
    Cross-addiction, multiple addictions, dual diagnoses.
    Addictive behavior not involving chemicals, etc.
    The nature and processes of addiction and recovery.
    The issues of dysfunctional families, codependence, children of alcoholics.
Write and share one's chemical history, the progression of addiction, and the consequent
    problems.
Read appropriate books and discuss their contents.

Therapeutic Activities

Define, in one's own words, all the words in one of the Twelve Steps.
Interview five peers on powerlessness, their understanding of the Twelve Steps, etc.
List five examples of one's personal unmanageableness.
Identify specific negative consequences of one's substance use.
Keep a "feelings journal" and make at least two entries a day.
Interview counselors on how to deal with anger.
Interview peers about a positive and a negative quality of oneself.
Write a "feelings letter" to one's mother.

Therapeutic Planning

Prepare an aftercare plan including a daily plan, home group meetings, how to attend (#)
    of meetings per week for a total of (#) meetings/weeks/days.
Recognize and plan to prevent how becoming Hungry, Angry, Lonely, Tired leads to drink-
    ing.
Relapse prevention (Marlatt & Gordon, 1985): Learn abstinence violation effect statements
    and counters, identify high-risk situations, rehearse coping responses.
Develop multiple alternatives to chemical use for high-risk situations (e.g., recreation skills,
    time management planning, calling on one's support system); use Stress Inoculation
    Training (Meichenbaum, 1985).

For Adult Children Of Alcoholics

Write letters to one's parents about feelings of inadequacy, history of emotional/physical/
    sexual abuse or neglect, abandonment, etc.

25.7. TREATMENT PLAN COMPONENTS FOR CRISIS INTERVENTIONS

Acknowledge/appreciate/validate/take seriously the subject's distress. (Do not argue or get into a power struggle.)
Encourage ventilation of feelings.
Reassure subject/family of your continued availability.
Reinforce/support all positive responses.
Reinforce/support problem-solving efforts.
Offer alternative methods of coping.
Negotiate a contract of not doing anything to worsen the situation for a period of time.
Negotiate what to do during periods when feeling bad.
Provide assured and continual support.

25.8. CHECKLIST OF STRENGTHS

Alternative terms for strengths include the following:

Assets, resources, capacities, talents, competencies, unrecognized resources, protective/generative factors.

Social/Community *See also Chapter 15, "Social/Community Functioning."*

Has multiple, extensive, accessible support systems.
Has long-term relationships; supportive, capable spouse/partner.
Membership in viable groups or communities.

Interpersonal *See also Chapter 16, "Couple and Family Relationships."*

Socially skilled, competent, assertive, respectful, offers and accepts feedback, tolerant.
Social competence/intelligence, popular, likeable.
Friendly, comfortable, outgoing, extraverted, sense of humor, shares, helpful.
Social sensitivity, aware of impact on others, empathic, good listener, concern for others, supports others, maintains appropriate boundaries.
Nurturing, compassionate, generous, modest, not egotistical.
Strong, self-assertive, powerful, dominant, acting as leader.

Occupational/Educational *See also Chapter 17, "Vocational/Academic Skills."*

Income, financial resources, savings, insurance.

Personality *See also Chapter 13, "Personality Patterns."*

Shows integrity, honesty; trustworthy; accepts responsibility for own behavior; dependable, reliable, stable, decisive.
Spiritual/religious faith, hopeful, optimistic.
Understands interactions of cognitions, affects, and behaviors; understands own motivations.
High task motivation, ambitious, hard-working, school/career success.
History of triumphs over challenges, nonavoidance/counterphobic, coped effectively with losses, benefited from previous counseling, no or minimal substance abuse/dependence.
Self-confidence and esteem, accurate self-perceptions, positive self-regard.

Resilience, hardiness, coping skills, good adjustment, normal, well-adjusted, happy, satisfied.
Satisfying recreation.

Affective   *See also Chapter 10, "Emotional/Affective Symptoms and Disorders."*

Awareness/comfort with feelings in self and others, expressive, range of affects.
Controls/modulates impulses; thinking and feeling are integral.
Tolerates painful emotions.
Emotionally intelligent.

Cognitive   *See also Chapter 11, "Cognition and Mental Status."*

Can attend and concentrate, recall.
Intellectually competent, intelligent, skillful, rational, scientific, articulate.
Creative, imaginative.
Adaptable, flexible, talented, common-sensical, good reality testing, accurate appraisal of demands, realistic.

Physical

Healthy, energetic, normal weight, exercises, sleeps well, good hygiene, well-being, maturity.

25.9. OUTCOME MEASURES/GOAL ACHIEVEMENTS

The evaluation of the effects of one's work is a professional and ethical as well as a scientific obligation. As part of the privilege of being in clinical practice, we owe our current and future patients the most effective care, and we owe ourselves the feedback to guide the development of our skills. Much guidance is available for the clinician who wishes to evaluate his/her own practice (Clement, 1999).

Many aspects of treatment can be evaluated. To select goals, refer to appropriate sections of this book for each kind of goal. Clients and MCOs focus most on the goal of symptom reduction. This book contains much detail about particular symptoms from which to develop goals: Emotional/affective symptoms are presented in Chapter 10, cognitive ones in Chapter 11, personality disorder symptoms in Chapter 13, and most of the other symptoms in Chapter 12. In addition, Chapter 5, "Referral Reasons," describes many symptomatic behaviors. Use the index for more specific areas. For the goals of increasing functionality, Chapter 14 covers ADLs, Chapter 15 social/community functioning, Chapter 16 relationships, and Chapter 17 vocational and academic functioning.

Common Foci of Outcome Evaluations

Clinicians and MCOs define outcomes from very different perspectives. Clinicians tend to focus on building realistic self-esteem; providing a supportive context for the exploration of feelings/history; bolstering defenses and preventing further decompensation; improving insight; increasing behavior controls, coping skills, and the tolerance of stressors at work/home; improving sexual adjustment; etc. The most common focus of MCOs is client satisfaction with services. This has most often been defined in its more easily measured but less clinical aspects, such as physical accessibility, scheduling/availability, comfort of setting, etc. In parallel, MCOs have asked providers for information about the availability of crisis services, the levels and varieties of care/service, consultation and transfer to other providers, record keeping and information transfer, etc. More recently, MCOs have been asking clients whether they would return for care or recommend the service to another, about their comfort with level of autonomy/control, and about their relationship with the providers (including respect, trust, competence, availability, etc.). Obviously, these additional factors are difficult to assess, and the measurements are open to interpretation.

As competition rises, MCOs will emphasize the "quality" of their services. "Quality" in this context is most often defined as the lessening of symptoms—their lessened duration, intensity, or frequency, or their increased latency (time between onset of stressors and onset of symptoms). MCOs are also interested in improvement in clients' level of functioning—that is, their fulfilling of life roles.

The larger picture of assessing the role of therapy in improving the quality of life; reducing other health care costs; lengthening lifespan; and increasing human happiness, satisfaction, and productivity has yet to be addressed by MCOs. However, Frisch (1992) has made an excellent start.

Goal Attainment Scaling

The strengths of Goal Attainment Scaling, a little-known method for assessing outcomes, are its simplicity and flexibility: Any kind of goal, in any paradigm, in any area, with any definition can be used. All that is needed is the ability to specify five levels of outcome (least favorable likely outcome, less than expected, expected, more than expected, and most favorable likely outcome) for each of at least three goals. Each level is given a relative weight. At review time the current status of each goal is assessed, and a simple mathematical formula determines the success of the intervention. For more information, see Kiresuk and Sherman (1968).

26

Formats for Reports, Evaluations, and Summaries

This chapter offers templates, formats, or outlines for many kinds of reports to organize and convey your information for specific audiences, purposes, or paradigms. Although neuropsychological, forensic, developmental, vocational, rehabilitation, and some other specialized psychiatric nursing and psychosocial evaluations are beyond the scope of this book, you will find guidance here for common reports and some examples of uncommon but heuristic alternatives.

26.1. A STANDARD FORMAT FOR REPORTS OF EVALUATIONS

The sequential structure of this book can also be used.

Use your agency's letterhead, or your own letterhead with credentials of relevance. Give the title or type of report as the heading. Then provide the following:

Name of person to whom report is being sent.
Name of subject of report; case/identification number; subject's gender and age.
Date(s) of examination(s) and report.
Evaluator's name (if not the same as the name on the letterhead).

The report itself should cover these areas:

1. Identification.
   a. Referral source and reason.
   b. Presenting problem.
   c. History of presenting problem.
   d. Treatment of presenting problem.
   e. Other problems.
2. Physical and behavioral description.
   a. Appearance.
   b. Behavioral observations.
   c. Interpersonal observations.
3. Mental status.
   a. Mood and affect.
   b. Cognitive aspects of mental status.
4. Health and habits.
   a. Medical status.
   b. Nutritional behaviors.
   c. Drugs and alcohol.
5. Legal issues.
   a. Aggressive behavior.
   b. Suicide.
   c. Child protective services.
6. Current living situation.
   a. Education.
   b. Work.
   c. Family.
   d. Deaths/losses/separations.
   e. Economic functioning and support.
   f. Financial competence.
7. Diagnostic impressions.
   a. Reliability.
   b. Summary of findings.
   c. Diagnoses.
   d. Dynamics/case formulation.
8. Recommendations and disposition.
   a. Treatment recommendations.
   b. Motivations for treatment.
   c. Barriers to treatment.

Sundberg (1977) adds these topical headings to those above:

Family constellation.	Birth and development.
Early recollections.	Sexual development.
Marital/couple and family data.	Self-description.
Recreation and interests.	Choices and turning points in life.
View of the future.	Any further material points.

26.2. FORMAT FOR A COMPREHENSIVE CASE SUMMARY

This very elaborate outline is modified from Wolberg (1954). It is also called a "source-oriented record," the "treatment team format," or the "orthopsychiatric format." Although it is perhaps best suited to research or teaching settings, it is included here so that you can see the most encompassing and classic style.

1. Chief Complaint.
2. History and development of complaint (date of onset, circumstances under which complaint developed, progression from the onset to the time of the initial interview).
3. Other complaints and symptoms (physical, emotional, psychic, and behavior symptoms other than those of the complaint factor).
4. Medical, surgical, and (in women), gynecological history.
5. Environmental disturbance at onset of therapy (economic, work, housing, neighborhood, and family difficulties).
6. Relationship difficulties at onset of therapy (disturbances in relationships with people; attitudes toward the world, authority, and self).
7. Heredity, constitutional, and early developmental influences (significant physical and psychiatric disorders in patient's family, SocioEconomic Status of family, important early traumatic experiences and relationships, neurotic traits in childhood and adolescence).
8. Family data (mother, father, siblings, spouse, children—ages, state of health, personality, adjustment, and patient's attitude toward each). Summary of social service contacts.
9. Previous attacks of emotional illness (as a child and later). When did patient feel himself/herself to be completely free from emotional illness?
10. Initial interview (brief description of condition of patient at first contact, including clinical findings).
11. Initial assessment of mental status: Level of insight and motivation at onset of therapy. (How long did the patient feel that he/she needed treatment? For what? Awareness of emotional nature of problem? Willingness to accept psychotherapy?)
12. Previous treatments. (When did the patient first seek treatment? What treatment did he/she get? Any hospitalizations?)
13. Clinical examination (significant findings in physical, neurological, laboratory, psychiatric, and psychological examinations).
14. Differential diagnosis (at time of initial interview).
15. Estimate of prognosis (at time of initial interview).
16. Psychodynamics/dynamic formulation and psychopathology.
17. Course of treatment: Treatment plan and goals, recommendations, disposition.
    a. Type of therapy employed, frequency, total number of sessions, response to treatment.
    b. Significant events during therapy, dynamics that were revealed, verbatim report of important dreams, nature of transference and resistance.
    c. Progress in therapy, insight acquired, translation of insight into action, change in symptoms, mental status, attitudes toward and relationships with people.
18. Condition on discharge (areas of improvement, remaining problems).
19. Recommendations to patient.
20. Statistical classification.

26.3. FORMAT FOR PSYCHODYNAMIC EVALUATIONS: DEVELOPMENTAL MODEL

Huber (1961) offers an outline for what he calls the "sequential report," which combines the chronological (to understand causation) with the topical (to understand the presentation) and frames the questions of dynamics.

1. Intellectual functioning.
   Level of present functioning, comparison with his group.
   Level of capacity.
   Reasons for failure to function up to capacity.
   Areas of strength and weakness.
2. Dynamics.
   What is he/she attempting to accomplish with her/his present mode of behavior?
   What thoughts and feelings is she/he having?
   What events or people produce conflict? Anxiety?
   Major and minor conflicts.
   People with whom the conflicts are manifested.
   Times and places where the conflicts arise.
   How did her/his present situation arise? What pressures and supports were given by significant figures? What was the sequence of learning the defenses, symptoms, adaptations, etc.?
3. Methods of handling conflicts.
   Overt behavior manifesting anxiety, defense mechanisms, symptoms.
4. Strengths and weaknesses in relation to goals.
   Needs and wishes, both manifest and latent.
   Strengths for pursuing them: What are the pressures, supports, and strengths (environmental and intrapsychic) that can change her/his life?
   Weaknesses: What can produce dangerous and/or crippling behaviors (suicide, psychotic reactions, psychosomatic difficulties, antisocial acts)?
   What does she/he need to function more effectively?
   How much impairment is there? What is the nature of the impairment?
5. Recommendations.
   Therapy/no therapy, environmental change.
   Form(s) of therapy.
   Predictions about therapy.

26.4. FORMAT FOR PSYCHODYNAMIC EVALUATIONS: STRUCTURAL MODEL

Much of the following is adapted by permission from Kellerman and Burry (1997).

Structure of the Personality

1. Psychosexual developmental levels, character/personality structure, identity.
2. Areas of conflict, adaptive and maladaptive techniques, mechanisms of defense/adaptation.
3. Ego strength, primary and secondary autonomous ego functioning, integrative/synthetic/adaptive ego functions.
4. Intellectual aspects of the personality.
5. Affective aspects of the personality.

6. Object relationships, potential for acting out.
7. Estimate of treatability, transference issues.

Topics to be Addressed in a Report

Anxiety

Signal anxiety/inner tension evoked by internal threat (fantasies, impulses) or external threat (other people or demands of life).
How is it manifested?
How is anxiety experienced: Consciously? Acted out? Somatized?

Impulses vs. Control

IMPULSES (ENERGIZED EMOTIONS)

Anger: Hostility, fantasy, rumination, aggression, sarcasm, quarrelsomeness, passive–aggressive behaviors.
Sexuality: Libidinous impulses and wishes for gratification, pleasure fantasies, power themes, sexual fantasies, sexual variations, acting out (compulsive masturbation, perversions, promiscuity).
Impulse-dominated personality.

CONTROL MECHANISMS

Cognitive/intellectual: Concentration, attention, achievement, integration.
Ego and superego: Goal pursuit, frustration tolerance, taking actions.
Individual defense mechanisms (for anxiety management, emotion associated with the anxiety).
Character traits (patterns for binding anxiety): Sublimating, impulsive, pleasure-dominated, anger-dominated, fear-dominated, dependency-dominated.
Fantasy.
Fears/phobic reactions.
Control-dominated personality.

Defense Mechanisms

Acting out, acting in	Identification	Repression
Compartmentalization	Insulation, emotional	Resistance
Compensation, over-compensation	Intellectualization	Restitution
	Internalization	Splitting
Denial (see Section 12.10)	Introjection	Sublimation
Denial in fantasy	Isolation (of affect)	Substitution
Displacement	Projection	Suppression
Dissociation	Rationalization	Symbolization
Fantasizing	Reaction formation	Turning against the self
Fixation	Regression	Undoing

DSM-IV proposes these additional or redefined mechanisms (in its Appendix B):

Affiliation	Help-rejecting complaining	Passive aggression
Altruism	Humor	Projective identification
Anticipation	Idealization	Self-assertion
Autistic fantasy	Omnipotence	Self-observation
Devaluation		

Correspondence of Diagnosis and Defense/Coping Mechanisms

Diagnosis	*Preferred defenses*
Hysteric	Denial, repression
Obsessive–compulsive	Intellectualization, isolation, undoing, rationalization, sublimation
Passive–aggressive	Displacement
Depression	Compensation, turning against the self
Narcissistic disturbance	Compensation
Paranoid	Denial, reaction formation, projection
Borderline	Splitting
Psychopathic personality	Regression
Mania	Reaction formation, compensation, sublimation

26.5. BEHAVIORAL DIAGNOSIS

Kanfer and Saslow (1965) offer an alternative to the usual dynamic and personological perspectives for clinical evaluations and interventions. The following summarizes their approach.

The Problem

I. Count the excesses, deficits, and qualities of the maladaptive behavior(s).
II. Circumstantial/functional analysis.
    A. Original initiating circumstances.
    B. Antecedent-maintaining and -inhibiting circumstances.
        1. Environment: Location, time.
        2. Physical: Illness, injury, sleep, diet, exercise, chemical intake.
        3. Social: Others present, and their actions.
        4. Affect, mood.
        5. Cognitive: Thoughts, meanings, ideas about self, situation, others.
        6. Other factors: Values, attitudes, opinions.
    C. Sequence: What happened, what happens, and what can upset the sequence.
    D. Payoffs, reinforcements (immediate and long-term).
    E. Competing or enhancing higher-level cognitive functions: Ideals, values, self-talk.

The Person

III. Skills.
    A. Self-control: Sex, aggression, self-injurious habits, persistence, delay of gratification, relaxation.
    B. Expressive: Sex, aggression, any strong emotion, artistic activities (art, music, dance), religion, humor.
    C. Cognitive: Self-awareness, psychological-mindedness, academic intelligence, job skills, verbal and analytical facility.
    D. Physical: Strength, coordination, attractiveness.
    E. Social.
    F. Payoffs in past for exercising skills.
IV. Reaction to incentives and aversions: Techniques for changing behavior used in the past.
    A. Reinforcements: What has worked or would work to change behavior (self-image, goal achievement, approval, money, access to activity, free time, power, competition, status, etc.).

B. Withdrawal of reinforcements or punishment: Time out, being ignored, withdrawal of privileges, reactions toward punisher and punishment.
C. Schedule of reinforcement, subgoals, step size, etc.

The Environment

V. Psychosocial–cultural context.
A. Social class: Expectations of authority, therapy, opportunities, previous treatment.
B. Effects of changes on family, friends, coworkers, bosses, etc.
C. Health behaviors.

The Future

VI. Predicted response to various kinds of interventions.
A. Environmental manipulation.
B. Therapy.
VII. Prognosis.
A. Changeability of maintaining circumstances and skills.
B. Habit strength.
C. Cost of interventions.

26.6. THEMES FOR EVALUATIONS FROM AN EXISTENTIAL PERSPECTIVE

Enhancing the capacity for self-awareness so as to make choices and live more fully.
Acceptance of responsibility: Because we are free to act, we must accept responsibility for our actions. We cannot change without accepting this responsibility.
Striving for an identity from within rather than based on others' expectations.
The continuous search for the meaning of one's life: "What do I want from this life? Where is my source of meaning?"
Acceptance of anxiety as a normal, inescapable part of living.
Fuller awareness of death and nonbeing.

26.7. ADLERIAN EVALUATIONS[1]

Life Style Analysis

Activity level and radius: Friendships, social life, occupation, recreation, love, and sex.
Degree of cooperation and social interest: Thinking about needs and feelings of others, actions to help others.
Courage and conquests.
Discouragements and stopping points.
Excesses and omissions.
Level and type of intelligence.
Emotions and feelings: Conjunctive and disjunctive, depth and range.
Scheme of apperception: Antithetical scheme of apperception, perceived minus and plus situations.

---

[1]These are courtesy of Henry T. Stein, PhD, of San Francisco, CA.

Use of capabilities: Intelligence (social purpose), abilities and talents (socially useful and useless), feelings and emotions (move ahead or stop), and memory and imagination (encouragement/discouragement).

Pattern of dealing with tasks and difficulties: Childhood prototype, adolescent experimentation, repetitive adult style.

Inferiority feelings, compensatory goal, and style of life: Inferiority feelings (what to avoid, painful insecurity); fictional goal of superiority (imagined compensation, security and success); style of life (how to get to goal and deal with life's major tasks: social relationships, occupation, love, and sex); connection of presenting problem with life style and goal; use of symptoms to excuse avoidance of normal tasks.

Theory

Interpersonal focus: Social beings moving through and interacting with their environments.

Goals of psychotherapy: Expansion of the individual, self-realization, enhancement of social interest, enhancement of choices (ability to choose to shape the internal and external environment, and to choose posture adopted toward life's stimuli).

Terms and Concepts

Inferiority, superiority, and their complexes.
Compensation, overcompensation.
Life style, style of life.
Confluence and transformation of drives.
Masculine protest.
Fictionalism, fictional finalisms.
Striving for perfection, self-enhancement.
Social embeddedness, social interest.
Early/first recollections.

26.8. TRANSACTIONAL ANALYSIS[2]

Almost all clinical models examine only the individual. Eric Berne's (1964) TA combines interactional and psychodynamic perspectives.

Ego States: Parent, Child, Adult; contaminations, exclusions; critical, nurturing; defining/structuring;
Adapted child, Natural Child, Little Professor.
Strokes: Stroke Economy, Stroke Hunger, for being/doing, conditional/unconditional, discounting, compromise.
Transactions: Complimentary, crossed, ulterior, congruent, angular, duplex.
Relationships: Companionate, intimate, symbiotic.
Scripts, counterscript, script injunction, positive script decisions, messages.
Ways of structuring time: Withdrawal, intimacy, ritual, activities, pastimes, games, rackets.

Pastimes: PTA, Psychiatry, Small Talk (General Motors, Who Won, Grocery, Kitchen, Wardrobe, How To, How Much?, Do You Know?, Ever Been?, What Became Of?, Morning After, Martini).

[2]Resources for TA materials include these: For information, International Transactional Analysis Association, 436 14th St., Suite 1301, Oakland, CA 94612–2710; (510) 625-7720; e-mail, ITAA@ITAA-net.org.

Games:
    Degrees of games: Hard, soft, ulterior transactions.
    Elements of games: Steps, Gambits, Moves, Payoffs.
    Types of games:
        Alcoholic games: Roles for the game of Alcoholic include Alcoholic, Patsy, Connection, Rescuer, Persecutor. (Variations of this game include Drunk and Proud; Lush; Wino; High and Proud; etc.—for these and other games alcoholics play, see Steiner, 1971.)
        Marital games: Corner; Courtroom; Frigid Woman; Frigid Man; Harried; If It Weren't for You; Look How Hard I've Tried; Sweetheart.
        Sexual games: Let's You and Him Fight; Perversion; Rapo; Stocking Game; Uproar.
        Party games: Ain't It Awful; Blemish; Schlemiel; Anti-schlemiel; Why Don't You—Yes, But; You Got Me into This; You Got Yourself into This; There I Go Again.
        Underworld games: Cops and Robbers; How Do You Get Out of Here; Let's Pull a Fast One on Joey.
        Consulting room games: Greenhouse; Stupid; Wooden Leg; Do Me Something; Indigence; Peasant; I'm Only Trying to Help You; Psychiatry.
        Good games: Busman's Holiday; Cavalier; Happy to Help; Homely Sage; They'll Be Glad They Knew Me.
        Other games: Kick Me; Harass; I Am Blameless; NIGYSOB (Now I've Got You, Son Of a Bitch); See What You Made Me Do; Debtor; Creditor.

Rackets: Stamp Collecting, Nobody Loves Me.

26.9. NURSING DIAGNOSES AND TREATMENT PLANNING[3]

Each profession approaches the facts of abnormal behavior from its own perspective, history, and traditions. Many clinicians are surprised to find that nursing thinks clearly and comprehensively (nursing diagnoses) and productively (nursing care plans) about psychological conditions, and that many nurses are trained and certified as psychiatric specialists.[4]

Nursing diagnoses tend to be quite behavior-specific and can add "potential for" additional behaviors of concern, such as suicide or substance abuse.

Biopsychosocial History and Assessment[5]

1. Identifying information.
2. Predisposing factors: Genetic influences, past experiences, current resources.
3. Precipitating event.
4. Patient's perception of the stressor.
5. Adaptation responses: Psychosocial, physiological.
6. Summary of initial psychosocial/physical assessment: Diagnoses (DSM-IV) and other concerns (such as "potential for . . . "; see above).

---

[3]I am most grateful to Patricia Hurzeler, MS, APRN, CS, of Bloomfield, CT, for these suggestions.

[4]The basic psychiatric credential is Certified Specialist, which requires 2 years of supervised practice beyond the Master of Science in Nursing level. With courses in medication, etc., nurses are called Advanced Practice Registered Nurses and can prescibe in 36 states.

[5]This format is from the nursing faculty of Butler County Community College, El Dorado, KS, and is based on the stressor/adaptation model.

Components of a Nursing Diagnosis: The PES Model

1. Health <u>P</u>roblems: Human response to actual or potential health problems as assessed by the nurse.
   1A. "Related to":
2. <u>E</u>tiology: Past experiences of individual, genetic influences, current environmental factors, or pathophysiological changes.
   2A. "<u>E</u>videnced by":
3. Clustered <u>S</u>igns or symptoms/defining characteristics: What the client says and what the nurse observes about the existence of a problem.

Nursing Care Plan

1. Selected and prioritized nursing diagnoses.
2. Goal/objectives: In behavioral/objective terminology, measurable, for evaluating effectiveness of interventions. "Long-term" usually means "by discharge from treatment."
3. Interventions with their rationales.
4. Desired patient outcomes/discharge criteria.
5. Date of evaluation.
6. Medication information.
7. Revisions of plan on evaluation dates.

26.10. CHILD ASSESSMENT OUTLINE

Jenkins et al. (1990) offer this format for the psychiatric assessment interview of a child, which is adapted by permission here.

Meeting the Child and Each Caregiver, and Establishing Rapport

1. Meet the child and accompanying adults.
2. Find out why the child thinks he/she is being seen.
3. Discuss the nature and procedures of the interview.
4. Explain that information given is confidential, with the exception of information needed to protect the child and others from imminent harm.

Developmental History

Family

1. Child's attitude toward each parent.
2. Child's relationship with sibling(s).
3. Family psychiatric history.
4. History of parents' childhoods:
   a. Relationships with their parents and siblings.
   b. Discipline methods used; evidence of abuse or dysfunction.
   c. Levels of education and current occupation(s).
5. Circumstances of patient's birth; if adopted, circumstances and motivation for adoption.

Developmental Milestones

1. Physical:
   a. Pregnancy, delivery, feeding, and weaning; neonatal illnesses.
   b. Early or significant medical illnesses or injuries.
   c. Neuromuscular development of speech, motor milestones (sitting, standing, walking, first words, play).

2. Behavioral:
   a. Toilet training and other training—response to discipline, methods used.
   b. Reactions to beginning day care and school; adaptation.
   c. Sleep patterns, sleep disturbances.
   d. Phobias.
   e. Habit patterns (e.g., bedwetting and thumb sucking).

Significant Events

Ask about moves, parents' illnesses, deaths, divorces, violence, etc.

Current Level of Functioning (as Compared with Peers)

1. School performance.
2. Hobbies and extracurricular activities.
3. Peer relationships.
4. Relationships with adults other than parents.
5. Unusual habits and habit disorders.
6. Aims and ambitions.
7. Current health and medications.

Interview with the Child

Child's Ideas about the Problem

1. Expectations for outcome.
2. What the child would like to change in self or others.
3. "What problems have we not talked about yet?"

Symptom Review

1. Vegetative symptoms.
2. Anxiety symptoms.
3. Psychotic symptoms.
4. Suicidal ideation, self-injurious acts, acts of violence.
5. Ruminations, preoccupations, obsessions, rituals, compulsions.
6. Substance abuse.
7. Victimization experiences.

Mental Status Examination   *See Section 26.11, just below.*

Drawings

House–Tree–Person.
Self-portrait.
Kinetic Family Drawing.

Developmental Status

Consider development achieved, as compared to the child's age peers, in these areas:

1. Motor: Coordination, fine and gross.
2. Cognitive.
3. Social.
4. Communication.
5. Psychological, social, interpersonal.
6. Identity.

Other Information That May Be Sought

1. Psychological testing.
2. Medical consultations—pediatric, neurological.
3. School records, interview with teachers.
4. Interviews with other significant adults (noncustodial parents, grandparents, social worker).
5. Records of previous treatment or evaluations.

26.11. CHILD'S MENTAL STATUS EVALUATION REPORT

Simmons (1987) offers this format, which is adapted by permission:

Appearance.
Mood or affect.
Orientation and perception.
Coping mechanisms:
    a. Major defenses.
    b. Expression and control of affectional and aggressive impulses.
Neuromuscular integration.
Thought processes and verbalizations: Speech quality, vocabulary.
Fantasy as seen in:
    a. Dreams.
    b. Drawings.
    c. Wishes.
    d. Play.
Superego functioning:
    a. Ego ideals and values.
    b. Integration into personality.
Concepts of self:
    a. Object relations.
    b. Identification.
Awareness of problems.
Estimate of intelligence.
Summary of MSE.

26.12. VOCATIONAL AND NONCLINICAL PERSONALITY EVALUATIONS

Huber (1961) quotes these skeletal industrial/organizational report outlines:

From Roher et al.:

1. Intelligence.
2. Emotional control.
3. Skill in human relations.
4. Insight and self-criticism.
5. Organization and planning ability, direction of others.
6. Recommendations and prognosis (for candidates) or conclusions and prognosis (for noncandidates).

From Fear (1958):

1. Test results: Mental ability, numerical ability, verbal ability, clerical aptitude (or other appropriate testing), social intelligence.
2. Evaluation: Work history, education and training, early home background, present social adjustment, personality, motivation, and character.
3. Summary of assets and liabilities.
4. Summary.

From Richardson et al.:

1. Intellectual functioning.
2. Relations with others.
3. Work characteristics.
4. Aspirations and drive.
5. Interests and values.
6. Personal adjustment.
7. Family background.
8. Potential and recommendations.

Huber (1961) also suggests asking the reader or recipient of the report these questions:

"Describe the characteristics of the most satisfactory/ideal candidate in this job."
"What characteristics of this person stand in the way of your hiring him/her without any hesitation?"
"What specific questions keep coming into your mind about this candidate?"
"What do you not want to see in a candidate for this job?"

26.13. FORMATS FOR THERAPY NOTES

See also Zuckerman (1997) for guidance, forms, and examples of formats, and Wiger (1998) for suggestions and examples of good and bad notes.

First decide on the answers to these questions: (1) To/for whom am I writing? (2) For what purpose am I making these notes? (3) What is my system for recording data?

Include the content (facts, actions, words) and some interpretations, and keep these distinguished.

Format for Individual Psychodynamic Therapy Note

Wolberg (1954) suggests including the following:

1. Present state of symptoms/complaint (absent, improved, the same, worse).
2. How the patient feels (mood and emotion).
3. Important life situations and developments since the last visit and how they were handled.
4. Content of the session.
5. Insight; translation of insight into action.
6. Significant transference and resistance reactions: Appointments (timely, tardy, attitude), communicativeness, relationship with therapist.
7. Dreams (in the patient's words).

Huber (1961) adds:

8. Countertransference reactions.
9. Goals of therapy (as seen by the therapist).

FORMATS FOR REPORTS

A Simple Format

Huber (1961) suggests this alternative format. The tips in brackets indicate my way of noting various elements.

Content (or behavior): What each did and said. [✔ I record these with no modifiers.]

What the therapist thought and felt about the content and may have said to the patient. [✔ I put these in parentheses.]

What the therapist thought and felt about the patient, the interview, the content—and probably did not tell the patient. [✔ I put these comments in square brackets, along with my observations and hypotheses about games played, emotional and cognitive styles, etc.]

Outside: Anything bearing on the therapy that happened outside the interview. Menninger (1952) adds to this: Compliance with the therapeutic program, steps taken to overcome the patient's resistance and who took them, telephone calls, consultations with colleagues and the results.

Plans for the next interview (promises made, what to pursue, questions). [✔ I use the headings "HW" for work to be done by either of us, and "RX" for topics to be followed up.]

27

Listing of Common Psychiatric and Psychoactive Drugs

27.1. LISTING OF MEDICATIONS BY BOTH TRADE AND GENERIC NAMES

This listing is intended only as a guide for the clinician through the often confusing mass of names of medications. It is far too basic to be used for prescription guidance or medication evaluations.

Use this list to quickly find the generic and trade names for a drug when you have only one name, and to learn the drug's major uses. The first and second columns include both generic and trade names in alphabetical order. Uncapitalized, lower-case words are generic names; capitalized words are trade names. For example, "acetazolamide" is the generic name of the first drug listed, and "Diamox" is its trade name. Both "acetazolamide" and "Diamox'" appear in the first column's alphabetical listing, under "A" and under "D." If you look for the trade name in the first column, the second column will offer the generic name, and vice versa. When a drug has several trade names, they are listed next to the generic name's entry, and cross-referenced at each trade name's entry. The major uses for each drug are given in the the third column. A single drug may be used for diverse purposes. The "Major uses" column reflects this diversity. While most of these drugs have major psychiatric uses, some with psychoactive effects have common nonpsychiatric uses, such as antihistamines (e.g., diphenhydramine/ Benadryl) or appetite suppressants (e.g., phentermine/Adipex-P). The list that follows includes such drugs and lists their major *nonpsychiatric* use to alert you to check on possible psychoactive effects. Do not assume that the functions listed are the only uses of these drugs.

Names of medications		Major uses
acetazolamide	Diamox	Anticonvulsant
acetophenazine	Tindal	Antipsychotic
Adapin	doxepin	Antidepressant
Adderall	amphetamine & dextroamphetamine	<u>C</u>entral <u>N</u>ervous <u>S</u>ystem stimulant
Adipex-P	phentermine	Appetite suppressant
Akineton	biperiden	Anti-Parkinsonian
Aldomet	methyldopa	Anti-Parkinsonian, antihypertensive
alprazolam	Xanax	Anxiolytic, hypnotic
Alurate	aprobarbital	Sedative/hypnotic
amantadine	Symadine, Symmetrel	Anti-Parkinsonian, antiviral
Ambien	zolpidem	Hypnotic
amitriptyline	Elavil Endep	Antidepressant
amobarbital	Amytal	Sedative/hypnotic
amoxapine	Asendin	Antidepressant
amphetamine	Adderall, Benzadrine, Biphetamine	CNS stimulant
Amytal	amobarbital	Sedative/hypnotic
Anafranil	clomipramine	Antidepressant, Antiobsessive
Android	methyltestosterone	Male replacement hormone
Antabuse	disulfiram	Blocks alcohol metabolism
aprobarbital	Alurate	Sedative/hypnotic
Arco-Lase	pentobarbital	Sedative/hypnotic
Aricept	donepezil	Anti-Alzheimer's
Artane	trihexyphenidyl	Anti-Parkinsonian
Asendin	amoxapine	Antidepressant
Atarax	hydroxyzine	Antihistamine, antianxiety
Ativan	lorazepam	Anxiolytic, hypnotic
Aventyl	nortriptyline	Antidepressant
baclofen	Lioresal	Muscle relaxant
Banobese	phentermine	Appetite suppressant
Benadryl	diphenhydramine	Antihistamine/decongestant
Benzadrine	amphetamine	CNS stimulant
benztropine	Cogentin	Anti-Parkinsonian
biperiden	Akineton	Anti-Parkinsonian
Biphetamine	amphetamine & dextroamphetamine	CNS stimulant
bromocriptine	Parlodel	Anti-Parkinsonian
bupropion	Wellbutrin	Antidepressant
	Zyban	Antismoking
BuSpar	buspirone	Anxiolytic, hypnotic
buspirone	BuSpar	Anxiolytic, hypnotic
butabarbital	Butisol	Sedative
butaperazine	Repoise	Antipsychotic
Butisol	butabarbital	Sedative
carbamazepine	Tegretol, Epitol	Anticonvulsant, mood stabilizer
carbidopa & levodopa	Sinemet	Anti-Parkinsonian
carbimid, calcium	Temposil	Alcohol challenge reaction
Carbolith	lithium carbonate	Antimanic, mood stabilizer, potentiates antidepressants
carphenazine	Proketazine	Antipsychotic
Catapres	clonidine	Anti-ADHD, antianxiety, antihypertensive
Celexa	citalopram	Antidepressant
Centrax	prazepam	Anxiolytic, hypnotic

Names of medications		Major uses
chlorprothixene	Taractan	Antipsychotic
chloral hydrate	Noctec	Hypnotic
chlordiazepoxide	Librium, Mitran	Anxiolytic, hypnotic
chlordiazepoxide & amitriptyline	Limbitrol	Antidepressant
chlormezanone	Trancopal (no longer available)	Antianxiety
chlorpromazine	Thorazine, Ormazine, Promaz	Antipsychotic
Cibalith-S	lithium citrate	Antimanic, mood stabilizer, potentiates antidepressants
citalopram	Celexa	Antidepressant
clomipramine	Anafranil	Antidepressant, antiobsessive
clonazepam	Klonopin, Rivotril	Anticonvulsant, anxiolytic, hypnotic, mood stabilizer
clonidine	Catapres	Anti-ADHD, antianxiety, antihypertensive
clorazepate	Tranxene	Anxiolytic, hypnotic
Clozaril	clozapine	Antipsychotic
clozapine	Clozaril	Antipsychotic
Cogentin	benztropine	Anti-Parkinsonian
Cognex	tacrine	Antidementia
cyclobenzaprine	Flexeril	Muscle relaxant
cycrimine	Pagitane	Anti-Parkinsonian
Cylert	pemoline	Anti-ADHD, potentiates antidepressants
Cytomel	liothyronine (T_3)	Thyroid hormone replacement, potentiates antidepressants
Dalmane	flurazepam	Hypnotic
danazol	Danocrine	Male replacement hormone
Danocrine	danazol	Male replacement hormone
Dantrium	dantrolene	Muscle relaxant
dantrolene	Dantrium	Muscle relaxant
Darvon	propoxyphene	Opioid analgesic
Daxoline	loxapine	Antipsychotic
Deaner	deanol	CNS stimulant
deanol	Deaner	CNS stimulant
Decadron	dexamethasone	Diagnostic test for depression
Demerol	meperidine	Opiate analgesic
Depakene	valproic acid	Anticonvulsant, mood stabilizer, antimanic
Depakote	divalproex	Anticonvulsant, mood stabilizer, antimanic
deprenyl	selegiline	Anti-Parkinsonian
Deprol	meprobamate & benactyzine	Antianxiety
desipramine	Norpramin, Pertofrane	Antidepressant
Desoxyn	methamphetamine	Anti-ADHD
Desyrel	trazodone	Antidepressant, hypnotic
dexamethasone	Decadron	Corticosteroid, diagnostic test for depression
Dexedrine	dextroamphetamine	Anti-ADHD, potentiates antidepressants
dextroamphetamine	Dexedrine, Adderall	Anti-ADHD, potentiates antidepressants
Diamox	acetazolamide	Anticonvulsant
diazepam	Valium, T-Quil, Valrelease, Zetran	Anxiolytic, hypnotic, muscle relaxant
dichloralphenazone	Midrin	Analgesic, sedative
Dilantin	phenytoin	Anticonvulsant

LISTING OF DRUGS

Names of medications		*Major uses*
diphenhydramine	Benadryl	Antihistamine
disulfiram	Antabuse	Antialcohol
divalproex	Depakote, Epival	Anticonvulsant, mood stabilizer
Dolophine	methadone	Blocks narcotics craving
Dopar	levodopa	Anti-Parkinsonian
Doral	quazepam	Sedative/hypnotic
Doriden	glutethimide	Sedative/hypnotic
doxepin	Sinequan, Adapin	Antidepressant
droperidol	Inapsine	Antipsychotic, antianxiety
Duralith	lithium carbonate	Antimanic, mood stabilizer, potentiates antidepressants
Effexor	venlafaxine	Antidepressant
Elavil	amitriptyline	Antidepressant
Eldepryl	selegiline	Anti-Parkinsonian, antidepressant
Endep	amitriptyline	Antidepressant
Epitol	carbamazepine	Anticonvulsant, mood stabilizer
Epival	divalproex	Mood stabilizer
ergoloid	Gerimal, Hydergine	Relieves vascular headache
Equanil	meprobamate	Antianxiety
Eskalith	lithium carbonate	Antimanic, potentiates antidepressants, mood stabilizer
estazolam	ProSom	Sedative/hypnotic
estrogen	Menrium, Premarin	Female replacement hormone
ethchlorvynol	Placidyl	Hypnotic
ethopropazine	Parsidol	Anti-Parkinsonian
Etrafon	perphenazine & amitriptyline	Antidepressant, anxiolytic, antipsychotic, antiemetic
Fastin	phentermine	Appetite suppressant
felbamate	Felbatol	Mood stabilizer, anticonvulant
Felbatol	felbamate	Mood stabilizer
Flexeril	cyclobenzaprine	Muscle relaxant
Fluanxol	flupenthixol	Antipsychotic
flumazenil	Romazicon	Benzodiazepine antagonist
fluoxetine	Prozac	Antidepressant, antiobsessive, antibulimic
flupenthixol	Fluanxol	Antipsychotic
fluphenazine	Prolixin, Permitil, Modecate	Antipsychotic
flurazepam	Dalmane	Hypnotic
fluvoxamine	Luvox	Antidepressant, antiobsessive
gabapentin	Neurontin	Mood stabilizer, anticonvulsant
Gemonil	metharbital	Sedative, hypnotic
Gerimal	ergoloid	Relieves vascular headache
glutethimide	Doriden	Sedative/hypnotic
Habitrol	nicotine	Nicotine substitute
Halcion	triazolam	Sedative/hypnotic
halazepam	Paxipam	Anxiolytic, hypnotic
Haldol	haloperidol	Antipsychotic
haloperidol	Haldol	Antipsychotic
Hydergine	ergoloid	Relieves vascular headache
hydroxyzine	Atarax, Marax, Vistaril	Anxiolytic, hypnotic, antihistamine
imipramine	Tofranil, Janimine	Antidepressant
Imitrex	sumatriptan	Antimigraine
Inapsine	droperidol	Antipsychotic, antianxiety, antiemetic
Inderal	propranolol	Antihypertensive, antimigraine
Intensol	chlorazepam	Antianxiety

Names of medications		Major uses
Janimine	imipramine	Antidepressant
Kemadrin	procyclidine	Anti-Parkinsonian
Klonopin	clonazepam	Anticonvulsant, anxiolytic, hypnotic, mood stabilizer
Lamictal	lamotrigine	Mood stabilizer, anticonvulsant
lamotrigine	Lamictal	Mood stabilizer, anticonvulsant
L-dopa, levodopa	Larodopa, Dopar	Anti-Parkinsonian
Larodopa	L-dopa	Anti-Parkinsonian
levodopa	Dopar	Anti-Parkinsonian
levodopa & carbidopa	Sinemet	Anti-Parkinsonian
Levothroid	levothyroxine	Thyroid hormone replacement, potentiates antidepressants
levothyroxine	Synthroid, Levothroid, Thyrar, Levoxy	Thyroid hormone replacement, potentiates antidepressants
Levoxy	levothyroxine	Thyroid hormone replacement, potentiates antidepressants
Librax	clidinium & chlordiazepoxide	Anticholinergic
Librium	chlordiazepoxide	Anxiolytic, hypnotic
Limbitrol	chlordiazepoxide & amitriptyline	Antidepressant
Lioresal	baclofen	Muscle relaxant
liothyronine (T₃)	Cytomel, Triostat	Thyroid hormone replacement, potentiates antidepressants
Lithane	lithium carbonate	Mood stabilizer
lithium carbonate	Carbolith, Duralith, Eskalith, Lithane, Lithizine, Lithobid, Lithonate, Lithotabs	Antimanic, mood stabilizer, potentiates antidepressants
lithium citrate	Cibalith-S	Antimanic, mood stabilizer, potentiates antidepressants
Lithizine	lithium carbonate	Antimanic, mood stabilizer, potentiates antidepressants
Lithobid	lithium carbonate	Antimanic, mood stabilizer, potentiates antidepressants
Lithonate	lithium carbonate	Antimanic, mood stabilizer, potentiates antidepressants
Lithotabs	lithium carbonate	Antimanic, mood stabilizer, potentiates antidepressants
Lopressor	metoprolol	Antianxiety, antihypertensive
lorazepam	Ativan, Intensol	Anxiolytic, hypnotic
Loxapac	loxapine	Antipsychotic
loxapine	Loxitane, Daxoline	Antipsychotic
Loxitane	loxapine	Antipsychotic
Ludiomil	maprotiline	Antidepressant
Luminal	phenobarbital	Sedative/hypnotic
Luvox	fluvoxamine	Antidepressant, antiobsessive
maprotoline	Ludiomil	Antidepressant
Marax	hydroxyzine	Anxiolytic, hypnotic
Mazanor	mazindol	Appetite suppressant, psychostimulant
mazindol	Mazanor, Sanorex	Appetite suppressant, psychostimulant
Mebaral	mephobarbital	Sedative/hypnotic, antianxiety, anticonvulsant
Mellaril	thioridazine	Antipsychotic

Names of medications		*Major uses*
Menrium	estrogen	Female replacement hormone
meperidine	Demerol	Opiate, analgesic
mephenytoin	Mesantoin	Anticonvulsant
mephobarbital	Mebaral	Sedative/hypnotic, antianxiety, anticonvulsant
meprobamate	Miltown, Equanil	Antianxiety
meprobamate & benactyzine	Deprol	Antianxiety
Mesantoin	mephenytoin	Anticonvulsant
mesoridazine	Serentil	Antipsychotic
metoprolol	Lopressor	Antianxiety, antihyperensive
methadone	Dolophine	Blocks narcotics craving
methaqualone	Quaalude (no longer available)	Sedative/hypnotic
methamphetamine	Desoxyn	CNS stimulant
metharbital	Gemonil	Sedative/hypnotic
methyldopa	Aldomet	Antihypertensive
methylphenidate	Ritalin	Anti-ADHD, potentiates antidepressants
methyltestosterone	Android	Male replacement hormone
methyprylon	Noludar	Sedative/hypnotic
midazolam	Versed	Antianxiety
Miltown	meprobamate	Antianxiety
mirtazapine	Remeron	Antidepressant
Mitran	chlordiazepoxide	Anxiolytic, hypnotic
Moban	molindone	Antipsychotic
modafinil	Provigil	For narcolepsy
Modecate	fluphenazine	Antipsychotic
molindone	Moban	Antipsychotic
morphine	Roxanol	Analgesic, narcotic
Myidone	primidone	Anticonvulsant
Mysoline	primidone	Anticonvulsant
naloxone	Narcan	Blocks opioid effects
naltrexone	ReVia, Trexan	Blocks alcohol craving
Narcan	naloxone	Blocks opioid effects
Nardil	phenelzine	Antidepressant
Navane	thiothixene	Antipsychotic
nefazodone	Serzone	Antidepressant
Nembutal	pentobarbital	Sedative/hypnotic
Neurontin	gabapentin	Mood stabilizer
nicotine	Habitrol	Nicotine substitute
nifedipine	Procardia	MAOI reaction antidote
Noctec	chloral hydrate	Sedative/hypnotic
Noludar	methyprylon	Sedative/hypnotic
Norpramin	desipramine	Antidepressant
nortriptyline	Aventyl, Pamelor	Antidepressant
Nozinan	methotrimeprazine	Antipsychotic
Obenix	phentermine	Appetite suppressant
Oby-Cap	phentermine	Appetite suppressant
olanzapine	Zyprexa	Antipsychotic
Orap	pimozide	Antipsychotic
Ormazine	chlorpromazine	Antipsychotic
oxazepam	Serax	Anxiolytic, hypnotic
Pagitane	cycrimine	Anti-Parkinsonian
Pamelor	nortriptyline	Antidepressant
Paral	paraldehyde	Sedative/hypnotic

Names of medications		*Major uses*
paraldehyde	Paral	Sedative/hypnotic
Parlodel	bromocriptine	Anti-Parkinsonian
Parnate	tranylcypromine	Antidepressant
paroxetine	Paxil	Antidepressant
Parsidol	ethopropazine	Anti-Parkinsonian
Paxil	paroxetine	Antidepressant
Paxipam	halazepam	Anxiolytic, hypnotic
pemoline	Cylert	Anti-ADHD
pentazocine	Talwin	Analgesic
pentobarbital	Nembutal, Quadrinal, Arco-Lase	Sedative/hypnotic
Permitil	fluphenazine	Antipsychotic
perphenazine	Trilafon	Antipsychotic
perphenazine & amitriptyline	Etrafon, Triavil	Antidepressant
Pertofrane	desipramine	Antidepressant
phenelzine	Nardil	Antidepressant
phenobarbital	Solfoton, Luminal	Sedative/hypnotic
phentermine	Adipex-P, Fastin, Banobese, Obenix, Oby-Cap	Appetite suppressant
phenytoin	Dilantin	Anticonvuslant
pimozide	Orap	Antipsychotic
pindolol	Visken	Potentiates antidepressants
Placidyl	ethchlorvynol	Sedative/hypnotic
prazepam	Centrax	Anxiolytic, hypnotic
primidone	Myidone, Mysoline	Anticonvulsant
Procardia	nifedipine	Antianginic, MAOI reaction antidote
procyclidine	Kemadrin	Anti-Parkinsonian
Proketazine	carphenazine	Antipsychotic
Prolixin	fluphenazine	Antipsychotic
Promaz	chlorpromazine	Antipsychotic
promazine	Sparine	Antipsychotic
propoxyphene	Darvon	Opioid analgesic
propranolol	Inderal	Antihypertensive, antimigraine
ProSom	estazolam	Sedative/hypnotic
protriptyline	Vivactil, Triptil	Antidepressant
Provigil	modafinil	For narcolepsy
Prozac	fluoxetine	Antidepressant, antiobsessive, antibulimic
Quaalude	methaqualone (no longer available)	Sedative/hypnotic
Quadrinal	pentobarbital	Sedative/hypnotic
quazepam	Doral	Sedative/hypnotic
Remeron	mirtazapine	Antidepressant
remoxipride	Roxiam	Antipsychotic
Repoise	butaperazine	Antipsychotic
reserpine	Ser-Ap-Es, Serpasil	Antihypertensive, antipsychotic
Restoril	temazepam	Sedative/hypnotic
ReVia	naltrexone	Blocks alcohol craving
Rhotrimine	trimipramine	Antidepressant
Risperdal	risperidone	Antipsychotic
risperidone	Risperdal	Antipsychotic
Ritalin	methylphenidate	Anti-ADHD, potentiates antidepressants
Rivotril	clonazepam	Anxiolytic, hypnotic, mood stabilizer
Roxanol	morphine	Analgesic, narcotic

Names of medications		*Major uses*
Roxiam	remoxipride	Antipsychotic
Sanorex	mazindol	Appetite suppressant, psychostimulant
secobarbital	Seconal	Sedative/hypnotic
secobarbital & amobarbital	Tuinal	Sedative/hypnotic
Seconal	secobarbital	Sedative/hypnotic
selegiline	Eldepryl	Anti-Parkinsonian, antidepressant
Serax	oxazepam	Anxiolytic, hypnotic
Ser-Ap-Es	reserpine	Antihypertensive, antipsychotic
Serentil	mesoridazine	Antipsychotic
Serlect	sertindole	Antipsychotic
Serpasil	reserpine	Antihypertensive, antipsychotic
sertindole	Serlect	Antipsychotic
sertraline	Zoloft	Antidepressant
Serzone	nefazodone	Antidepressant
sildenafil	Viagra	Erectile dysfunction
Sinemet	carbidopa & levodopa	Anti-Parkinsonian
Sinequan	doxepin	Antidepressant
Solfoton	phenobarbital	Sedative/hypnotic
Sparine	promazine	Antipsychotic
Stelazine	trifluoperazine	Antipsychotic
sumatriptan	Imitrex	Antimigraine
Surmontil	trimipramine	Antidepressant
Symadine	amantadine	Anti-Parkinsonian antiviral
Symmetrel	amantadine	Anti-Parkinsonian antiviral
Synthroid	levothyroxine	Thyroid hormone replacement, potentiates antidepressants
tacrine	Cognex	Antidementia
Talwin	pentazocine	Analgesic
Taractan	chlorprothixene	Antipsychotic
Tegretol	carbamazepine	Anticonvulsant, mood stabilizer
Temaz	temazepam	Sedative/hypnotic
temazepam	Restoril, Temaz	Sedative/hypnotic
Temposil	calcium carbimid	Alcohol challenge reaction
thioridazine	Mellaril	Antipsychotic
thiothixene	Navane	Antipsychotic
Thorazine	chlorpromazine	Antipsychotic
Thyrar	levothyroxine	Thyroid hormone replacement, potentiates antidepressants
Tindal	acetophenazine	Antipsychotic
Tofranil	imipramine	Antidepressant
T-Quil	diazepam	Anxiolytic, hypnotic, muscle relaxant
Trancopal	chlormezanone (no longer available)	Antianxiety
Tranxene	clorazepate	Anxiolytic, hypnotic
tranylcypromine	Parnate	Antidepressant
trazodone	Desyrel	Antidepressant, hypnotic
Trexan	naltrexone	Blocks alcohol craving
Triavil	perphenazine & amitriptyline	Antidepressant, antipsychotic
triazolam	Halcion	Hypnotic
trifluoperazine	Stelazine	Antipsychotic
triflupromazine	Vesprin	Antipsychotic
trihexyphenidyl	Artane	Anti-Parkinsonian
Trilafon	perphenazine	Antipsychotic

Names of medications		*Major uses*
trimipramine	Surmontil, Rhotrimine	Antidepressant
Triostat	liothyronine (T$_3$)	Thyroid hormone, potentiates antidepressants
Triptil	protriptyline	Antidepressant
Tuinal	secobarbital & amobarbital	Sedative/hypnotic
Valium	diazepam	Anxiolytic, hypnotic, muscle relaxant
Valrelease	valproic acid	Anticonvulsant, mood stabilizer, antimanic
Valproate	valproic acid	Anticonvulsant, mood stabilizer, antimanic
valproic acid	Depakene, Valrelease, Valproate	Anticonvulsant, mood stabilizer, antimanic
venlafaxine	Effexor	Antidepressant
Versed	midazolam	Antianxiety
Vesprin	triflupromazine	Antipsychotic
Viagra	sildenafil	Erectile dysfunction
Visken	pindolol	Potentiates antidepressants
Vistaril	hydroxyzine	Anxiolytic, hypnotic
Vivactil	protriptyline	Antidepressant
Wellbutrin	bupropion	Antidepressant
Xanax	alprazolam	Anxiolytic, hypnotic
yohimbine	Yocon, Yohimex	Erectile dysfunction
Yocon	yohimbine	Erectile dysfunction
Yohimex	yohimbine	Erectile dysfunction
Zetran	diazepam	Anxiolytic, hypnotic, muscle relaxant
Zoloft	sertraline	Antidepressant, antiobsessive
zolpidem	Ambien	Hypnotic
Zyban	bupropion	Nicotine substitute
Zyprexa	olanzapine	Antipsychotic

Psychoactive drugs not currently available in the United States: clovoxamine, femoxetine, isocarboxazid (Marplan), nisoxetine, oxaprotiline, mianserin, viloxazine, sulpiride, amisulpiride, fluperlapine, moclobemide (Aurorix), phentermine (Zantryl, Ionamin), raclopride, clopenthixol, pipamperone, zopiclone (Imovane).

27.2. YOUR LIST OF ADDITIONAL MEDICATIONS

Use this space to list medications applicable to your practice setting.

27.3. YOUR LIST OF STREET DRUGS' NAMES

Because the names of street drugs change frequently and are often local, you may want to make your own list here. Lewis (1990) provides a good beginning.

LISTING
OF DRUGS

27.4. RESULTS OF MEDICATION TREATMENT: DESCRIPTORS

Tolerated without difficulty, rapid and dramatic improvement, abatement of symptoms, symptomatology improved.

Highly sensitive to all medications, multiple/distressing side effects, quite difficult to find a medication regimen that was tolerated, distressing and extreme reactions to all medications tried despite changes in dosage and schedule, adverse drug reactions.

Contraindicated, use not advisable because . . . (specify).

Polypharmacy, more than one/several/multiple drugs being taken, drug interactions, drug augmentation.

27.5. RESOURCES FOR THE CLINICIAN

Information on uses, side effects, and interactions of medications can of course be found in the latest editions of the *Physicians' Desk Reference* and the *PDR Guide to Drug Interactions, Side Effects, Indications, Contraindications.*

Many pharmaceutical companies supply pocket guides for medications, and the books below will supply more information.

Bentley, K. J., & Walsh, M. (1996). *The social worker and psychotropic medication: Toward effective collaboration with mental health clients, families, and providers.* Pacific Grove, CA: Brooks/Cole.
　　Obviously aimed at social workers, this text offers, besides a primer on medications, an inclusive approach of partnership among clients, families, social workers, and prescribers to address concerns about medications through consumer and family psychoeducation.

Bezchlibnyk-Butler, K. Z., & Jeffries, J. J. (1999). *Clinical handbook of psychotropic drugs* (9th rev. ed.). Seattle, WA: Hogrefe & Huber.
　　Lots of objective data displayed in 140 pages of tables for easy access, and organized by disorder. No narrative explanation or interpretation, but bits of advice on interactions, comparisons, side effects, etc.

Gelenberg, A. J., & Bassuk, E. M. (Eds.). (1997). *The practitioner's guide to psychoactive drugs* (4th ed.). New York: Plenum Press.
　　A classic text, mainly for prescribing professionals.

Gitlin, M. J. (1996). *The psychotherapist's guide to psychopharmacology* (2nd ed.). New York: Free Press.
　　A clearly written book about medications for each disorder. It offers explanations of pharmacodynamics, working collaboratively with psychopharmacologists, choosing among treatment options, and case studies.

Janicak, P. G., Davis, J. M., Preskorn, S. H., & Ayd, Jr., F. J. (1993). *Principles and practice of psychopharmacotherapy.* Baltimore: Williams & Wilkins.
　　While not the latest, this book may be the best. It offers a comprehensive picture of all aspects, clearly organized and well written. Unique features include treatments for different stages of a disorder, decision trees, multiple strategies, and coverage of pregnant and HIV+ patients.

Maxmen, J. S., & Ward, N. G. (1995). *Psychotropic drugs: Fast facts* (2nd ed.). New York: Norton.
　　A massive (400-page) collection of facts, with much guidance and many cautions in a very accessible outline format.

Preston, J., O'Neal, J. H., & Talaga, M. C. (1994). *Handbook of clinical psychopharmacology for therapists.* Oakland, CA: New Harbinger.
　　A brief guide covering pharmacology, treatment of common disorders, and dosing guidelines.

There are many other books, and new ones come out monthly, so just visit your favorite bookstore or Web site for the most current information.

LISTING
OF DRUGS

28

Psychiatric Masquerade
of Medical Conditions

28.1. INTRODUCTION

The well-trained and responsible clinician must consider all possible causes of a client's symptoms: developmental, dynamic, existential, learned, cultural, and medical/physiological.

"Psychiatric masquerade" is the commonly accepted term for the situation in which a patient presents to the clinician with psychological or psychiatric symptoms caused by a medical condition or illness that is not immediately (and, sadly, sometimes never) recognized. In other words, it is the case in which a medical condition wears the "mask" of a psychiatric condition. Adams (1991) notes that calling it "psychiatric masquerade" focuses on the presentation; if we were to focus on the causation, we would call it "medical masquerade." It is not to be confused with malingering (see Section 12.21).

Although there are numerous excellent articles and books that describe the psychological effects of medical conditions or of medications, they are useless to the professional who sees only the patient presenting with psychiatric symptoms, unaccompanied by a medical diagnosis. However, as clinicians, all of us have the ethical obligation to be sensitive to the possibility of masquerade and to investigate any such possibilities appropriately.

348

The listings below are not meant to be complete or in any way to replace a thorough medical workup, nor are they in order of importance or frequency. They are merely meant to raise the practitioner's awareness of the possible physical illness basis of some psychiatric symptoms he/she is likely to see in clinical practice. With this sensitization, the clinician can make a better-focused referral to the appropriate medical practitioner.

Good general references in this area are Pincus and Tucker (1985), Asad (1994), Morrison (1997), and Taylor (1990). The latter two are highly recommended for a nonmedical audience, as well as for their focus on the most common problem presentations. Lishman (1998) is an encyclopedic resource. The *Merck Manual of Diagnosis and Therapy* (Berkow, 1999) is another excellent and standard resource and is commonly available.

Drug Interactions

The interactions of substances, especially medications, is a complex subject, and new information is constantly being added. There are many articles, a number of books, and several computer databases for reference. Ask your local medical librarian for the most current and usable materials and consult with a pharmacist.

28.2. ANXIETY

See Section 10.3, "Anxiety."

Medications/Substances That May Induce Anxiety

Anticholinergics and antihistamines.
Antidepressants: Fluoxetine and other Selective Serotonin Reuptake Inhibitors, Mono-Amine Oxidase Inhibitors, tricyclic antidepressants (especially early in therapy).
Benzodiazepines (paradoxical reactions, withdrawal states).
Euphoriants and hallucinogens: Cannabis, LSD, mescaline, psilocybin, phencyclidine (PCP).
Hormones: Androgens, estrogens, progesterones, corticosteroids, thyroid supplements.
Neuroleptics.
Stimulants and sympathomimetics: Amphetamines, cocaine, amethylphenidate, pemoline, ephedrine, pseudoephedrine, phenylpropanolamine, xanthine derivatives (caffeine, theobromine, theophylline).
Withdrawal states (especially from alcohol, sedatives, narcotics).
Others: Cycloserine, metrizamide, quinacrine, nasal decongestant sprays.

Medical Conditions That May Present as/with Anxiety

Mitral Valve Prolapse, adrenal tumor, alcoholism, carcinoid syndrome, Central Nervous System degenerative diseases, Cushing's disease, coronary insufficiency, delirium, hypoglycemia, hyperthyroidism, Meniere's disease (early stages), postconcussion syndrome, chronic obstructive lung disease, AIDS, diabetes, fibromyalgia.

28.3. SEXUAL DYSFUNCTION

About 100 medications may cause sexual dysfunction. A good listing can be found in "Drugs That Induce Sexual Dysfunction" (1987). The book by Crenshaw and Goldberg (1993) is complete and highly recommended.

28.4. DEPRESSION
See Section 10.5, "Depression."

Medications/Substances That May Induce Depression

Antiarrhythmics: Digitalis, disopyramide, nifedipine.
Anticonvulsants.
Antihypertensives: Clonidine, guanethidine, hydralazine, methyldopa, prazosin, propranolol, and other β-blockers; reserpine; trichloromethiazide.
Antimicrobials: Cycloserine, isoniazid, metronidazole, nalidixic acid.
Anti-Parkinsonian agents: Levodopa, amantadine, carbidopa.
Chemotherapeutic agents: Asparaginase, vinblastine, vincristine.
Hormone preparations: Corticosteroids, oral contraceptives, thyroid supplements.
NonSteroidal Anti-Inflammatory Drugs.
Sedatives: Alcohol, barbiturates, benzodiazepines, hypnotics, marijuana, hallucinogens.
Withdrawal states (especially from cocaine and other stimulants, amphetamines).
Other: Cimetidine, ranitidine, disulfiram, levodopa, α-methyldopa, carbidopa, metoclopramide, metrizamide, cholinesterase inhibitor insecticides.

Diseases That May Present as/with Depression

Influenza, tuberculosis, general paresis/tertiary syphilis, hypothyroidism, Cushing's disease, Addison's disease, Parkinson's disease, Systemic Lupus Erythematosus, Rheumatoid Arthritis, stroke, Multiple Sclerosis, End-Stage Renal Disease (with hemodialysis),[1] cerebral tumors, sleep apnea, early stages of dementing diseases, epilepsy, diabetes, hypothyroidism, hyperthyroidism, brain trauma, Lyme disease.

28.5. MANIA
See Section 10.7, "Mania."

Medications/Substances That May Induce Mania

Amphetamines, bromides, cocaine, isoniazid, procarbazine, corticosteroids, levodopa, MAOI, tricyclic antidepressants, methylphenidate, over-the-counter stimulants/appetite suppressants, vitamin deficiencies, excess of fat-soluble vitamins.

Diseases That May Present as/with Mania

Influenza, general paresis/tertiary syphilis, St. Louis encephalitis, Q fever, thyrotoxicosis, rheumatic chorea, stroke, Multiple Sclerosis, cerebellar/diencephalic/third-ventricle tumors, hyperthyroidism, Cushing's disease, hyperparathyroidism.

28.6. ORGANIC BRAIN SYNDROME/DEMENTIA
See Section 11.6, "Dementia."

Medications/Substances That May Induce Delirium, Hallucinations, or Paranoia

Antiarrhythmics: Digitalis, lidocaine, procainamide, quinacrine.
Anticholinergics.

---

[1] I am grateful to Renee F. Bova-Collis of Richmond, VA, for pointing this out.

Anticonvulsants.

Antidepressants: Tricyclics, MAOIs, SSRIs.

Antimicrobials, antiparasitics, antivirals: Amantadine, amphotericin B, metronidazole, thiabendazole, cycloserine, isoniazid, chloroquine, hydroxychloroquine, dapsone, penicillin G procaine.

Antihistamines: H_2 blockers (cimetidine, rantidine).

β-blockers.

Chemotherapeutic agents (especially intrathecal administration): Asparaginase, cisplatin, vincristine.

Euphoriants and hallucinogens: Cannabis, LSD, mescaline, psilocybin, PCP.

Hormone preparations: Corticosteroids.

NSAIDs.

Sedatives: Alcohol, barbiturates, benzodiazepines, hypnotics.

Stimulants and sympathomimetics: Amphetamines, cocaine, methylphenidate, pemoline.

Withdrawal states (especially from alcohol, sedatives).

Other: Albuterol, bromides, bromocriptine, disulfiram, levodopa, carbidopa, methyldopa, methysergide, metrizamide.

Neurological Conditions That Commonly Exhibit Psychological Symptoms

Bondi (1992) offers this basic orienting information to this issue (adapted here by permission):

Neurological conditions have a base rate of 2.5% of general population.

General symptoms: Paranoia, attentional deficits, mood swings, euphoria, sleep disturbance, personality changes, depression, impaired memory, anxiety, apathy, violence.

Temporal lobe epilepsy/complex partial seizure disorder → global diminution in sexual behavior, impulsive–irritable behaviors, especially in a context of hyperethical and hyperreligious history, hypergraphia, and overconcern and overemphasis on the trivial.

Frontal lobe damage → apathy (empty indifference as contrasted with the depressive's preoccupation with worry), total loss of initiative, euphoria, lack of adult restraint/tact, incontinence.

Traumatic head injury → like frontal lobe damage as well as depression (psychomotor retardation, apathy, lack of initiative, blunted or flat affect), and memory dysfunction.

Huntington's disease → intermittent mood disorder with onset before the chorea and dementia. Besides the affective components, there may be paranoia, delusions, hallucinations, and mood swings. Always seek a family history.

Hypothyroidism → progressive cognitive deterioration, insidious onset, sluggishness, lethargy, poor attention and concentration, memory disturbances.

Multiple Sclerosis → muscle weakness, fatigue, double vision, numbness, paresthesia, pain, bowel and bladder dysfunction, sexual disturbance. Euphoria and/or depression, "conversion" symptoms.

Headache:

- If it is the worst ever experienced by the patient, a new type of headache, or accompanied by neurological signs, it is much more likely to be organic than one which is dull, generalized, familiar, or present for a year.
- Tumor-caused headaches have no one quality. They may occur on awakening and recede during the day; they are often bifrontal or bioccipital, lateralized or localized, ameliorated or exacerbated by changes in body position.

Some Clues Suggestive of Organic Mental Disorder

The following is adapted by permission from Hoffman and Koran (1984).

Psychiatric symptom onset after age 40.
Psychiatric symptoms beginning . . .
  a. during a major illness.
  b. while taking drugs known to cause mental symptoms (see above).
  c. suddenly, in a patient without prior psychiatric history or known stressors.
A history of . . .
  a. alcohol or drug abuse.
  b. a physical illness impairing a major organ's function, e.g., hepatitis.
  c. taking multiple medications (prescribed or over-the-counter).
  d. poor response to apparently adequate psychiatric treatment.
A family history of . . .
  a. degenerative or inheritable brain disease.
  b. metabolic disease (diabetes, pernicious anemia, etc.).
Mental signs including . . .
  a. altered level of consciousness.
  b. fluctuating mental status.
  c. cognitive impairment.
  d. episodic, recurrent, or cyclic course.
  e. visual, tactile, or olfactory hallucinations.
Physical signs that include . . .
  a. signs of organ malfunction that can affect the brain.
  b. focal neurological deficits.
  c. difuse subcortical dysfunction (slowed speech/mentation/movement, ataxia, incoordination, tremor, chorea, asterixis, dysarthria, etc.).
  d. cortical dysfunction (dysphasia, apraxias, agnosia, visuo-spatial deficits, or defective cortical sensation, etc.).

Treatable/Possibly Reversible Causes of OBS

The following list is adapted by permission from Slaby et al. (1994):

Addison's disease, some angiomas of the cerebral vessels, anoxia secondary to chronic cardiac or respiratory disease, cerebral abscess, some cerebral neoplasias, chronic subdural hematomas, electrolyte imbalance, endogenous toxins (as with hepatic or renal failure), exogenous toxins such as carbon monoxide, hypothyroidism, hypoglycemia, cerebral infections (such as tuberculosis, syphilis, parasites, or yeasts), intracranial aneurysms, normal-pressure hydrocephalus, pseudodementia (e.g., schizophrenia or depression), vitamin deficiencies, Wilson's disease.

Irreversible Causes of OBS

The following list is reprinted by permission from Slaby et al. (1994):

Alcoholic encephalopathy, Alzheimer's disease, arteriosclerosis, cerebral metastases, some primary cerebral neoplasms, Creutzfeldt–Jakob disease, dementia pugilistica, familial myoclonus epilepsy, Friedreich's ataxia, Huntington's chorea, Kuf's disease, Marchiafava–Bignami disease, multiple myeloma, multiple sclerosis, collagenoses, Parkinsonism/dementia complex of Guam, Pick's disease, postconcussion syndrome, presenile dementia with motor neuron disease, presenile glial dystrophy, primary parenchymatous cerebellar atrophy with dementia, primary subcortical gliosis, progressive supranuclear palsy, sarcoidosis, Schilder's disease, senile dementia, trauma, simple presenile dementia.

28.7. PSYCHOSIS

Medications/Substances That May Induce Psychosis

Sympathomimetics (e.g., cocaine, "crack," many over-the-counter cold medications).
Antinflammatory drugs: Steroids.
Anticholinergics: Anti-Parkinsonian agents (especially levodopa, in schizophrenic patients).
Hallucinogens.

Medical Conditions That May Present as/with Psychosis

Addison's disease, CNS infections, CNS neoplasms, CNS trauma, Cushing's disease, folic acid deficiency, Huntington's chorea, Multiple Sclerosis, myxedema, pancreatitis, pellagra, pernicious anemia, porphyria, Systematic Lupus Erythematosus, temporal lobe epilepsy, thyrotoxicosis.

28.8. MEDICATION-INDUCED AND TOXIN-INDUCED PSYCHIATRIC CONDITIONS
See also Section 12.34, "Side Effects of Medications."

The following quick reference list is adapted by permission from Estroff and Gold (1986).

The key to the abbreviations in the middle columns below is as follows: P, psychoses; M, mania; A, anxiety; D, depression; O, organic mental disorder; H, hallucinations and similar effects. Other conditions and effects are described in the far right column.

Psychiatric Medications

Tricyclic anti- depressants	P	M		O	H—Visual	
MAOI antidepressants	P	M	A			Agitation, insomnia.
Antipsychotics				D	O	Oversedation, Neuroleptic Malignant Syndrome.
Sedatives/hypnotics						Oversedation, disinhibition.
Benzodiazepines	P			D		
Disulfiram	P	M	A	D	O	

Antihypertensives

Reserpine	P			D	O	
α-methyldopa	P			D	O	Nightmares, disordered sleep.
Clonidine	P	M	A	D		Sedation, fatigue.
Propranolol					H—Hypnopompic H—Hypnagogic	Nightmares, fatigue.

Cardiovascular Medications

Medication	P	M	A	D	O	H	Notes
Lidocaine	P						
Procainamide	P	M					
Disopyramide	P					H–Auditory, visual	
Digitalis	P					H–Auditory, visual	Mutism, lability, mood swings.

Neurological Medications

Medication	P	M	A	D	O	H	Notes
Phenytoin	P				O		Visual, tactile, and somatic delusions.
Barbiturates				D	O		Tearfulness, hyperactivity, aggression in children.
Primidone	P	M			O		Mood swings, personality changes, paranoia.
Ethosuzimide	P	M	A	D		H	Aggression, night terrors, lethargy.
Carbamazepine	P		A				Restlessness, drowsiness.
Baclofen	P	M		D		H–Auditory, visual	
Levodopa	P	M		D	O	H–Auditory	Vivid dreams and visual illusions.
Bromocriptine	P	M			O		Vivid dreams.
Anticholinergics	P		A	D	O		Prominent anxiety.

Gastrointestinal Medications

Medication	P	M	A	D	O	H	Notes
Cimetidine	P			D	O	H–Auditory, visual	

Over-the-Counter Medications

Medication	P	M	A	D	O	H	Notes
Phenyl-propanolamine	P			D			
Ephedrine	P			D			
Pseudoephedrine	P			D			
Aminophylline	P			D			

Nonsteroidal Anti-Inflammatory Drugs

Medication	P	M	A	D	O	H	Notes
Indomethacin	P		A	D			Agitation, hostility, depersonalization.
Sulindac	P			D			Angry/combative/homicidal/obsessive talking.

Anticancer Medications

Medication	P	M	A	D	O	H	Notes
Steroids	P	M		D			
Decarbazine				D	O		
Hexamethylamine				D	O	H	
Methotrexate					O		
5 FU					O		Labile mood.
Vincristine				D	O	H	
Vinblastine			A	D			

	P	M	A	D	O	H	Symptoms
Mithramycin			A				Agitation, irritability.
Asparaginase				D	O		Personality changes,
Procarbazine		M					Drowsiness.

Anesthetic Medications

	P	M	A	D	O	H	Symptoms
Nalophine						H—Auditory, visual	Panic, suffocation, fear of impending death.
Levorphan							Fears, "queer" behavior.
Atropine							Postanesthetic excitement.
Scopolamine							Postanesthetic excitement.
Cyclopropane							Postanesthetic excitement.
Halothane				D	O		Anger, tension, fatigue.
Isoflurane				D	O		Anger, tension, fatigue.
Pentazocine							Overactive/rambling/crazy thoughts, fear of dying.

Antibiotic Medications

	P	M	A	D	O	H	Symptoms
Iproniazid	P	M			O	H	
Isoniazid	P			D	O	H—Auditory, visual	Catatonia.
Cycloserine	P	M	A	D	O		Nervousness, irritability.
Penicillin G procaine	P	M			O	H	Extreme agitation, fear of impending death.
Amphotercin B					O		
Chloroquine	P	M				H	
Quinacrine	P	M				H	

Heavy Metals and Toxins

	P	M	A	D	O	H	Symptoms
Lead							Lowered IQs and hyperactivity in children.
Mercury	P		A	D	O		Extreme anxiety, strange form of xenophobia.
Arsenic	P	M		D	O	H—Visual	
Manganese	P	M		D			Destruction of nigrostriatum.
Bismuth	P		A	D	O	H—Visual	
Thallium	P			D	O		
Aluminum				D	O	H	
Tin (organic)				D			Unprovoked rage attacks.
Magnesium	P			D	O		
Copper	P	M		D	O	H	
Vanadium	?			D			
Cadmium							Learning disabilities in children.
Bromine	P	M		D	O	H—Auditory, visual	
Carbon monoxide	P			D	O		Catatonia, panic attack.
Carbon dioxide							Panic attack
Volatile hydrocarbons		M	A	D	O	H—Auditory, visual	Conduct disorder, panic, personality change.

Appendices

A

Abbreviations
in Common Use

Throughout the book, initials of common acronyms are capitalized and underlined. The abbreviations presented below include many in common use, as well as some I personally find useful. In each pair of columns, the full term is given on the left and the abbreviation on the right. I have not attempted to give either the full terms or the abbreviations in alphabetical order.

A.1. CLINICIANS/MENTAL HEALTH PROFESSIONALS

Academic Degrees

Master of Arts	MA	Doctor of Medicine	MD
Master of Science	MS	Doctor of Osteopathy	DO
Bachelor of Social Work	BSW	Doctor of Philosophy	PhD
Master of Social Work	MSW	Doctor of Psychology	PsyD

Psychiatry, Psychology, and Psychotherapy

Psychiatrist	ψi
Psychologist	ψo
American Psychiatric Association	APiA
American Psychological Association	APoA
National Certified School Psychologist	NCSP

American Board of Medical Psychotherapists   ABMP
Licensed Marriage and Family Therapist   LMFT

Social Work

Titles may differ by state.

Licensed Social Worker   LSW
Clinical or Certified Social Worker   CSW
Licensed Certified Social Worker   LCSW
Licensed Independent Clinical Social Worker   LICSW
Licensed Graduate Social Worker   LGSW
Licensed Social Work Associate   LSWA
Academy of Certified Social Workers   ACSW

Counseling

Again, titles may vary.

National Certified Counselor   NCC
National Board Certified Counselor   NBCC
National Certified Career Counselor   NCCC
National Certified School Counselor   NCSC
National Certified Gerontological Counselor   NCGC
Certified Communication Counselor   CCC
Certified Clinical Mental Health Counselor   CCMHC
Certified Rehabilitation Counselor   CRC
Certified Alcoholism Counselor   CAC
Master Addictions Counselor   MAC
Licensed Chemical Dependency Counselor   LCDC

Chemical Dependency Work

See also the last three counseling titles, above.

Certified Chemical Dependency Supervisor   CCDS
Chemical Dependency Associate   CDA
Certified Prevention Specialist   CPS
Certified MICA (Mentally Ill Chemical Abuser) Specialist CMS
Certified Addictions Specialist   CAS

Nursing

Public Health Nurse   PHN
Certified, Registered Nurse Practitioner   CRNP
Certified Specialist (in psychiatric nursing)   CS
Advanced Practice Registered Nurse   APRN

Other

Speech and Language Pathologist   SLP
Certified Employee Assistance Professional   CEAP
Licensed Psychological Examiner   LPE
Art Therapist   AT
Occupational Therapist   OT
Physical Therapist   PT

A.2. TREATMENT

Interview	IV	Psychotherapy	P/T	Psychoanalysis	P/A
Summary	Σ	Treatment	Rx, Tx	Therapist	Th
History	Hx	Prognosis	Px	History of	h/o
Homework	HW	Symptom	Sx	Discontinue/ed	d/c
Not otherwise specified	NOS	Diagnosis	Dx	Discharge/ed	d/ch
		Intelligence	I	Prior to admission	PTA
Within normal limits	WNL	Against medical advice	AMA		

A.3. DIAGNOSES AND CONDITIONS

Needless to say, only a small sampling of the many possible abbreviations in this category can be provided here.

Heart attack	H/A	Headache	h/a
Closed head injury	CHI	Low back pain	LBP
Mitral valve	MVP	Hypertension/high blood pressure	HBP
Cerebral vascular accident	CVA		
Diabetes mellitus	DM	Chronic obstructive pulmonary disease	COPD
Seizures	sz		
Gunshot wound	GSW	Motor vehicle accident	MVA
		Motorcycle accident	MCA

Anxiety	A̲	Panic	P̲
Alcohol and other drugs	AOD	Paranoia	Pa
Generalized anxiety disorder	GAD	Drug and alcohol	D+A
Chronic undifferentiated schizophrenia	CUS or CUSc	Depression	D̲
		Temper tantrum	tt
Delusions and hallucinations	D+H	Toilet training	TT
Bipolar disorder	Bip	Rule out	R/O

A.4. RELATIONS

Husband	H	Wife	W	Brother-in-law	bil
Brother	B	Sister	S	Sister-in-law	sil
Grandparent	GP[1]	Daughter	d	Son	s
Mother	Mo	Father	Fa	Household	HH
Boyfriend	bf	Girlfriend	gf		

A.5. GENERAL AIDS TO RECORDING

About	c.	Primary	1°	Secondary	2°
At	@	Therefore	∴	Change	Δ
With	c̄	Without	s̄ or w/o	Within	w/i or c̄/in
After, by history, post	p̄ or s/p	Before, ante	ā		

[1]Grandparents may be further specified as follows: maternal grandmother/grandfather, MGM/MGF; paternal grandmother/grandfather, PGM/PGF.

ABBREVIATIONS

Date of birth	DOB	Died	D	Date of death	DOD
		Divorced	d or d/		
Anyone	AO	No one	NO	Everyone	EO
Question	?, Q	Times 3	× 3	Present,	⊕
Increasing	↑	More, greater,	>	positive for	
Decreasing	↓	larger		Not present,	∅ or ⊖
Frequency	f	Less, lesser,	<	absent	
Number	#	smaller			
Disorder	d/o	Did not show	DNS	Return to	RTW
Signs and	S+S	Failed to keep	FTKA	work	
symptoms		appointment		Return to	RTC
Intake	ntk	Did not keep	DNKA	clinic	
Withdrawal/	w/d	appointment			
withdrew					

A.6. LEGAL TERMS

Involuntary deviate sexual intercourse	IDSI	Corrupting the morals of a minor	CMM
Indecent assault	IA	Underage drinking/drinker	UAD
Intravenous drug user	IVDU		

A.7. MEDICATION REGIMENS

Every day	q.d.	Every 4 hours	q.q.h.	At night/	h.s.
Every morning	o.m.	After meals	p.c.	bedtime	
Twice a day	b.i.d.	Whenever	p.r.n.	As much	q.s.
Three times	t.i.d.	needed		as required	
a day		Intramuscular	i.m.	By mouth	p.o.
Four times a day	q.i.d.	Intravenous	i.v.		

A.8. EDUCATIONAL SERVICES

In this section, acronyms for disability categories are linked by arrows with acronyms for the appropriate services.

Multidisciplinary team	MDT		Multidisciplinary evaluation	MDE
Individual educational plan or program	IEP		Notice of recommended assignment	NORA
Learning-disabled	LD	→	Learning support	LS
Educable mentally retarded	EMR	→	Learning support	LS
Socially and emotionally maladjusted/disturbed	SEM/ SED	→	Emotional support	ES
Trainable mentally retarded	TMR	→	Life skills support	LSS
Severely/profoundly mentally retarded	SMR/ PMR	→	Multihandicapped support	MHS

Hearing-impaired	HI	→	Sensory-impaired support	SIS
Visually impaired	VI	→	Sensory-impaired support	SIS
Speech- and language-impaired	SLI	→	Speech and language support	SLS
Physically handicapped	PH	→	Physical support	PS
Multihandicapped	MH	→	Multihandicapped support	MHS

ABBREVIATIONS

B

Conversions of Scores Based on the Normal Curve of Distribution

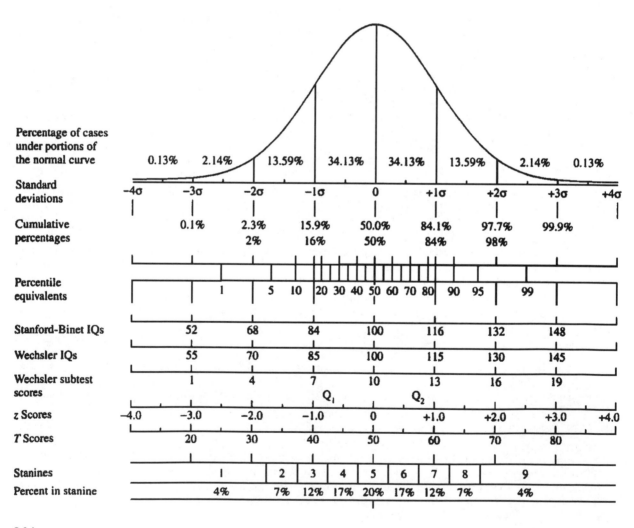

Percentage of cases under portions of the normal curve	0.13%	2.14%	13.59%	34.13%	34.13%	13.59%	2.14%	0.13%
Standard deviations	−4σ	−3σ	−2σ	−1σ	0	+1σ	+2σ	+3σ	+4σ
Cumulative percentages		0.1%	2.3% / 2%	15.9% / 16%	50.0% / 50%	84.1% / 84%	97.7% / 98%	99.9%
Percentile equivalents		1	5 10	20 30 40 50 60 70 80	90 95	99
Stanford-Binet IQs		52	68	84	100	116	132	148
Wechsler IQs		55	70	85	100	115	130	145
Wechsler subtest scores		1	4	7	10	13	16	19
z Scores	−4.0	−3.0	−2.0	−1.0 Q₁	0	+1.0 Q₂	+2.0	+3.0	+4.0
T Scores		20	30	40	50	60	70	80
Stanines		1	2 3 4	5 6 7 8	9
Percent in stanine		4%	7% 12% 17%	20% 17% 12% 7%	4%

364

C

Annotated Readings in Assessment, Interviewing, and Report Writing

ASSESSMENT

Clement, P. W. (1999). *Outcomes and incomes: How to evaluate, improve, and market your psychotherapy practice by measuring outcomes.* New York: Guilford Press.

    This book offers dozens of assessment tools specially designed to show changes in symptoms and other client aspects of therapeutic interest. Using one or two of these with each client allows the therapist to document initial levels, change in therapy, and further benefits. Clement also provides all the assistance needed to easily use his tools to evaluate one's clinical practice.

Fischer, J., & Corcoran, K. (1995). *Measures for clinical practice: A sourcebook.* New York: Free Press.

    If you need a questionnaire for your clinical work and want one with reliability and validity studies, it is probably in here.

Grotevant, H. D., & Carlson, C. I. (1989). *Family assessment: A guide to methods and measures.* New York: Guilford Press.

    When you need measures for evaluating families, either for clinical work or for research, this is your best resource for tools and perspectives.

Groth-Marnat, G. (1997). *Handbook of psychological assessment* (3rd ed.). New York: Wiley.

    The current standard concerning testing and evaluation. Comprehensive, up-to-date, solid data-based weighing of the tests. Strong on integrating data from different sources. For the beginner through the skilled clinician.

Hurt, S. W., Reznikoff, M., & Clarkin, J. F. (1991). *Psychological assessment, psychiatric diagnosis, treatment planning.* New York: Brunner/Mazel.

    Case studies in the use of psychological assessment in the development both of diagnoses and of treatment plans.

Lezak, M. D. (1995). *Neuropsychological assessment* (3rd ed.). New York: Oxford University Press.

    The standard in this area. For the beginner through the skilled clinician.

Meehl, P. (1996). *Clinical vs. statistical prediction: A theoretical analysis and a review of the evidence.* Northvale, NJ: Aronson. (Original work published 1954)

    Still in print because it tells the truth: Mechanical formulas weighing objective data are more accurate than any clinician using his/her favorite test, etc. We clinicians don't like to hear that as we become more experienced, our confidence in our judgments rises, but the judgments do not become more valid. Read this before you go much further.

INTERVIEWING

Hersen, M., & Van Hasselt, V. B. (Eds.). (1998). *Basic interviewing: A practical guide for counselors and clinicians.* Mahwah, NJ: Erlbaum.

    The next step up from Lukas's book: confidentiality; beginning and terminating the interview; rapport; social, medical, and presenting histories; the MSE; dealing with the defensive or overtalkative client; writing it all up.

Hughes, J. N., & Baker, D. B. (1991). *The clinical child interview.* New York: Guilford Press.

    The interviewing skills to use with children from preschool to high school. Tailored to school psychologists, but also more widely useful to child mental health professionals from all orientations. Hughes and Baker teach you how to adapt your strategies to a child's cognitive and linguistic skills and developmental levels.

Lukas, S. (1993). *Where to start and what to ask: An assessment handbook.* New York: Norton.

    She starts the beginner or student out right, with specific tools and usable guidance for gathering the information and integrating it into a coherent assessment.

Morrison, J. (1995a). *The first interview: Revised for DSM-IV.* New York: Guilford Press.

    If you are less interested in diagnosing and more interested in the dynamics of the interview, get ready to enjoy Morrison's gifts as a teacher. This book gives especially good advice on handling the many kinds of difficult interview situations clients can present. Rich with perfectly structured cases.

Morrison, J. (1995b). *DSM-IV made easy: The clinician's guide to diagnosis.* New York: Guilford Press.

    Do not go to DSM-IV to learn to diagnose. All that you need is easily accessible right here. It is like looking over the shoulder of a superb clinician, diagnostician, and interviewer at work. Just paging through it, even over familiar terrain, makes me feel smarter. For example, the discussions of "rule-outs" expand my understanding of dynamics, and the discussions of medical disorders that might be present sharpen my skills. Hundreds of perfectly constructed vignettes invite practice and consideration.

Rogers, R. (1995). *Diagnostic and structured interviewing: A handbook for psychologists.* Odessa, FL: Psychological Assessment Resources.

    All interviews, even yours, are horribly unreliable. They can be improved by standardizing the questions and the categories of response. This is the best book on structured MSE and on the dozen general and specialized structured interviews available.

Shea, S. C. (1998). *Psychiatric interviewing: The art of understanding.* Philadelphia: Saunders.

    A big book (750 pages) but not intimidating. Absolutely comprehensive, yet simple and clear.

Trzepacz, P. T., & Baker, R. W. (1993). *The psychiatric mental status examination.* New York: Oxford University Press.

    Just on the MSE, and under 200 pages, but everything you need to know on doing and interpreting it.

REPORT WRITING

Ownby, R. L. (1997). *Psychological reports: A guide to report writing in professional psychology* (3rd ed.). New York: Wiley.

    The appendix on diagnosing problems in one's own report is clever and very useful. Many sample reports.

Feedback Solicitation Form

Dear Fellow Clinician,

I created this book to meet my needs as a clinician writing reports and gave it my best shot. I really would appreciate your best shot too, so that it may be further developed to aid all of us. New versions can be designed to meet our needs better if we work together. If you will send your suggestions, modifications and ideas (perhaps by photocopying the relevant pages), and they are adopted, I will give you credit in the revised editions and send you a free copy of the next edition.

Ed Zuckerman
P.O. Box 222, Armbrust, PA 15616
Fax: (724) 838-8339
E-mail: edzuckerman@information4u.com
or edzuckerma@aol.com

Would you answer a few questions for me so I can better understand your professional life, please?

Your name: _____

Your professional title: _____

Years in practice when you bought this book: _____ Today's date: _____

Your mailing address: _____

_____

Your phone/fax numbers: _____

Your e-mail address(es): _____

How often do you refer to this book? (Check one.)

☐ Whenever I evaluate people.   ☐ Fairly often, when I need some specific ideas and wording choices.
☐ Every time I write a report.   ☐ Never now, but it was useful when I was learning to write reports.
☐ Other times: _____

How do you use it?

☐ I use it for questions in evaluating people.   ☐ I use it to teach evaluation or report writing.
☐ I use it to structure my report writing.   ☐ I refer to it for specific information and wording choices.
☐ Other use(s): _____

What is your overall evaluation of the *Clinician's Thesaurus*, 5th Edition, in just a few words?

_____

_____

I would suggest the following changes:

Increase these sections: _____

_____

Add coverage of the following: _____

_____

Decrease or eliminate these sections: _____

_____

As a clinician, I really wish there were a "tool" to: _____

_____

About the *Clinician's Electronic Thesaurus, Version 5.0*

If you write your reports on a computer and find this book helpful, the *Clinician's Electronic Thesaurus, Version 5.0* (CET 5.0) can make your report writing even easier. CET 5.0 is an easy-to-use computer program, available on CD-ROM, that is filled with over 20,000 terms, standard phrasings, and common concepts—as found in Part II of this book. The computer disk is also fully searchable and fully compatible with any Windows™ word processing software. Terms can be quickly found, copied, and then pasted into your own word processing documents. As with the book version, the computerized thesaurus covers the appropriate terms to describe almost any clinical situation from intake and diagnostic work-up to psychological evaluations, psychosocial narratives, treatment plans, progress notes, case summaries, and closings.

You will never need to type the same paragraph again. With no size limits, CET 5.0 can store all of your favorite wordings so you can use them repeatedly. You can store technical terms, localized referral statements, complex treatment plans, test interpretation statements, or any other text. Then with only a few mouse clicks you can find them under your preferred headings.

CET 5.0 is completely customizable by you for you. You can move text around or delete it (and reinstall it from the CD-ROM if you need it later). You can add new chapters, sections, and subsections to what is already present in the book. You can also change the fonts, font sizes, and formatting to highlight your preferred word choices in the text windows.

ADDITIONAL PRODUCTIVITY FEATURES

- Easy-access definitions of 500+ mental health and drug and alcohol terms.
- Ability to copy and paste more than one item at a time from the thesaurus into your document.
- **Find** command that searches the whole thesaurus to locate key words. You can then find similar words nearby.
- Fully compatible with Windows 95 and Windows 98 features.

CET 5.0 is very simple to learn and use. It has a foolproof installation with our custom installer. Technical support is provided by Guilford by phone, fax, and e-mail. CET 5.0 works with your word processor's resources, including spell check, page formatting, and printing. A full set of Help files are available within the program under the Help menu. Witty documentation with many examples and tips is included with the CD-ROM.

HARDWARE REQUIREMENTS

- IBM or IBM-compatible PC with a Pentium chip or above.
- A hard disk with at least 5 megabytes (MB) of available space
- At least 8 MB of RAM
- A CD-ROM drive of any speed

SOFTWARE REQUIREMENTS

- Microsoft Windows 95/98 or higher
- Any word processing program running under Windows

Want to see how this program can make your life easier? You can download a demonstration of the software at www.guilford.com/framesoft.html and click on *Clinician's Electronic Thesaurus* (you will need WinZip to decompress the downloaded files).

References

Ables, B., Brandsma, J., & Henry, G. M. (1983). An empirical approach to the mental status examination. *Journal of Psychiatric Education, 7*(3), 232–239.

Ackerman, N. (1982). *The strength of family therapy.* New York: Brunner/Mazel.

Ackerman, R. J. (1987). *Children of alcoholics: A bibliography and resource guide.* Pompano Beach, FL: Health Communications.

Ackley, D. C. (1997). *Breaking free of managed care.* New York: Guilford Press.

Adams, D. (1991). Factitious disorders and malingering: Choosing the appropriate role for the psychologist. *American Psychological Association Division 29 Newsletter,* pp. 10–13.

Adorno, T. W., Frenkel-Brunswik, E., Levinson, D. J., & Sanford, R. N. (1950). *The authoritarian personality.* New York: Harper & Row.

Akiskal, H. S., Khani, M. K., & Scott-Strauss, A. (1979). Cyclothymic temperamental disorders. *Psychiatric Clinics of North America, 2,* 527–554.

Alden, L. E. (1992). Cognitive–interpersonal treatment of avoidant personality disorder. In L. Vandecreek, S. Knapp, & T. L. Jackson (Eds.), *Innovations in clinical practice: A source book* (Vol. 11). Sarasota, FL: Professional Resource Press.

Allen, J. G., Buskirk, J. R., & Sebastian, L. M. (1992). A psychodynamic approach to the master treatment plan. *Bulletin of the Menninger Clinic, 56,* 487–510.

American Psychiatric Association. (1994). *Diagnostic and statistical manual of mental disorders* (4th ed.). Washington, DC: Author.

Archibald, H. C., & Tuddenham, R. D. (1965). Persistent stress reaction after combat. *Archives of General Psychiatry, 12,* 475–481.

Asaad, G. (1994). *Understanding mental disorders due to medical conditions or substance abuse: What every therapist should know.* New York: Brunner/Mazel.

Association of Sleep Disorders Centers. (1979). Classification of sleep and arousal disorders. *Sleep, 2*(1), 5–122.

Barkley, R. A. (1994). *ADHD in adults* [Manual accompanying videotape]. New York: Guilford Press.

Barkley, R. A. (1998). *Attention-deficit hyperactivity disorder: A handbook for diagnosis and treatment* (2nd ed.). New York: Guilford Press.

Barth, R. J., & Kinder, B. N. (1987). The mislabeling of sexual impulsivity. *Journal of Sex and Marital Therapy, 13,* 15–23.

Bateson, G. (1972). *Steps to an ecology of mind.* San Francisco: Chandler.

Beavers, R. W. (1990). *Successful families.* New York: Norton.

Beck, A. T. (1987). *Beck Hopelessness Scale.* San Antonio, TX: Psychological Corporation.

Beck, A. T., Kovacs, M., & Weisman, A. (1979). Assessment of suicidal ideation: The Scale for Suicide Ideators. *Journal of Consulting and Clinical Psychology, 47,* 343–352.

Beck, A. T., Rush, A. J., Shaw, B. F., & Emery, G. (1979). *Cognitive therapy of depression.* New York: Guilford Press.

Beck, A. T., Schuyler, D., & Herman, I. (1974). Development of suicide intent scales. In A. T. Beck, H. L. P. Resnick, & D. J. Lettieri (Eds.), *The prediction of suicide.* Bowie, MD: Charles Press.

Beck, A. T., Ward, C. H., Mendelson, M., Mock, J., & Erbaugh, J. (1961). An inventory for measuring depression. *Archives of General Psychiatry, 4,* 561–571.

Beck, J. C. (1990). The potentially violent patient: Clinical, legal and ethical implications. In E. Margenau (Ed.), *The encyclopedic handbook of private practice.* New York: Gardner Press.

Bellack, A. S., & Hersen, M. (1985). *Dictionary of behavior therapy techniques.* New York: Pergamon Press.

Benjamin, L. S. (1996). *Interpersonal diagnosis and treatment of personality disorders* (2nd ed.). New York: Guilford Press.

Berg, I. K., & Miller, S. D. (1992). *Working with the problem drinker*. New York: Norton.

Berkow, R. (1999). *The Merck manual of diagnosis and therapy* (17th ed.). Rahway, NJ: Merck.

Bernard, S. D. (1991). A substance use checklist. In P. Keller & S. R. Heyman (Eds.), *Innovations in clinical practice: A source book* (Vol. 10). Sarasota, FL: Professional Resource Exchange.

Berne, E. (1964). *Games people play*. New York: Grove Press.

Bernstein, E. M., & Putnam, F. W. (1986). Development, reliability, and validity of a dissociation scale. *Journal of Nervous and Mental Disease, 174*, 727–735.

Bernstein, J. G. (1989). Prescribing antipsychotics. *Drug Therapy, 9*, 79.

Blakiston's Gould medical dictionary (3rd ed.). (1972). New York: McGraw-Hill.

Bleuler, F. (1968). *Dementia praecox, or the group of schizophrenias* (J. Zinkin, Trans.). New York: International Universities Press. (Original work published 1911)

Bondi, M. (1992). Distinguishing psychological disorders from neurological disorders: Taking Axis III seriously. *Professional Psychology: Research and Practice, 23*(4), 306–309.

Bowlby, J. (1969). *Attachment and loss: Vol. 1. Attachment*. New York: Basic Books.

Braun, P. R., & Reynolds, D. J. (1969). A factor analysis of a 100-item fear survey inventory. *Behaviour Research and Therapy, 7*, 399–402.

Breznitz, S. (1988). The seven kinds of denial. In C. Spielberger et al. (Eds.), *Stress and anxiety* (Vol. 2). Washington, DC: Hemisphere.

Brodwin, S. K., Brodwin, M. G., & Liebman, R. (1992a). Initial case assessment forms in rehabilitation counseling. In L. Vandercreek, S. Knapp, & T. L. Jackson (Eds.), *Innovations in clinical practice: A source book* (Vol. 11). Sarasota, FL: Professional Resource Press.

Brodwin, S. K., Brodwin, M. G., & Liebman, R. (1992b). Job analysis procedures in rehabilitation counseling. In L. Vandercreek, S. Knapp, & T. L. Johnson (Eds.), *Innovations in clinical practice: A source book* (Vol. 11). Sarasota, FL: Professional Resource Press.

Broverman, I. D., Broverman, D. M., Clarkson, F. E., Rosencrantz, P. S., & Vogel, S. R. (1970). Sex-role stereotypes and clinical judgements of mental health. *Journal of Consulting and Clinical Psychology, 34*, 1–7.

Brown, T. (1996). *Brown Attention Deficit Disorder Scales*. San Antonio, TX: Psychological Corporation.

Burgess, T., & Holmstrom, B. (1974). Rape trauma syndrome. *American Journal of Psychiatry, 131*(9) 981–986.

Burns, D. D. (1980). *Feeling good*. New York: Morrow.

Callahan, E. J., Hamilton-Oravetz, S., & Walker, A. (1992). Psychotherapeutic intervention for unresolved grief in primary care medicine. In L. Vandecreek, S. Knapp, & T. L. Jackson (Eds.), *Innovations in clinical practice: A source book* (Vol. 11). Sarasota, FL: Professional Resource Press.

Campbell, R. J. (1996). *Psychiatric dictionary* (7th ed.). New York: Oxford University Press.

Cameron, N., & Rychlak, J. F. (1968). *Personality and psychopathology*. Boston: Houghton Mifflin.

Carey, K. B., & Teitelbaum, L. M. (1996). Goals and methods of alcohol assessment. *Professional Psychology: Research and Practice, 27*(5), 460–466.

Cass, V. C. (1979). Homosexual identity formation: A theoretical model. *Journal of Homosexuality, 4*(3), 219–235.

Cermak, T. L. (1991). *Evaluation and treating adult children of alcoholics II*. Minneapolis, MN: Johnson Institute.

Cleckley, H. M. (1976). *The mask of sanity* (5th ed.). St. Louis, MO: C. V. Mosby.

Clement, P. W. (1999). *Outcomes and incomes: How to evaluate, improve, and market your psychotherapy practice by measuring outcomes*. New York: Guilford Press.

Conners, K. (1996). *Conners' Rating Scales–Revised*. Toronto: Multi-Health Systems.

Coons, P. M., & Milstein, V. (1986). Psychosexual disturbances in multiple personality: Characteristics, etiology, and treatment. *Journal of Clinical Psychiatry, 47*, 107–110.

Costa, P. T., Jr., & McCrae, R. R. (1987). Validation of the five factor model of personality across instruments and observers. *Journal of Personality and Social Psychology, 52*, 81–90.

Costa, P. T., Jr., & McCrae, R. R. (1992). *NEO-PI-R professional manual*. Odessa, FL: Psychological Assessment Resources.

Coulehan, J., & Block, M. (1987). *The medical interview: A primer for students of the art*. Philadelphia: Davis.

Crenshaw, T. L., & Goldberg, J. P. (1993). *Sexual pharmacology: Drugs that affect sexual functioning*. New York: Norton.

Davis, P., Morris, J., & Grant, E. (1990). Brief screening tests vs. clinical staging in senile dementia of the Alzheimer type. *Journal of the American Geriatric Society, 38*(2), 129–135.

Davis, T. C., Long, S. W., Jackson, R. H., et al. (1993). The Rapid Estimate of Adult Literacy in Medicine: A shortened screening instrument. *Family Medicine, 25,* 391–395.

Derogatis, L. R. (1977). *SCL-90 administration, scoring and procedures manual I for the R(evised) version.* Baltimore: Johns Hopkins University School of Medicine.

Drugs that induce sexual dysfunction. (1987). *Medical Letter on Drugs and Therapeutics, 29,* 65–70.

Durkheim, E. (1966). *Suicide: A study in sociology* (J. Spaulding & G. Simpson, Trans.). New York: Free Press. (Original work published 1897)

Ebert, B. W. (1987). Guide to conducting a psychological autopsy. *Professional Psychology: Research and Practice, 18*(1), 52–56.

Edinger, J. D. (1985). Sleep history questionnaire for evaluating insomnia complaints. In P. A. Keller & L. G. Ritt (Eds.), *Innovations in clinical practice: A source book* (Vol. 4). Sarasota, FL: Professional Resource Exchange.

Ellis, A. (1976). The biological basis of human irrationality. *Journal of Individual Psychology, 32,* 145–168.

Erikson, E. (1963). *Childhood and society* (rev. ed.). New York: Norton.

Erkinjunti, T., Sulkava, R., Wilkstrom, J., & Autio, L. (1987). Short Portable Mental Status Questionnaire as a screening test for dementia and delirium among the elderly. *Journal of the American Geriatrics Society, 35*(5), 412–416.

Esser, T. J. (1974). *Effective report writing in vocational evaluation and work adjustment training.* (Available from Materials Development Center, Department of Rehabilitation and Manpower, University of Wisconsin, Menomonie, WI 54751)

Estroff, T. W., & Gold, M. S. (1986). Medication-induced and toxin-induced psychiatric disorders. In I. Extein & M. S. Gold (Eds.), *Medical mimics of psychiatric disorders.* Washington, DC: American Psychiatric Press.

Farberow, N. (Ed.). (1980). *The many faces of suicide: Indirect self-destructive behavior.* New York: McGraw-Hill.

Favier, C. M. (1986). The mental status examination—revised. In P. A. Keller & L. G. Ritt (Eds.), *Innovations in clinical practice: A source book* (Vol. 5). Sarasota, FL: Professional Resource Exchange.

Feuerstein, M., & Skjei, E. (1979). *Mastering pain.* New York: Bantam Books.

Firestone, L. (1991). *Firestone Voice Scale for Self-Destructive Behavior.* (Available from The Glendon Association, 2049 Century Park East, Suite 3000, Los Angeles, CA 90067)

Folstein, M. F., Folstein, S. E., & McHugh, P. R. (1975). Mini-Mental State: A practical method for grading the cognitive state of patients for the clinician. *Journal of Psychiatric Research, 12,* 189–198.

Forgatch, M. S., & Patterson, G. R. (1989). *Parents and adolescents living together: Vol. 2. Family problem solving.* Eugene, OR: Castalia.

Frisch, M. B. (1992). Clinical validation of the Quality of Life Inventory. *Psychological Assessment, 4*(1), 92–101.

Gardner, H. (1983). *Frames of mind: The theory of multiple intelligences.* New York: Basic Books.

Garner, D. M., & Garfinkel, P. E. (1979). The Eating Attitudes Test: An index of the symptoms of anorexia nervosa. *Psychological Medicine, 9,* 273–279.

Geller, J. A. (1992). *Breaking destructive patterns.* New York: Free Press.

Gilliam, J. E. (1995). *Attention Deficit/Hyperactivity Disorder Test.* Odessa, FL: Psychological Assessment Resources.

Goldberg, C. (1995). The daimonic development of the malevolent personality. *Journal of Humanistic Psychology, 35*(3), 7–36.

Goldberg, L. R. (1992). The development of markers for the Big Five factor structure. *Psychological Assessment, 4,* 26–42.

Goleman, D. (1988, November 1). Narcissism looming larger as root of personality woes. *The New York Times,* pp. C1, C16.

Gonsalves, C. (1992). Psychological stages of the refugee process: A model for therapeutic interventions. *Professional Psychology: Research and Practice, 23*(5), 382–389.

Goodman, W. K., Rasmussen, S. A., Pnce, L. H., Mazure, C., Heninger, C. R., & Charney, D. S. (1989). *Yale–Brown Obsessive Compulsive Scale.* (Available from Clinical Neuroscience Research Unit, Connecticut Mental Health Center, 34 Park Street, New Haven, CT 06508)

Grant, I., & Martin, A. (1994). Neurocognitive disorders associated with HIV-1 infection. In I. Grant & A. Martin (Eds.), *Neuropsychology of HIV infection.* New York: Oxford University Press.

Greenberg, L. M., & Waldman, I. W. (1993). Developmental normative data on the Tests of Variables of Attention (TOVA). *Journal of Child Psychology and Psychiatry, 34,* 1019–1030.

Greenwood, D. U. (1991). Neuropsychological aspects of AIDS dementia complex: What clinicians need to know. *Professional Psychology: Research and Practice, 22*(5), 407–409.

Greist, J. H., Jefferson, J. W., & Marks, I. M. (1986). *Anxiety and its treatment: Help is available.* Washington, DC: American Psychiatric Press.

Grotevant, H. D., & Carlson, C. I. (1989). *Family assessment: A guide to methods and measures.* New York: Guilford Press.

Groth-Marnat, G. (1997). *Handbook of psychological assessment* (3rd ed.). New York: Wiley.

Group for the Advancement of Psychiatry (GAP). (1990). *Casebook in psychiatric ethics.* New York: Brunner/Mazel.

Gruber, H. E., & Von Eiche, J. J. (1977). *The essential Piaget.* New York: Basic Books.

Hackett, T. P. (1978). The pain patient: Evaluation and treatment. In T. P. Hackett & N. H. Cassem (Eds.), *Massachusetts General Hospital handbook of general hospital psychiatry.* St. Louis, MO: C. V. Mosby.

Hagen, C., Malkmus, D., & Durham, P. (1979). Levels of cognitive functioning. In *Rehabilitation of the head injured adult: comprehensive physical management.* Downey, CA: Los Amigos Research & Education Insitute, Rancho Los Amigos National Rehabilitation Center.

Haley, J. (1984). *Ordeal therapy.* San Francisco: Jossey-Bass.

Hamilton, M. (1960). A rating scale for depression. *Journal of Neurology, Neurosurgery and Psychiatry, 23,* 56–62.

Hare, R. D. (1980). A research scale for the assessment of psychopathy in criminal populations. *Personality and Individual Differences, 1,* 111–119.

Hase, H. D. (1992). McGill Pain Questionnaire: Revised format. In L. Vandecreek, S. Knapp, & T. L. Jackson (Eds.), *Innovations in clinical practice: A source book* (Vol. 11). Sarasota, FL: Professional Resource Press.

Hays, A. (1984). The Set Test to screen mental status quickly. *Geriatric Nursing, 5*(2) 96–97.

Hersen, M., & Turner, S. (Eds.). (1994). *Diagnostic interviewing* (2nd ed.). New York: Plenum Press.

Hoffman, R. S., & Koran, L. M. (1984). Detecting physical illness in patients with mental disorders. *Psychosomatics, 25,* 654–660.

Horacek, H. J. (1992, September). Neurobehavioral perspective may help in treating ADDH. *Psychiatric Times, 9*(9), 32–35.

Horvath, A. T. (1995). Enhancing motivation for treatment of addictive behavior: Guidelines for the psychotherapist. *Psychotherapy, 30,* 475–480.

Huber, J. T. (1961). *Report writing in psychology and psychiatry.* New York: Harper.

Hyler, S. E., & Spitzer, R. T. (1978). Hysteria split asunder. *American Journal of Psychiatry, 135,* 1500–1504.

Jacobs, J. W., Bernhard, M. R., Delgado, A., & Strain, J. J. (1977). Screening for organic mental syndromes in the medically ill. *Annals of Internal Medicine, 86,* 40–46.

Jahoda, M. (1958). *Current concepts of positive mental health.* New York: Basic Books.

Jellinek, E. M. (1960). *The disease concept of alcoholism.* New Haven, CT: Hillhouse Press.

Jenkins, S. C., Gibbs, T. P., & Szymanski, S. R. (1990). *A pocket reference for psychiatrists.* Washington, DC: American Psychiatric Press.

Kalichman, S. (1995). *Understanding AIDS: A guide for mental health professionals.* Washington, DC: American Psychological Association.

Kalichman, S. (1996). *Answering your questions about AIDS.* Washington, DC: American Psychological Association.

Kanfer, F. H., & Saslow, K. (1965). Behavioral analysis: An alternative to diagnostic classification. *Archives of General Psychiatry, 12,* 529–538.

Kaplan, H. S. (1983). *The evaluation of sexual disorders: Psychological and medical aspects.* New York: Brunner/Mazel.

Kaplan, R. E. (1983). A woman's view of DSM-III. *American Psychologist, 38,* 786–792.

Karpel, M. A. (1994). *Evaluating couples: A handbook for practitioners.* New York: Norton.

Kaslow, F. (1995). *Projective genogramming.* Sarasota, FL: Professional Resources Press.

Kellerman, H., & Burry, A. (1997). *Handbook of psychodiagnostic testing: An analysis of personality in the psychological report* (3rd ed.). Boston: Allyn & Bacon.

Kennedy, J. A. (1992). *Fundamentals of psychiatric treatment planning.* Washington, DC: American Psychiatric Press.

Kennedy, W. A. (1965). School phobia: Rapid treatment of fifty cases. *Journal of Abnormal Psychology, 70,* 285–289.

Kinston, W. (1988). The family health scales for global assessment of family functioning. In P. A. Keller & S. R. Heyman (Eds.), *Innovations in clinical practice: A source book* (Vol. 7). Sarasota, FL: Professional Resource Exchange.

Kiresuk, T. J., & Sherman, R. E. (1968). Goal Attainment Scaling: A general method for evaluating comprehensive community mental health programs. *Community Mental Health Journal, 4,* 443–453.

Kohlberg, L. (Ed.). (1984). *The psychology of moral development: The nature and validity of moral stages.* San Francisco: Harper & Row.

Kral, V. A. (1978). Benign sensecent forgetfulness. In R. Katzman, R. F. Terry, & K. L. Bick (Eds.), *Alzheimer's disease: Senile dementia and related disorders.* New York: Raven Press.

Kratochwill, T., & Bergan, J. (1990). *Behavioral consulting in applied settings: An individual guide.* New York: Plenum Press.

Krupp, K. B., Mendelson, W. B., & Friedman, R. (1991). An overview of chronic fatigue syndrome. *Journal of Clinical Psychiatry, 52*(10), 403–410.

Kübler-Ross, E. (1969). *On death and dying.* New York: Macmillan.

L'Abate, L. (1994). *Family evaluation: A psychological approach.* Newbury Park, CA: Sage.

Langer, E., & Rodin, J. (1976). Effects of choice and enhanced personal responsibility for the aged: A field experiment in an institutional setting. *Journal of Personality and Social Psychology, 34,* 191–199.

Lasswell, M., & Brock, G. (Eds.). (1989). *AAMFT forms book.* Washington, DC: American Association for Marriage and Family Therapy.

Lawson, G., Ellis, D., & Rivers, P. C. (1984). *Essentials of chemical dependency counseling.* Rockville, MD: Aspen.

Lazarus, A. A. (Ed.). (1976). *Multimodal behavior therapy.* New York: Springer.

Lazarus, A. A. (1981). *The practice of multimodal therapy.* New York: McGraw-Hill.

Leary, T. (1957). *Interpersonal diagnosis of personality: A functional theory and methodology for personality evaluation.* New York: Ronald Press.

Lefkovitz, P. M., Morrison, D. P., & Davis, H. J. (1982). The Assessment of Current Functioning Scale (ACFS). *Journal of Psychiatric Treatment and Evaluation, 4*(3), 297–305.

Lesieur, H. R., & Blume, S. E. (1987). South Oaks Gambling Screen (SOGS): A new instrument for the identification of pathological gamblers. *American Journal of Psychiatry, 144,* 1184–1188.

Levenstein, J. (1994). Treatment documentation in private practice: I. The PIC Treatment Plan. *Independent Practitioner, 14,* 181–185.

Levin, H. S., O'Donnell, V. M., & Grossman, R. G. (1979). The Galveston Orientation and Amnesia Test (GOAT): A practical scale to assess cognition after head injury. *Journal of Nervous and Mental Disease, 167,* 675–684.

Lewinsohn, P. M., Rohde, P., & Seeley, J. R. (1996). Adolescent suicidal ideation and attempts: Prevalence, risk factors, and clinical implications. *Clinical Psychology: Science and Practice, 3*(1), 25–46.

Lewis, J. A. (1990). A psychosocial and substance use history form. In P. Keller & S. Heyman (Eds.), *Innovations in clinical practice: A source book* (Vol. 9). Sarasota, FL: Professional Resource Exchange.

Lidz, T., & Fleck, S. (1985). *Schizophrenia and the family* (2nd ed.). New York: International Universities Press.

Lishman, W. (1998). *Organic psychiatry: The psychological consequences of cerebral disorder* (3rd ed.). Oxford: Blackwell Scientific.

Logue, M. B., Sher, K. J., & Frensch, P. A. (1992). Purported characteristics of adult children of alcoholics: A possible "Barnum effect." *Professional Psychology: Research and Practice, 23*(3), 226–232.

Lopez-Ibor, J. J., Jr. (1990). The masking and unmasking of depression. In J. P. Feighner & W. F. Boyer (Eds.), *The diagnosis of depression.* New York: Wiley.

Lubin, B. (1965). Adjective checklists for measuring depression. *Archives of General Psychiatry, 12,* 57–62.

Lukas, C., & Seiden, H. M. (1990). *Silent grief: Living in the wake of suicide.* New York: Bantam.

Mahler, M. (1975). *The psychological birth of the human infant.* New York: Basic Books.

Makover, R. B. (1996). *Treatment planning for psychotherapists.* Washington, DC: American Psychiatric Press.

Mapou, R. L., & Law, W. A. (1994). Neurobehavioral aspects of HIV disease and AIDS: An update. *Professional Psychology: Research and Practice, 25*(2), 132–140.

Maris, R. W., Berman, A. L., Maltsberger, J. T., & Yufit, R. I. (Eds.). (1992). *Assessment and prediction of suicide.* New York: Guilford Press.

Marlatt, G. A. (Ed.). (1998). *Harm reduction: Pragmatic strategies for managing high-risk behaviors.* New York: Guilford Press.

Marlatt, G. A., & Gordon, J. R. (Eds.). (1985). *Relapse prevention: Maintenance strategies in the treatment of addictive behaviors.* New York: Guilford Press.

Marsh, D. T. (1992a). *Families and mental illness: New directions in professional practice.* New York: Praeger.

Marsh, D. T. (1992b). Working with families of people with serious mental illness. In L. Vandecreek, S. Knapp, & T. L. Jackson (Eds.), *Innovations in clinical practice: A source book* (Vol. 11). Sarasota, FL: Professional Resource Press.

Martin, P. R. (1993). *Psychological management of chronic headaches.* New York: Guilford Press.

Maslow, A. H. (1962). *Toward a psychology of being.* Princeton, NJ: Van Nostrand.

Masters, W. H., & Johnson, V. E. (1970). *Human sexual inadequacy.* Boston: Little, Brown.

McCarney, S. B. (1995). *The Attention Deficit Disorder Evaluation Scale.* Columbia, MO: Hawthorne Educational Services.

McGoldrick, M., & Gerson, R. (1985). *Genograms in family assessment.* New York: Norton.

McIntosh, J. L. (1995). Suicide prevention in the elderly (age 65–99). *Suicide and Life-Threatening Behavior, 25*(1), 180–192.

McLemore, C., & Benjamin, L. S. (1979). Whatever happened to interpersonal diagnosis?: A psychological alternative to DSM-III. *American Psychologist, 34,* 17–34.

Meehl, P. (1996). *Clinical vs. statistical prediction: A theoretical analysis and a review of the evidence.* Northvale, NJ: Aronson. (Original work published 1954)

Meichenbaum, D. (1985). *Stress inoculation training.* New York: Pergamon Press.

Melton, G. B., Petrila, J., Poythress, N. G., & Slobogin, C. (1997). *Psychological evaluations for the courts: A handbook for mental health professionals and lawyers* (2nd ed.). New York: Guilford Press.

Melzack, R., & Wall, P. D. (1983). *The challenge of pain.* New York: Basic Books.

Menninger, K. A. (1952). *A manual for psychiatric case study.* New York: Grune & Stratton.

Menninger, W. C. (1967). *Psychiatrist for a troubled world.* New York: Viking Press.

Milgram, S. (1974). *Obedience to authority.* New York: Harper & Row.

Miller, A. G. (1986). *The obedience experiments: A case study of controversy in social science.* New York: Praeger.

Miller, L. (1993). Psychotherapeutic approaches to chronic pain. *Psychotherapy, 30,* 115–124.

Miller, P. S., Richardson, S. J., Jyu, C. A., Lemay, J. S., et al. (1988). Association of low serum anticholinergic levels and cognitive impairment in elderly presurgical patients. *American Journal of Psychiatry, 145*(3), 342–345.

Miller, S. G. (1994). Borderline personality disorder from the patient's perspective. *Hospital and Community Psychiatry, 45*(12), 1215–1219.

Miller, W. R., & Rollnick, S. (1991). *Motivational interviewing: Preparing people to change addictive behavior.* New York: Guilford Press.

Millon, T. (1986). Personality prototypes and their diagnostic criteria. In T. Millon & G. Klerman (Eds.), *Contemporary directions in psychopathology.* New York: Guilford Press.

Millon, T., & Everly, G. S. (1985). *Personality and its disorders.* New York: Wiley.

Minuchin, S. (1974). *Families and family therapy.* Cambridge, MA: Harvard University Press.

Monahan, J. (1981). *Predicting violent behavior: An assessment of clinical techniques.* Beverly Hills, CA: Sage.

Morey, L. C., & Ochoa, E. S. (1989). An investigation of adherence to diagnostic criteria: Clinical diagnosis of the DSM-III personality disorders. *Journal of Personality Disorders, 3,* 180–192.

Morrison, J. (1995a). *The first interview: Revised for DSM-IV.* New York: Guilford Press.

Morrison, J. (1995b). *DSM-IV made easy: The clinician's guide to diagnosis.* New York: Guilford Press.

Morgan, J. P. (1991). What is codependency? *Journal of Clinical Psychology, 47,* 720–729.

Mosak, H., & Shulman, B. (1988). *Manual for life style assessment.* Muncie, IN: Accelerated Development.

Mosher, D. L. (1968). Measurement of guilt in females by self-report inventories. *Journal of Consulting and Clinical Psychology, 32,* 690–695.

Mueller, J. (1995). The mental status examination. In H. H. Goldman (Ed.), *Review of general psychiatry* (4th ed.). Los Altos, CA: Lange.

Nadelson, T. (1986). The false patient: Chronic factitious disease, Munchausen syndrome, and malingering. In J. L. Haupt & H. K. H. Brodie (Eds.), *Consultation–liaison psychiatry and behavioral medicine.* Philadelphia: Lippincott.

Nathan, P. E., & Gorman, J. M. (Eds.). (1998). *A guide to treatments that work.* New York: Oxford University Press.

NiCarthy, G., & Davidson, S. (1989). *You can be free: An easy to read handbook for abused women.* Seattle, WA: Seal Press.

Nietzel, M. T., & Himelein, M. J. (1987). Crime prevention through social and physical environmental change. *Behavior Analyst, 10*(1), 69–74.

Norman, W. T. (1963). Toward an adequate taxonomy of personality attributes: Replicated factor structure in peer nomination personality ratings. *Journal of Abnormal and Social Psychology, 66,* 574–583.

O'Brien, P. E., & Gaborit, M. (1992). Codependency: A disorder separate from chemical dependency. *Journal of Clinical Psychology, 48,* 129–136.

Okpaku, S. O. (1998). *Clinical methods in transcultural psychiatry.* Washington, DC: American Psychiatric Press.

O'Rourke, N., Tuokko, H., Hayden, S., & Beattie, B. L. (1997). *Early identification of dementia: Predictive validity of the Clock Test. Archives of Clinical Neuropsychology, 12*(3), 257–267.

Ownby, R. L. (1997). *Psychological reports: A guide to report writing in professional psychology* (3rd ed.). New York: Wiley.

Paniagua, F. (1998). *Assessing and treating culturally diverse clients: A practical guide* (2nd ed.). Thousand Oaks, CA: Sage.

Pankratz, L. (1998). *Patients who deceive: Assessment and management of risk in providing health care and financial benefits.* Springfield, IL: Thomas.

Patterson, G. R., & Forgatch, M. S. (1987). *Parents and adolescents living together: Vol. 1. Living together.* Eugene, OR: Castalia.

Paul, G. L. (1966). *Insight vs. desensitization in psychotherapy: An experiment in anxiety reduction.* Stanford, CA: Stanford University Press.

PDR guide to drug interactions, side effects, indications, contraindications (54th ed.). (2000). Oradell, NJ: Medical Economics.

Pelonero, A. L., Levenson, J. L., & Pandurangi, A. K. (1998). Neuroleptic malignant syndrome: A review. *Psychiatric Services, 49*(9), 1163–1172.

Perry, H. S. (Ed.). (1953). *The collected works of Harry Stack Sullivan.* New York: Norton.

Pfeiffer, E. (1975). A short, portable mental status questionnaire for the assessment of organic brain deficit in elderly patients. *Journal of the Geriatric Society, 23,* 433.

Physicians' desk reference (PDR) (54th ed.). (2000). Oradell, NJ: Medical Economics.

Pies, R. (1993). The psychopharmacology of PTSD. *Psychiatric Times, 10*(6), 21–24.

Pincus, H. H., & Tucker, G. J. (1985). *Behavioral neurology* (3rd ed.). New York: Oxford University Press.

Pomeroy, W. B., Flax, C., & Wheeler, C. C. (1982). *Taking a sex history: Interviewing and recording.* New York: Free Press.

Potter-Effron, R. T. (1989). Shame and guilt: Definitions, processes, and treatment issues with AODA clients. In R. T. Potter-Effron & P. S. Potter-Effron (Eds.), *The treatment of shame and guilt in alcoholism counseling.* New York: Haworth Press.

Prochaska, J. P., DiClemente, C. C., & Norcross, J. (1992). In search of how people change: Applications to addictive behaviors. *American Psychologist, 47*(9), 1102–1114.

Putnam, F. W. (1989). *Diagnosis and treatment of multiple personality disorder.* New York: Guilford Press.

Putnam, F. W. (1991). Recent research on multiple personality disorder. *Psychiatric Clinics of North America, 14*(3), 489–502.

Putnam, F. W. (1997). *Dissociation in children and adolescents.* New York: Guilford Press.

Reimer, T., Brink, P. J., & Saunders, J. M. (1984). Cultural assessment: Content and process. *Nursing Outlook, 32*(2), 78–82.

Reisberg, B. (1983). Clinical presentation, diagnosis, and symptomology of age-associated cognitive decline and Alzheimer's disease. In B. Reisberg (Ed.), *Alzheimer's disease.* New York: Free Press.

Reisberg, B. (1985). Alzheimer's disease updated. *Psychiatric Annals, 15,* 319–322.

Reisberg, B., Ferris, S., deLeon, M. J., & Crook, T. (1982). The Global Deterioration Scale for assessment of primary degenerative dementia. *American Journal of Psychiatry, 139*(9), 1136–1139.

Reynolds, W. M. (1987). *Suicide ideation questionnaires.* Odessa, FL: Psychological Assessment Resources.

Robertson, D., Rockwood, K., & Stolee, P. (1982). A short mental status questionnaire. *Canadian Journal on Aging, 1*(1–2), 16–20.

Rogers, R. (1984). Toward an empirical model of malingering and deception. *Behavioral Science and the Law, 2,* 544–559.

Rogers, R. (1995). *Diagnostic and structured interviewing: A handbook for psychologists.* Odessa, FL: Psychological Assessment Resources.

Rogers, R. (Ed.). (1997). *Clinical assessment of malingering and deception* (2nd ed.). New York: Guilford Press.

Rosenthal, N. E. (1998). *Winter blues* (rev. ed.). New York: Guilford Press.

Ross, C. A. (1989). *Multiple personality disorder: Diagnosis, clinical features, and treatment.* New York: Wiley.

Ross, C. A., Miller, S. D., Reagar, P., Bjornson, L., Fraser, G. A., & Anderson, G. (1990). Structured interview data on 102 cases of multiple personality disorder from four centers. *American Journal of Psychiatry, 147,* 596–601.

Roth, A., & Fonagy, P. (1996). *What works for whom?* New York: Guilford Press.

Rubinow, D. R., & Roy-Byrne, P. (1984). Premenstrual syndrome: Overview from a methodological perspective. *American Journal of Psychiatry, 141,* 163–171.

Samenow, S. (1980). *Inside the criminal mind.* New York: Times Books.

Satir, V. (1967). *Conjoint family therapy.* Palo Alto, CA: Science & Behavior Books.

Sattler, J. M. (1992). *Assessment of children* (3rd ed.). San Diego, CA: Jerome M. Sattler.

Schaef, A. W. (1986). *Codependency: Misunderstood–mistreated.* San Francisco: Harper & Row.

Schneider, K. (1959). *Clinical psychopathology.* New York: Grune & Stratton.

Schutz, W. C. (1958). *FIRO: A three dimensional theory of interpersonal behavior.* New York: Rinehart.

Severino, S., & Moline, M. L. (1989). *Premenstrual syndrome: A clinician's guide.* New York: Guilford Press.

Shapiro, D. (1965). *Neurotic styles.* New York: Basic Books.

Sher, K. J. (1991). *Children of alcoholics: A critical appraisal of theory and research.* Chicago: University of Chicago Press.

Shneidman, E. S. (Ed.). (1980). *Death: Current perspectives.* Palo Alto, CA: Mayfield.

Shneidman, E. S., Farberow, N., & Lifman, R., E. (Eds.). (1970). *The psychology of suicide.* New York: Science House.

Shoben, E. J. (1956). *The psychology of adjustment: A dynamic and experiential approach to personality and mental hygiene.* Boston: Houghton Mifflin.

Simmons, J. E. (1987). *Psychiatric examination of children.* Philadelphia: Lea & Febiger.

Slaby, A. E., Liev, J., & Tancredi, L. R. (1994). *Handbook of psychiatric emergencies* (4th ed.). Norwalk, CT: Appleton & Lange.

Sobell, M. B., & Sobell, L. C. (1993). *Problem drinkers: Guided self-change treatment.* New York: Guilford Press.

Sovner, R., & Hurley, A. D. (1983). The mental status examination: I. Behavior, speech, and thought. *Psychiatric Aspects of Mental Retardation Newsletter, 2*(2), 5–8.

Sperry, L., Gudeman, J. E., Blackwell, B., & Faulkner, L. R. (1992). *Psychiatric case formulations.* Washington, DC: American Psychiatric Press.

Stedman's medical dictionary (26th ed.). (1999). Baltimore: Williams & Wilkins.

Stedman's psychiatry/neurology/neurosurgery words (2nd ed.). (1999). Baltimore: Lippincott, Williams & Wilkins.

Steinem, G. (1980). Erotica and pornography: A clear and present difference. In L. Lederer (Ed.), *Take back the night: Women on pornography.* New York: Morrow.

Steiner, C. (1971). *Games alcoholics play.* New York: Grove Press.

Sternberg, R. J., & Grigorenko, E. L. (1997). Are cognitive styles still in style? *American Psychologist, 52*(7), 700–712.

Stuart, R., & Jacobson, B. (1991). *Couple's pre-counseling Inventory.* Champaign, IL: Research Press.

Sue, D., & Sue, D. W. (1999). *Counseling the culturally different: Theory and practice* (3rd ed.). New York: Wiley.

Sundberg, N. F. (1977). *Assessment of persons.* Englewood Cliffs, NJ: Prentice-Hall.

Swenson, C. H., Nelson, M. K., Warner, J., & Dunlap, D. (1992a). Scale of Marriage Problems: Revised. In L. Vandecreek, S. Knapp, & T. L. Jackson (Eds.), *Innovations in clinical practice: A source book* (Vol. 11). Sarasota, FL: Professional Resource Press.

Swenson, C. H., Nelson, M. K., Warner, J., & Dunlap, D. (1992b). Scale of Feelings and Behavior of Love: Revised. In L. Vandecreek, S. Knapp, & T. L. Jackson (Eds.), *Innovations in clinical practice: A source book* (Vol. 11). Sarasota, FL: Professional Resource Press.

Tanner, J. M. (1962). *Growth at adolescence* (2nd ed.). Oxford: Blackwell Scientific.

Taylor, R. L. (1990). *Distinguishing psychological from organic disorders: Screening for psychological masquerade.* New York: Springer.

Teasdale, G., & Jenvet, B. (1974). Assessment of coma and impaired consciousness. *Lancet, 2*(7872), 81–83.

Thomas, A., & Chess, S. (1977). *Temperament and development.* New York: Brunner/Mazel.

Thomas, A., Chess, S., & Birch, H. G. (1968). *Temperament and behavior disorders in children.* New York: New York University Press.

Thorndike, R. L., Hagen, E. P., & Sattler, J. M. (1986). *Stanford–Binet Intelligence Scale* (4th ed.). Itasca, IL: Riverside.

Toman, W. (1993). *Family constellations* (4th ed.). New York: Springer.

Trzepacz, P. T., & Baker, R. W. (1993). *The psychiatric mental status examination.* New York: Oxford University Press.

Tseng, W.-S., & Streltzer, J. (1997). *Culture and psychopathology: A guide to clinical assessment.* New York: Brunner/Mazel.

Turk, D. C., & Melzack, R. (1992). *Handbook of pain assessment.* New York: Guilford Press.

Tyrer, P., Fowler-Dixon, R., Ferguson, B., & Keleman, A. (1990). A plea for the diagnosis of hypochondrical personality disorder. *Journal of Psychosomatic Research, 34*(6), 637–642.

Ullman, R. K., Sleator, E. K., & Sprague, R. L. (1991). *ADDH Comprehensive Teacher's Rating Scale (ACTeRS).* Champaign, IL: MetriTech.

Walker, L. (1984). *The battered woman syndrome.* New York: Springer.

Walker, L. (1991). PTSD in women: Diagnosis and treatment of battered woman syndrome. *Psychotherapy, 28,* 21–29.

Wallack, J., Bialer, O., & Prenzlauer, S. (1995). Psychiatric aspects of HIV infection and AIDS: An overview and update. In A. Stoudemire & B. Fogel (Eds.), *Medical–psychiatric practice* (Vol. 3). Washington, DC: American Psychiatric Association.

Watzlawick, P. (1977). *The interactional view.* New York: Norton.

Wechsler, D. (1981). *Manual for the Wechsler Adult Intelligence Scale–Revised.* New York: Psychological Corporation.

Wechsler, D. (1991). *Manual for the Wechsler Intelligence Scale for Children–Third Edition.* San Antonio, TX: Psychological Corporation.

Wechsler, D. (1998). *Manual for the Wechsler Memory Scale–Third Edition.* San Antonio, TX: Psychological Corporation.

Weinberg, T. S., Williams, C. T., & Moser, C. (1984). The social constituants of sadomasochism. *Social Problems, 31,* 379–389.

Whelihan, W., Lesher, E. L., & Kleban, M. H. (1984). Mental status and memory assessment as predictors of dementia. *Journal of Gerontology, 39*(5), 572–576.

Wiger, D. (1998). *The psychotherapy documentation primer.* New York: Wiley.

Wilson, S. J. (1980). *Recording guidelines for social work.* New York: Free Press.

Wolberg, L. R. (1954). *The technique of psychotherapy.* New York: Grune & Stratton.

World Health Organization. (1992). *International classification of diseases* (10th rev.): *Chapter V. Mental and behavioral disorders.* Geneva: Author.

Wynne, L. C. (Ed.). (1988). *The state of the art in family therapy research.* New York: Family Process Press.

Zimmerman, I. L., & Woo-Sam, J. M. (1973). *Clinical interpretation of the Wechsler Adult Intelligence Scale.* New York: Grune & Stratton.

Zuckerman, E. L. (1997). *The paper office* (2nd ed.). New York: Guilford Press.

Zung, W. W. (1965). A self-rating depression scale. *Archives of General Psychiatry, 12,* 63–70.

Index